Cisco Enterprise Management Solutions, Volume I

Michael Wynston

Cisco Press
201 West 103rd Street
Indianapolis, IN 46290 USA

Cisco Enterprise Management Solutions, Volume I

Michael Wynston

Copyright© 2001 Cisco Systems, Inc.

Cisco Press logo is a trademark of Cisco Systems, Inc.

Published by:
Cisco Press
201 West 103rd Street
Indianapolis, IN 46290 USA

Printed in the United States of America 1 2 3 4 5 6 7 8 9 0

Library of Congress Cataloging-in-Publication Number: 00-105175

ISBN: 1-58705-006-4

Warning and Disclaimer

This book is designed to provide information about Cisco Enterprise Management Solutions using the Resource Manager Essentials 3.X application. Every effort has been made to make this book as complete and as accurate as possible, but no warranty or fitness is implied.

The information is provided on an "as is" basis. The authors, Cisco Press, and Cisco Systems, Inc. shall have neither liability nor responsibility to any person or entity with respect to any loss or damages arising from the information contained in this book or from the use of the discs or programs that may accompany it.

The opinions expressed in this book belong to the author and are not necessarily those of Cisco Systems, Inc.

Feedback Information

At Cisco Press, our goal is to create in-depth technical books of the highest quality and value. Each book is crafted with care and precision, undergoing rigorous development that involves the unique expertise of members from the professional technical community.

Readers' feedback is a natural continuation of this process. If you have any comments regarding how we could improve the quality of this book, or otherwise alter it to better suit your needs, you can contact us through e-mail at ciscopress@mcp.com. Please make sure to include the book title and ISBN in your message.

We greatly appreciate your assistance.

Publisher	John Wait
Editor-In-Chief	John Kane
Cisco Systems Program Manager	Bob Anstey
Executive Editor	Brett Bartow
Acquisitions Editor	Amy Lewis
Managing Editor	Patrick Kanouse
Development Editors	Howard Jones
	Chris Cleveland
Production Editor	Marc Fowler
Copy Editor	Chuck Gose
Technical Editors	Mark Basinski
	Michael Carrick
	Paul L. Della Maggiora
	Dennis Klama
Team Coordinator	Tammi Ross
Book Designer	Gina Rexrode
Cover Designer	Louisa Klucznik
Production Team	Octal Publishing, Inc.
Indexer	Larry Sweazy

CISCO SYSTEMS

Corporate Headquarters
Cisco Systems, Inc.
170 West Tasman Drive
San Jose, CA 95134-1706
USA
http://www.cisco.com
Tel: 408 526-4000
        800 553-NETS (6387)
Fax: 408 526-4100

European Headquarters
Cisco Systems Europe
11 Rue Camille Desmoulins
92782 Issy-les-Moulineaux
Cedex 9
France
http://www-europe.cisco.com
Tel: 33 1 58 04 60 00
Fax: 33 1 58 04 61 00

Americas Headquarters
Cisco Systems, Inc.
170 West Tasman Drive
San Jose, CA 95134-1706
USA
http://www.cisco.com
Tel: 408 526-7660
Fax: 408 527-0883

Asia Pacific Headquarters
Cisco Systems Australia,
Pty., Ltd
Level 17, 99 Walker Street
North Sydney
NSW 2059 Australia
http://www.cisco.com
Tel: +61 2 8448 7100
Fax: +61 2 9957 4350

Cisco Systems has more than 200 offices in the following countries. Addresses, phone numbers, and fax numbers are listed on the Cisco Web site at www.cisco.com/go/offices

Argentina • Australia • Austria • Belgium • Brazil • Bulgaria • Canada • Chile • China • Colombia • Costa Rica • Croatia • Czech Republic • Denmark • Dubai, UAE • Finland • France • Germany • Greece • Hong Kong • Hungary • India • Indonesia • Ireland Israel • Italy • Japan • Korea • Luxembourg • Malaysia • Mexico • The Netherlands • New Zealand • Norway • Peru • Philippines Poland • Portugal • Puerto Rico • Romania • Russia • Saudi Arabia • Scotland • Singapore • Slovakia • Slovenia • South Africa • Spain Sweden • Switzerland • Taiwan • Thailand • Turkey • Ukraine • United Kingdom • United States • Venezuela • Vietnam • Zimbabwe

Trademark Acknowledgments

About the Authors

Michael Wynston, CCIE #5449, joins Netigy with over 7 years experience in instructing, planning, designing and implementing Enterprise Networks. Michael has joined Netigy as a Principal Consultant specializing in Cisco solutions. He is a subject matter expert in Cisco Network Management, Switching, and routing. Michael has spent the last three years as a Certified Cisco Systems Instructor at Global Knowledge Network, where he taught customized classes to employees of the largest enterprises and service providers in North America. Michael is also a published author with both Global Knowledge and Cisco Press. Michael has his Cisco Certified Internetworking Expert (CCIE), Cisco Certified Systems Instructor (CCSI), Microsoft Certified Systems Engineer (MCSE), and Microsoft Certified Trainer (MCT) certifications.

About the Technical Reviewers

Mark Basinski, CCIE #4422, is a senior support engineer for Cisco Systems' Technical Assistance Center (TAC) specializing in network management products and issues since 1997. His previous experience includes stints as a software developer for telecommunications products and as a senior member of the Network Operations staff at the University of Arizona. Mark was part of the team that developed the new NMS CCIE Recertification Exam.

Mike Carrick is a Cisco Certified Systems Instructor with Global Knowledge Network and teaches the Cisco Enterprise Management Solutions course. He has over 18 years in the data communications industry, having spent most of his time managing and designing networks for the Department of Veterans Affairs, where he used a variety of network management products and public domain utilities. He holds a Master's Degree in Telecommunications Management from Golden Gate University.

Paul L. Della Maggiora, CCIE #1522, is a Technical Marketing Engineer for Cisco's Performance Design and Verification Center. He has also served as an Escalation Engineer and NMS team lead for the TAC and Product Marketing Engineer since joining Cisco is 1994. For the past 10 years, Paul has worked as a network manager, network engineer, and network designer. Paul is also the recent author of the Cisco Press book, *Performance and Fault Management*. He has a Bachelor's degree in Computer Science from the University of South Carolina.

Dennis Klama is a Communications and Network Architect for Global Knowledge, Cisco's largest worldwide training partner. He has been working in the networking industry since 1985. His consulting services include analyzing user requirements, procedures and problems to automate processing, and improving production and workflow in existing information processing systems. Dennis is also a Certified Cisco Systems Instructor (CCSI), teaching networking professionals how to configure their products and identify network management requirements in a variety of environments. He teaches the Cisco Enterprise Management Solutions course on a regular basis. Dennis has a wealth of network configuration and management experience. Previous to joining Global Knowledge, he worked for Focus Technologies and McMaster University in Canada, installing and running CiscoWorks software, configuring essential TCP/IP services, and deploying and managing campus network services with Cisco products.

Dedications

This book is dedicated to my daughter and hero Remy Jordan. I have learned what is truly important by being with you. I love you more than anything; thank you for being here.

"I'll show you everything with arms wide open"—Creed, Human Clay

Acknowledgments

To the people who helped make this book happen:

My family: To my wife for reading everything before I sent it in. For all the nights and weekends we spent inside. Thank you, I love you.

The Cisco Press team: To Brett Bartow who made this project possible and kept it together. Thanks to Paul Della Maggiora who was my inside man; without you I would still have huge holes in my knowledge and this book would not have been as useful as it is. To Amy Lewis who stepped up to the plate when we needed more help. To Howard Jones, thanks for reading my words and making them sound better.

Thanks to Chuck Terrien for getting me started as a Cisco Instructor.

Thanks to the Cisco team at GKN for all of your support.

Lastly, thanks to all of my students who provided ideas on what needs to be in the book.

Contents at a Glance

Table of Contents

Introduction

The *Cisco Enterprise Management Service, Volume One* Coursebook educates readers on installing, configuring, running, and troubleshooting the Resource Manager Essentials 3.X application. From the numerous detailed examples this book presents you will learn do the following:

- Install both the CiscoWorks 2000 CD-One and Resource Manager Essentials.
- Configure Cisco hardware for SNMP management.
- Create a set of managed devices in an inventory.
- Manage device configurations, software images, operating systems, Syslog messages, and access-control lists.
- Maintain the Resource Manager Essentials' server.
- Troubleshoot a Resource Manager Essentials' environment that is not operating properly.

Fifteen chapters cover the general objectives for the book:

- **Chapter 1**, "Network Management Concepts," presents an introduction to the concepts of network management. This chapter teaches the reader what SNMP is and why network management is conducted.

- **Chapter 2**, "Cisco Network Management Products," provides an overview of the CiscoWorks 2000 product line. At the conclusion of this chapter you will be able to identify the different components of the CiscoWorks 2000 suite of applications.

- **Chapter 3**, "Configuring Cisco Devices for Network Management," details the numerous commands an administrator needs to be familiar with in order to enable the different SNMP management features on various hardware platforms. At the end on this chapter the reader will be able to enable SNMP, SNMP Trap, Syslog, and RMON services on the different platforms of Cisco Routers and Cisco Switches.

- **Chapter 4,** "CiscoWorks 2000 Server and Resource Manager Essentials Installation," introduces the Resource Manager Essentials application to the reader. After completing this chapter, the reader will be familiar with the structure and purpose of the Resource Manager Essentials application.

- **Chapter 5**, "CiscoWorks 2000 Resource Manager Essentials 3.X," provides detailed steps of the installation requirements for the CiscoWorks 2000 CD-One and Resource Manger Essentials applications on the Windows NT and Solaris platforms. The system requirements for both the server and client are also addressed. The reader will be able to successfully install both the CiscoWorks 2000 CD-One and Resource Manager Essentials applications upon completion of this chapter.

- **Chapter 6**, "Resource Manager Essentials System Administration." The first task after installation is to set up the server for use by creating users, assigning roles, and configuring system settings such as SNMP timeouts. After completing this chapter, you will be able to create users' and assign the users permissions. The reader will also be able to configure system settings such as SNMP timeouts and proxy settings.

- **Chapter 7**, "Resource Manager Essentials Inventory Management." This chapter provides the reader with the necessary skills to implement a Resource Manager Inventory. Topics covered include how to import inventory information, how to add information manually, how to keep the information up to date, and how to generate reports on the inventory. The reader will also be able to create views to control how inventory is accessed and modified.

- **Chapter 8**, "Device Configuration Management," discusses how to manage configuration files in the Resource Manager Essentials environment. The NetConfig and Config Editor tools are explained in detail. The **CWConfig** command-line application is covered to provide the reader with the necessary information to deploy configuration changes from the CWConfig command-line tool.

- **Chapter 9**, "Software Image Management," explains how to manage software deployment through the Resource Manager Essentials application. Integration with the CCO web site and bug analysis is also covered. Deploying new software images and retaining a current inventory are explained in detail.

- **Chapter 10**, "Syslog Analysis," presents the reader with information on how to configure and manage Syslog services in the Resource Manager Essentials application. The configuration of Syslog filters and reports is covered. The reader will also learn how to direct messages at a remote Syslog Analyzer and Collector.

- **Chapter 11**, "Change Audit Services," details information on how to manage change information in the Resource Manager Essentials database. Chapter 11 also discusses how to control aging and filtering of Change Audit records. In addition, this chapter presents information on how to generate reports on the changes to managed devices.

- **Chapter 12**, "Access-Control List Manager," outlines why Access-Control List management is important in any routed network. This chapter presents the Access-Control List Management application. The reader will be able to create, modify, and download TCP/IP, IPX, and Rate-Limit access-lists. Concepts such as how access-lists can be made modular through access-control entities, and how to create network classes are also covered in this chapter.

- **Chapter 13**, "Availability and Connectivity Tools," covers how to use the included connectivity tools such as ping and traceroute. The Resource Manager Essentials' Availability Tools are explained. The reader will be able to configure devices in views for polling of availability. The different polling intervals and applications such as availability polling and protocol distribution are presented.

- **Chapter 14**, "Additional CiscoWorks 2000 Tools." Integration with third-party applications through management connections is covered. In addition, integration with CCO and the different tools is discussed. The reader will be able to manage a case with the TAC, use the CCO Troubleshooting Engine and other CCO tools from Resource Manager Essentials.

- **Chapter 15**, "Troubleshooting Resource Manager Essentials," provides detailed instructions on how to troubleshoot the different Resource Manager Applications. Each application is covered along with necessary files and steps to correct problems that might be encountered in the day-to-day administration of the Resource Manager Essentials application. This chapter also covers topics such as log file and database management that are necessary to keep the server running well.

Who Should Read This Book?

This book was written for administrators responsible for implementing the Resource Manager Essentials 3.X application in a CiscoWorks 2000 Environment. This text can also be used to complement the Cisco Enterprise Management Solution class. An administrator who is responsible for implementing the Resource Manager Essentials application and cannot arrange to attend the official Cisco Enterprise Management Solutions class can use this book in conjunction with the online documentation to implement the application.

This book focuses on implementing the Resource Manager Essentials application. The reader should be familiar with Cisco network solutions, along with the following concepts:

- Basic router and switch configuration

- TCP/IP operation and configuration

- Routing protocols RIP, EIGRP, etc.

- Layer 3 protocols such as TCP/IP and IPX

- Using Windows NT and/or Solaris as a network administrator

Icons Used in This Book

Router

Bridge

Hub

DSU/CSU

Catalyst switch

Multilayer switch

ATM switch

ISDN switch

Communication server

Gateway

Access server

PC

PC with
software

Sun
Workstation

Mac

Terminal

File server

Web
server

CiscoWorks
Workstation

Printer

Laptop

IBM
mainframe

Front End
Processor

Cluster Controller

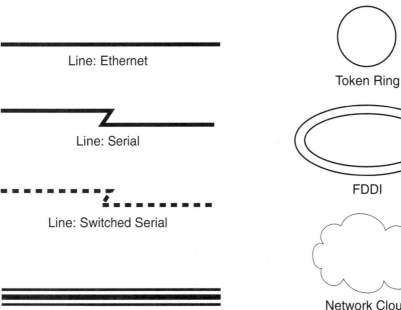

Line: Ethernet

Line: Serial

Line: Switched Serial

Frame Relay Virtual Circuit

Token Ring

FDDI

Network Cloud

Command Syntax Conventions

The conventions used to present command syntax in this book are the same conventions used in the IOS Command Reference. The Command Reference describes these conventions as follows:

- Vertical bars (|) separate alternative, mutually exclusive elements.

- Square brackets [ ] indicate optional elements.

- Braces { } indicate a required choice.

- Braces within brackets [{ }] indicate a required choice within an optional element.

- **Boldface** indicates commands and keywords that are entered literally as shown. In actual configuration examples and output (not general command syntax), boldface indicates commands that are manually input by the user (such as a **show** command).

- *Italics* indicate arguments for which you supply actual values.

Topics covered in this chapter include the following:

- Why Conduct Network Management?
- Components for Successful Network Management
- Management Protocols
- SNMP (Simple Network Management Protocol)
- Remote Monitoring (RMON)

## CHAPTER 1

Network Management Essentials

This chapter introduces the concepts and terms of network management. These concepts and terms are designed to help build a proper foundation for the rest of the book, which explains how to use the applications of CiscoWorks 2000 Resource Manager Essentials. The information in this chapter will help you properly understand some of the decisions made in the design, use, and implementation of the applications.

Why Conduct Network Management?

In an ideal world, network management would be unnecessary. Networks would be able to detect potential problems and instantaneously send a fix over the LAN or WAN. Continual advances in technology, however, have not eliminated the need for critical network management. Rather, the complexity and size of today's networks have greatly increased the necessity for expert network managers.

As a network administrator, you may take a "wait and see" attitude toward your network, or you may prefer to avoid problems in advance. Often network managers are not given the appropriate tools to do their job as efficiently as possible. A lack of tools gives the network administrator no opportunity for preventative action. Rather, an administrator practicing "wait and see" finds him or herself always putting out the fire and never preventing one in the first place.

If given the right tools, however, taking a proactive approach to network management and foreseeing a problem before one arises is easy.

So let's study why properly managing an enterprise network is crucial to a successful network operation. By examining the need for network management, the financial investment required for network management, and the solutions provided by network management products, the benefits of a properly managed enterprise network become apparent.

The Need

The first issue to address is the need for network management. Understanding the need for network management illuminates the dangers of doing without it.

The evolution of networks has often occurred without a distinct plan. Through the years, users were probably added to the network based on any available connection and not according to their function or intended network use. As problems started to occur, the usual solution was to simply add more bandwidth. Although adding more bandwidth served as an intermediate solution, the reasons for such high-link utilization were not addressed.

In today's society the network has become a vital part of business. The network has evolved into an indispensable business resource. Unfortunately, the tools needed to properly manage a network have not kept pace with both the growth of the network itself and the users' ever-increasing dependency on it. The network manager faces a seemingly never-ending uphill battle of network management.

The IS department faces a number of obstacles:

- Technology advancing more quickly than skill level of management team
- The ever-increasing number of management tasks
- Wide choices of incompatible tools
- Limited time, staff, and expertise

This combination causes the IS team to be in a constant state of reaction. By the time the user informs the team of a potential network problem, the problem has often escalated and affected the entire network population. For any company, a down network means lost revenue and unhappy users and customers. The reactive management team is now under intense pressure to hurry up and fix the problem. The lost revenue is blamed on the network outage and by extension, the IS department.

Keeping the network up and running is the IS department's responsibility and is therefore expected by management and end users. Often the IS department finds itself without the tools needed to properly manage the network. Furthermore, the lack of expertise and time limits the management team's ability to prevent network problems. The IS department is all too often in a no-win situation, lacking tools, time, and expertise. The ideal scenario would be for the IS team to be alerted to potential network problems before the entire network population is affected. By being proactive, the network is always up and becomes invisible to the user. Downtime would no longer be an issue.

The Dangers

Without proper network management, a network faces a number of dangers. These dangers are typically encountered because of a lack of information about the current state of network resources.

Lack of Consistent Service

In the Enterprise Service Provider arena, network downtime can mean the loss of many customer connections. The deciding factor in many service contracts today is not only price but also a guaranteed level of service. An administrative team with the proper monitoring and management tools can anticipate bandwidth and other resource needs in a proactive fashion.

Without the proper tools, an organization will ultimately experience network down time. An extended network outage can have significant side effects. An industry study of Fortune 100 companies' networks revealed:

- An average of 23 failures per year
- Five hours downtime per failure
- Cost = $3.5 million per company

Imposed Fines

The financial industry relies heavily on networks for money transfers. Financial companies cannot afford to have their network down; end-of-day postings need to take place or the Federal Trade Commission could fine the company.

Possible Loss of Life

NASA's mission critical network has a requirement of 99.98% availability. As satellites pass overhead, only a limited amount of time is available to download all the data. This information is used to support military operations abroad. The network must be ready!

The 911-phone system saves countless lives every day. As recently as February 1, 1999 in New York City, a small period of 911 outages created a host of life-threatening situations in which proper care was not easily obtained. Service outages such as this lead to permanent injury and loss of life.

Reduced Productivity

Large enterprises are not the only ones that rely on their networks to be up and running. Any company, large or small, that has servers and printers on a network will come to a stand still if the network is down.

The Benefits

The benefits of network management are inherent, just as managing anything is. Specifically, network management ensures consistent level of service, promotes bandwidth conservation, provides cost/labor efficiency, maintains industry standards, and ensures network security. The sections that follow elaborate on aspects of these benefits of network management.

Ensuring Consistent Level of Service

Providing a network administrator with the proper management tools can have incalculable benefits. The most obvious benefit is reduced downtime. The ability to monitor network links and devices all at once can lead to proactive bandwidth and device management.

Saving on Bandwidth Expenditures

The solution in many networks when a link is congested is to provide more bandwidth to the users without understanding the need first. With the proper tools an evaluation of needs and resources can be made. After analysis it may be discovered that other underutilized links could provide the additional needed bandwidth. This discovery would eliminate the need to purchase more bandwidth. The analysis could also reveal that the traffic is not mission-critical and could be removed from the network. Proper network management applications allow an administrator to address issues and not just put out fires.

The simple, but costly, solution to a poorly performing network had traditionally been to add more bandwidth. By monitoring traffic flows and the activity on your network, the network manager can make a more informed decision—thereby eliminating the need to purchase additional bandwidth. Some typical questions the network manager might be faced with include the following:

- Why are the routers dropping packets?
- Why is response time slow?

By monitoring your network, you will be able to avoid spending dollars on unnecessary bandwidth and equipment. By being well informed about the traffic characteristics, you will be able to implement strategies to improve performance, such as segmenting the network, adding routing filters, relocating servers, and implementing VLAN groups.

Reducing Labor Costs

Could you imagine *manually* testing connectivity to *all* your critical devices or measuring network throughput? The fact is you probably wouldn't perform these important tasks at all; you would rather wait and reactively respond to complaints from the network users. In some situations administrators are forced to spend time learning scripting languages to perform these tasks in a somewhat automated fashion. All the while, the simplest of network management tools could complete these tasks easily.

In a great number of networks even the simplest changes must be done at only certain hours to prevent downtime. To accomplish these tasks, an administrator must often interrupt outside activities to perform operating system upgrades or configuration changes.

Automating repetitive tasks and scheduling other tasks allows an administrator more time for important tasks such as technology selection and network design. By providing a more efficient method for completing these tasks, fewer administrators are needed to manage the network; this can reduce labor costs without increasing workload on current administrators. An organization can do more with fewer resources expended.

With network management tools in place, you can automate repetitive tasks and schedule other tasks to execute at off hours. In addition, the tools can warn you when reaching critical thresholds in device utilization, error counts, and so on. This advanced warning improves your response time to technical issues.

Maintaining Industry Standards

Using standard off-the-shelf products significantly reduces software costs. Products have come a long way to become interoperable with other products. Ideally, we would like to use one platform to manage all resources. A solution that integrates all the aspects of network management into a single platform can provide many additional benefits to a system built piecemeal.

Keeping Systems Secure

In an age when commerce over the Internet has become commonplace, security can no longer take a back seat to other network issues. Without proper network management, security policies are implemented haphazardly. A security policy built only after an intrusion or lapse has taken place does not address the full needs of network security.

Processes such as changing passwords on routers and switches typically only happen in moments of crisis. Many organizations have routers, switches, and servers reporting significant events to Syslog servers. Without constant monitoring of these messages, a possible intrusion could go undetected for days and possibly only discovered when a problem arose. Managing systems in a network requires the use of SNMP. SNMP community strings are as important as the passwords used for telnet and often go unprotected and unchanged. This could lead to open security holes that an administrator is unaware of. For example, a Catalyst 5000 has SNMP enabled by default. The community strings for read-write, which are set to private by default, could allow outside intruders to configure these devices.

Another measure of security is implemented through access-lists. An access-list could permit traffic that should not be allowed if not properly configured. Access-lists are also constantly being updated to accommodate new applications and their traffic needs. Without proper management, access-lists could grow to unmanageable lengths and contain numerous undiscovered holes.

An Investment Worth Paying For

Network management does not come cheap. A medium size network management setup comes at a high price. Table 1-1 provides some estimated prices (not including volume discounts).

Table 1-1   *The Cost of Network Management*

Network Management Component	Resource	Cost
Hardware	One Dual Processor Pentium III PC with 1GB of RAM and 25GB of hard disk storage, tape drive for backup and a network adapter.	$10,000
	RMON Probes with LAN and WAN links (Five).	$75,000
Software	Third Party Management tools.	$30,000
	CiscoWorks 2000 RWAN and Campus.	$20,000
Outsourcing	2-fulltime support engineers for one year.	$180,000

For the medium-size network sketched out in Table 1-1, an initial investment of $315,000 in network management is not something to take lightly; however, you need to counter this cost against the potential losses over several years.

Components for Successful Network Management

A network management platform must provide a number of services to be a complete management solution. These components are based upon industry standards, which help to provide a foundation for the necessary components.

Visibility

The key to a successful network management plan is surprisingly simple—visibility. The more access you have to your network's behavior and configuration, the more swiftly problems can be resolved. Network management does not eliminate or automatically solve network problems. Rather, proper management affords you the ability to attack a potential problem before it becomes an actual problem.

Total visibility of the network extends through the seven-layers of the OSI reference model. This visibility allows you to determine if slow client-server response is due to network loading or an improperly configured protocol.

To provide visibility, network management platforms must provide three basic services:

- **Monitoring**—This is the means by which management information is collected or retrieved from the device or object being managed.

- **Device manipulation or control**—The ability to modify a device's configuration and status from a Management Station.

- **Reporting**—This is the means by which a device or object relays abnormal events.

Standards Requirements

A network management platform is much more than a topology map with colored devices. The International Organization for Standardization (ISO) Network Management Forum has categorized the objectives of a network management system into five functional areas. This list provided the industry with a standard model for describing network management. The functional areas are as follows:

- **Fault Management**—The process of detecting, isolating, and correcting network problems and beginning recovery from them.

- **Performance Management**—The process of analyzing and controlling data throughout a network to provide end users with consistent, reliable service.

- **Configuration Management**—The process of obtaining information from a network and setting up devices based on that information. Configuration management allows centralized control over the configuration of network devices.

- **Accounting Management**—The process of measuring resource utilization on a network to establish metrics, determine costs, bill users, and check quotas.

- **Security Management**—The process of controlling access to network resources and sensitive information. This control is affected by limiting access to network devices, applications on a given device, and network protocols.

Deployment Plan

The needs, risks, requirements, and benefits should now be easy to realize. With these concepts understood, the next question is how can these goals be achieved in a scalable fashion across a large enterprise network?

Management Protocols

Industry network management protocol standards such as SNMP and RMON provide the means to enable these services and standards through a network management platform.

Implementing a network management platform requires an implementation plan and an understanding of how network management platforms operate.

Most network management platforms function using a combination of industry standard and proprietary protocols as their means of communication with an agent. These protocols are typically implemented through Transmission Control Protocol/Internet Protocol (TCP/IP).

The most common network management protocol is SNMP; it has become the *de facto* standard for use in today's network management solutions.

Each managed device is viewed as having thousands of variables that quantify the state of the device. By reading the values of these variables, the managed device is *monitored*. By writing the values of these variables the managed device is *controlled*.

The MIB

A *Management Information Base (MIB)* is a precise definition of the information variables accessible through a network management protocol like SNMP.

The OSI management model uses MIB to store the structured information representing network elements and their attributes. The structure itself is called SMI (Structure of Management Information). The MIBs that a device supports reside in the device itself. A process on that device, referred to as an *agent*, is used to access the different variables within the MIB. SNMP is used to send and receive information about these variables to and from the management station.

A unique *object identifier*, which is a number in dot notation that traverses the SMI tree, identifies each MIB object. Each object identifier is appended with an instance to differentiate it from multiple occurrences of the same object. The distinguishing variable appended to the object is called the *instance*. For example, each router interface would collect the same set of values to distinguish between the interfaces that use the object's instance. Simple objects with only one occurrence in the managed node have an instance of 0. In the RMON MIB, for example, all statistics are in the Statistics table and have an OID of 1.3.6.1.2.1.16.1. The list of Ethernet statistics entries adds .1 to the end of the statistics table. In the etherStatsTable an instance is added to represent each interface and might, for example, be a .1. Then the statistic adds an instance for each variable in the table. For example, .6 would represent broadcast packets received. The complete identifier for etherStatsBroadcastPkts is 1.3.6.1.2.1.16.1.1.1.6.

Each object identifier is described using Abstract Syntax Notation (ASN.1). This notation format is referred to as *dotted notation*.

MIBs are highly structured depositories for information about a device. Many standard MIBs exist, but more proprietary MIBs are available to uniquely manage different companies' devices. Proprietary MIBs are defined in the same method as industry standard MIBs and use SNMP in the same manner.

The MIB implemented by almost all network devices is the Internet MIB II. MIB II support requires, at a minimum, support for RFC 1213 (the MIB II RFC). The RFC for MIB I and MIB II have been superceded by RFCs 1573 and 2233. Agents have been written to support MIB II for most devices that support TCP/IP. For information on Cisco support of RFC 1213, 1573, 2233, and many other RFCs, check the Cisco ftp site at ftp://www.cisco.com/pub/mibs/schema. This site contains the different schema files for Cisco hardware.

Many other standard MIBs exist—RMON, Host, Router, Ethernet 802.2, and Token Ring are just a few. Over 200 different RFCs describe the SNMP protocol and its derivatives. Many organizations have also defined proprietary MIBs for their own devices, such as the LAN Manager MIB for Windows NT stations and the Cisco hardware MIBs for router and switch devices. Table 1-2 shows some commonly found devices that would be monitored in a network and which object typically is most important to monitor.

Table 1-2   *Devices That Should Be Monitored*

Device	MIB Variables to Monitor
Router	Free buffers, congestions, errors, drop packets.
	Detect loopback, non-routed requests.
Bridge	Dropped packets, error rate.
	Unauthorized users.
UPS	Wattage level, peak current level, changes in input voltage.
Server	Number of processes, CPU and disk utilization.
HUB	Collisions or port threshold, intruders and port security.

Each managed object within an MIB has a unique object identifier. An object identifier is simply a string of non-negative values that traverse a SMI tree (see Figure 1-1).

Figure 1-1 *Sample of the Internet MIB for TCP/IP*

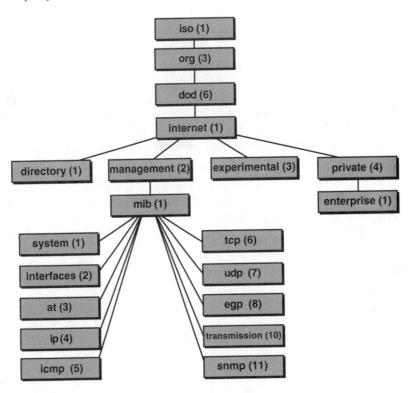

The boxes in the graph represent branches. Each end branch would support multiple leaves or the actual MIB variables.

The Cisco MIB

The *Cisco MIB* is defined as the ninth subordinate of the enterprise branch. A good portion of the Cisco MIB is defined in three subtrees of the SMI identifier 1.3.6.1.4.1.9 or iso.org.dod.internet.private.enterprise.cisco. The three subtrees are local (2), temporary (3), and ciscoMgmt (9).

The local subtree contains MIB objects defined prior to Cisco IOS Software Release 10.2. These MIB objects implemented the SNMPv1 SMI. Beginning with Cisco IOS Software Release 10.2, however, Cisco MIBs are defined according to the SNMPv2 SMI. The temporary subtree was used for experimental objects prior to IOS 10.2.

MIBs defined with SNMPv2 SMI are placed in the ciscoMgmt subtree. MIBs currently defined in the local subtree are being gradually deprecated by Cisco and replaced with new objects defined in the ciscoMgmt subtree. The local subtree is used by IOS 10.2 and earlier.

IOS 10.2 is currently EOL. The ciscoMgmt subtree is the main subtree for new MIB development.

The Cisco MIBs are available from the Cisco web site at www.cisco.com/public/sw-center/netmgmt/cmtk/mibs.shtml. These MIBs can be loaded by an Network Management Station (NMS) if it supports loading outside MIBs. MIB files maintain certain syntax. The Cisco MIB follows the syntax as specified in RFC 1902-1908. RFC 1902-1908 has made these RFCs obsolete; the Cisco MIB will soon be updated to support these new formats. Very few syntax differences occur between the revisions.

Cisco's MIB variables can be mapped to the ISO functional areas previously described and are used to manage your network.

SNMP

The industry standard management protocol is SNMP. SNMP provides a number of services for managing devices in the network. These services are provided by the different components of the SNMP protocol.

SNMP Messages

The simplicity of SNMP is seen in the simple set of operations available in the protocol. In SNMP all actions take place in the form of messages between the management station and the agent on the managed device. SNMP uses three types of messages—Get, Set, and Trap.

When a management station wishes to access information on an agent, it issues a Get request. When the management station wants to change the value of an MIB variable, it issues a Set request. The agent can also be programmed to respond to changes in the values of a local variable and will generate a message to the management station called a Trap. SNMPv2 adds the GetBulk message types, which reduces the repetitive requests and replies, therefore improving the performance when retrieving large amounts of date (in other words, tables). Figure 1-2 shows the different SNMP message types and their direction between the management station and the agent.

SNMP Community-Strings

The next SNMP components are community strings. In the SNMP community, strings serve a similar purpose to network passwords. Two types of SNMP community strings exist—a *read-only* and a *read-write* community string. The message type issued determines the community string used. When the management station issues a GET request the read-only community string is used. When the management station issues a SET request, the read-write community string is used. When the agent sends a TRAP, it uses the read-only community string.

Figure 1-2   *SNMP Message Types*

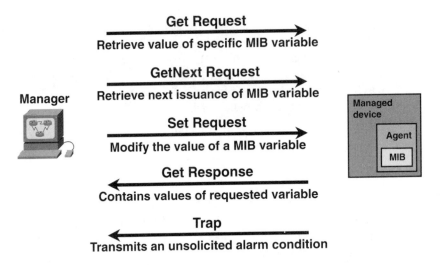

In SNMP v1 and v2, these community strings are sent across the network in every SNMP message and are in clear text format as depicted in Figure 1-3.

The roles that the components in Figure 1-3 have are as follows:

- **Manager**—Polls agents on network; correlates and displays information.
- **SNMP**—Protocol for message exchange (IP-to-UDP-to-SNMP).
- **Agents**—Collect and store information; respond to Manager requests for information; generate traps.
- **MIBs**—Database of objects (information variables) with access controlled by read-write community strings.

The danger created by the vulnerability of clear text community strings has led many networking vendors to only implement read-only capability in a device. Someone eavesdropping on a conversation between the management station and the agent could acquire these community strings from the packets. With the community strings, the eavesdropper could reconfigure network devices where these strings are used. This explanation is why periodic changing of community strings is recommended as frequently as changing passwords.

SNMP in Action

SNMP was designed to be simple to use and implement. SNMP requires few resources to implement efficiently. The industry acceptance of SNMP as the network management protocol of choice has led to its evolving feature set.

Figure 1-3   *A Network Manager Uses SNMP to Retrieve the Information from the Managed Device*

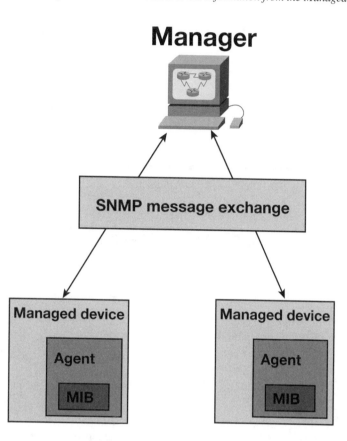

SNMP is the transport mechanism that allows retrieval of management information (MIB variables). SNMP uses User Datagram Protocol (UDP) transport of the IP protocol. See Figure 1-4 for an example of how MIBs are retrieved via SNMP.

SNMP Traps and Alarms

The job of the manager is to determine whether the value returned signifies a potential problem or not. The administrator can also configure traps triggered by these values. This decision is normally based upon configured thresholds set by the network administrator. When a value exceeds the threshold or falls below it the administrator can define an alarm. Typically the network management station contains some capability to respond to the alarms by executing a script or by sending an email or page.

Figure 1-4   *MIB Variable Retrieval via SNMP*

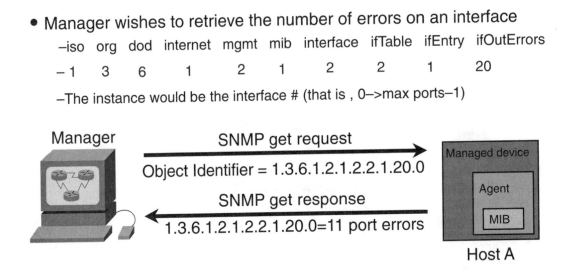

- Manager wishes to retrieve the number of errors on an interface
  - –iso org dod internet mgmt mib interface ifTable ifEntry ifOutErrors
  - – 1 3 6 1 2 1 2 2 1 20
  - –The instance would be the interface # (that is , 0–>max ports–1)

If the variable is a counter type (like ifOutErrors), the management station will need to take two samples of this variable and subtract them to determine the variable's rate. Remember, counter type variables continuously increase until they have been reset by a power cycle or have exceeded the counter limit.

SNMP Issues

Network management traffic bandwidth utilization has long been a troubling subject for network managers. Figure 1-5 depicts that even with minimal management efforts, a WAN link can be quickly and easily saturated.

This highlights the need to determine proper polling intervals. Because of the potential for management traffic to eat up bandwidth, a network management strategy must ensure that only relevant data is collected and only as often as is absolutely necessary. Additional polling problems that could be caused are excessive CPU utilization caused by the device constantly checking statistics.

Note that this method of polling for values can be resource intensive. Wouldn't it be nice to have something that only informed the manager of when a problem is starting to occur? In other words, a method to make the network intelligent instead of relying solely upon the network management station. This can be accomplished by using events and alarms on the agent, rather then polling. Some agents can be programmed to check their own variables and send traps based upon configured thresholds. This setup can help to reduce constant polling traffic.

Figure 1-5   *How Polling Can Consume Bandwidth on Slow WAN Links*

Example:

1 manager, multiple managed devices
64 kbps access link
1 request = 1 KB packet (avg.)
1 poll = getreq + getresp = 2KB
Assume 1 object polled/managed device

% of bandwidth utilized

Number of stations being polled				
10	50	25	12.5	8.3
20	100	50	25	16
30	150	75	37	25
	5	10	20	30

Polling interval in seconds

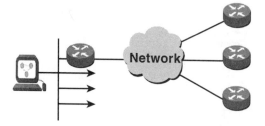

Remote Monitoring

SNMP is defined to monitor and manage devices. However, SNMP lacks the capacity to monitor the network that the device is attached to. To properly provide visibility to all levels of the OSI seven-layer model, a separate protocol based upon the foundation of SNMP has been defined. Remote Monitoring (RMON-1 and RMON-2) are a specific implementation used to manage the network itself.

The RMON MIB was designed to manage the network itself. Internet MIB I/II could be used to check each machine's network performance, but would lead to large amounts of bandwidth for management traffic. By using RMON, you see the wire view of the network and not just a single host's view. RMON has the capability to set performance thresholds and only report if the threshold is breached, again helping to reduce management traffic (effectively distributing the network management intelligence). RMON agents can reside in routers, switches, and dedicated boxes. The RMON-1 agents gather nine (ten with Token Ring) groups of statistics. RMON-2 agents add nine more groups to the RMON-1 specification. The agents then forward this information upon request from a management station.

The SMI for RMON variables begin with 1.3.6.1.2.1.16 or iso.org.dod.internet.mgmt. mib.rmon. The original RMON MIB implementation utilized a large number of tables making memory a premium. RMON agents must look at every frame on the network. The higher the traffic levels, the more important performance becomes. An RMON performance could be classified based on processing power and memory.

RMON-1

RMON-1 consisted of nine groups of variables as specified in RFC 1757 and 1513. A tenth group was added for Token Ring support with counters specific to Token Ring environments. Table 1-3 lists the ten RMON groups and provides a brief description of their use.

Table 1-3   *RMON-1 Groups*

RMON-1 Group	Function
statistics	Real-time/current statistics
history	Statistics over time
alarm	Predetermined threshold watch
host	Tracks individual host statistics
hostTopN	"N" statistically most active hosts
matrix	A < > B-conversation statistics
filter	Packet structure and content matching
capture	Collection for subsequent analysis
event	Reaction to predetermined conditions
tokenRing	Token Ring-RMON extensions

Remember that visibility is the key to successful network management. RMON-1 can only provide visibility into the data link and physical layers of the OSI reference model. Potential problems occurring at the higher layers still require capture and decode tools. Although RMON-1 could provide information about traffic statistics, the information had limited use due to this lack of visibility. An administrator might discover an inordinate amount of traffic to or from a particular device but would be unable to decipher OSI Layer 3 or higher information. The RMON working group went back to the drawing board.

RMON-2

The RMON working group created and standardized RMON-2, which adds to RMON-1 visibility in the upper layers. The RMON-2 MIB implementation strategy was changed from that of RMON-1 to avoid an excess number of tables. Tables are, however, still used but much more efficiently.

RMON-2 now lets administrators collect statistics beyond the segment. (See Figure 1-6.) Because RMON-1 only observed data link layer addressing, it limited the scope of a conversation to a single segment. Conversations can be viewed at the network layer, not just at the MAC layer (host-to-router). Network layer addresses go end to end in a conversation extending the scope past one segment.

Figure 1-6   *The Advantage of Extending the Scope of RMON-1 to RMON-2 by Going Beyond the Segment*

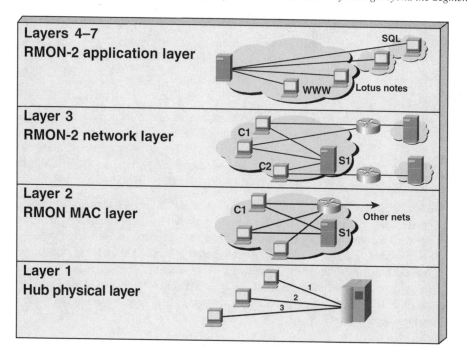

RMON-2 adds nine more groups to the original RMON-1. RMON-2 is an addition to RMON-1, not a replacement of RMON-1. Table 1-4 lists the additional groups extended to those listed in Table 1-3 and provides a brief description of each one.

Table 1-4   *RMON-2 Groups*

RMON-2 Group	Function
protocolDir	Probe's master list of protocols
protocolDist	Segment protocol statistics
addressMap	Host-to-MAC address matching list
nlHost	Host in/out: network layer statistics
nlMatrix	A < > B: network layer statistics
alHost	Host in/out: application layer statistics
alMatrix	A < > B: application layer statistics
usrHistory	Data logging: user specified variables
probeConfig	Probe configuration standards

With the additional groups, an administrator can now view not only data link layer statistics but also information from the higher layers. This provides maximum visibility into the network. Conversations can now be identified by network addresses and transport layer information, such as ports or socket numbers, which can help to identify applications.

Summary

A properly executed network management initiative can reduce capital equipment costs, administrative overhead, and provide for a proactively managed environment helping to avoid problems. Without proper network management software, an administrator wastes time on repetitive tasks and spends the remaining time putting out fires that might have been avoided with the proper information from a management station.

With the right network management software and strategy, a network administrator can better manage the resources of a network. A network management station uses software to provide information about the network via SNMP to perform queries in the network. SNMP is the industry standard protocol used to gather information and configure devices in the network. RMON puts forth information about what the network is being used for by providing a view of the wire itself. Both SNMP and RMON use MIBs to define databases of objects each can query and community strings to control access to the individual agents on the devices.

After the decision has been made to implement a network management solution, a proper product suite needs to be selected. In the next chapter, an overview of the different CiscoWorks 2000 suites will explain how the different suites fit into a Cisco network management solution.

Topics covered in this chapter include the following:

- Overview of Cisco Network Management Products
- CiscoWorks 2000 Product Family
    - CD-One
    - CiscoView Web
    - Resource Manager Essentials
    - TrafficDirector
    - Service Level Manager
    - Blue Maps and SNA View
    - Voice Manager
    - CiscoWorks for Windows 5.0

## CHAPTER 2

Cisco Network Management Products

Network management is important to all business operations, from Fortune 100 Companies to small businesses.

Today's mission-critical network environments not only move data but also voice and video. The reliance on network appliances in every organization heightens the need for a suitable network management application.

Cisco Systems has addressed the need for network management by offering applications for all levels of network size and application. Before proceeding into the Resource Manager Essentials application, a brief overview of the products in the Cisco network management arena is important. This information not only explains which application is the best choice for an organization, but also discusses the future direction of network management in a Cisco Systems powered network.

Overview of Cisco Network Management Products

Cisco Systems manufactures many types of devices and software to support a converged network. The software and equipment Cisco offers to its customers includes routers, switches, network security appliances, telephony hardware, voice and video application servers, and much more. The diversity of the Cisco product line enables Cisco to provide their customers with a complete end-to-end single vendor solution.

This diversity can increase the complexity of network design, deployment, and operation. To aid customers in managing their networks, Cisco provides many different solutions. Training for Authorized Training partners, books from Cisco Press, and other instructional tools can prepare the network administrator to manage a network. As the network gets larger, however, even the most talented of network administrators can become overwhelmed. Most of the devices are managed through a command line interface or web interface one device at a time. As discussed in Chapter 1, "Network Management Essentials," this type of micromanagement can become time consuming and inefficient.

One of the main objectives of the Cisco network management products is to ease the burden on the administrator without any loss of control. Many of the Cisco network management applications are purposely designed with features to support managing multiple devices simultaneously. For example, using a View in Resource Manager Essentials, an administrator can change settings on multiple devices simultaneously. In addition, applications such as Cisco QOS Policy Manager allow an administrator to deploy organization-wide policies for network use.

Configuring devices in one application lowers the time an administrator has to spend on low-level tasks and therefore concentrates on getting the most out of the technology. Many of the new applications being developed by Cisco today are either web-based or client-server based.

This chapter describes some of the applications Cisco has developed to ease the administrative burden. Many of the applications are described under the heading of CiscoWorks 2000. The Cisco network management product suite is in the process of migrating over to a single web-based management environment. The CiscoWorks 2000 environment is the foundation for this application platform.

The CiscoWorks 2000 Product Family

One major issue with implementing network management across many different classes of devices is the lack of a central management console with a consistent interface. One of the goals in the design of the CiscoWorks 2000 suite is to overcome this hurdle.

CiscoWorks 2000 has three major incarnations:

- CiscoWorks 2000 Routed Wide Area Network (RWAN)
- CiscoWorks 2000 Local Area Network Management Solution (LMS)
- CiscoWorks 2000 Service Level Manager (SLM)

These bundles serve as the foundation for the CiscoWorks 2000 management framework.

All the bundles have certain applications in common. Central components across the three bundles are CD-One, Resource Manager Essentials, and TrafficDirector. CD-One contains the CiscoWorks 2000 Server Console and CiscoView Web. Resource Manager Essentials is a centralized device and inventory management system. TrafficDirector is an RMON management station.

CD-One

CD-One is the first CD used in installation of the CiscoWorks 2000 product suite. CD-One contains the Common Management Framework (CMF). The CMF contains the common components used by the CiscoWorks 2000 products: user management, web-server, Java Run Time engine, CORBA (Common Object Request Broker Agent), and the ANI (Asynchronous Network Interface) process. CD-One also contains CiscoView Web.

CiscoWorks 2000 uses this combination of industry standard and open technologies to implement a network management platform that supports the Common Information Model

(CIM). *CIM* is an object-oriented conceptual model for the information and is required to manage many common aspects of complex computer systems, defined by the Desktop Management Task Force (DMTF).

Ongoing development of CIM is part of an industry-wide initiative for enabling enterprise management of devices and applications. A primary goal of CIM is the presentation of a consistent view of the managed environment independent of the various protocols and data formats supported by those devices and applications. Many network infrastructure and management software providers have accepted CIM as an information model for enterprise management tools.

The schema for network integration defined in this specification and CIM are complementary. The extended schema is primarily concerned with the expression and management of policy in both enterprise and service provider networks. CIM is primarily concerned with the management of individual components in the context of the enterprise. The enhanced, integrated network and directory service and CIM have many information needs in common.

The schema for integrating networks and the directory service incorporates concepts from both X.500 and CIM. The use of CIM promotes synergy between integrated, enhanced network and directory applications and management applications that use CIM:

- CIM and applications written to use CIM are natural sources of information for the directory.

- The directory is a natural source of information for CIM and applications written to use CIM. It adds models for defining and enforcing policy.

- Network applications integrated with the directory benefit from CIM. CIM applications benefit from network applications integrated with the directory with minimal effort on the application developer's part because the directory-enabled network schema is an extension of the CIM schema. Thus, there is no need for cumbersome information mapping.

Having one centralized management console makes an administrator's job easier. One network management console with one security model allows an administrator to assign a user's roles based upon the user's network responsibilities. The CiscoWorks 2000 Security can also be integrated with MS Active Directory, Netscape Directory, NT Native, RADIUS, and TACACS+. This configuration allows users to use a common user name and allows administrators to ease password administration.

Needing only one web server address to access all network management resources makes it easier for users. Connections to external third party web-based applications can be integrated to provide access from the CiscoWorks 2000 Server Console. Figure 2-1 shows the CiscoWorks 2000 Server console.

Figure 2-1   *The CiscoWorks 2000 Server Console*

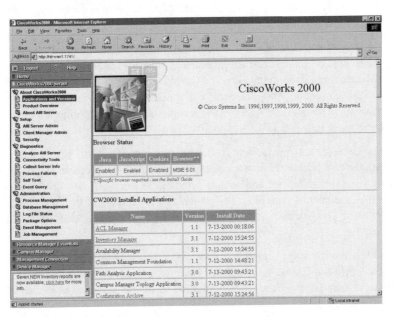

CiscoView Web

CiscoView is a graphical device management application. Using specific definition files for each device, the chassis of that device is represented in the application. The representation of the chassis is the same as the physical view of the actual device. Ports and interfaces are shown in their present real-time state. Using SNMP, CiscoView exposes different configuration and monitoring tools. These tools are specific to each device. This graphical interface allows an administrator a non-command line method for configuring basic device attributes. Figure 2-2 shows a Cisco 2612 router being managed by CiscoView. CiscoView Web Server is a web-based implementation of the familiar product CiscoView.

CiscoView is a central component of the CiscoWorks 2000 suite and appears in RWAN, LMS, and CiscoWorks for Windows 5.0. In CiscoWorks for Windows, CiscoView is again a standalone application.

CiscoView is also one of the applications that can be integrated into third party management platforms. In CiscoWorks for Windows 5.0, CiscoView can be launched from the What's Up Gold application by selecting any Cisco device being monitored, for example.

As an application in the RWAN and LMS suite, CiscoView can be launched from the version of Internet Explorer and Netscape Navigator browsers listed in the release notes.

Figure 2-2   *The CiscoView Web Application*

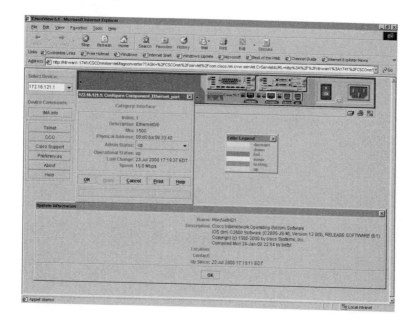

In applications like HP Openview, CiscoView can be launched from a remote server by using a http link to the CiscoView Server. Resource Manager Essentials Device Center can also launch the CiscoView application.

Resource Manager Essentials

Resource Manager Essentials is a fully web-based device and inventory management application. Resource Manager Essentials is also the main subject of this book, and provides many different features, such as inventory management, software management, configuration management, and Syslog message management. In the RWAN application suite, the Access-Control List Manager application is also included. Figure 2-3 shows the Resource Manager Essentials Application menus.

For a more detailed overview of Resource Manager Essentials see Chapter 5, "CiscoWorks 2000 Resource Manager Essentials 3.X."

Figure 2-3   *Resource Manager Essentials*

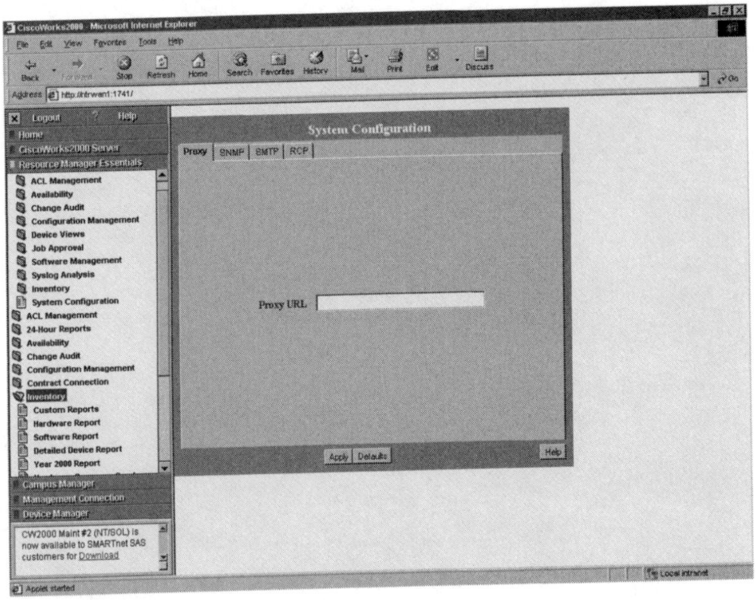

TrafficDirector

TrafficDirector is an RMON management station that enables an administrator to monitor and record information about network usage, events, and trends, and identify and isolate many fault conditions in data communication networks. To provide these capabilities, TrafficDirector is dependent on the RMON capabilities of the device it manages. Traffic-Director is not a promiscuous Ethernet sniffer. Without an RMON agent in the target device, TrafficDirector does not provide any information.

The TrafficDirector application consists of a centralized, SNMP-compatible network management console and data-gathering agents located at various points on a network. Figure 2-4 shows the TrafficDirector application monitoring a Catalyst 2924XL switch.

An administrator can use the TrafficDirector application to perform several basic functions:

- Monitoring network traffic and measuring data flow on probes and catalyst switches.
- Setting limit conditions on network traffic and generating alarms if those limits are exceeded.

- Capturing and displaying fully decoded network traffic, collecting statistical data, and recording it for later examination from RMON probes only.

- Obtaining real-time updates from all segments of a widely dispersed enterprise network by monitoring multiple agents. Using TCP/IP connectivity, TrafficDirector can gather statistics from agent in an enterprise location.

Figure 2-4   *TrafficDirector*

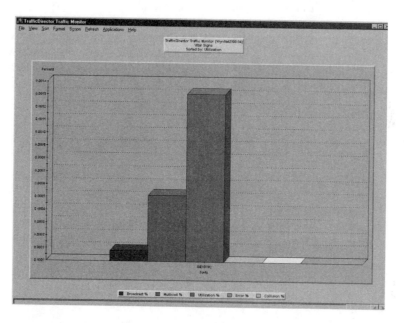

At the time of this writing TrafficDirector is one of the few remaining applications of the CiscoWorks 2000 suite that is not web-based. The TrafficDirector application must be installed on the station where the administrator plans to implement network monitoring.

CiscoWorks 2000 RWAN Bundle

CiscoWorks 2000 RWAN bundle includes the central CiscoWorks 2000 applications CD-One, CiscoView, Resource Manager Essentials, and TrafficDirector. Added into RWAN are the Access-Control List Manager (ACL) and Internetwork Performance Monitor (IPM).

RWAN has been specifically designed for management of routed wide-area networks. ACL Manager provides a web-based interface to manage TCP/IP and IPX access lists. ACL Manager makes managing security policies easier across multiple devices. The IPM tool is used to perform response time analysis in multiprotocol networks. IPM can analyze protocol latency on routers.

Access-Control List Manager

The ACL Manager application is designed for the experienced network administrator who already understands the structure and uses of ACLs. This application allows users to create, modify, and deploy ACLs to multiple devices through a Windows Explorer-type interface. ACL Manager supports IP and IPX ACLs.

With ACL Manager, an administrator can create ACL uses for traffic filtering and line access. Although an administrator cannot create all types of ACL uses, all existing types of ACL uses are recognized and tracked. This means that if an ACL is used in a category other than traffic filtering or line access, the ACL references in those statements will be changed if the ACL name is changed. ACL Manager also allows comments to be associated with an ACL or access control entry (ACE) so that an administrator can audit and track changes on a per-ACL or ACE-basis. Figure 2-5 shows the Access-Control List Manager application.

Figure 2-5 *Access-Control List Manager*

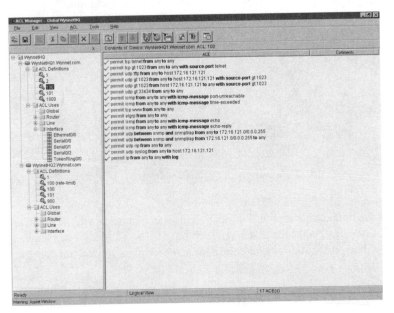

Internetwork Performance Monitor

IPM is a client server-based application. The client and server component can run on two different systems.

The client application is installed separately from the server. IPM is a network management application that enables you to monitor the performance of multiprotocol networks. IPM measures the latency and availability of IP networks on a hop-by-hop (router-to-router) basis. IPM also measures latency between routers and the mainframe in Systems Network Architecture (SNA) networks.

Use IPM to perform the following tasks:

- Troubleshoot problems by checking the network performance between devices.
- Send Simple Network Management Protocol (SNMP) traps and SNA alerts when a user-configured threshold is exceeded, a connection is lost and reestablished, or a timeout occurs.
- Analyze potential problems before one occurs by accumulating statistics, which can be used to model and predict future network topologies.
- Monitor latency errors between two network end points.
- Monitor jitter availability and errors between two network end points.

The IPM Server component is currently only supported on the UNIX platform. At the time this book was written, a version was in development for the Windows NT platform.

CiscoWorks 2000 LMS

The *CiscoWorks 2000 LMS* product suite includes all of the CiscoWorks 2000 foundation products: CD-One, CiscoView, Resource Manager Essentials and TrafficDirector. Added to the foundation are Campus Manager and Content Flow Monitor.

The Campus Manager application integrates into the CiscoWorks 2000 console to provide management capabilities for a Routed/Switched LAN network. The Content Flow Monitor is a web-based manager of Cisco Load Balancing Services.

Campus Manager

The *Campus Manager* Application includes three components: Topology Services, Path Analysis, and User Tracking. The ANI process serves these applications the necessary information about managed network devices. The ANI server provides network discovery services to the Campus applications. The discovery process uses the Cisco Discovery Protocol (CDP) to locate and recognize Cisco devices in a routed and switched network.

Topology Services

Topology Services is an application that enables an administrator to manage and discover devices in Layer 2 and Layer 3 networks.

With Topology Services, an administrator can manage and create VLANs (virtual local area networks) for Ethernet, Token Ring, and ATM LANE-based networks. By using topology services, an administrator can create VLANs in multiple VTP (Virtual Trunking Protocol) Domains. Ports across multiple switching platforms can also be assigned to VLANs.

Topology Services also provide a logical view of both Layer 2 and Layer 3 connected devices. These connections are displayed in topology maps selected from the Topology Services applications. By selecting a VLAN, or a Layer 2 or Layer 3 network, a new map is generated displaying only relevant devices. Figure 2-6 shows the Topology Service Map for a Layer 2/3 network.

Figure 2-6 *Topology Services*

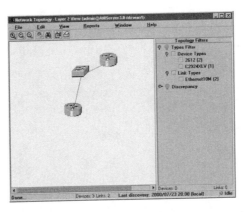

In a switched environment Spanning-Tree management can also be a burden. The topology maps can display Spanning-Tree port states, such as forwarding or blocking, and also which device is the root of the tree.

Path Analysis

Many network administrators are familiar with the traceroute tool. Traceroute will discover the Layer 3 paths through a TCP/IP network. In today's switched environment, the Layer 3 path is not necessarily a correct representation of the number of Layer 2 devices a packet must pass through from source to destination.

The Path Analysis tool overcomes these shortfalls in the traceroute tool.

Path Analysis will trace the path of a frame through Layer 2 and Layer 3 devices using information provided by the ANI services. By using TCP/IP addresses or hostnames, the Path Analysis tool can discover the path between both Layer 2 and Layer 3 devices. For the Path Analysis tool to properly show the trace, the devices must be in the CiscoWorks 2000 LMS database. Therefore because only Cisco Devices are discovered in the topology services on Cisco devices, the Path Analysis tool will show the Layer 2 paths. Figure 2-7 shows the Path Analysis application.

Figure 2-7   *Path Analysis*

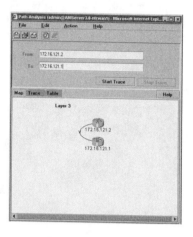

Path Analysis presents the information in both graphical and text format. When the path is completely traced, CiscoView, Telnet, and the Cisco Visual Switch Manager can be invoked to manage the devices in the path.

One significant advantage to Path Analysis is that the trace does not have to source from the CiscoWorks 2000 server or client. The path can trace through any managed device in the network.

User Tracking

As the network grows more complex, troubleshooting client connectivity becomes more difficult. To properly troubleshoot a client connection an administrator needs to know the following information about the client:

- User name
- TCP/IP address
- Hostname
- MAC Address
- VLAN
- Default gateway
- Switch port
- Switch

- VTP Domain
- Last logon time

By using User Tracking, the information above can be dynamically discovered easing the administrative burden. The information is gathered using the discovered devices in the Topology Map. This information is generated automatically at scheduled intervals. Figure 2-8 shows the User Tracking application after it has discovered the host NTRWAN1 and user mwyns.

Figure 2-8   *User Tracking*

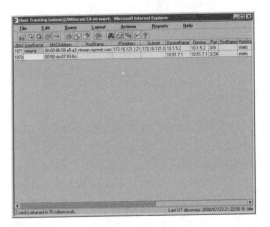

The user information can be queried to locate certain devices in the network. The tool can be helpful in providing information normally beyond the scope of the local user's knowledge to provide.

Content Flow Monitor

Content Flow Monitor (CFM) is a web-based status monitoring application within the CiscoWorks2000 product family for managing Cisco server load balancing devices. CFM leverages Cisco's ContentFlow Architecture (CoFA) to intelligently discover the roles and relationships of server load balancing devices.

CFM monitors the content delivery network and presents up-to-date aggregated device health status, service availability, detailed device configuration, and real-time performance statistics. CFM reduces network management complexity and provides status-monitoring capabilities for Cisco server load balancing devices.

CFM supports the following content delivery network architectures:

- *Standalone LocalDirector* is a turnkey solution with an embedded operating system. It is used for easy installation and low management with advanced load balancing features, such as SSL sticky and packet coloring. It is a local load balancer and supports up to 240-Mbps throughput and 18,000 connections per second.

- *MultiNode Load Balancing (MNLB)* is a load balancing solution that uses a multinode architecture with multiple load balancing devices working in tandem to achieve the highest level of availability, scalability, and performance for server applications.

You can use CFM to monitor the following entities:

- **Services manager**—The brains of server load balancing. A services manager makes load-balancing decisions based on application availability, server capacity, and load distribution algorithms, such as round robin or least connections. Using load balancing and server/application feedback, the services manager determines a real server for the packet flow and sends this information to the requesting forwarding agent. Once the optimal destination is decided, all other packets in the packet flow are directed to a real server by the forwarding agent increasing packet throughput.

- **Forwarding agent**—Packet redirector that forwards packets based on decisions made by the services manager. The forwarding agent filters packets coming into the virtual network and sends packets without a known server destination to the services manager.

- **Real server**—Physical computing engine or part of a physical-computing engine that offers one or more application services to a set of clients in the network. This includes Windows NT or Solaris servers.

- **Virtual server**—Presents a single virtual IP address that represents an application server farm for clients.

Service Level Manager

Today's enterprise users and Internet service customers rely on the network as an integral component of their corporate infrastructure. As a result, they need to monitor service contract agreements with their service providers and verify that defined network performance levels are being fulfilled. The Cisco Service Level Manager (SLM) provides the ability to monitor such service provider performance.

The SLM application concentrates its monitoring on the WAN edge, the boundary where the enterprise network meets service provider WAN services

Using SLM, you can define Service Level Contracts (SLCs) with service providers in a common language and a style that both the service provider and the service customer can recognize.

SLCs are used to describe the connectivity and performance agreements for a WAN service from a service provider to a service customer. SLCs comprise Service Level Agreements (SLAs) that measure performance between a pair of devices defined by the end user to represent any two hardware components connected by a network. Device pairs can include routers, servers, workstations, and so on. Using SLM, you can monitor the percentage of SLA conformance for that SLC.

The SLC can include a single SLA or multiple SLAs. After the SLC and its SLAs are defined, SLM initiates the appropriate network-based collection of data and testing to verify that the SLAs are being met. The data is stored and reports are generated from Java applets. There is almost no limit to the number of SLCs that can be created or the number of SLAs contained within an SLC. The SLM application is capable of monitoring 500 operations.

When an SLC is created, the SLM server contacts the Management Engine 1100 (ME 1100) Series to gather data. Data polling is performed periodically and the results are stored in the SLM database.

In addition to monitoring current service-level performance, service customers have the ability to realize long-term, service-level performance, and thus determine patterns and trends associated with network use.

The Management Engine 1100 Series

The *Management Engine (ME) 1100 Series* is a network appliance that performs distributed data collection and aggregation functions for network management applications. The ME 1100 Series is used by the SLM to collect performance data needed to monitor service level agreements that you have established with your service providers. Several ME 1100 Series can be deployed in your network.

Each ME 1100 Series collects the appropriate service-level metrics from its assigned set of Service Assurance (SA) Agent-enabled network devices using SNMP. The SLM application periodically collects data so as not to overload the network. Data is collected using HTTP data stream and XML format. This distributed architecture enables localized collection of management data across virtual private networks (VPNs) and firewalls.

CiscoWorks Blue Maps and SNA View

CiscoWorks Blue Maps and *CiscoWorks Blue SNA View* provide a set of UNIX Motif and web-based applications for diagnosing problems and managing integrated networks. CiscoWorks 2000 Blue Maps integrates into the CiscoWorks 2000 environment as an extended SNA specific add-in. These managed networks are based on SNA and TCP/IP environments.

SNA View is a web-based application. The SNA View web server runs in a UNIX workstation gathering information about routers and SNA LUs and PUs from the SNA View and Maps database. When you link to the SNA View web page, you can display SNA session paths.

CiscoWorks Blue Maps is a set of applications that let you manage Cisco routers in an IBM SNA network. Each Map's application focuses on a particular protocol: DLSw, RSRB, or APPN. Maps display graphical views of SNA networks connected with Cisco routers. These views are dynamically updated to provide snapshots of the network as it appears at any time.

Maps also let an administrator see beyond the routers to the SNA PUs and LUs that use the DLSw, RSRB, or APPN protocols. Maps' mainframe component discovers the PUs and LUs from VTAM information at the mainframe, monitors those PUs and LUs, and reports their changing status to the Maps workstation applications to update the Maps database and the graphical maps.

CiscoWorks 2000 Voice Manager 2.X

CiscoWorks 2000 Voice Manager 2.X (CVM) is a client-server, web-based voice management solution used by network administrators to configure and manage voice ports and create and modify dial plans on voice-enabled Cisco routers. Using CVM, network administrators can

- Manage the configuration of FXO, FXS, E&M, and ISDN voice interfaces on voice-enabled routers.
- Create and manage local (POTS) dial plans on voice-enabled routers.
- Create and manage VoIP, VoFR, and VoATM network dial plans on voice-enabled routers.
- Generate detailed reports using Telemate.net Quickview.

Key Features in CVM

CVM is a client-server, web-based voice management solution. The following list describes some of the key features of CVM:

- **Voice Port Management**—Manage the configuration of FXO, FXS, E&M, and ISDN configurations in single or batch mode.
- **Dial Plan Management**—Create and manage local dial plans and VoIP, VoFR, and VoATM network dial plans.

- **Report Generation**—See the Telemate.net Quickview documentation for complete details of the reports you can generate. Reports can be generated on Internet calls based upon destination, gateway, length, calling card number, costing, and many other categories.

- **Multiple Platform Support**—CVM clients can run in web browsers running Windows 95, Windows NT, or Solaris platforms.

- **Integration with Cisco Works 2000 CD-One**—CVM is integrated with CiscoWorks2000 CD-One, which provides a common platform for running different applications that manage a wide variety of router functions.

- **Scalability**—CVM can scale to support combinations of the following voice-enabled Cisco routers: Cisco 1700 series, Cisco 2600 series, Cisco 3600 series, Cisco MC3810 multiservice access concentrator, Cisco AS5300 series universal access server, and Cisco 7200/7500 series.

CiscoWorks for Windows 5.0

CiscoWorks for Windows 5.0 is a comprehensive network management solution that provides a powerful set of monitoring and configuration tools to simplify the administration of small to medium business networks and workgroups containing Cisco internetworking products switches, routers, hubs, and access servers.

CiscoWorks for Windows comprises the following tools:

- **CiscoView Version 5.0**—Provides graphical back-panel and front-panel views of Cisco devices; dynamic, color-coded graphical displays to simplify device-status monitoring; device-specific component diagnostics, device configuration, and application launching.

- **WhatsUp Gold Version 4.05 from Ipswitch, Inc.**—Provides network discovery, mapping, monitoring, and alarm tracking.

- **Threshold Manager**—Enhances the capability to set thresholds on Cisco Remote Monitoring-enabled devices, reducing management overhead, and improving trouble-shooting capabilities.

- **StackMaker**—Allows users to combine multiple Cisco devices of specific types into a single stack and visually manage them in a single window.

- **Show Commands**—Display detailed router system and protocol information without requiring the user to remember complex Cisco IOS command-line languages or syntax.

CiscoWorks for Windows 5.0 runs on Windows NT 4.0, Windows 95, and Windows 98. As a standalone application an administrator can install this suite on their personal station or laptop for mobile network analysis and management.

Summary

This chapter provided the reader with an understanding of the direction and options for the Cisco Management Application suites that fall under the CiscoWorks 2000 umbrella. Many of these applications are web-based and designed on industry standards such as Java, CORBA, XML, SNMP, and CIM. This design provides Cisco and their customers with an extensible platform for future development. This chapter also provided brief overviews of the different products that fall into the product line and an explanation of the function and purpose.

With an understanding of the family of CiscoWorks 2000 Network Management Products, it is apparent that Cisco has addressed the management needs of today's environment, while providing an easy to learn and use web-based management structure. As one of the core products in the CiscoWorks 2000 management suite, Resource Manager Essentials provides a centralized inventory and device management platform. The remainder of this book focuses on CiscoWorks 2000 Server and Resource Manager Essentials. The CiscoWorks 2000 Campus Manager, CiscoView 5.0, TrafficDirector, and Internetwork Performance Monitor are the subject of a second volume in the Cisco Enterprise Management Solution set.

Now that the reader understands why network management is necessary and how Cisco provides solutions, the following chapters focus on implementation. The next chapter gets the ball rolling with how to configure devices for network management.

Topics covered in this chapter include the following:

- **SNMP Connectivity**—Configuring SNMP on IOS- and COS-based devices
- **CDP Configuration**—Configuring CDP on IOS-based router devices and COS-based Catalyst switch devices
- **RMON Traffic Analysis**—Performing RMON on IOS-based routers and Catalyst switches
- **The Catalyst Switch Network Analysis Module**—Configuring SPAN and RMON support for the Network Analysis Module
- **Configuring VLAN Virtual Trunking Protocol**—Configuring VTP on a Catalyst switch and on a Catalyst LANE module
- **Syslog Analysis**—Configuring logging levels and setting the location of the logging server
- **Configuring Remote Copy Service on IOS-Based Devices**

## CHAPTER 3

Configuring Devices for Network Management

This chapter details the necessary commands used to configure various network devices for network management. In addition, suggestions and background are provided on how the different commands can be configured.

SNMP Connectivity

Prior to managing the devices in the network, each device must first be configured for SNMP and RMON network management. Separate processes exist for configuring each of the network devices. IOS-based devices have similar configuration commands, while switches and ATM devices are configured differently. (ATM devices 1010 and 8500 run IOS and thus are configured similarly to IOS devices.) The SwitchProbe uses a menu-based system for configuration. All devices, however, do require similar information.

The first step for configuring a device is to review the community strings. Community strings are used as the passwords to access the SNMP and RMON agents on the devices. Community strings should not be easy to guess and should be changed on a regular basis. A community string must be chosen for read-only or GET access to a device. Another community string must then be chosen for read-write or GET and SET access to a device. On the Catalyst switch another string, referred to as read-write-all, must also be chosen. This string is required when SNMP is used to change any SNMP parameters on a Catalyst Switch. Do this as an additional measure of security.

The information in the packets goes across the network in clear text. In an environment with VLANs, it is suggested to do all management in a separate VLAN, which only administrators can access. This setup lowers the possibility of an eavesdropper obtaining the community strings for illicit use.

After selecting the community strings, an administrator must decide which traps the devices will raise. Each device can have the traps set according to the device's functions and importance. Mission critical devices should raise more traps than edge or closet devices. If all possible traps were enabled on all the devices in a network, the network management station could become overwhelmed.

Trap information is sent to a management station. Be sure to have all the TCP/IP addresses of the appropriate devices in order to configure the trap destinations on each of the devices.

Configuring SNMP on IOS-Based Devices

Configuring SNMP support on IOS-based devices involves configuring community strings, trap support, and certain IOS specific options list system reloads.

Configuring Community Strings on IOS-Based Devices

To configure IOS-based router devices the following commands are used to set the community strings. The commands are the same on an LS1010 ATM switch.

```
Router(config)# snmp-server community public ro
Router(config)# snmp-server community private rw
```

SNMP community strings are sent across the network in clear text. The best way to protect an IOS-based device from unauthorized SNMP management is to build a standard IP access list that includes the source address of the management station(s). Multiple access lists can be defined and tied to different community strings. If logging is enabled on the access list then log messages will be generated every time the device is accessed from the management station. The log message will record the source IP address of the packet. To tie an access list to an SNMP community string, use the syntax shown above with a standard access list number at the end of the statement.

Configuring Traps on IOS-based devices

The next step in configuration is to enable traps on the agent. Depending on the traps the device supports the agent can then be configured to send information to the Management Station. On IOS-based devices, traps must be enabled in global configuration mode and also on interfaces. The traps supported depend on the feature set of the router IOS. An abbreviated list for version 11.2(14) follows. On the interface, traps must be enabled to obtain link up-down messages.

- Configuration changes
- ISDN status
- Frame Relay information
- BGP
- Syslog
- SNMP authentication
- Response time reporter

To enable traps on router interfaces and all other available traps, use the command sequence shown in Example 3-1. Use other interface numbers in place of Ethernet 0 to enable on each interface.

Example 3-1   *Enabling Traps on Router Interfaces*

```
Router(config)#interface Ethernet 0
Router(config-if)#snmp trap link-status
Router(config-if)#exit
Router(config)#snmp-server enable traps
```

Not all SNMP traps have to be enabled. Enabling only certain traps can cut down on the number of unnecessary notifications sent to the SNMP management station. Instead of a carriage return after the **snmp-server enable traps** command, an administrator can specify specific traps to be enabled. Without specific traps listed in the command, all traps are enabled.

On IOS-based routers, a special authentication trap can be raised when incorrect community strings are passed to the agent in an SNMP message, which follows:

```
Router(config)#snmp trap-authentication
```

On IOS-based routers, reloading the device by the SNMP Management Station must also be specifically enabled through the appropriate command as follows:

```
Router(config)# snmp-server system-shutdown
```

Configuring Trap Destinations on IOS-Based Devices

The next step on the router would be to specify the destination for trap messages when a significant event occurs on the agent.

```
Router(config)# snmp-server host ip-address-of-NMS public
```

If only specific traps have been enabled then these traps can be directed at different SNMP management stations. Add to the end of the above command the specific trap type to direct that trap at that NMS. Enter **?** after the community string to get a list of available traps.

Setting the SNMP Location, Contact, and Chassis ID on IOS-Based Devices

The SNMP location, contact, and system ID can be displayed on the management station to better understand the purpose of the device being managed. To do this, you need to enter the following commands:

```
Router(config)#snmp-server contact contact-name
Router(config)#snmp-server location device-physical-location
Router(config)#snmp-server chassis-id CEMSRouter
```

Verifying SNMP on IOS-Based Devices

After SNMP has been configured on IOS-based devices, it should be verified for completeness using the **show snmp** command as illustrated in Example 3-2.

Example 3-2 *Verifying SNMP Configuration*

```
Router#show snmp
Chassis: CEMSRouter
Contact: Michael Wynston
Location: Edison,NJ
0 SNMP packets input
    0 Bad SNMP version errors
    0 Unknown community name
    0 Illegal operation for community name supplied
    0 Encoding errors
    0 Number of requested variables
    0 Number of altered variables
    0 Get-request PDUs
    0 Get-next PDUs
    0 Set-request PDUs
0 SNMP packets output
    0 Too big errors (Maximum packet size 1500)
    0 No such name errors
    0 Bad values errors
    0 General errors
    0 Get-response PDUs
    0 SNMP trap PDUs

SNMP logging: enabled
    Logging to 172.16.121.121, 0/10, 0 sent, 0 dropped.
```

Configuring SNMP Support on Catalyst Switch COS-Based Devices

Configuring SNMP support on Catalyst Operating System-based devices require similar information as IOS devices. The commands, however, differ between the two platforms.

Configuring SNMP Community Strings on COS-Based Devices

To configure COS-based Catalyst switch devices, the following commands are used to set the community strings:

```
Console>(enable) set snmp community read-only public
Console>(enable) set snmp community read-write private
Console>(enable) set snmp community read-write-all secret
```

CAUTION   On the Catalyst switch, SNMP is enabled by default with community strings set to

Read-only: public

Read-write: private

Read-write-all: secret

With these community strings and the IP address of your switch's management interface, anyone would be able to reconfigure the device. Changing the community strings on the Catalyst switch immediately after setting the device on the network is very important.

Configuring Traps on COS-Based Devices

After community strings have been set, the next step is to enable SNMP traps on the agent. The Catalyst OS supports a wide range of trap options. Traps on the switch will monitor for Telnet logins, Spanning Tree changes, module and chassis changes, and many other significant events. To enable traps use the following command, in enable mode, in the COS:

```
Console>(enable) set snmp trap enable all
```

Configuring Trap Destinations on COS-Based Devices

The final step for enabling SNMP on the Catalyst switch is to configure the destination for SNMP traps. To configure the destination for SNMP traps use the following command, in enable mode, in the COS:

```
Console>(enable) set snmp trap ip-address-of-NMS public
```

Setting the SNMP Contact, Location, and Chassis-ID on COS-Based Devices

The SNMP location, contact, and system ID can be displayed on the Management Station to better understand the purpose of the device being managed. To configure the location, contact, and system ID on the Catalyst switch, use the following commands:

```
Console>(enable) set system name name_string
Console>(enable) set system location location_string
Console>(enable) set system contact contact_string
```

CDP Configuration

The network discovery process used by CiscoWorks 2000 LAN Management Service requires that CDP be enabled on all participating devices. CDP is enabled on all Cisco devices by default. If CDP has been disabled, however, it can be enabled again by using only a few commands on all Cisco routers and switches.

Enabling CDP on IOS-Based Devices

CDP can be enabled on IOS-based devices on each interface or globally for the whole router. Timers can also be configured to control CDP updates. To enable CDP on IOS-based devices, you would enter the following command:

```
Router(config)# cdp run
```

To enable CDP on each interface, you would enter:

```
Router(config-if)# cdp enable
```

Verifying CDP on IOS-Based Devices

CDP can verify that a link is up and also verify the Layer 3 addresses of the connected neighbors. CDP can also be used to verify that cable connections have been done correctly (see Example 3-3).

Example 3-3   *Verifying CDP Configuration on IOS-Based Devices*

```
Router# show cdp interface
Serial0 is up, line protocol is up
  Encapsulation is HDLC
  Sending CDP packets every 30 seconds
  Holdtime is 180 seconds
```

Enabling CDP on COS-Based Devices

On COS-based devices, CDP can be enabled or disabled on each port or globally on all ports on the switch using the following command:

```
Console>(enable) set cdp enable all
```

Verifying CDP on COS-Based Devices

As demonstrated by Example 3-4, CDP can be used to verify important information on a COS device, such as:

- Ports connecting devices
- Platform type
- Capabilities
- System name
- Layer 3 IP address (shown in detail output)

Example 3-4 *Verifying CDP Configuration on COS-Based Devices*

```
Console> (enable) show cdp neigh
Capability Codes: R - Router, [ic:ccc] T - Trans Bridge, B - Source Route Bridge
                  S - Switch, H - Host, I - IGMP, r - Repeater

Port    Device-ID              Port-ID           Platform             Capability
------  ---------------------  ----------------  -------------------  ----------
 1/1    007599811(CEMS)        1/1               WS-C5000             T B S
 1/2    007599811(CEMS)        1/2               WS-C5000             T B S
```

RMON Traffic Analysis

After SNMP has been configured on both routers and switches, the next step is to enable RMON on supporting devices. SNMP is designed for device management and analysis. RMON operates in a fashion similar to SNMP but manages and analyzes the wire between devices. RMON information is accessible through an RMON management station, such as TrafficDirector.

Most Cisco devices ship with some level of RMON support. On Catalyst switches, this RMON support is referred to as the mini-RMON. The mini-RMON agent has support for four RMON 1 groups' statistics, history, alarms, and events. On Cisco 2500 series routers only, support is included for all nine RMON 1 groups. On other Cisco routers support is included only for alarms and events.

RMON on an IOS-Based Router Device

Cisco routers have support for RMON-1 through events and alarms. Routers ordered with the additional RMON support license have support for all RMON-1 groups; without the license, only the mini-RMON support is provided. The Threshold Manager application plug-in for CiscoView can be used to graphically configure alarm thresholds on the routers. The alarms can be used to raise traps, which are sent to a management station. Cisco 2500 series router platforms also have support for packet analysis as described in RFC 1577 RMON on their Ethernet interfaces. This support allows for remote packet capture through TrafficDirector.

Use the commands discussed in the following sections to configure RMON on Catalyst switches and Cisco routers.

Configuring RMON on IOS-Based Devices

On IOS-based devices, RMON alarms and events must be enabled using many complicated parameters that specify interface, thresholds, and time measures as either absolute or delta. For complete syntax, consult the release notes for the IOS version. Tools such as

TrafficDirector can be used to graphically create these alarms and events. Example 3-5 shows the **rmon** command options

Example 3-5 **rmon** *Command Options for Configuration*

```
Router(config)# rmon ?
  alarm      Configure an RMON alarm
  event      Configure an RMON event
  queuesize  Size of the RMON packet queue
```

Configuring RMON Packet Analysis on 2500 Series Routers

To configure RMON to capture all packets on a 2500 series router, use the following command on any Ethernet interface:

```
Router(config-if)# rmon promiscuous
```

To configure RMON to capture only packets destined for the router interface, use the following command on any Ethernet interface:

```
Router(config-if)# rmon native
```

Do not enable the RMON capture capabilities on a busy production router. The capture process uses system memory and CPU. These resources are not as strong in the 2500 series router. If enabled on a busy production router, this process could cause serious performance degradation.

RMON on COS-Based Catalyst Switch Devices

All Catalyst switches have at a minimum an embedded mini-RMON agent. With additional software licensing, a Network Analysis Module, and a NetFlow Feature Card, extended VLAN and traffic analysis support is also available. This statistical information can be obtained by any RMON management platform including TrafficDirector or Sniffer Pro 3.0. To configure RMON on a COS-based device, enter the following command:

```
Console>(enable) set snmp rmon enable
```

The Catalyst Switch Network Analysis Module

The Network Analysis Module for the Catalyst 5000 Family enables users to monitor network applications, analyze network traffic patterns, troubleshoot protocol-related problems, and perform trend analysis for capacity planning. This module provides a fully integrated RMON, RMON2, NetFlow, and VLAN monitoring solution for the Catalyst 5000 Family of LAN switches. The Network Analysis Module is a component of the Cisco Systems' enterprise traffic-monitoring solutions and complements the mini-RMON agent available on every Ethernet, Fast Ethernet, and Gigabit Ethernet switch port of the Catalyst 5000 Family.

With the CiscoWorks 2000 Campus Traffic Management application, the network analysis module can be transparently roved to any switch port or VLAN to provide full seven-layer monitoring and powerful drill-down troubleshooting. The Network Analysis Module supports simultaneous monitoring of multiple ports or VLANs and maintains independent RMON/RMON2 MIB group statistics for each data source. The module also performs NetFlow-to-RMON2 proxy for standards-based access to the Layer 3 traffic statistics. Using a Supervisor Engine III with a NetFlow Feature Card (NFFC or NFFC2), these statistics can be gathered at backplane speeds. To attach to the RMON agents on the NAM (Network Analysis Module), use the TCP/IP address of the switch's SCO interface and the community strings set on the switch.

Configuring Switched Port Analyzer for the Network Analysis Module

The Network Analysis Module uses the Switched Port Analyzer (SPAN) feature to gather traffic and statistics information from the Catalyst Switch. The SPAN source can be set to any port, VLAN, or group of ports in the same VLAN on the switch. To analyze traffic from multiple VLANs, use a trunk port as the data source. The destination for the SPAN command will be the slot number where the NAM is located followed by a 1 as the port number.

Configure the SPAN tool to mirror traffic to the NAM. The first parameter is the source the second is the slot where the NAM is inserted followed by port 1. For example, the following command configures SPAN for the NAM with VLAN 1 as the source with the NAM in slot 7:

```
Console#(enable) set span 1 7/1 both
```

Configuring RMON Support for the Network Analysis Module

When a NAM is present in the switch, the extended RMON agent is automatically enabled. This can be verified in the output of the **show snmp** command. When the NAM is present in the switch, the output of **show snmp** will display Extended RMON: Enabled. To enable other RMON features for VLANs and NetFlow refer to the configuration examples that follow.

Enabling the VLAN Agent Option

The extended VLAN agent option enables the NAM to aggregate statistics by VLAN, as well as by port. This action is very resource intensive for the NAM and should not be enabled on a switch with a very heavy load. Example 3-6 shows how to enable the VLAN agent option.

Example 3-6 *Enabling the VLAN Agent Option*

```
Console> (enable) set snmp extendedrmon vlanagent enable
Snmp extended RMON vlanagent enabled
Console> (enable) show snmp
RMON:                        Disabled
Extended RMON:               Enabled
Extended RMON Netflow:       Disabled
Extended RMON Vlanmode:      Disabled
Extended RMON Vlanagent:     Enabled
```

Enabling the VLAN Monitor Option

The VLAN monitor option allows the NAM to aggregate statistics by VLAN when the SPAN source is a trunk port. Example 3-7 shows how to enable the VLAN monitor option.

Example 3-7 *Enabling the VLAN Monitor Option*

```
Console> (enable) set snmp extendedrmon vlanmode enable
Snmp extended RMON vlanmode enabled
Console> (enable) show snmp
RMON:                        Disabled
Extended RMON:               Enabled
Extended RMON Netflow:       Disabled
Extended RMON Vlanmode:      Enabled
Extended RMON Vlanagent:     Disabled
```

Enabling the NetFlow Monitor and Data Export Options

The NetFlow option requires a NFFC or NFFC2 card on the Supervisor III module on the switch. Using the NetFlow monitoring option also requires an additional software license. To enable the monitor option, you must obtain a password from a Cisco Sales representative. The password is tied to the MAC address of the Network Analysis Module. You can enable the NetFlow option after obtaining the password. The monitor also requires that NetFlow data export (NDE) be enabled on the switch. The data from NDE will be automatically sent to the NAM when present. Example 3-8 shows how to enable the NetFlow monitor and NDE options.

Example 3-8 *Enabling the NetFlow Monitor and NDE Options*

```
Console> (enable) set mls nde enable
Console> (enable) set snmp extendedrmon netflow enable password
Snmp extended RMON netflow enabled
Console> (enable) show snmp
RMON:                        Disabled
Extended RMON:               Enabled
Extended RMON Netflow:       Enabled
Extended RMON Vlanmode:      Disabled
Extended RMON Vlanagent:     Disabled
```

Syslog Analysis

SNMP generates traps to a management station when configured for certain thresholds on individual counters or when a significant event occurs. To generate SNMP traps, the agent must first be configured with the proper community strings and the administrator must also be aware of the different MIBs supported on the agent to know which events can generate traps.

Syslog messages are generated based upon logging levels configured on the router or switch. The messages are normally sent only to the console of the device. Sending messages to the console of the router or switch generates significant CPU utilization to display the messages. For this reason, Catalyst switches have their logging levels set very low by default. This hinders administrator awareness to significant events on the device unless the event is configured to raise a trap. On routers and switches, the messages to the console can go unseen unless an administrator is continually monitoring the console environment. To improve awareness, messages can be directed to the console, the Syslog Server, or to both. This process is easy to configure and simple to understand. Only two steps are involved to enable this feature on a router or switch. The administrator must set a logging level and a logging device.

Logging levels are used to create different messages for various events. The more severe the event is the lower the corresponding logging level number will be. On a Cisco router the level is set the same for all system features. On a Catalyst switch the level can be set differently for each feature. This situation provides the administrator with a precise ability to control the number and types of messages generated by switches.

Configuring Logging Levels

The first step to configuring the amount of generated messages by the router and switch is to set the logging level or levels. Table 3-1 lists the logging levels for both routers and switches.

Table 3-1   *Router and Switcher Logging Levels*

Logging Level	Keyword	Description
0	Emergencies	System unusable
1	Alerts	Immediate action required
2	Critical	Critical condition
3	Errors	Error conditions
4	Warnings	Warning conditions
5	Notifications	Normal but significant condition
6	Informational	Informational messages
7	Debugging	Debugging messages

Setting the proper logging level is very important. Typically the level to the server should not be set higher than 6. Debugging level 7 messages can generate thousands of messages in a very short time. The logging messages are generated for all levels equal to and below the configured logging level.

Configuring the Logging Level on the Router

To enable logging on an IOS-based device, use the following commands. The first command enables logging, and the second sets the logging level.

```
Router(config)# logging on
Router(config)# logging trap informational
```

Configuring the Logging Level on the Switch

On the Catalyst switch, setting the logging level also includes selecting which facilities to change the level of. The basic command syntax to do this is as follows:

```
Console>(enable) set logging level facility severity [default]
```

Table 3-2 lists the different facilities available to set logging levels for on the switch.

Table 3-2   *Logging Level Facilities*

Facility Name	Definition
all	All facilities below
cdp	Cisco Discovery Protocol
dtp	Dynamic Trunking Protocol
drip	Dual Ring Protocol
dvlan	Dynamic VLAN
earl	Enhanced Address Recognition Logic
fddi	Fiber Distributed Data Interface
filesys	Flash file system
ip	IP permit list
kernel	Kernel
mgmt	Management messages
mcast	Multicast messages
pagp	Port Aggregation Protocol
protfilt	Protocol filtering
pruning	VTP pruning
rmon	Remote monitoring

Table 3-2   *Logging Level Facilities (Continued)*

Facility Name	Definition
security	Port security
snmp	Simple Network Management Protocol
spantree	Spanning-Tree Protocol
sys	System
tac	TACACS+
tcp	Transmission Control Protocol
telnet	Terminal Emulation Protocol in the TCP/IP protocol stack
tftp	Trivial File Transfer Protocol
vmps	VLAN Membership Policy Server
vtp	VLAN Trunking Protocol

The default parameter signifies to preserve the settings between reloads. The factory default would set most of the logging levels back to 2.

Setting the Location of the Logging Server

To configure messages to be sent to a server, the server's TCP/IP address must be configured on the router and switch. The TCP/IP address entered in the router and switch should be the address of the Resource Manager Essentials Server. To accommodate networks with multiple Management Stations, both the router and switch accept multiple destinations. Switches will accept up to three addresses, while routers will accept more than ten. The logging messages use UDP as their transport protocol to the server. The messages are sent to port 514 on the logging server.

To configure the logging server address on IOS-based devices, enter the following command:

```
Router(config)# logging ip-address-of-Essentials-Server
```

To configure the logging server address on COS-based devices, enter the following command:

```
Console>(enable) set logging server ip-address-of-Essentials-Server
```

Summary

This chapter covered how to configure SNMP and RMON capabilities on both COS-based and IOS-based devices. When enabling SNMP on all devices there are many common aspects this chapter covered, such as traps, community strings, and RMON features. Be sure to choose community strings carefully because they are the keys to you SNMP kingdom. The chapter concluded with a discussion about enabling Syslog features on both IOS and COS devices.

The network devices have now been configured for network management. The next step is to set up the management station. This step will be covered in Chapter 4, "CiscoWorks 2000 Server and Resource Manager Essentials Installation."

Topics covered in this chapter include the following:

- Pre-installation Tasks
- Pre-installation Verification
- Upgrading Prior Versions of CiscoWorks
- The Installation Process
- Integrating with Network Management Platforms
- Client Installation and Setup

## CHAPTER 4

CiscoWorks 2000 Server and Resource Manager Essentials Installation

Prior chapters dealt with configuring devices for network management and why network management is performed. Now that the devices are ready to be managed, the process of installation is next to be discussed. The installation process is straightforward and does not require significant experience in the target installation operating system. Some system checks of the operating system must be made first.

If an upgrade installation is being performed, then understanding what the installation process does to prior versions is also important. When installing with other network management platforms, certain additional files and prerequisites must be met. Once the installation process is complete, verifying the installation and access from a client is necessary.

Pre-Installation Tasks

The installation requirements such as minimum CPU, memory, hard drive space, and operating system version should be checked when choosing the target server on which to install the application. Certain aspects of the target system are independent of the operating system and server hardware. Verification of TCP/IP address, hostname, and network connectivity should be made before the installation process starts. The first step is choosing a target platform.

Choosing a Target Platform

One of the first questions in choosing to deploy CiscoWorks 2000 Server is the choice of server operating system. Currently CiscoWorks 2000 Server RWAN (Routed Wide Area Network) and LMS (LAN Management Solution) are supported on two operating systems:

- Solaris 2.6
- Windows NT 4.0

A separate package has been developed for HP-UX and AIX. The requirements for these products are outside the scope of this book. Please consult the installation guide and release notes for detailed install instructions.

The variety of supported platforms can lead to a difficult decision for a first-time installation. The different platform choice affects the day-to-day administration of the server. Platform application support is similar from one platform to another. Therefore, the choice does not have to be made based on application support.

The best way to make the decision should be the level of comfort with the target server platform and potential training costs. If network administrators are already familiar with one platform then that is the best platform to select. An important aspect of the application is that almost all administration of the server is conducted through the web-based interface, which is the same across all platforms. The knowledge of the target operating system is most important at the time of installation.

System Platform Requirements

There are two different system platform requirement types—minimum operating system software revisions along with any patch requirements and minimum hardware requirements. Following the minimum software requirements for each platform is important. The hardware requirements are minimums and should be used as minimum requirements for the platform.

Table 4-1 provides details for the current minimum software and hardware requirements. These minimum requirements are based upon networks with 500 devices.

Table 4-1   *System Installation Requirements*

Application	CiscoWorks 2000 RWAN Entire Package		CiscoWorks 2000 LMS Entire Package		CiscoWorks 2000 Campus Manager	
Operating System	Minimum Software	Minimum Hardware	Minimum Software	Minimum Hardware	Minimum Software	Minimum Hardware
Windows NT Server or Workstation 4.0	Windows NT 4.0 Service Pack 5	Intel Pentium III 400 MHz processor 256 MB memory 2GB on the installation partition	Windows NT 4.0 Service Pack 5	Intel Pentium III 550 MHz processor 512 MB memory 6 GB on the installation partition	N/A	Same as LMS
Solaris 2.6	Sun Solaris 2.6 with the following patches: 105210-17, 105490-05, 105529-07, 105568-13, 1015181-11	Sun SPARC Ultra 60 MP (MP optional) or higher 512 MB memory 6 GB on the installation partition	Sun Solaris 2.6 with the following patches: 105181-11, 105210-17, 105490-05, 105529-07, 105568-13	Sun SPARC Ultra 60 MP or higher 512 MB minimum memory 6 GB on the installation partition	N/A	Same as LMS

Table 4-1   *System Installation Requirements (Continued)*

Application	CiscoWorks 2000 RWAN Entire Package		CiscoWorks 2000 LMS Entire Package		CiscoWorks 2000 Campus Manager	
Operating System	Minimum Software	Minimum Hardware	Minimum Software	Minimum Hardware	Minimum Software	Minimum Hardware
AIX	N/A	N/A	N/A	N/A	AIX 4.33	RS6000 PowerPC Model 604e 233 MHz 256 MB of Memory 4 GB on the installation partition
HP-UX	N/A	N/A	N/A	N/A	HP-UX 11.0	HP J2240 236 MHz 256 MB of memory 4 GB on the installation partition

Check the Cisco website or product documentation for updated requirement information.

After the minimum requirements have been met, the pre-installation verification can begin.

NOTE   Solaris-required patch 105490-05 has been superceded by 107733-06. The original version of RWAN had problems with this but the update (contains CD-One second edition) can work around this. This is documented in Cisco bug CSCdp81495.

Pre-Installation Verification

Prior to performing the installation, a number of steps must be completed to verify the system is ready for installation. The first step is to verify that the target system has sufficient resources and operating system software versions as detailed in Table 4-1. This section provides details for verifying system requirements for Solaris and Windows NT as shown in this section. For HP-UX and AIX, please consult the product documentation for the operating system.

To verify the operating system version and patches on Solaris use the **showrev –p** command.

Under Windows NT use the Start; Programs; Administrative Tools; Windows NT Diagnostics; select the tab labeled Version to verify the system version and service pack number. Figure 4-1 shows the displayed version and service pack for the target Windows NT platform.

Verify sufficient hard disk space is available on the target directory on the server. On Solaris Systems, use the **df –k** *directory* command to verify available disk space. On the Windows NT system use the **dir** *directory* command.

Figure 4-1   *Windows NT Version Information*

Under Windows NT, the Java Virtual Machine provided by Internet Explorer 5.0 is required. Supported Java Virtual Machines are 5.0.0.3167 through 5.0.0.3186.

The Java Console is not enabled by default in Internet Explorer. To enable the Java Console select the Start menu; Settings; Control Panel; Internet Options; Advanced Tab. Then scroll to the Microsoft VM section and check the Java Console Enabled checkbox. The Java console requires restarting the operating system.

Verify that the port numbers used by CiscoWorks 2000 are not already in use on the target system. In addition to normal network ports for applications such as SNMP, TFTP, and Syslog, additional ports are listened to by CiscoWorks 2000, including the following:

- **42340/tcp**—CiscoWorks2000 Daemon Manager (the tool that manages server processes).

- **42341/tcp**—Open Server Gateway.

- **42342/udp**—Osagent.

- **42343/tcp**—Jrun.

- **1741/tcp**—The port used for the CiscoWorks2000 HTTP server; used when accessing CiscoWorks.

These ports are documented for Windows NT and Solaris. This list does not include normal network ports for such services as TFTP and Syslog.

The port used for the CiscoWorks website can be modified. If port 80 is not in use, then under Solaris the installation will present an option to use port 80 for the website. If another port is desired, modify the *httpd.conf* file. Under Windows NT the http.conf file can also be modified to use a different port. After the port has been changed stop and restart the CiscoWorks 2000 services. See the instructions below for the necessary steps.

Do not use dynamic DHCP addressing on the CiscoWorks 2000 Server. The TCP/IP address is written into the *httpd.conf* file in Solaris. Another issue is that if the Management Station loses connectivity to the DHCP server, then it could lose the address it is using and cause serious problems with connectivity to the server. If the address is changed under Solaris then this file must be updated and the daemons must be restarted. The httpd.conf file is located in the *opt/CSCOpx/objects/web/conf/httpd.conf* directory. To stop and then start the CiscoWorks Daemons use the following commands as root:

```
# /etc/init.d/dmgtd stop
# /etc/init.d/dmgtd start
```

The TCP/IP address is also used on managed devices as a destination for SNMP traps and Syslog messages. Changing the address would create an administrative burden to update all of the managed devices.

Under Windows NT, the system Computer Name is written into the database and httpd.conf file. For this reason changing the computer name after installation will cause many features to stop operating. For additional information about changing the Computer Name after installation, see Chapter 15, "Troubleshooting Resource Manager Essentials."

Upgrading Prior Versions of CiscoWorks

CiscoWorks 2000 RWAN, LMS, and Campus Manager will not run on a machine with a prior version of CiscoWorks installed. When CiscoWorks 2000 RWAN, LMS, or Campus Manager is installed on a server with a prior version of the application installed, all prior data will be migrated to the new version but the prior version will be disabled.

Upgrading is supported from 2.X versions of Resource Manager Essentials and CWSI. Prior to installation of any new version, all older versions must be uninstalled. If a version older then 2.X of Resource Manager Essentials or CWSI is on the server, backup all data prior to performing an upgrade. The older data can then be migrated to the newer application version. Do not perform any installation steps before backing up all old data. An 2.X upgrade will automatically migrate data to the newer version and all older applications will be disabled.

The setup engine of the new version does the work of uninstalling prior versions. A dialog box will appear listing all prior application versions on the target system that will be uninstalled. Figure 4-2 shows the message that appears on the Windows NT platform if CWSI 2.4 and RME 2.2 are installed on the target system.

Figure 4-2   *Uninstall Confirmations*

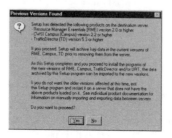

All databases, ANI settings, community-strings, user and host information, and application-specific data files are preserved and migrated to the new version as soon as the installation is complete. The original data is left on the server in a backup directory. The old data is broken up into folders that represent each area of the original install. Figure 4-3 shows the folder list after the data is backed up. The default folder name for the backed up data is *CW2000\OldData*.

The database size and the number of devices determine the length of processing time for upgrading the database. An upgrade of a database with 500 or more devices can take over an hour to complete.

Figure 4-3 *Prior Version Data*

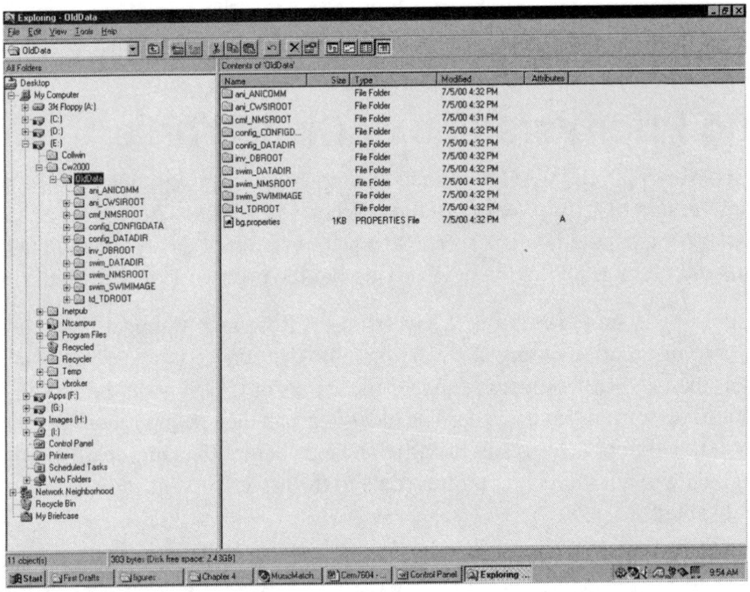

The Installation Process

After the pre-installation checklist has been verified, the installation process can begin. The installation process begins with CD-One. CD-One includes CiscoWorks 2000 Server and CiscoView. After CD-One has been installed, Resource Manager Essentials can be installed.

The CD-One Solaris Installation Process

To begin the installation, insert the CD-One disc into the target server or mount a remote network drive that contains the installation media. Under Solaris, mount the CD-ROM using instructions provided with the operating system. To begin the installation, implement the following steps:

Step 1 To begin the installation processes run the *setup.sh* script.

Step 2 A message requests the target directory for installation. The default is */opt/CSCOpx*. Press enter to accept the default directory for installation.

Step 3 The installation process runs a series of checks to verify the system meets the minimum requirements.

Step 4 Choose an installation option to install CD-One, Integration Utility, or all of the above. If the Integration Utility is installed then a message will appear to perform integration either during the installation or skip the integration. Integration is discussed later in the chapter. Choose either option because if integration is skipped it can always be done later after the installation is complete. There is no advantage to doing it at either time.

Step 5 After the installation is complete, check the log file for error messages. The log file is located in */var/tmp/ciscoinstall.log*. Each time an installation is performed, information is appended to this file.

After the installation is complete, verify the installation by checking the */var/tmp/ciscoinstall.log* file for any error messages. If port 80 is not in use on the target server then it will be used to host the CiscoWorks 2000 environment. If connect to the server at *http://hostname/*. If port 80 was not available, port 1741 will be used. If port 1741 was used then connect to the server at *http://hostname:1741*. The port number can be changed. See instructions earlier in the chapter about the httpd.conf file.

The CD-One installation process modifies the following files:

- /etc/services
- /etc/inetd.conf
- /etc/syslog.conf
- /var/sadm/install/admin/default

The Resource Manager Essentials for Solaris Installation Process

When the CD-One installation is complete, mount the CD-ROM for Resource Manager Essentials 3.X. If an upgrade was performed then information from the prior version will be upgraded at the conclusion of the Resource Manager installation.

The system requirements at the time of writing are listed in Table 4-1. Table 4-2 lists some performance recommendations for installing Resource Manager on Solaris.

Table 4-2 *Solaris Performance Recommendations*

Minimum System Configuration	Availability	Syslog	Configuration	Inventory
Ultra 10 Memory: 256 MB Swap Space: 512 MB Available Disk Space: 4 GB	0–100	0–50,000	0–500	0–500
Ultra 10 Memory: 384 MB Swap Space: 768 MB Available Disk Space: 6 GB	100–500	50,000– 150,000	500–2500	500–2500
Ultra 60 (dual processor) Memory: 512MB Swap Space: 1024 MB Available Disk Space: 4 GB	500–1000	150,000	2500–5000	2500–5000

The installation places files under the same directory as the CD-One installation directory. Perform the following steps to launch the installation process:

Step 1 Become the superuser by entering the command **su** and the root password or log in as root. The command prompt changes to the # sign.

Step 2 If the /cdrom directory does not already exist, enter the following command to create it:

```
# mkdir /cdrom
```

Step 3 Mount the CD-ROM drive.

Step 4 The vold process manages the CD-ROM device and performs the mounting. The CD-ROM might automatically mount onto the */cdrom/cdrom0* directory.

Step 5 If you are running File Manager, a separate File Manager window displays the contents of the CD-ROM.

Step 6 Start the installation program. For a local installation, enter:

```
# cd /cdrom/cdrom0/
# ./setup.sh
```

The installation process will present three options for installation components:

- Resource Manager Essentials
- Resource Manager Essentials Incremental Device Support
- All of the Above

You should choose the third option. The system will then display any information about prerequisites. The installation will proceed and return to a system prompt when complete. Check the */var/tmp/ciscoinstall.log* file for any error messages.

After the installation is complete, connect to the port CiscoWorks 2000 is installed on to verify the installation of Resource Manager Essentials. Also ensure DNS name resolution is working correctly to simplify connecting to the server and communication to the network devices.

Allowing the User Bin to Use **at** and **cron**

Software Management uses **at** and **cron** to schedule Software Management image transfers to devices. The process that performs the download is executed as bin so the user bin must be allowed to use **at** and **cron**.

To allow the user bin to use **at**:

Step 1 If an *at.deny* file exists in the */usr/lib/cron* directory, make sure bin is not listed in it. If necessary, remove bin from the *at.deny* file using a text editor.

Step 2 If an *at.allow* file exists in the */usr/lib/cron* directory, make sure bin is listed in it. If necessary, add bin to the *at.allow* file using a text editor.

Step 3 If neither an *at.allow* nor an *at.deny* file exist in the directory */usr/lib/cron*, create an *at.allow* file and add bin to it using a text editor.

To allow the user bin to use **cron**:

Step 1 If a *cron.deny* file exists in the */usr/lib/cron* directory, make sure bin is not listed in it. If necessary, remove bin from the *cron.deny* file using a text editor.

Step 2 If a *cron.allow* file exists in the */usr/lib/cron* directory, make sure bin is listed in it. If necessary, add bin to the *cron.allow* file using a text editor.

Step 3 If neither a *cron.allow* nor a *cron.deny* file exists in the */usr/lib/cron* directory, create a *cron.allow* file and add bin to it using a text editor.

The CD-One Windows NT Installation Process

To begin the installation insert the CD-One disk locally or map a remote drive to the software location. Some specific requirements for the Windows NT platform are shown in the following list:

- The software cannot be installed on a Windows NT Primary or Backup Domain Controller. The installation process will stop if the server is a PDC or BDC.

- The software should be installed on a partition formatted with NTFS. Installing the software on NTFS will consume less space then on a FAT partition. The install process will also set permissions on the files if the install is performed on an NTFS.

- The installation requirements for Windows NT 4.0 are different for the CD-One from LMS and RWAN. LMS CD-One Second-Edition requires Windows NT 4.0 with service pack 5 but will install with Service Pack 6 (sp6).

CAUTION   Do not attempt to install with sp6! The install may succeed, but the product is not supported in this configuration! The install script permits install, not because the product can run with sp6, but in order to prevent installation failure in the event that the sp6 check fails for unforeseen reasons.

- RWAN CD-One First Edition requires Windows NT with service pack 5—it will not install with any other service pack. Even though the product will allow installation with Service Pack 6, only Service pack 5 is currently supported. Cisco strongly recommends using Service Pack 5.

To begin the installation, implement the following steps:

Step 1   If Auto-Play is enabled, the installer screen will appear when the CD is inserted. Click the install button.

Step 2   If the Auto-Play feature is disabled then from the Start; Run menu; type *X:\setup.exe,* where X is the drive with the software.

Step 3   Select Typical installation to start copying files. To change the installation directory or any install components select Custom installation.

Step 4   If a Custom Installation is selected then the option to change the directory and installation components is displayed. The installation components are CD-One and Integration Components or Integration Components only.

Step 5   If a prior version of CiscoWorks 2000 is present on the system then all applications will be uninstalled first by the installation routine. The data from the prior version will be backed up to a local directory on the system to be restored when Resource Manager Essentials is installed.

Step 6   After the installation is done copying files, an option will be presented to perform integration with another NMS system. Figure 4-4 shows the list of available integration packages that come with CiscoWorks 2000.

Figure 4-4   *The Integration Options*

Select Later to integrate with a third-party NMS after installation. Select Now to integrate with a third-party NMS platform now. The integration process is explained later in this chapter.

Step 7   After the install is complete, reboot the system.

After the installation is complete, verify the installation by checking the server console at *http://hostname:1741*. The default login is the admin user name and admin password (the password is case-sensitive). Figure 4-5 shows the CiscoWorks 2000 server console after the install of CD-One is complete.

If there were any installation errors, check the log at *X:\cw2000_in001.log*; the log file is located on the drive where the install was performed. Figure 4-6 shows a sample of what the install log contains. Notice on the lines highlighted that a prior version of CiscoWorks was located.

Figure 4-5   *The CiscoWorks 2000 Console*

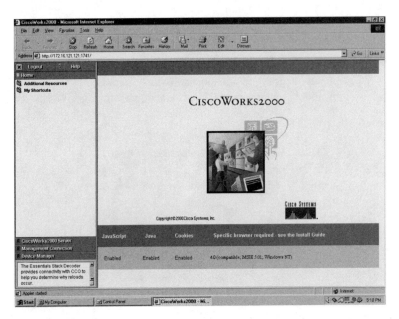

Figure 4-6   *The cw2000_in001.log File*

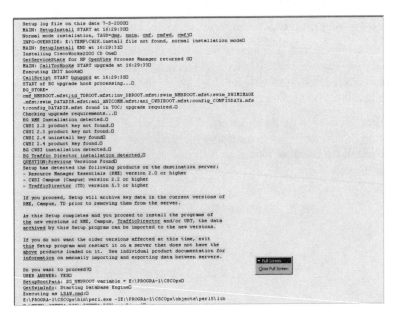

Verify that the necessary services were installed at a command prompt by typing:

`net start`

The following bulleted list shows the services that should be installed:

- Apache WebServer
- CMF rsh/rcp service
- CMF Syslog service
- CMF tftp service
- CW2000 Daemon Manager
- CW2000 VisiBroker Smart Agent
- JRUN Proxy Server for CW2000

The Resource Manager Essentials for Windows NT Installation Process

After the installation of CD-One is complete, the installation of Resource Manager Essentials can begin. Mount the CD-ROM or remote network drive where the installation media is located. If this is an upgrade, the data preserved during the installation of CD-One will be upgraded at the end of the installation.

The system requirements are similar to the requirements listed in Table 4-1. Table 4-3 shows some performance recommendations for installing Resource Manager on Windows NT.

Table 4-3   *Windows NT Performance Recommendations*

Minimum System Configuration	Availability	Syslog	Configuration	Inventory
Pentium II 300 Memory: 256 MB Swap Space: 1025 MB Available Disk Space: 4 GB	0–100	0–50,000	0–500	0–500
Pentium III 450 Memory: 384 MB Swap Space: 1024 MB Available Disk Space: 9 GB	100–500	50,000– 150,000	500–2500	500–2500
Pentium III 550 Memory: 512 MB Swap Space: 1024 MB Available Disk Space: 9 GB	500–1000	150,000	2500–5000	2500–5000

The installation process will provide the option of installing Resource Manager Essentials and Incremental Device Support. For the installation to complete successfully, both must be installed on the target system. After the installation is done copying files, the Resource Manager is then ready for use. Verify the installation process by launching the CiscoWorks 2000 console. The address is *http://hostname:1741*. The default login is the admin user name and admin password. As a reminder, the password is case-sensitive. Figure 4-7 shows the CiscoWorks 2000 Server console after the Resource Manager installation.

Figure 4-7 *The CiscoWorks 2000 Console*

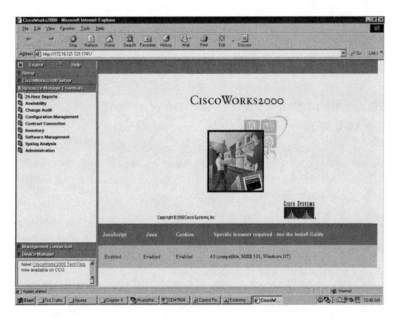

If there were any errors during the installation, check the log file CW2000_in002.log file. Figure 4-8 shows the log file of the Resource Manager Essentials installation. A message is displayed during the installation about upgrading the data at the end of the install. At the end of the log file is the insert and update statements used to upgrade the data from the different database tables.

After the installation is complete (or during the installation), choosing to integrate with third-party network management platforms can extend the functionality of the current management platform.

Figure 4-8   *The Resource Manager Installation Log*

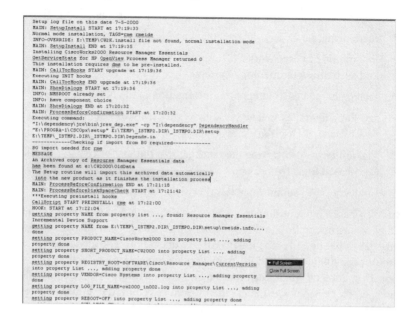

Integrating with Network Management Platforms

One of the tools installed with CD-One is the Network Management Integration Module (NMIM). The NMS integration tool provides web-based integration for third-party NMS platforms from such leading vendors as Hewlett Packard, Tivoli, Computer Associates, Fujitsu, and BullSoft. This web-based integration improves location options for the NMS platforms and is no longer required to be on the same system as CiscoWorks 2000. By using a Network Management Adapter provided by the third-party development company, the platform can take advantage of resources on the CiscoWorks 2000 server. The benefits provided by integration with a third-party system are as follows:

- Launch of CiscoView 5.0 from the NMS maps or menus.

- Launch of the device center of Resource Manager Essentials 3.x from the NMS maps or menus.

- New Web-based integration of CiscoWorks2000 solutions and NMSs.

- Greater flexibility in the physical location of CiscoWorks2000 and NMSs.

- Greater flexibility in operating system deployment.

- Quicker time to market for CiscoWorks2000/NMS support.

- MIB registration with NMS platform 1.

- Cisco-provided icons display on NMS maps 1.

- Incremental new Cisco device support via Cisco Connection Online (CCO).

- Incremental new Cisco management application integration via CCO.

- Integration of CiscoWorks2000 applications and NMSs residing on different servers and even different operating systems.

- Dynamic updates to integration information in the NMS.

- Dynamic upgrades to new versions of the NMS without reinstalling or waiting for a new release of CiscoWorks2000 software.

- Flexibility in customizing the management intranet environment using completely Web-based tools from Cisco.

- Frequent NMS support updates downloaded from CCO Software Center.

The Web-based Integration Tool can be installed on a remote server from the CD-One and choosing integration tool only. A network management adapter written by the third-party developer provides the link to CiscoWorks 2000. The advantage is that updates to CiscoWorks 2000 or to the third-party application will not affect the other. One issue in prior integration efforts occurred when one vendor would release an update that required a new operating system. Customers then would be required to either update the operating system and lose the integration features or not get access to new features in the applications new version. The new web-based integration eliminates this dilemma. Customers can now use almost any Network Management System and get integration with CiscoView and the Device Center. The CiscoWorks 2000 Server launches all the applications through URL links. Third-party developers can add the integration anywhere in their applications.

The following steps add a third-party integration. (In this case, the integration is for the *What's Up Gold* application from IPSwitch.) The Integration adapter is not included with CiscoWorks 2000 CD-One and must be imported from the CiscoWorks 5.0 for Windows CD.

Step 1 Launch the Integration Tool from either the CiscoWorks 2000 Server or the NMS. Figure 4-9 shows the Integration Tool initial screen.

Figure 4-9 *The NMS Integration Application*

Step 2   In the Integration Tool, select a location for the adapter—either the local file system or the CCO web site.

Step 3   Specify the default application to launch when the NMS double-clicks on a Cisco device—either CiscoView 5.0 or Resource Manager Essentials Device Center. Figure 4-10 shows the Resource Manager Device Center as the default application launched by the adapter.

Figure 4-10   *The Default Application*

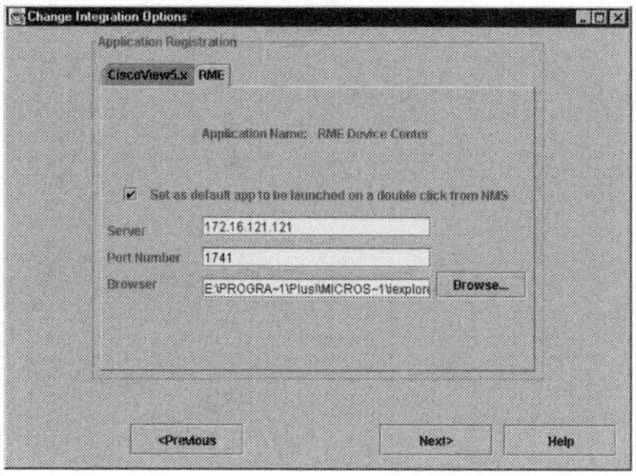

Step 4   Specify the host name or IP address of the CiscoWorks 2000 server and the port number the server is listening on. Specify the browser to launch the application in.

Step 5   Select an adapter from the available list of adapters and click on **integrate**. Figure 4-11 shows the browse window used to add the *.jar* file for the *What's Up Gold* adapter.

Figure 4-11   *The Browse File Dialog Box*

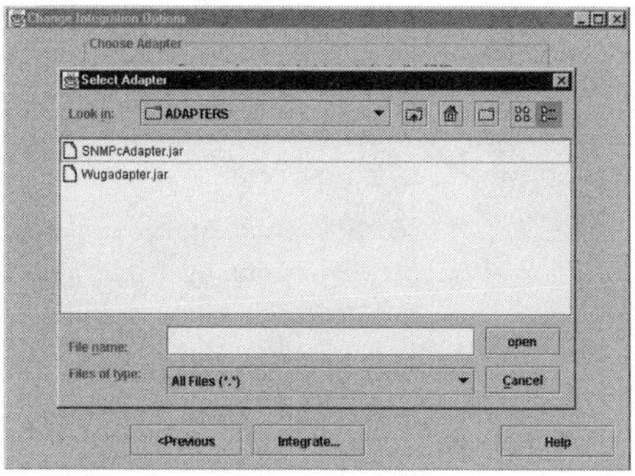

Step 6   The description for the adapter is displayed by selecting the adapter from the list. Figure 4-12 shows the description for the *What's Up Gold* adapter.

Figure 4-12   *The What's Up Gold Adapter*

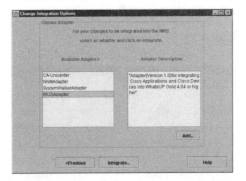

Step 7   Click the Integrate button to begin integration process. When the integration is completed successfully a message displays, stating that the adapter execution is complete.

After the application is installed, clients can connect to the server. To achieve maximum performance, minimum requirements for the client must be addressed.

Client Installation and Setup

CiscoWorks 2000 is a web-based application so the primary client requirement is the browser. The application does have minimum resource requirements for clients. Table 4-4 shows a list of supported client operating systems and the hardware requirements for the release available during this writing. Please consult release notes for the version you are running.

Table 4-4   *Minimum Client Requirements*

Requirement Type	Minimum Requirement
System Hardware and Software	Client System:
	IBM PC-compatible computer with 300 MHz Pentium processor running Windows NT 4.0, Windows 95, or Windows 98.
	Solaris SPARCstation or Sun Ultra 10 running Solaris 2.5.1 or Solaris 2.6.
	IBM RS/ 6000 workstation running AIX 4.3.1 or 4.3.2.
	HP-UX workstation running HP-UX 10.20 or 11.0.
	Color monitor with video card set to 256 colors.

Table 4-4   *Minimum Client Requirements (Continued)*

Requirement Type	Minimum Requirement
Memory (RAM)	128 MB
Browser	Netscape Navigator 4.6.1.
	(Windows NT, Windows 95/98, Solaris 2.5.1, Solaris 2.6)
	Microsoft Internet Explorer 5.0.
	JVM versions 5.0.0.3167 through 5.0.0.3186 are supported.
	(Windows NT, Windows 95/98)

The client can download certain Java classes to improve the local performance. The classes are controlled from the Client Application Manager.

Managing the Client Application Manager

Applications that create their own environment on the client require that the client download many Java class lib files from the server.

This download process happens every time the application is launched. This can cause application load times that sometimes take over five minutes depending upon the application. The CAM (Client Application Manager) can help alleviate this constant downloading of applications. It downloads many of the required Java classes into a permanent storage location on the client. Whenever an application that uses the CAM is launched, the client will examine to see if the classes have been downloaded. If the classes have been downloaded, the application start time improves significantly.

CAUTION   Lab testing by Cisco has shown the Internet Explorer does not benefit from the CAM because it caches many of the same files the CAM does. A significant benefit is realized in Netscape because it does not cache the Java class libraries like Internet Explorer. The CAM, however, can also cause conflicts. If applications are updated at the server, the CAM must be uninstalled or the updated applications will not operate properly. For example, if updating Resource Manager Essentials from 3.0 to 3.1, the CAM must be removed and reinstalled.

For the CAM to be set up properly, the client must connect to the server by a host name, not a TCP/IP address. The name is used in the server registration process. Connecting via an IP address sometimes causes the setup of the CAM to fail. The server name can be resolved either through DNS or a local host file.

If the CAM is not installed, implement the following steps to set it up:

Step 1 In the CiscoWorks 2000 Server Console select CiscoWorks 2000 Server; Setup; Client Manager Admin. Figure 4-13 shows the Client Application Manager default state with no Java applications downloaded.

Figure 4-13 *The Client Application Manager*

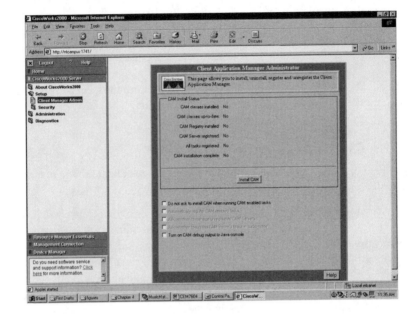

Step 2 The Client Application Manager will appear. Click the Install CAM button if it has not been previously installed.

Step 3 The Installation progress will be displayed in the status window. Choose a directory to install the CAM classes. The classes are server-, user-, and browser-specific and need to be reinstalled for each. Figure 4-14 shows the Choose Directory to Place CAM Registry dialog box for placing the CAM files.

Figure 4-14 *The CAM Destination Directory*

Step 4 When the CAM process is complete, all browser windows need to be closed for the CAM to take effect the next time the system is started. Figure 4-15 shows the Client Application Manager after the CAM install is complete. The CAM also lists how many applications have been registered.

Figure 4-15 *The CAM Fully Installed*

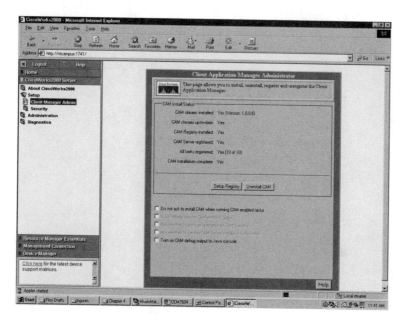

Step 5 If the CAM is not installed, then each time an application that uses the CAM is started the user will be prompted to install the CAM. To prevent this, select the option not to be prompted again to install the CAM.

Step 6 To uninstall the CAM, use the Client Application Manager Admin page and click Uninstall CAM to remove the CAM.

The files for the CAM take less then 5 MB to install all the possible tasks. Some of the tasks that use CAM are the ACL Manager, CiscoView, and the Topology Services in the LAN Management Services. If the browser is left open, the launch time of the application is reduced each time the application is launched.

Summary

After the installation is complete and clients have been properly configured to access the server, the next steps are to start building a Resource Manager Essentials environment. This will be the focus of the following chapters, except Chapter 15, which focuses on trouble-shooting. The next chapter will provide an overview of the Resource Manager Essentials application to make the reader more familiar with the capabilities and functions of Resource Manager Essentials.

Topics covered in this chapter include the following characteristics of CiscoWorks 2000 Resource Manager Essentials 3.X:

- The Concept
- The Architecture
- The Applications

## CHAPTER 5

CiscoWorks 2000 Resource Manager Essentials 3.X

This chapter provides an overview of the different applications of Resource Manager Essentials 3.X. In addition, the chapter provides background on the functional architecture of the Resource Manager Essentials Server.

CiscoWorks 2000 Resource Manager Essentials 3.X: The Concept

The Essentials product, a member of the CiscoWorks 2000 management family, is a suite of client/server management applications that delivers a web-based solution for managing Cisco networks. Essentials applications provide you with the means to configure, deploy, monitor, and troubleshoot small- to large-scale enterprise networks.

Resource Manager Essentials applications provide the network monitoring and fault information you need to track devices critical to network uptime and application availability. They also provide tools you can implement to rapidly and reliably deploy Cisco software images, and view and change configurations of Cisco routers and switches. Essentials applications, together with links to the Cisco Connection Online (CCO) service and support, automate software maintenance to help you maintain and control your enterprise network.

Resource Manager Essentials has incorporated distributed management capabilities. Now Resource Manager Essentials can provide distributed polling and data collection and provide trap-handling services.

Resource Manager Essentials have the capability to manage multiple devices in one job for software, fault, availability, configuration, and management. A job-oriented environment allows an administrator to assign responsibilities for creating and executing tasks within the Resource Manager framework.

Resource Manager Essentials is aimed at supporting large enterprise networks. This is achieved by using client/server architecture with distributed processing entities.

Running the client interface in a browser allows Resource Manager Essentials to offload the chore of producing the client interface. This action saves precious CPU cycles and leaves more memory for the application. Resource Manager Essentials also has the ability to use

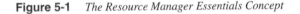

distributed Syslog servers to filter messages before they reach the server. Offloading the Syslog message filtering alleviates the overhead incurred by local message filtering. Figure 5-1 illustrates the concept of how Resource Manager Essentials functions.

Figure 5-1 *The Resource Manager Essentials Concept*

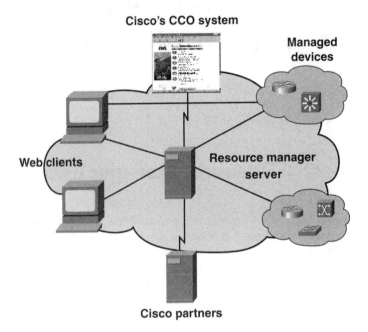

CiscoWorks 2000 Resource Manager Essentials 3.X: The Architecture

The same Internet technologies that have fueled the explosion of bandwidth intensive applications in the network provide some of the solutions to the problems facing network management today. The Web introduces a new scalable network management framework to build from. The Web changes the way we manage networks. No longer does the network manager need to sit in a room surrounded by consoles doing swivel chair management. Next generation network managers can dial in from home or from a hotel using nothing more than their standard browser.

The Web is the console for today's network manager. It decreases the dependency on the platform and console, and reduces the pains of integrating tools and other applications by providing hyperlinks that transparently take the user to other applications and information resources.

Resource Manager Essentials is based on a client-server architecture built on a web server. With version 3.X, this architecture has been expanded to include the CiscoWorks 2000 Server. The Resource Manager Essentials Server is configured to collect information on managed Cisco devices. The administrator configures the collection schedule. Access to the devices is through common protocols such as SNMP, RCP, and TFTP. During the installation process the platform is configured to support these protocols. Access to the server by clients is through a Web-based browser such as Netscape or Internet Explorer.

Command-line tools are also provided to allow an administrator to script certain routines to happen at some scheduled interval or when a Syslog message is received. Tools such as cwconfig allow an administrator to use scripts to update and collect configuration files.

The architecture of the Resource Manager Essentials Server is dependent on a number of components. The data is stored in a Sybase SQL Anywhere database located on the server. The database and applications are composed of a variety of Perl scripts and Java applets. This modular architecture allows updates to individual features of add-in applications without changing the foundation of the product.

Both the client and server components can be scaled, allowing multiple web-based clients to simultaneously access a management server residing on the network. As the number of devices in the network increases, additional servers or collection points can be added with little impact to the client browser application. The servers are unaware of each other so an administrator must ensure the proper devices report to the correct server. Administrators can create a web page that directs users to the correct server. Figure 5-2 illustrates the architecture Resource Manager Essentials and where the server comes into play.

Figure 5-2   *The Architecture of the Resource Manager Essentials Server*

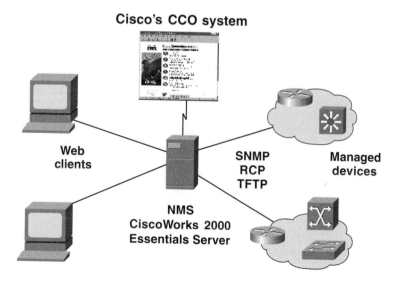

Resource Manager Essentials also features a drop-in capability. New or updated application or device support can be added by using the drop-in feature. Drop-in packages can be part of the Essentials suite, such as Software Management, or additional applications not included in the suite, such as Access-List Control Manager. Drop-in packages are available from CCO on the Essentials home page by selecting the following from the CiscoWorks 2000 Server console:

Home; Additional Resources; Enterprise Network Management

CiscoWorks 2000 Resource Manager Essentials 3.X: The Applications

Resource Manager Essentials have a number of features provided to make network management easier and more efficient. The remainder of the chapters in this book covers each of the features listed in Table 5-1 in great depth. Explanations will be provided on how to configure each feature for proper operation, what options are available, and how to troubleshoot problems when the features do not perform as expected.

Table 5-1   *CiscoWorks 2000 Resource Manager Essentials 3.X: The Applications*

Application	Description	Related Chapter in This Book
Inventory Management	Resource Manager Essentials manage inventory information for all of the Cisco devices in the network. The inventory stores information on chassis, modules, the operating system, and many other aspects of the device. Through polling, the inventory of managed devices is being continually updated.	Chapter 7
Device Configuration NetConfig	The Device Configuration tool archives Cisco device configuration files and lets you modify, search for, compare, and import configuration files. The Device Configuration application gives you access to the configuration files for all Catalyst Switches and Cisco Routers in your Essentials inventory. The configuration archive polls your network and collects and stores all new and changed device configuration files. By maintaining the latest configuration for all devices, this can greatly increase the speed of recovery from a disaster like losing a device configuration or having to swap a device due to a hardware failure. The NetConfig application allows you to change configuration files on network devices through predefined or custom templates.	Chapter 8

Table 5-1   *CiscoWorks 2000 Resource Manager Essentials 3.X: The Applications (Continued)*

Application	Description	Related Chapter in This Book
Software Image Management	The Software Image Management tool provides rapid, reliable deployment of software images. The Essentials Software Management application reduces the cost and time needed to deploy and maintain your Cisco routers, access servers, and switches. As new product features or enhancements are released, Software Management allows you to query your network and take a snapshot of your devices, their versions, and their memory configurations. You can then compare your environments to up-to-date image information on CCO. Images can be downloaded from CCO and then staged for deployment to selected devices in a controlled manner.	Chapter 9
Syslog Analysis	The Syslog Analyzer provides a rapid collection of error conditions. Using the advanced features of the Cisco IOS software, Essentials looks at Syslog events, explains probable causes, and also offers recommendations for resolution. The distributed Syslog service accommodates offloading message collection and filtration to other servers in the network.	Chapter 10
Change Audit Services	Change Audit Services tracks network changes by providing other Essentials applications a place to log network change information. Change Audit monitors your software image distribution and download history events from Software Management, tracks any configuration file changes, and monitors inventory additions, deletions, or changes.	Chapter 11
Access-Control List Manager	Access-Control list manager (ACLM) provides a graphical tool for managing access-lists on routers. Using ACLM an administrator can centralize access-list management and ensure consistent security policies across the network. ACLM also makes constructing or modifying access-lists simpler through the ability to specify traffic type as building blocks in access-lists. The ACLM will also optimize access-lists and remove unnecessary statements.	Chapter 12
Device Availability and Connectivity Tools	The monitoring dashboard can track availability of mission critical devices in the network. Device response time is also monitored to detect periods of link saturation. Protocol Distribution can provide analysis of individual desktop protocols and their impact on the network.	Chapter 13

continues

Table 5-1   *CiscoWorks 2000 Resource Manager Essentials 3.X: The Applications (Continued)*

Application	Description	Related Chapter in This Book
Resource Manager Tools	The CCO integration delivers CCO service and support to your desktop. Essentials provides direct access to CCO information about software image updates and bug notes and streamlines problem resolution through 24 hours a day, seven days a week access to the Cisco Technical Assistance Center (TAC). Resource Manager Essentials also provides easy access to diagnostic and debugging tools, information on TAC cases, and its software.	Chapter 14
	Other assorted tools provide methods for testing network connectivity through **ping** and **traceroute**. The new **network show** commands display output from assorted **show** commands executed from within Resource Manager.	

Summary

The CiscoWorks 2000 application Resource Manager Essentials is now installed. The administrator is familiar with the process of building the environment from the information in this chapter. The next step is to set up the Resource Manager Environment for user access and non-inventory administration tasks. The next chapter covers administrative tasks not related to the inventory of managed devices. Topics such as backing up the database and setting up proxy server connections must be covered to provide an operation platform before loading inventory information.

Topics covered in this chapter include the following:

- Common Resource Manager Administration Tasks
- Accessing the Essentials' Server
- Desktop Enhancements
- User Management
- Administrative Tools
- Managing the Database

## CHAPTER 6

Resource Manager Essentials System Administration

Managing the Resource Manager Environment should not consume more time than the effort saves. Resource Manager is designed to reduce the time an administrator spends managing the system. This is accomplished by having all the common administration tasks in a single Admin folder. Administration of the Resource Manager Environment should not require more than a cursory knowledge of the platform it runs on. For this reason, all the necessary tools for performing administration are contained within the Resource Manager environment. The administration is entirely web-based to enable the administrator to perform the necessary management from anywhere in the environment.

This chapter details the necessary tools for day-to-day server administration of users, server settings, and data management.

The Common Resource Manager Administration Tasks

The first task of the administrator is to set up user accounts on the server. Administration of these accounts, such as changing passwords and roles, is also a responsibility of the administrator.

After users have been configured for the system, the next task is to configure the system itself. This task entails setting up proxy web support, SMTP, SNMP timeouts, and other application parameters. Each application that performs periodic tasks must also have the schedule configured for when these periodic tasks occur. Aside from the day-to-day operations, an administrator may also have to perform some troubleshooting of the RME (Resource Manager Essentials) server. Tools are also included to perform this task, such as tools to test connectivity, process status, log files, server status, and more. Managing the applications and troubleshooting are discussed in their respective chapters.

Accessing the Essentials' Server

Typically, you will install the software using the default port 80. If another application is already using port 80 then the server will use port 1741. See the information in Chapter 4, "CiscoWorks 2000 Server and Resource Manager Essentials Installation," on how to change the port number. When using a web browser for which you do not need to specify the port number, the browser assumes port 80. To access Essentials, enter the URL of the Essentials' server in your web browser as follows:

- **http://server_name**—Web browser uses default port 80.

- **http://server_name:port**—The default port setup during installation is 1741.

For login, the administrator (User Name: admin, Password: admin) can create new users and change passwords, as well as other functions. Figure 6-1 shows the initial login screen with the user name and password dialog boxes circled.

Figure 6-1 *The Initial Login Screen*

One of the first administrative acts after login should be to change the admin password from admin to another password to secure the system. Select CiscoWorks 2000; Setup; Security; Modify My Profile. Change the password for the admin account.

The network desktop is composed of a series of windows that let you navigate among various network management tasks. Each window consists of two frames.

The left frame contains a navigation tree, buttons, and a message window. The tree structure consists of one or more drawers. Each drawer contains associated applications, which in turn contain options. For example, clicking the Resource Manager Essentials Drawer and opening the Administration folder displays the administration options. In Figure 6-2, the admin login account has been used to access the Resource Manager Essentials portion of the application. Clicking the Software Management folder displays the Software Management options. Located above the navigation tree are two buttons: Logout and Help.

Figure 6-2   *After the Login Has Completed*

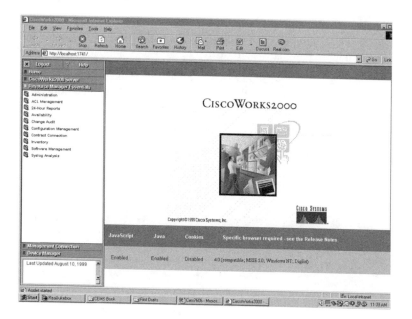

The message window is a web-based "tips-of-the-day" window. Product upgrade information, product tips, and other support information that can make an administrator more productive are displayed in this window. Cisco messages are automatically updated to CCO users daily. You do not need to have access to the Internet for this window to work. If you do not have CCO access, however, your messages will be limited to the messages shipped with the product. To turn off the messages, click on the square in the message window. The square changes to a different colored circle and the window freezes until you click the circle to turn the messages back on.

Administrators can add messages to the ticker window by modifying the UserMessageFile. This file is a text file in the *%NMSROOT%\lib\classpath\com\cisco\nm\cmf\servlet\msgdir* directory. This file does not have an extension on it. If the file is modified using Notepad as the text editor, it will add a *.txt* extension. Make sure the file does not have a file extension. An administrator can use this to make users aware of new reports or server maintenance schedules.

The right frame contains explanations and wizard steps to complete the task. Selecting an application on the left generates an application response in the right window.

Desktop Enhancements

A number of enhancements have been included to make Resource Manager easier to navigate. Channel-based navigation tools use a common web paradigm to make the application more familiar to administrators who are frequent web users.

An administrator can also add links into Resource Manager either to plug-in applications built for integration or to hyperlinks for other web-based applications on the network. The process for accomplishing this is covered in Chapter 13, "Availability and Connectivity Tools."

The quick device window enables an administrator to quickly enter the names of one or more devices to get quick information without using the query window. (See Figure 6-3.)

Figure 6-3   *A Query Window*

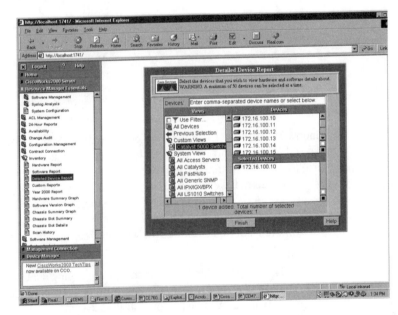

Resource Manager Essentials now caches a selection so that it remembers what you were working with. This caching speeds up the workflow considerably as you move between the tools, especially if you are working on the same collection of devices.

Device views have been split into user and system folders. The views added by the user go into the custom folder. The views that come with RME go into the system folder. In Figure 6-3, the folders are displayed in the query window.

New icons have been added for different devices. If you manage by IP address, there are icons to designate whether the device is a router, a switch, or a generic SNMP device.

User Management

Security has been integrated into the CiscoWorks 2000 Server console. The same user, who is created with access to Resource Manager Essentials, is also allowed to access the CiscoWorks 2000 server. In prior versions of Resource Manager Essentials only the RME application was web based. In the current release most of the suite is now web enabled. Many of the administration features such as login security, database backups, and process management are no longer specific to Resource Manager. The hosting environment is now called CiscoWorks 2000 Server. Resource Manager Essentials is now an application that exists in the CiscoWorks 2000 environment.

There are five groupings of access privileges, called roles, in CiscoWorks 2000. These roles have assigned permissions. Roles can be combined to provide the proper combination of permissions. Access to application options is determined by the roles assigned to a user's login. The role controls what parts of the database and scripts the user can access. The user's desktop options are made available based upon their roles.

User Roles

The access privileges assigned to the roles are not cumulative. There is not a hierarchy of roles, where each role includes all of the privileges of the roles below it. Instead each role is associated with a number of tasks the user can perform. The roles and respective tasks are static. The only exception to this is when add-ins are created with the Cisco Management Connection. Cisco Management Connection applications can be assigned by an administrator to specific roles. However, administrators can assign users to more than one role.

The five roles defined by Cisco are listed as follows:

- **Help Desk**—All users have this role assigned automatically. This role provides help desk technicians enough permission to run most reports but not modify the environment or devices through jobs other Resource Manager applications. Because every user has the Help Desk role, these permissions could be implied permissions for all users. Although Help Desk role can run CiscoView and Network Show commands, they cannot use most of the Configuration Management applications. The Help Desk role is best suited for general administrators who need only the most basic information.

- **Approver**—The Approver role is combined with the Help Desk role to add more functionality to the Help Desk Role. Although the Approver role can approve jobs this is only if they are on the approver list. The Approver role can not create approval lists. Above the Help Desk role they have the ability to create and modify views, schedule Access-Control list download jobs, and use NetConfig. This is typically combined with either Help Desk or Network Operator.

- **Network Operator**—The Network Operator role has the same permissions as Help Desk and has the added abilities to make more use of the configuration archive, manage jobs, create custom reports, but still not create any except in NetConfig. It is usually combined with System Admin to provide a System Admin with more rights but not complete control.

- **Network Admin**—The Network Admin role is assigned carefully. It contains all of the permissions of Network Operator and more. The holder of this role can complete almost any task except create, modify or delete users, start or stop a server process, and many of the tasks under the Administration folder. It should be assigned to the administrator who should be able to use all of the applications but not change many administrative settings. Usually combined with System Admin to create a user that can do anything, or used on its own to create a power user.

- **System Admin**—The System Admin can use all the administrative functions but none of the actual applications. Kind of meaningless on its own, as the System Admin could create a user to perform any function they could not perform. It is usually combined with Network Admin to provide an admin the ability to do anything.

To match the roles to the Essentials' tasks, view the Permissions Report as displayed in Table 6-1 under CiscoWorks 2000 Server; Setup; Security; Permissions Report.

Table 6-1 *The Permissions Report*

Drawer	Folder	Sub Folder	Task	System Admin	Network Admin	Network Operator	Approver	Help Desk
Home								
	Additional Resources							
			Cisco's Home Page (CCO)	X	X	X	X	X
			Enterprise Network Management	X	X	X	X	X
			Documentation	X	X	X	X	X
			Service and Support	X	X	X	X	X
			Partners and Resellers	X	X	X	X	X
	My Shortcuts							
			Delete Shortcut	X	X	X	X	X
CiscoWorks 2000 Server								
		About CiscoWorks 2000						

Table 6-1   *The Permissions Report (Continued)*

Drawer	Folder	Sub Folder	Task	System Admin	Network Admin	Network Operator	Approver	Help Desk
			Applications and Versions	X	X	X	X	X
			Product Overview	X	X	X	X	X
			Client Manager Admin	X	X	X	X	X
	Setup							
		Security						
			Permissions Report	X	X	X	X	X
			Who Is Logged On	X	X	X	X	
			Modify My Profile	X	X	X	X	X
			Add Users	X				
			Modify Delete Users	X				
	Administration							
		Process Management						
			Start Process	X				
			Stop Process	X				
			Process Status	X	X	X	X	X
		Database Management						
			Back Up Data Now	X				
			Schedule Backup	X				
			Log File Status	X	X	X	X	X
			Package Options	X	X			
		Event Management						
			Event Admin Channel	X				

continues

Table 6-1 *The Permissions Report (Continued)*

Drawer	Folder	Sub Folder	Task	System Admin	Network Admin	Network Operator	Approver	Help Desk
			Event Consumer Admin	X				
			Job Admin	X	X	X		
	Diagnostics							
		Connectivity Tools						
			Traceroute	X	X	X	X	X
			Ping	X	X	X	X	X
			NSLookup	X	X	X	X	X
			Management Station to Device	X				
			Collect Server Info	X	X	X		
			Process Failures	X	X	X		
			Self Test	X	X	X		
			Event Query	X				
Resource Manager Essentials								
	24-Hour Reports							
			Change Audit Report	X	X	X	X	X
			Syslog Messages	X	X	X	X	X
			Reloads Report	X	X	X	X	X
			Offline Device Report	X	X	X	X	X
			Configuration Sync Report		X	X		
			Software Upgrade Report	X	X	X	X	X
	Availability							
			Reachability Report	X	X	X	X	X

Table 6-1 *The Permissions Report (Continued)*

Drawer	Folder	Sub Folder	Task	System Admin	Network Admin	Network Operator	Approver	Help Desk
			Availability Report	X	X	X	X	X
			Reloads Report	X	X	X	X	X
			Offline Device	X	X	X	X	X
			Protocol Distribution Graph		X	X		
	Change Audit							
			Exceptions Summary	X	X	X	X	X
			Search Change Audit	X	X	X	X	X
			All Changes	X	X	X	X	X
	Configuration Management							
			Search Archive by Device		X	X		
			Search Archive By Pattern		X	X		
			Startup/Running Out of Sync Report		X	X		
			Custom Reports		X	X		
			Compare Configurations		X	X		
			Update Archive		X	X		
			NetConfig	X	X	X	X	
			Network Show Commands	X	X	X	X	X
			Netsys Report		X	X		
	Contract Connection							
			Check Contract Status	X	X	X	X	

continues

Table 6-1 *The Permissions Report (Continued)*

Drawer	Folder	Sub Folder	Task	System Admin	Network Admin	Network Operator	Approver	Help Desk
		Inventory						
			Hardware Report	X	X	X	X	X
			Software Report	X	X	X	X	X
			Detailed Device Report	X	X	X	X	X
			Custom Reports	X	X	X	X	X
			Year 2000 Report		X	X		
			Hardware Summary Graph	X	X	X	X	X
			Software Version Graph	X	X	X	X	X
			Chassis Summary Graph	X	X	X	X	X
			Chassis Slot Summary		X	X		
			Chassis Slot Details		X	X		
			Scan History	X	X	X	X	X
	Software Management							
		Library						
			Add Images		X			
			Browse Images		X			
			Search for Images		X			
			Synchronization Report		X	X		
		Distribution						
			Distribute Images		X			
			CCO Upgrade Analysis		X			

Table 6-1   *The Permissions Report (Continued)*

Drawer	Folder	Sub Folder	Task	System Admin	Network Admin	Network Operator	Approver	Help Desk
			Library Upgrade Analysis		X			
		Job Management						
			Browse Jobs	X	X	X	X	X
			Consolidated Job Report	X	X	X	X	X
			Mail or Copy Log File	X				
		History						
			Browse History	X	X	X	X	X
			Search History by Device	X	X	X	X	X
			Search History by User	X	X	X	X	X
		Bug Report						
			Browse Bugs		X			
			Browse Bugs by Device		X			
			Locate Devices by Bugs		X			
	Syslog Analysis							
		Severity Level Summary		X	X	X	X	X
		Standard Reports		X	X	X	X	
		Custom Reports		X	X	X	X	
		Custom Report Summary		X	X	X	X	
		Unexpected Device Report						
	Administration							

continues

Table 6-1 *The Permissions Report (Continued)*

Drawer	Folder	Sub Folder	Task	System Admin	Network Admin	Network Operator	Approver	Help Desk
		Availability						
			Change Polling Options	X				
		Change Audit						
			Define Exceptions Summary	X				
			Delete Change History	X				
			Administer Change Audit	X				
	Configuration Management							
			General Setup	X				
			Import from CiscoWorks	X				
			Archive Status	X				
	Network Show							
			Define Command Set	X	X			
			Assign Users	X	X			
	Device Views							
			Browse Dynamic Views	X	X	X	X	X
			Browse Device Membership	X	X	X	X	X
			Add Static Views	X				
			Add Dynamic Views	X				
			Change Static Views	X				
			Delete Views	X				
	Inventory							

Table 6-1   *The Permissions Report (Continued)*

Drawer	Folder	Sub Folder	Task	System Admin	Network Admin	Network Operator	Approver	Help Desk
			List Devices	X	X	X	X	X
			Add Devices	X				
			Import from File	X				
			Import from Local NMS	X				
			Import from Remote NMS	X				
			Import Status	X				
			Delete Devices	X				
			Delete Device Status	X				
			Change Device Attributes	X				
			Check Device Attributes	X				
			View Check Results	X				
			Export to File	X				
			Custom Reports	X	X	X		
			Inventory Change Filter	X				
			Schedule Collection	X				
			Update Inventory	X				
			Inventory Poller	X				
	Job Approval							
			Edit Preferences	X	X			
			Approve or Reject Jobs	X	X		X	
			Create Approval List	X	X			

continues

Table 6-1 *The Permissions Report (Continued)*

Drawer	Folder	Sub Folder	Task	System Admin	Network Admin	Network Operator	Approver	Help Desk
			Edit Approval List	X	X			
	Software Management							
			Edit Preferences	X				
			Schedule "Browse Bugs" Job	X				
			Schedule Synchronization Job	X				
			Update "Upgrade Path" Info	X				
	Syslog Analysis							
			Syslog Collector Status	X	X	X		
			Change Storage Options	X				
			Define Custom Report	X	X			
			Define Message Filter	X				
			Define Automated Action	X				
			Change User URL	X				
			System Configuration	X				
Management Connection								
	Case Management							
			Open Case	X	X	X		
			Query or Update Case	X	X	X		
	CCO Tools							
			Tech Tips	X	X	X	X	X
			Troubleshooting	X	X	X	X	X

Table 6-1   *The Permissions Report (Continued)*

Drawer	Folder	Sub Folder	Task	System Admin	Network Admin	Network Operator	Approver	Help Desk
			Bug Toolkit	X	X	X	X	X
			Open Forum Q&A	X	X	X	X	X
			Open A TAC Case	X	X	X	X	X
			Query A TAC Case	X	X	X	X	X
			Browse CCO IOS Software	X	X	X	X	X
			Browse CCO Switch Software	X	X	X	X	X
			Browse CCO 700 Series Software	X	X	X	X	X
			Browse CCO Microcom Firmware	X	X	X	X	X
			Browse CCO MICA Portware	X	X	X	X	X
			Browse CCO CIP Microcode	X	X	X	X	X
	Device Navigator							
			Browse Device		X	X		
			Configure Fallback Port		X			
	Administration							
			Create	X				
			Import	X				
			Delete	X				
			Export	X				
			Modify	X				
			Set HTTP Proxy	X				

continues

Table 6-1 *The Permissions Report (Continued)*

Drawer	Folder	Sub Folder	Task	System Admin	Network Admin	Network Operator	Approver	Help Desk
Device Manager								
			CiscoView	X	X	X	X	X
	Administration							
		CiscoView Server Admin						
			Setting debug options and display log	X				

Default Users

Two default logins were created for the CiscoWorks 2000 Server. Guest and Admin were designed to provide initial access into the system. The guest account is assigned to the Help Desk role and therefore has some permissions. This account has no default password. The admin account has all roles assigned to it and has all possible permissions. The default password for admin is admin.

CAUTION The admin and guest accounts exist on all CiscoWorks 2000 Servers. If your server is accessible from the Internet, this could pose a security hazard. Anyone with knowledge of the admin or guest account could possibly gain unauthorized access to the system. For this reason, change the password immediately for the admin and the guest account.

Adding Users

To add a user account, the admin account or another account with System Admin privileges must be used. By default, all accounts are assigned the Help Desk role. Additional roles can be added to an account to further enhance its capabilities.

User Profiles

Users cannot modify accounts other than their own unless they have the System Admin role. Users, however, always have permission to change their own profile. This permission allows an administrator to avoid micro-management of the user population. Users can change their own password, email address, CCO account, and CCO password. Users cannot modify their assigned roles or user name.

The CCO information of users is now part of the CiscoWorks 2000 user profile. CCO is the name attributed to most of the support resources on the Cisco website. This attribution makes the integration with CCO seamless. Users can access support services on the CCO site without having to log in outside of CiscoWorks. This allows users with their own accounts to avoid sharing their information with an administrator. In Figure 6-4, the modify user profile dialog box is displayed. The user can modify their information from this dialog box. Note that the user role section is grayed out, therefore rendering changes impossible.

Figure 6-4   *The Modify/Delete Users Dialog Box*

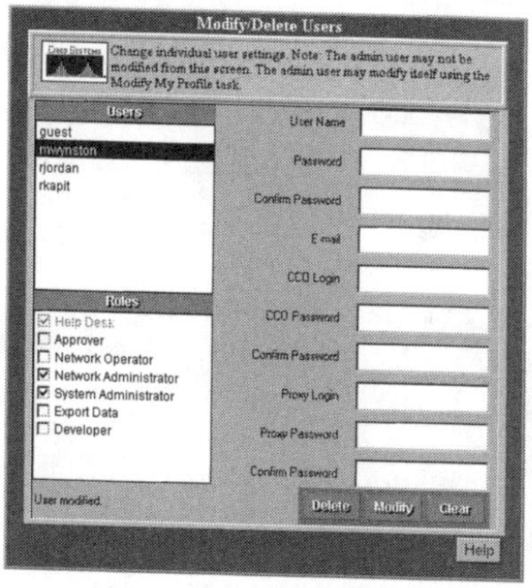

Administrative Tools

The CiscoWorks 2000 suite comes with a number of tools to administer the server and the database. Some tools are related to troubleshooting problems with the server and other tools are designed for maintenance. Troubleshooting tools are covered in Chapter 13, which discusses tools for troubleshooting processes, connectivity, and server settings. This section focuses primarily on maintenance tools.

Managing User Connections

One of the more difficult tasks in a distributed architecture is managing server maintenance. An administrator must take down a server from time to time and it is often difficult to determine when to do so. If a critical job is scheduled or a user is running a report, the user needs notice of when the server will be off-line. New to CiscoWorks 2000 Server is the ability to determine which users are logged into the system.

The "Who Is Logged On" application displays all users who are logged into the system. The user's last known TCP/IP address is displayed, as well as the time of last activity and login. All users' roles are also displayed to determine each user's respective permissions. The administrator can also send a message to all users currently logged into the system. The "Who Is Logged On" feature is available to every role except the Help Desk role. Figure 6-5 shows the "Who Is Logged On" application and a message that was sent from the application to the users.

Figure 6-5 *Who Is Logged On Application*

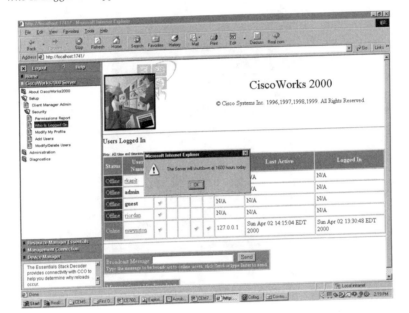

Configuring SNMP Timeouts on the Server

Multiple SNMP queries can be sent at one time. The process of querying devices is not a linear one. This process ensures that one slow responding device does not delay queries to other devices for a job or process. Two types of SNMP timeouts are available: the fast timeout and the slow timeout. Devices are first queried with the fast timeout. The default settings for fast timeouts are five seconds with two retries. The maximum setting for fast timeout is 90 seconds with six retries. This situation allows a device to time out quickly with only two retries. The slow SNMP timeout is set to twenty seconds with three retries. The maximum setting for slow timeout is the same as fast timeout, ninety seconds with six retries. Devices respond to SNMP queries at different speeds depending on device speed, network traffic, and network delays. To access the SNMP setting select Resource Manager Essentials; Administration; System Configuration; SNMP. Figure 6-6 shows the default SNMP settings.

Figure 6-6   *System Configuration: SNMP Default Timeout Settings*

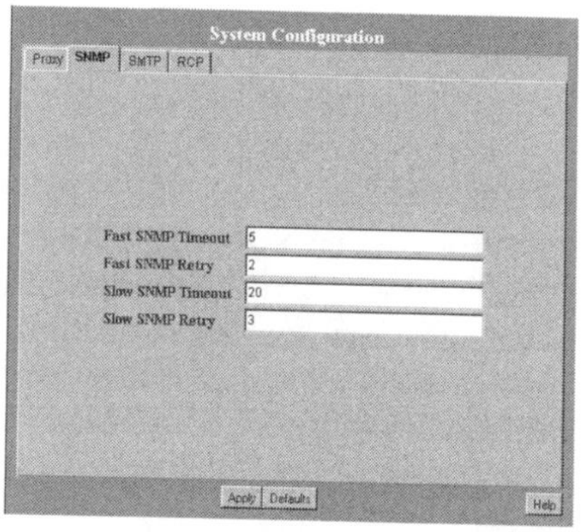

Configuring a Proxy Server

If the Resource Manager Essentials' server requires a Proxy Server to access the Internet, the address can be entered into the server's configuration. This allows networks that use firewalls or address translation to provide Resource Manager Access to the Internet for CCO integration and other Internet accessible tools. The application uses the settings configured on the server, not local client settings. A Proxy Server requiring authentication is supported. The Proxy Server settings can be configured for each user in their profile. In the user's profile, an administrator can enter the user's proxy user name and password. To configure the Proxy Server address use the console Resource Manager Essentials; Administration; System Configuration; Proxy.

Configuring the SMTP Settings

A number of applications in Resource Manager Essentials can be programmed to send information to the administrator by email. To enable this feature the server must be configured with the address of an SMTP server. Resource Manager Essentials uses the email address configured in the user profile for sending the message to the appropriate recipient. The SMTP server then forwards the email to the address as specified in the user's profile. To configure the SMTP settings, use the console Resource Manager Essentials; Administration; System Configuration; SMTP.

Configuring the RCP Username

The Software Image Management Application in Resource Manager Essentials includes the ability to copy files by RCP in addition to the standard TFTP options. RCP uses TCP to copy files to ensure reliability that is not normally available with TFTP, which uses UDP as the data transport. To configure the RCP username, use Resource Manager Essentials; Administration; System Configuration; RCP. The same username must also be set up on the router.

Managing the Database

The CiscoWorks 2000 Server uses the Sybase SQL Anywhere database engine to store the data on the server. Administration of the database consists mainly of backing up the data on a regular basis. Cisco does not openly publish the schema for the databases in the product. Cisco does not want customers to create application that go around Resource Manager Essentials because there is no way to ensure consistency from one version of Resource Manager to another. Manipulation of the database directly violates the support agreement and should not be attempted.

Backing Up the Database

Database Management backs up both the Resource Manager Essentials database and the Common Management Framework database, which is used by the CiscoWorks 2000 Server. The databases can be backed up either immediately or scheduled for backup on a set schedule. The scheduled backup can be done daily, weekly, or monthly. The application keeps prior generations of backups in case corrupt data is not immediately discovered.

To backup the database through a schedule, use CiscoWorks 2000 Server; Administration; Database Administration; Schedule Backup. Figure 6-7 shows the Set Backup Schedule screen and a backup scheduled to go weekly on Sunday at 2100 hours (9:00PM). By turning on the Generations feature, multiple database backups are saved.

Figure 6-7 *Scheduled Backup*

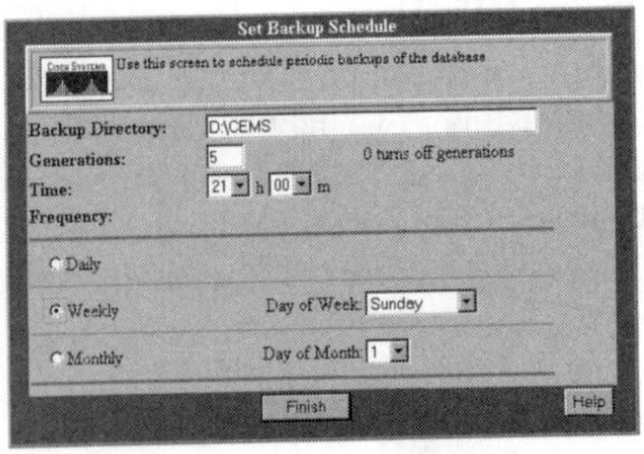

The database can be backed up immediately by choosing the Back Up Data Now application. This scenario creates an immediate backup of the database in a specified directory. This backup will overwrite any previous database backups in the directory. The application will place the files under a subdirectory named 0.

The database backup contains the necessary files to recreate the server on another machine. Files are compressed so the backup takes less space. Included in the backup are all database files, log files, configuration files, and software images. The software images take up substantial space in the backup, however, there is not an option to choose not to back up the software images.

Accessing the Database Using ODBC

On Windows NT-based systems the Sybase database engine is accessed through an ODBC connection. This setup allows an administrator with access to the CiscoWorks 2000 Server to access the database through applications other than the management console.

CAUTION   Accessing the database through applications other than the management console is not a supported method of accessing the database and should be used with extreme caution. Changing the database in any way outside of the application framework could prove to be disastrous to the server. This could also cause inconsistencies in the data. Doing any direct data manipulation is a violation of the support agreement.

The following information is subject to change at any time and should not be written into other applications.

To access the databases outside of the application framework, use any application that can access data through an ODBC connection. Using MSQuery32, an application that comes with Microsoft Office, is an easy way to perform this task. On the menu choose File; New Query. From the Choose Data Source window select **cmf** for the CiscoWorks 2000 Server database or **RME** for the Resource Manager Essentials Database. The ODBC will read the user name and password from the connection definition. If ODBC is not able to read the username and password the application will prompt for the information.

The connection definition is contained in a number of the PERL scripts used to connect to the database. For the **cmf** database the username is **cmfDBA**. The username for the **RME** database connection is DBA. The password for both connections is **c2kY2k**. The username and passwords are case-sensitive. Through this database access, an administrator may use various applications to query or report on the data in ways not available in the application framework.

In Figure 6-8, the RME database connection is open with the tables displayed.

Figure 6-8   *MSQuery32 Opening the RME Database*

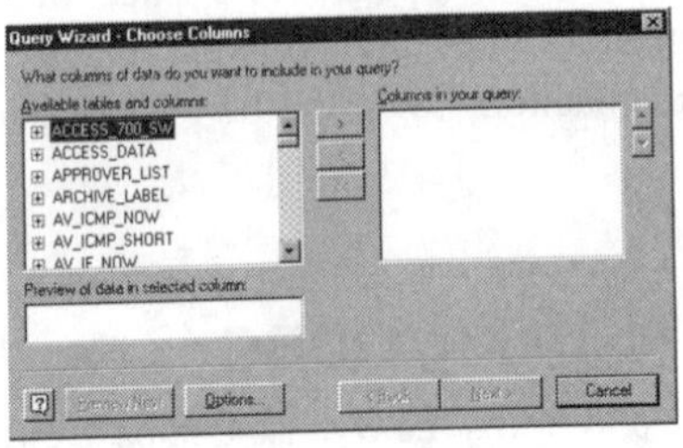

Restoring the Database from Backup

CiscoWorks 2000 comes with support to seamlessly restore a backup of a database into the server. This support allows for both disaster recovery and relocation of the database to another server. The restore feature only supports restoring the database from the same version and is not a method of upgrading the database. Before attempting to restore any of the databases, backing up the data still on the server is advisable.

CAUTION   The restore process starts with shutting down all CiscoWorks 2000 services that manage the database. This is done to unlock the file. Be sure that the server is not running any critical tasks before shutting the server down, and be sure to send users a message warning them that the server is going down.

Restoration Instruction for UNIX

On UNIX, take the following steps to stop the CiscoWorks 2000 services:

Step 1   Log in as the superuser and enter the root password.

Step 2   Stop all processes:

— On Solaris: /etc/init.d/dmgtd stop

— On AIX: /etc/rc.dmgtd stop

— On HP-UX: /sbin/init.d/dmgtd stop

Step 3   Restore the database:

```
$NMSROOT/bin/perl $NMSROOT/bin/restorebackup.pl [-force] [-s suite]
[-gen generationNumber] -d backup directory
```

Where **$NMSROOT** is the CiscoWorks2000 installation directory.

Table 6-2 explains the different **restore** command options.

Table 6-2   **restore** *Command Options*

Command Option	Description
-force	Optional. Forces restoration of an old schema. For example, if the backup has several generations, there may be a 1, 2, ...5. If generation 2 is a much older schema than 5, the **restorebackup** complains the schema is too old. The restorebackup process aborts. If a **restorebackup -force** is used then **restorebackup** prompts for confirmation and the old schema will be restored.
[**-s** *suite*]	Optional. By default, this option restores all suites' data. You can also specify a particular suite using this option. Refer to the appropriate user guide for suite-specific details.
[**-gen** *generationNumber*]	Optional. By default, it is the latest generation. If there are generations 1, 2, through 5, 5 will be the latest generation.
-d *backup directory*	Required. Which backup directory to use.
-h	Provides help when used with **-d** *<backup directory>* syntax. Shows correct syntax along with available suites and generations.

The following is an example of restoring the most recent copy of the database:

```
$NMSROOT/bin/perl $NMSROOT/bin/restorebackup.pl /var/backup
```

After the restoration is complete, verify through the log file that the restoration was successful:

Step 1   Examine the log file in the following location to verify that the database was restored:

```
/var/adm/CSCOpx/log/restorebackup.log
```

Step 2   Restart the system:

— On Solaris: */etc/init.d/dmgtd start*

— On AIX: */etc/rc.dmgtd start*

— On HP-UX: */sbin/init.d/dmgtd start*

Restoration Instructions on Windows NT

The process for the database restoration in Windows NT is similar to the Unix process. To restore the database from a backup, execute the following:

Step 1   At the command line, make sure you have the correct permissions.

Step 2   Stop all processes: **net stop crmdmgtd**

Step 3 Restore the database:

`%NMSROOT%\bin\perl %NMSROOT%\bin\restorebackup.pl [-force] [-s suite]`
`[-gen generationNumber] -d backup directory`

%NMSROOT% is the CiscoWorks2000 installation directory. Refer to Table 6-2 for command option descriptions.

Step 4 To restore the most recent version, enter the following command:

`%NMSROOT%\bin\restorebackup.pl drive:\var\backup\`

Step 5 Examine the log file in the following location to verify that the database was restored:

`%NMSROOT%\log\restorebackup.log`

Step 6 Restart the system:

`net start crmdmgtd`

In Figure 6-9, a restoration has been successfully completed. Contained on the screen display is the necessary command executed in the *%NMSROOT%* directory and the resulting log file.

Figure 6-9 *A Successful Restoration*

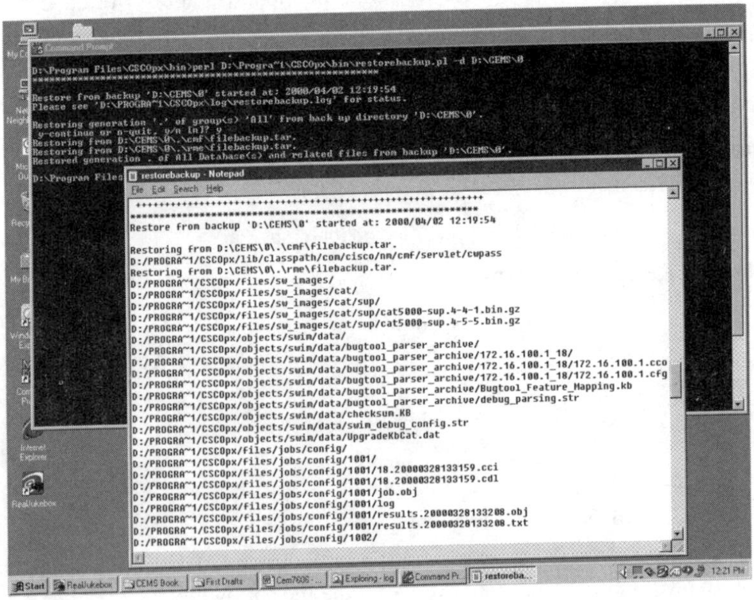

Backup and Restoration Tips

When performing scheduled backups with the Generations feature enabled, CiscoWorks 2000 follows the directory structure in Table 6-3 for database backups. This information is useful to know for restoration purposes.

Table 6-3   *The Backup Directory Structure*

Option	Description	Usage Notes
generationNumber	Number of backups.	For example, 1, 2, and 3, with 3 being the latest database backup.
suite	Application or suite.	CiscoWorks2000 server suite is cmf. Other optional suites are supported. Refer to the appropriate user guide for suite-specific details.
directory	What is being stored.	Directories include database and any suite applications.
filename	File that has been backed up.	Files include database (*.db*), log (*.log*), version (*DbVersion.txt*), manifest (*.txt*), tar (*.tar*), and data files (*datafiles.txt*).

Summary

This chapter instructed the reader about how to prepare the Resource Manager Essentials server for the management process. The reader can now create users, back up the database, access the database, and manage system configuration. These critical steps are often overlooked in many deployments until a problem arises the needs a database backup or accountability for who does what in the application. Performing these tasks before the problems appear follows the proactive nature of the application. The next chapter takes the reader through the process of now adding devices into the Resource Manager Essentials application.

Topics covered in this chapter include the following:

- Inventory Management Features
- Supported Devices
- Inventory Manager—Setup
- Populating the Network Inventory
- Updating the Inventory Information
- Inventory Manager Device Views
- Inventory Manager Reports
- Custom Reports

## CHAPTER 7

Resource Manager Essentials Inventory Management

The foundation for almost all Resource Manager Essentials functions begins with the inventoried devices managed by the database. These devices can then be accessed so that other features of Resource Manager Essentials, such as configuration management, software management, and device availability can be used. Resource Manager Essentials provide numerous methods for obtaining and querying inventory information.

Inventory Management Features

Resource Manager provides a variety of features, which makes inventory management quick and efficient.

Multidevice Management of Cisco and MIB II Devices

The inventory management tools can be used to manage multiple devices with one job. Using database queries defined as views, an administrator can update software, inventory, configuration information, and many other aspects with one job. Resource Manager has the capacity to also manage non-Cisco Internet MIB II-compliant devices. The support for non-Cisco devices is limited in functionality but when using the import tools and user-defined fields almost any information can be stored in the database.

Automated Device Inventory Update

Resource Manager provides a number of methods to keep inventory information up to date. Inventory is updated automatically by polling for changes and can also be triggered by an administrator to happen manually.

Automatic Change Reports

Resource Manager can generate reports on devices that have changed since the last inventory was taken. These changes can be based upon hardware or software changes.

User Defined Views

Users can create custom views of the inventory information. Custom queries allow quick access to the most frequently used devices, saving time otherwise spent creating ad-hoc queries. Users can select devices based on multiple criteria defined in the inventory.

Supported Devices

The inventory features of Resource Manager support all versions of Cisco software 11.0 and higher and almost all platforms of devices. For specific device support, check the release notes for the current release. As of this writing, a list of supported devices is available at www.cisco.com/univercd/cc/td/doc/product/rtrmgmt/cw2000/cw2000e/dev_sup/e3_1.html.

Inventory Manager—Setup

To use any of the inventory's management features, the login entered must have the System Admin role assigned. Only system administrators can import or add new device information, change the inventory-polling schedule, or edit device attributes.

Populating the Network Inventory

To use most of the features in Resource Manager, the database must be populated with inventory. Once inventory is loaded an administrator can use tools such as Software Image Management, Configuration Management, and Syslog Analyzer, among others.

No Autodiscovery of Devices

Resource Manager does not support network Auto discovery. Resource Manager Essentials depends on other applications such as the Asynchronous Network Interface (ANI) in the LAN Management Solutions or HP OpenView Network Node Manager to provide an automated network discovery. These and other applications have well-defined controls over devices that are Auto discovered. If no Auto discovery process is available, then the inventory must be built manually through a device import from another NMS or CSV file. An administrator can also manually input devices one at a time—this activity can be very time consuming.

Although Resource Manager does not perform Auto discovery, it only requires a device's TCP/IP address or DNS name and SNMP community-strings to begin the management process. This information can be imported from numerous management platforms, from a CSV (Comma Separated Value) file, or a DIF (Device Information Format) file. Once this information is provided the application will discover a device's attributes through SNMP.

Device Import

Resource Manager Essentials provides the capability to import inventory information from other Network Management Stations. Imports can be done from a network management application installed on the same server as CiscoWorks 2000 or from a remote server. The location for the import feature is restricted by the operating system where the Management Station is running.

The inventory information imported into Resource Manager will be used for all aspects of device management. Before performing any tasks, make sure the data being imported is clean. There should not be any duplicate devices, incorrect community-strings, or passwords. If the information imported into Resource Manager is of poor quality, any further queries of that same information will probably fail.

Duplicate devices are the most dangerous of problems. If a device is listed in the database with more than one valid name or TCP/IP address, it will be considered as two devices. Therefore, configurations will be stored twice, and all jobs directed at the device will be completed twice. This action can be disastrous in the case of software upgrades, which might leave the device in an unusable state. Resource Manager can detect a duplicate device if the DNS name ties to a TCP/IP address of another device or vice versa. If you are unsure of the quality of the data, use the feature of the Management Station to export the data for cleanup and then import the clean file as a CSV file into Resource Manager.

Device management is easier if DNS names are used instead of TCP/IP addresses. In the DNS server, a name can tie to multiple addresses on a device. Tying to multiple addresses on a device can provide a higher level of consistency than using TCP/IP addresses, which can change and cause the device to become unreachable. If the address changed on the DNS server, it is automatically updated at the Resource Manager Essentials server.

Remote Device Import for Resource Manager Essentials

The remote device import feature does not support importing from a remote Windows NT machine. Windows NT can only be the source of a local import. When performing an import, Resource Manager Essentials is mainly looking for a TCP/IP address or DNS name and SNMP community strings of Cisco devices. Resource Manager on Windows NT or Solaris can import from a remote UNIX server running any of the following applications:

- CiscoWorks for Switched Internetworks (CWSI)
- HP OpenView
- Tivoli NetView (AIX remote hosts only)
- CiscoWorks
- Cisco WAN Manager (CWM)
- CiscoWorks for Switched Internetworks (CWSI)(ANI Server 3.0 or later)

- HP OpenView (Version 5.01 or 6.0)
- Tivoli NetView (AIX remote hosts only)(Version 5.1 or later)
- CiscoWorks (Version 4.0)
- Cisco WAN Manager (CWM)(Version 9.2)

For updated information on supported platforms for remote import, check the release notes for the current version of Resource Manager Essentials.

Remote Device Import Requirements

The remote import process works the same whether Resource Manager is running under Windows NT or UNIX. Verify that the following requirements have been met before beginning the process to ensure a successful import.

- Verify that your device read and read-write try-strings are correct and accurate.
- Verify that your local Essentials' server has remote access to the remote username. You must be able to run the remote shell as the specified bin user on the remote host.

NOTE	Remote Shell is a UNIX Daemon (program) that runs as a process in the background and enables commands to be executed on the server remotely.

Before attempting to perform the remote import, check to see that user bin can log in to the UNIX server. Use the following process to check login and directory permissions:

- On UNIX:

  ```
  %su bin
  %remsh <host name> -l <remote login> ls <directory name>
  ```

- On Windows NT (must be logged on as user bin):

  ```
  %SystemRoot%\system32\rsh.exe <host name> -l <remote login> ls
  <directory name>
  ```

Table 7-1 provides directory name defaults, depending on your platform.

Table 7-1   *Directory Structure for Remote Import*

Platform	Operating System & Database	Default Directory
CiscoWorks	UNIX on HP OpenView, HP-UX 10	/opt/CSCOcwh
	UNIX on SunNet Manager	/opt/CSCOcws
	AIX	/usr/nms
CWSI 2.2	Windows NT	c:\CWSI22

Table 7-1   *Directory Structure for Remote Import (Continued)*

Platform	Operating System & Database	Default Directory
CWSI 2.1	Windows NT	c:\CWSI21
HP OpenView	UNIX and HP-UX	/opt/OV
	Windows NT	c:\OpenView
Tivoli NetView	Solaris	/usr/OV
Cisco WAN Manager	Solaris and Informix	/usr/users/svplus
	AIX and Informix	/usr/users/svplus

- Verify that both local and remote machines are in the network's Name Resolution Service, such as DNS or WINS.

- Verify that the remote UNIX Server is configured as follows:

  — A .rhosts file is in the remote user's home directory and contains an entry for the Essentials Server. The username entry should be bin.

  — The /etc/hosts.equiv file on the remote server does not contain any statements that disenable access by the Essentials Server.

  — For CiscoWorks, the remote user is a member of the CiscoWorks group. On UNIX, the remote user ID is part of cscworks (or the group entered when CiscoWorks was installed) in /etc/group.

  — For CiscoWorks, the Sybase server is running on the remote host and the Sybase database uses the default query server name CW_SYBASE.

  — For CWSI, the remote user is a member of the group bin and a member of the CWSI "Known Network" database group. This database group must have write access to the "Known Network" database.

  — For HP OpenView, HP OpenView is running on the remote host.

  — For Tivoli NetView, Tivoli NetView is running on the remote host.

  — For Cisco WAN Manager, the default user name is svplus.

Remote Import Procedure

Once the login and directory structure have been verified, the remote import process can begin. Use the following steps to carry out the remote import process.

Step 1   Select Resource Manager Essentials; Administration; Inventory; Import from Remote NMS. The Remote Database Import dialog box appears.

Step 2 Select the database you are importing from (CWSI, HP Openview, Tivoli NetView, CiscoWorks, or Cisco WAN Manager) using the NM Product drop-down list box. Only applicable products appear in this list.

Step 3 In the Host Name field, enter the network name of the host on which the remote NMS resides. In the User Name field, enter the name of the remote user.

Step 4 Click a radio button from the Reconciliation Criteria list. This specifies the conflict resolution method to apply if there is a conflict between a device you try to import and a managed device with the same host and domain names.

Step 5 Select Cisco Devices Only or Customize or both from Special Options, then click Next. If you are importing non-Cisco devices or you want to enter device information, click Customize.

Figure 7-1 displays the Remote Import dialog box. The Management Station is HP OpenView on host name MGMTSTN1.

Figure 7-1 *The Remote Import Dialog Box*

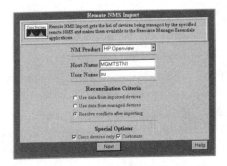

- If you select Cisco Devices Only, devices are filtered based on the SNMP MIB-II variable "sysObjectId." (Devices are not filtered on CWSI.)

- If you select Customize or CWSI, the Import Options dialog box appears. Enter the import options that apply to your NMS database.

- If you installed the NMS at a user-specified location (instead of the default), click Customize and enter the Source location.

- If you select Check Device Attributes, device attribute information is verified after the import.

The next steps manage how Resource Manager Essentials should handle duplicate devices added through the import process.

Step 1   Click a radio button in the Reconciliation Criteria list. This specifies the conflict resolution method to apply if a conflict occurs between a device you try to import and a managed device with the same hostname and domain name.

Step 2   Click **Finish**. The Add/Import Status summary displays the number of devices that are managed, alias, pending, conflicting, suspended, and not responding.

To verify the current import status, use the following steps. This window does not need to be left open during the import process. To return to the import status window select Resource Manager Essentials; Administration; Inventory; Import Status.

- You can click any of these statuses to view the devices in that state.

- If you selected Check Device Attributes, the number of device attribute errors is also shown. You can click this field to view details.

- Click Update to display the most recent information.

Importing from a Local Management Station

You can populate your Essentials server with device inventory data by importing the data from a supported network management system (NMS) database residing on the local host. Device import supports the following NMS databases:

- The ANI Discovery Process
- HP OpenView
- Tivoli NetView (Windows NT and AIX local hosts only)
- CiscoWorks (Solaris, AIX, and HP-UX local hosts only)
- Cisco WAN Manager (CWM)

The ANI import process is handled in the section entitled, "The ANI Synchronization Process."

Before Beginning a Local Import

In a fashion similar to a remote import, certain steps must be taken first to ensure a successful import:

Step 1   Verify that your device read community-strings are accurate.

Step 2   For HP OpenView, make sure HP OpenView is running on the local host.

Step 3   For CiscoWorks, verify the Sybase server is running on the local host and that the user bin is a member of the CiscoWorks group (defaults to cscworks).

As in a remote import, the data imported is only as good as the original data. As mentioned previously in Remote Import be sure to check that the data is clean before starting the import process.

Procedure for Local Import

To perform a local import from a locally installed NMS use the following steps:

Step 1   Select Resource Manager Essentials; Administration; Inventory; Import from Local NMS. The Local Database Import dialog box appears.

Step 2   Select the database you are importing from (HP OpenView, Tivoli NetView, CiscoWorks, or Cisco WAN Manager) using the NM Product drop-down list box. Only applicable products appear in this list.

Step 3   Click a radio button in the Reconciliation Criteria list. This list specifies the conflict resolution method to apply if there is a conflict between a device you try to import and a managed device with the same hostname and domain name.

Step 4   Select Cisco Devices Only or Customize or both under Special Options, then click Next. To change default import options, click Customize.

Figure 7-2 displays a local import from HP OpenView. Because the application is locally installed, the Hostname and Username do not have to be specified.

Figure 7-2   *The Local Import Dialog Box*

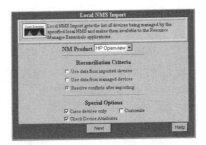

- If you select Cisco Devices Only, device filtering is performed only for CiscoWorks and HP OpenView. Note that if you performed a "quick sync" in CiscoWorks, device filtering will not work. (Devices are filtered based on the SNMP variable "sysObjectId.")
- If you select Customize, the Import options dialog box appears. Enter the import options that apply to your NMS database.

- If you installed the NMS at a user-specified location (instead of the default), click Customize and enter the Source location.

- If you select Check Device Attributes, device attribute information is verified after the import.

To complete the local import process, continue with the following step:

Step 5   Click **Finish**. The Add/Import Status summary displays the number of devices that are managed, alias, pending, conflicting, suspended, and not responding.

To verify the current import status:

- You can click any of these statuses to view the devices in that state.

- If you select Check Device Attributes, the number of device attribute errors is also shown. You can click this field to view details.

- Click Update to display the most recent information.

The status window does not need to be left open during the import process. To return to the import status window, select Resource Manager Essentials; Administration; Inventory; Import Status.

The ANI Synchronization Process

In the CiscoWorks 2000 suite LAN Management Solutions (LMS), Cisco included a way to automatically synchronize the autodiscovery process of ANI with the Resource Manager Essentials inventory database.

The ANI process is responsible for discovery in the CiscoWorks 2000 Topology Services application used to manage switches and VLANs. In prior versions the ANI process and Resource Manager Essentials had to be manually synchronized through an import process. Administrators would have to write their own scripts to keep the two applications synchronized. The added feature of automatic synchronization is a tremendous leap in easing the process of populating the inventory database.

The ANI Process

The ANI process is dependent on Cisco Discovery Protocol (CDP) in order to function properly. Many of the specifics of ANI are beyond the scope of this book. However, understanding how the ANI process does work in order to know how to make it work is important.

Before the ANI process can begin there are three things that must exist in the network:

- TCP/IP Connectivity to all devices that will be managed from the server. This connectivity must allow SNMP, Telnet, TFTP, and RCP at a minimum to each device.

- CDP (Cisco Discovery Protocol) must be enabled on each interface that needs to advertise its presence to another device. No Cisco device passes CDP traffic. This advertisement is set to a Cisco registered 40-bit MAC address. This address is listened to only by CDP-aware devices. Configuring CDP is discussed in Chapter 3 "Configuring Devices for Network Management."

- SNMP must be enabled in order for both the ANI and Resource Manager Essentials processes to communicate with the network devices.

After TCP/IP, CDP, and SNMP have been configured on the network devices, the next step is to configure the ANI process for Network Discovery.

Configuring the ANI Process

The ANI process is configured from the CiscoWorks 2000 Console. This process is broken down into configuring SNMP, configuring seed devices, and then general ANI settings. Configure the ANI process for network discovery using the following steps:

Step 1 Log in to the system as either the Admin account or with the System Admin role.

Step 2 Select CiscoWorks 2000 Server; Setup; ANI Server Admin. First select the SNMP Settings application. This application is pictured in Figure 7-3. The Modify SNMP Settings dialog box will appear. This application is modifying the anisnmp.conf file, located in the *%NMSROOT%\etc\cwsi* directory. Be careful when modifying this dialog because it directly modifies the file.

Figure 7-3 *The ANI SNMP Settings*

Step 3 In the SNMP Setting dialog click in the area of the string
"*.*.*.*:public::::::private". It is important not to accidentally delete
or add any colons—they are the data delimiters.

Step 4 The four asterisks represent the parts of a TCP/IP address. By using
multiple lines in a top-down fashion, an administrator can enter different
community strings for different devices. Use the asterisk as a wildcard in
the address.

Step 5 The next field is the read-only community string, then an unused field,
timeout, retries, unused, unused, and the read-write community string.
Remember the strings are case sensitive. An example using parameters
follows:

```
Read-only string: cisco
Read-write string: san-fran
Timeout: 10 seconds
Retries: 3
ANI SNMP settings- *.*.*.*:cisco::10:3:::san-fran
```

Once the ANI SNMP has been completed, the next steps configure ANI seed device
settings:

Step 1 Adding seed devices is completed by selecting CiscoWorks 2000 Server;
Setup; ANI Server Admin; Discovery Settings. Figure 7-4 shows the
Configure Discovery Settings dialog box.

Figure 7-4 *ANI Discovery Settings*

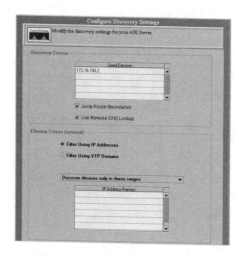

The Discovery Settings dialog box is broken into two parts—the
Discovery Criteria and Filtering Criteria.

The Discovery Criteria is where seed devices are listed. This is the TCP/IP address of the devices where the discovery process starts.

Step 2 Select Use Reverse DNS Lookup to resolve the TCP/IP addresses that are discovered against a DNS server. If no DNS Server is present, a local hosts file can also be used. Check the operating system documentation on how to configure a local host file.

Step 3 If the networks to be discovered are separated by routers, you must select Jump Router Boundaries to get the CDP neighbor information of Router interfaces and to discover Router-to-Router links.

Step 4 Filtering Criteria can be either VTP Domains or IP address, but not both.

VTP Domains are used in Catalyst switched networks to make VLAN administration more efficient. If devices are grouped into domains, use this to filter which domains are allowed in the discovery process.

To filter by IP address, list the TCP/IP addresses to either be excluded from discovery or included in discovery. If a device is encountered that is not in the allowed range, the discovery process will not go beyond that device.

Now that the SNMP and Seed device configurations are in place, here are some general ANI settings, such as discovery schedule and performance:

Step 1 To control the frequency of the discovery process, select CiscoWorks 2000 Server; Setup; ANI Server Admin; Discovery Schedule. Figure 7-5 shows the ANI Configure Discovery Schedule dialog box.

Figure 7-5 *ANI Configure Discovery Schedule Dialog Box*

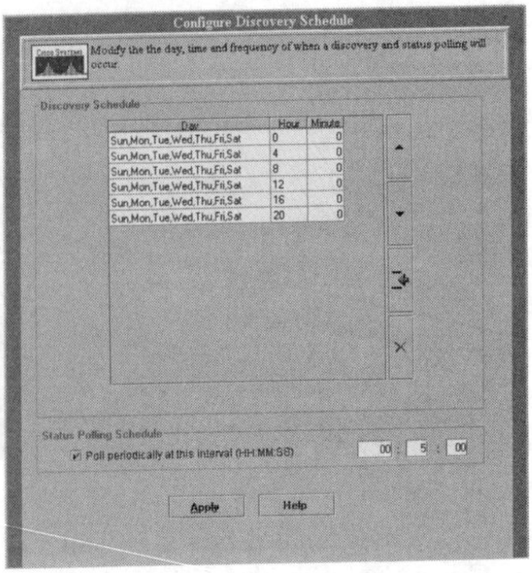

The Configure Discovery Schedule dialog box is broken into two sections. The Discovery Schedule sets how often the discovery process occurs. The Status Polling Schedule checks a device's status.

Step 2   The Discovery Schedule process is set by default to happen every four hours, Sunday-Saturday. Click in the Day, Hour, or Minute fields to change the schedule. Use the arrows on the side of the dialog box to change the order or insert new schedules.

Step 3   The Status Polling Schedule controls polling for the status of a device. This status is used to update the Topology Service and does not impact Resource Manager Essentials. The polling process should not be used to obtain real-time device status. The polling process should be used when the discovery process is run infrequently because the network is fairly static, but the Topology map needs to be updated. For a more efficient method of determining device status, use the Resource Manager Essentials Availability Tools discussed in Chapter 13, "Availability and Connectivity Tools." The polling process checks devices that have already been discovered for their availability. This is done by checking three things:

— Devices are checked for reachability.

— ifAdminStatus and ifOperStatus are updated for each interface connected to a link.

— Administrative and operational statuses are updated for each LANE component (LECS, LES/BUS, and LEC) on each reachable device.

Step 4   Last is to set ANI performance settings. This setting will impact the speed of the discovery process and also the overhead on the server. If discovery happens too frequently and the performance is set too high, this can cause a tremendous burden on the server. To configure performance settings select CiscoWorks 2000 Server; Setup; ANI Server Admin; Performance Settings. This setting will affect how many devices the ANI server will process at one time. The more devices the shorter the discovery process, but the greater the server overhead. Figure 7-6 shows the Configure Discovery Performance dialog box.

Figure 7-6 *ANI Server Performance Settings*

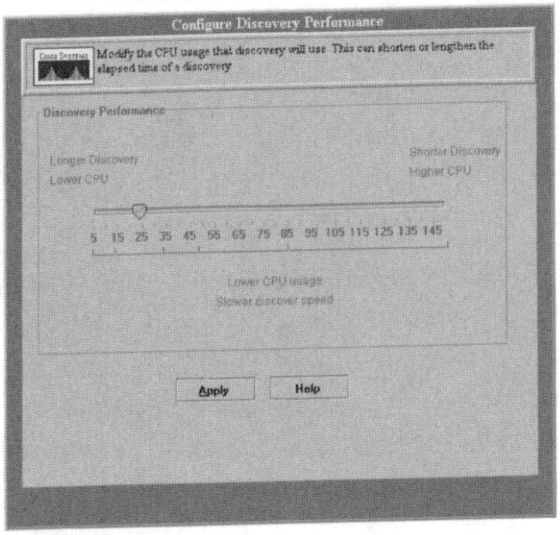

Step 5 Move the slider bar in the Configure Discovery Performance dialog box to the right to decrease the amount of time discovery takes. This will increase the load on the server. Slide the bar to the left to increase the discovery time but decrease the impact on the server. The recommended setting is between 35–49. If the setting is too high, the server could experience memory errors or even crash.

Once the ANI Discovery process is configured, the next step is to enable synchronization between the ANI database and Resource Manager Essentials.

Configuring ANI and Resource Manager Synchronization

To configure database synchronization select CiscoWorks 2000 Server; Setup; ANI Server Admin; Device Synchronization. The Device and Credential Synchronization dialog box will appear as shown in Figure 7-7.

The Device and Credential Synchronization dialog box is separated into two sections: Essentials Server and Configure Device, and Credential Synchronization.

The Essentials Server section can be filled in either with local server information or a remote Essentials Server. If the server is local, the application will fill in the necessary information once Device Synchronization is enabled. If the server is remote, then fill in the server DNS host name, port number the essentials server is installed on, and the admin login information.

Figure 7-7   *Device and Credential Synchronization Dialog Box*

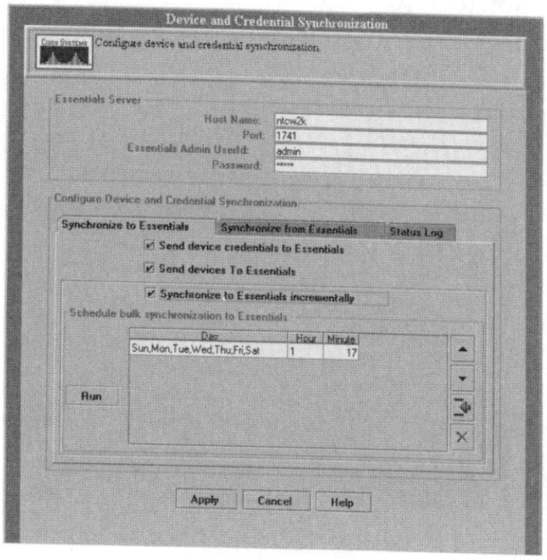

The Configure Device and Credential Synchronization section has three tabs in the dialog box: Synchronize to Essentials, Synchronize from Essentials, and Status Log. The check boxes under the Synchronize to Essentials tab are explained as follows:

- Select the check box "Send device credentials to Essentials" to send the SNMP community strings to Essentials from the ANI SNMP settings.

- Select the check box "Send devices to Essentials" to send the devices that have been discovered to the Essentials Device Import process. These devices will be treated as any other imported devices and will have their inventory added to the database.

- Select the check box Synchronize to Essentials Incrementally to send new devices to Essentials as they are discovered and not just at the scheduled synchronize time.

Click the Run button to run an immediate synchronization to Essentials from the ANI database.

Once the inventory information has been synchronized to the Resource Manager Essentials database from the ANI database, the administrator must still add information to the database about Telnet, TACACS, RADIUS, and enable passwords. This information is not in the ANI database but must be in the RME database for the application to function properly. See the section on Updating Inventory Information later in the chapter for instructions on how to add this information to the database.

Manually Adding Devices

If no other Management Platform is available as a source of information, then the information can be manually added to Resource Manager or imported through a CSV file. Manually adding information into Resource Manager is a simple process.

Adding Devices Through the Online Form

The only information required to add a device into Resource Manager is the TCP/IP address of the device and the device's community-strings. Figure 7-8 displays the Add a Single Device form in its initial state.

Figure 7-8 *The Add a Single Device Form*

Optionally an administrator can also specify additional information necessary for software upgrades, configuration management, and other features. The optional parameters are:

- TACACS username and password

- Telnet password

- Enable password

- External serial number

- RCP username and password

- User-defined fields

These additional fields can also be filled in after the device is added. Information such as Telnet, TACACS, and enable password must be added for Resource Manager to perform functions such as configuration file collection or software updates. If the information is specified later, it can be done through a view. Changing information through a view allows an administrator to change multiple devices at once.

Adding Devices Through a CSV or DIF File

In addition to filling out the online form, an administrator can create a CSV or DIF file with the appropriate information and add the devices all at once. The CSV and DIF have templates supplied with the CiscoWorks application. The template files are located in the *%NMSROOT%\example\import* directory. The name of the CSV example file is *device_CSV_sample.txt* and *device_IFF_sample.txt* for the DIF file. Both file types can perform the same functions. The type used is simply an administrative preference.

The CSV file is imported by Resource Manager and then broken down into a DIF file. A DIF file specifies the data already broken down in Resource Manager format. Figure 7-9 contains a sample CSV file used to import 18 devices along with the respective community-strings.

Figure 7-9   *A CSV File Used for Device Import*

```
cisco Systems NM data import, source = Hand edit; Version = 2.0; Type = Csv
Device Name,RO community string,RW community string
172.16.100.2,football,nfl
172.16.100.10,football,nfl
172.16.100.11,football,nfl
172.16.100.12,football,nfl
172.16.100.13,football,nfl
172.16.100.14,football,nfl
172.16.100.15,football,nfl
172.16.100.16,football,nfl
172.16.100.17,football,nfl
172.16.100.60,football,nfl
172.16.100.61,football,nfl
172.16.100.62,football,nfl
172.16.100.63,football,nfl
172.16.100.64,football,nfl
172.16.100.65,football,nfl
172.16.100.66,football,nfl
172.16.100.67,football,nfl
172.16.100.1,football,nfl
```

The top two lines are required for the import to process the file. The first line identifies the file as an import file. The second line is the column headings. One way of keeping Resource Manager Essentials synchronized with other NMS systems is to schedule imports of CSV files. This action can be done using the Perl script *crmimport.pl* and the operating systems scheduler services like the **AT** command. The crmimport.pl file is located in the bin subdirectory of the install directory, which is typically *CSCOPx*. If the local or remote system supports exporting the inventory to a CSV file, then the file can be copied to the server through a script that then calls the *crmimport.pl* script.

Conflict Resolution

Device conflicts occur when two devices share the same device and domain name; other information may differ. When individual devices are added, conflict checking is not performed. When importing devices from an NMS database or from a file, conflicts are checked. You must, however, determine how those conflicts are handled. Select the reconciliation method in the How to Resolve Conflicts dialog box.

Conflict Resolution can be done in one of the following three ways:

- Use data from imported devices. The system overwrites the existing managed device information with the new device information. Make sure that your imported devices have the correct community-strings. Otherwise, inventory collection does not work properly. If any other imported information is incorrect it can be changed later.

- Use data from managed devices. The system ignores the new information and continues to use the existing information.

- Resolve conflicts after importing (the default). The imported device is added to the list of conflicting devices. A dialog box displays the two sets of device information and prompts you to select the information to use.

Add/Import Status Summary

Once the import process has started, the status can be checked using the Add/Import Status Summary window. The device's current status can be determined from this window. The administrator can tell if a device is having difficulty being imported. Figure 7-10 displays the Add/Import Status Summary window after 18 devices have become managed with some devices reporting errors. If an import was started and you selected some other Resource Manager feature, you can return to the Add/Import Status Summary window through the following navigation: Resource Manager Essentials; Administration; Inventory; Import Status.

Figure 7-10 *The Add/Import Status Summary Dialog Box*

Table 7-2 explains the different conditions of the Add/Import Status Summary dialog box.

Table 7-2   *Conditions of the Add/Import Status Summary Dialog Box*

Condition	Description
Managed	Devices whose inventory information is tracked on the Essentials server.
Alias	Unmanaged devices that have the same interface information as a managed device but a different name reintroduced via a file add or import.
Pending	Unmanaged devices that can still become managed.
Conflicting	Unmanaged devices with the same domain naming system (DNS) and network host name as a currently managed device, but with one or more password elements that are different from the managed device.
Suspended	Unmanaged devices you have suspended in the Pending or Not Responding list, or a managed device you deleted from the Essentials Server.
Not Responding	Devices that are on an unknown host, are unavailable, are not responding to ICMP Echo requests, are not responding to SNMP Get requests, or do not support RFC 1213 (SNMP MIB II) attributes.
Device Attribute Errors	Devices that Resource Manager has been able to contact but has incorrect information for. This could be an SNMP community-string or any of the passwords that must also be provided. Select the hyperlink and the devices will be listed. Select the individual devices to resolve the incorrect information so that Resource Manager Essentials can import the device.

If a device is not responding an administrator can take the following actions:

- Resubmit, delete, or suspend the device(s).
- Change device passwords; Show details.
- Check read-write community-strings.

Updating the Inventory Information

Once the inventory has been populated with devices that need to be managed, the next step is to schedule inventory updates. The inventory update process is conducted in two ways: by scheduling inventory collection and inventory polling.

Inventory Polling

Keeping inventory up to date is a very important aspect of network management. Although Resource Manager does not automatically discover new devices it does monitor for changes in devices, already managed by Resource Manager. The process of updating the inventory should cause minimal network impact. The inventory information taken from devices when first added will generate significant traffic on the network.

Inventory polling updates the inventory without generating a strain on network resources. The inventory polling process uses an SNMP **get** request to discover devices that have either reloaded or recorded a change in the value of the chassis. The polling process uses the reload MIB, the OLD_CISCO_CHASSIS_MIB, and the CISCO_RHINO_MIB to check for changes in a device's physical attributes. If the returned value of the **get** request indicates a change, the Resource Manager Server requests a full inventory accounting. This request allows the inventory to maintain up-to-date information without retrieving a significant amount of information it does not need.

The inventory polling process can be scheduled to run at certain times hourly, daily, or weekly, or it can be disabled entirely. If the polling process detects a change, it immediately initiates an inventory collection. Figure 7-11 displays the Set Inventory Poller Schedule dialog box configured to run every seven days at 2:00 a.m. The detected changes can be monitored through inventory reports.

Figure 7-11 *The Set Inventory Poller Schedule Dialog Box*

Scheduling Inventory Collection

To verify that the inventory is current a periodic inventory update should be conducted. This ensures that if a prior polling process did not notice an inventory change, the information is updated. The inventory collection process updates the inventory of all managed devices.

In most networks, unless a new rollout of hardware is taking place, existing devices are very infrequently changed. To minimize unnecessary inventory traffic, schedule the polling to happen more frequently than the inventory collection process. The polling will catch most changes and the collection process will update those changes not caught in polling. In the event of a known hardware change, an administrator can always use the update feature to update the device immediately.

Inventory Manager Device Views

One of the most powerful features of the inventory management tools is the ability to query the information through views. An administrator can query the database through views without any knowledge of SQL scripting.

There are two types of views—static and dynamic. Resource Manager Essentials has predefined static and dynamic views that can be used to query the data. An administrator may create their own user views without changing the system's predefined views.

Becoming familiar with the process of creating and using views is important. Views are the window into the inventory used for almost all processes. Choosing devices for software updates, configuration modifications, availability, and other features is based upon views.

To determine which views a device shows up in, use the Browse Device Membership application. To access the Browse Device Membership application, use the console to select Resource Manager Essentials; Administration; Device Views. Figure 7-12 displays the Browse Device Membership Application with a Catalyst 5000 switch as the selected device.

Figure 7-12 *The Browse Device Membership Application*

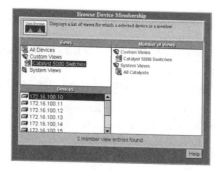

System Views

Resource Manager comes with system-defined views that group devices by their device type attribute. The views are useful in quickly answering questions like, "Which devices are routers?" or "Which devices are Catalyst Switches?"

Custom User Views

Custom views enable a user to develop queries that return the devices they need to manage. By developing Custom Views, users can create groups of devices that follow a certain type of device, or create a view that always manages the same devices regardless of their device type.

Static Views

Static views allow a user to select different devices and group them into a view for easier management. For example, a static view may group core routers and switches into one view. This static view would then include a number of different devices but could be managed as if just one view. Static views can be updated at a later time to include additional devices or to remove unwanted devices.

Dynamic Views

Dynamic Views allow an administrator to select a filter to apply to the inventory. The filter can then be used as criteria to query the inventory. The filter can be based upon any combination of the following criteria:

- Domain name
- Description
- Software Version
- User Field 1–4

The Domain Name is based on the DNS domain of the device. The Description is a list of the devices Resource Manager can manage, not the devices in the inventory. The software version is for IOS software only. It does not list COS software. The User Fields are from the inventory. Figure 7-13 displays the Add dynamic view dialog box, along with the filter criteria. Notice that only IOS software is listed in the Software column.

Resource Manager will cache the query last used to provide for quick access to that same view. This function can improve productivity by allowing quicker device selection.

Figure 7-13 *The Add Dynamic View Application*

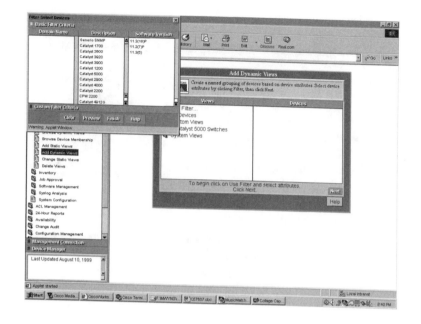

Inventory Manager Reports

The inventory manager comes with a number of useful predefined reports. The reports are listed in the following figures along with brief descriptions in the following tables. The reports that are available as both graphs and reports show the same information. Figure 7-14 shows the Detailed Device Report of a Catalyst 5000 Series Switch. The modules, serial numbers, software, firmware, and many other important pieces of information are displayed.

Use the information in Table 7-3 to determine which report to use to view different aspects of the inventory database.

Figure 7-14 *The Detailed Device Report*

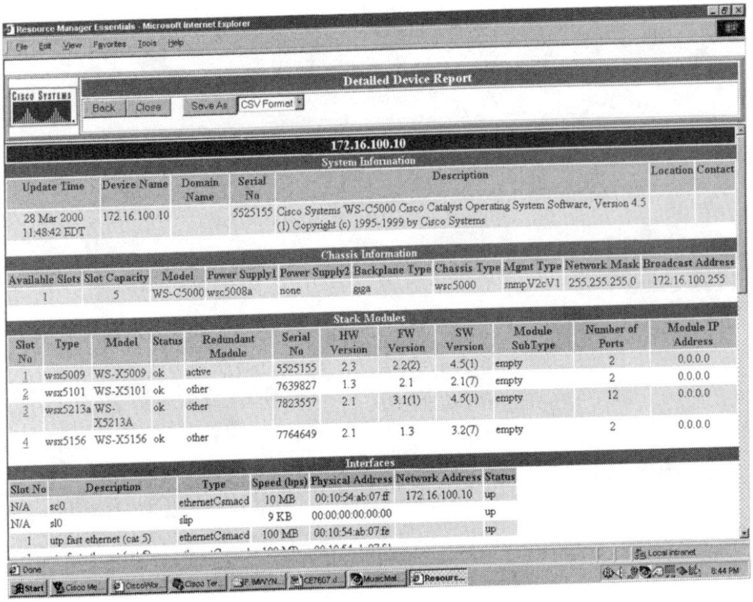

Table 7-3 *Inventory Manager Reports*

Report Name	Description
Scan History	The Scan History option lists all historical data associated with scheduled inventory collection. The report shows the last run duration, devices scanned, and average scan time.
Hardware Report	You can display detailed hardware information for your selected devices. The Hardware Report includes user-specified information for each device. The report contains a different table for each device class in your selection.
Software Report	You can display detailed software information for your selected devices. The Software report includes user-specified information for each device. The report contains a different table for each device class in your selection.
Detailed Device Report	You can display detailed hardware, software, chassis, and interface information for multiple devices.
Capacity Planning Report	For each device class supporting capacity planning, the Capacity Planning report shows the total number of devices and the number of devices with zero free slots, one free slot, two free slots, and four or more free slots.

Table 7-3   *Inventory Manager Reports (Continued)*

Chassis Capacity Report	You can display available capacity for selected devices. The Chassis Capacity Report shows the total slots, available slots, location, and user field information for each device.
Year 2000 Compliance	You can display a report showing which managed devices are compliant to the year 2000. Compliance is determined by device type and software version. To display an accurate year 2000 compliance report, you should have an up-to-date master definition file that lists which devices are compliant to the year 2000. Download the most recent definition file from CCO.

Custom Reports

A new feature in Resource Manager is the ability to generate custom reports. Custom Reports can be a very useful method for device analysis. Custom Reports enable an administrator to view selected criteria on devices limiting the scope to just a certain view rather than having to pick the information out from the more generalized reports. Custom Reports are created based first on views, then generated by report type and selection criteria.

Creating Custom Reports

To create a custom report, navigate to the following tool in Resource Manager, Resource Manager Essentials; Administration; Inventory; Custom Reports. The report types available are:

- IP Address Report
- User Field
- RAM Size
- Flash Size
- Hardware Version
- Card Type
- Port Count

The selection criteria are then based upon the report type. For example, the Port Count Report generates a list of cards in the selected devices and then creates a tally of how many ports are on each card. The Flash Size Report generates a report on devices by selecting the flash size. The IP Address report will generate a list of IP addresses on the selected devices. After the selection criteria have been chosen the report may be previewed before it is generated. Figure 7-15 demonstrates how to create a report of IP addresses of the routers in the inventory.

Figure 7-15   *Creating a Custom Report*

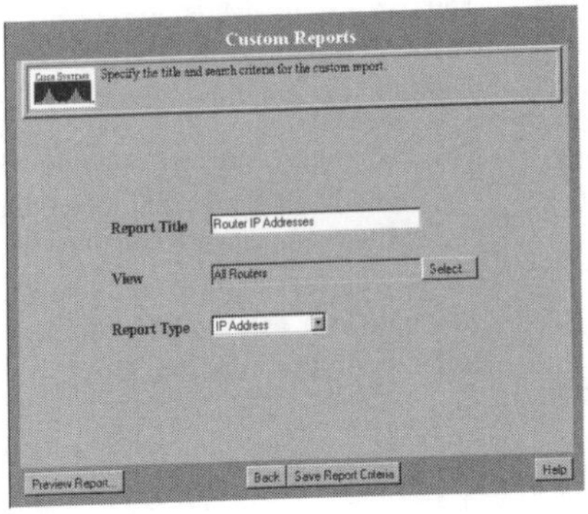

Generating Custom Reports

Custom Reports can be generated from Resource Manager Essentials by navigating to Resource Manager Essentials; Inventory; Custom Reports. The report can be run and then either printed or saved in CSV format. Figure 7-16 displays the output from the report generated in Figure 7-15. The report displays all IP addresses on the routers in the inventory and the interface the address is associated with. This report can be useful to determine that the address is associated with the correct interfaces. By clicking on the Device Name hyperlink, the Device Center will be launched. The Device Center provides an in-depth view of all information in the Resource Manager Essentials server about that device. Information such as configuration files, software files, and syslog messages are some of the details available in the Device Center.

Figure 7-16   *The Custom Report: Router IP Addresses*

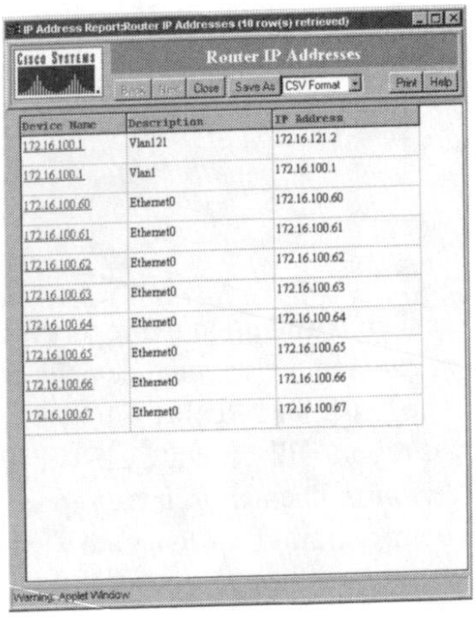

Custom Reports can also be generated from a command line. This tool is useful for generating a report in a script. For example, if the import process is carried out through a CSV file import using the *crmimport.pl* script, generating the custom report on IP address can help to determine which new devices have been added. Calling the *cwinvcreport.pl* script from the import script can automate the entire process. To generate the report, form a command line use the following command:

```
%NMSROOT%\bin\cwinvcreport [option] "reportname"
```

Table 7-4 explains the options available when generating an automated report.

Table 7-4   *cwinvcreport Command-Line Parameters*

Option	Description
-m *<email id>*	Redirects the output to an email recipient.
-o *<filename>*	Redirects the output to a file.
-l *<logfile>*	Redirects log messages and debug information to the log file.
-h	Displays a list of options.
-v	Displays the Inventory Custom Reports version number.
-r	Lists existing Inventory Custom Reports.
-d *[1-2]*	Sets debugging levels. 1 – preliminary level. 2 – detailed level.
"reportname"	The report name must be typed in double quotations.

Summary

This chapter detailed Resource Manager Essentials' Inventory Management features. These features all use device inventory to implement changes and create reports. This chapter also discussed how to import inventory from remote and local management stations, as well as how to add devices manually. Once the inventory was populated, the chapter described how a schedule could be set to keep the inventory information up to date. The last step discussed was how to use views and reports to analyze the inventory. In subsequent chapters, the inventory will be used to manage configuration files, update software, and test device availability and other tasks.

Topics covered in this chapter include the following:

- **Overview of Configuration Management**
- **The Architecture of Configuration Management**
- **Configuration File Management**—Covers supported devices, verifying inventory information, importing configurations from CiscoWorks UNIX, and configuration file management general setup process
- **The NetConfig Tool**—Covers NetConfig templates and creating a NetConfig job
- **The cwconfig Command-Line Tool**—Covers executing the cwconfig tool and using NetConfig with the cwconfig Tool
- **Configuration File Reporting**—Covers five different report/query types: search archive by device pattern, search archive by pattern, startup/running out of Sync, comparing configurations, and custom

## CHAPTER 8

Device Configuration Management

One of the most important yet time-consuming processes in network management is Configuration Management. In a network with a variety of devices, from routers and switches to access servers and firewalls, managing the configuration files can become a full-time job. The Configuration Management features of Resource Manager Essentials enables an administrator to perform a variety of functions on configuration files without the need to learn a scripting language to automate the process. Resource Manager Essentials provide a variety of powerful tools for Configuration Management. This chapter covers how these tools are utilized in the Resource Manager environment.

Overview of Configuration Management

Configuration Management provides easy access to the configuration files for all set command-based or IOS-based Catalyst Switches and Cisco Routers in your Essentials' Inventory.

Once a device is in a managed state the configuration files are automatically collected and stored on the Resource Manager Server. The configuration files are automatically updated by monitoring Syslog messages, SWIM jobs, checking for inventory changes, and scheduling polling. The Configuration Management background process manages the different aspects of keeping the archive up to date.

Once the configuration files are on the server, an administrator can perform a number of tasks with the files.

- **Run change reports**—Find changes made to config files to raise change awareness and administrator accountability.

- **Schedule automatic reports**—Generate reports for history tracking without constant administrative overhead of remembering to run the reports.

- **Query the configuration files**—Search config files or multiple files for any string in (or not in) the file. For example, "Which routers have OSPF configured?"

- **Compare configuration files**—"Why does the config work on router A and not router B?" Find out the differences by comparing configuration files.

- **Create custom reports**—Generate reports based upon text strings within the config files. For example, run a report on all routers running TACACS.

In addition to file management, Resource Manager also provides the NetConfig tool, which permits real-time changes and queries to the managed devices. The NetConfig tool allows an administrator to create custom templates in order for commands to be executed on both routers and switches. These templates are sets of commands used to make changes to one or multiple devices in the network.

The Architecture of Configuration Management

The *Change Agent*, also referred to as the *Probe*, controls the configuration file management process. The Change Agent communicates with other processes to maintain the Configuration Archive. There are a number of ways a router or switch can be configured. Changes can be made to a router or switch through the console, telnet, SNMP, or job processes like NetConfig. To monitor for changes, the Change Agent must be aware of all the methods available for configuring routers and switches.

To provide this type of support the Change Agent has a variety of methods for determining if a change has occurred:

- **Out of Band Console Syslog messages**—Every time an administrator leaves global configuration mode of the router, the configuration message is generated and sent to the Syslog service on Resource Manager.

- **Resource Manager Inventory of New Device**—When a new device is added the Inventory Management Agent will inform the Change Agent to collect the configuration.

- **SNMP Polling**—The Config MIB in 11.1 and higher versions of IOS can be used to poll devices for configuration changes.

- **Scheduled Retrieval**—The Change Agent can be configured to retrieve configuration files on a scheduled basis.

- **Software upgrade jobs created in SWIM**

The monitoring process is called the *ENCASE (Enterprise Network Change Audit Service Environment)* notification process. The ENCASE process is used by the Change Agent to monitor for changes to managed devices in the network.

Figure 8-1 explains how the different processes intercommunicate when a new device is added or when a change is made to an existing device.

Figure 8-1   *The Archive Process*

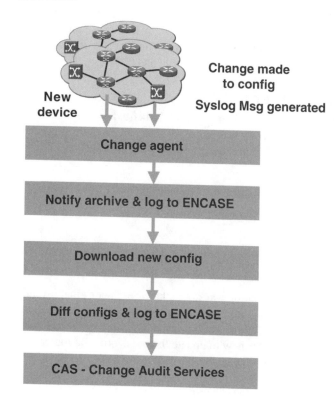

Configuration File Management

The first step in Configuration Management in Resource Manager Essentials is to set up the configuration archive. This process entails a number of steps, detailed as follows:

Step 1   Determining which devices are supported

Step 2   Validating inventory contains necessary information for device access

Step 3   Importing from CiscoWorks UNIX

Step 4   Configuring of Syslog message monitoring

Step 5   Changing device-polling options

Step 6   Setting aging options

Step 7   Changing the location for file storage

Step 8   Setting NetSys Integration Options

These steps are necessary for the proper creation and maintenance of the configuration archive. The configuration archive is necessary for all reports that evaluate anything but the real-time configuration. This archive is used by Resource Manager Essentials to differentiate between changes in configuration files from one version of the configuration file to another.

Verifying Inventory Information

Certain information is not always included when a device is added to the Resource Manager Essentials Server, unless it was included during an inventory import. To properly gather the configuration information, the server must have the following information about the managed devices:

- SNMP read and write community-strings
- User and privileged mode passwords
- Telnet password
- TACACS username and password when TACACS is used
- RCP user name and password when RCP is used

If the preceding information was not included in the original inventory, then it must be added to gather the configuration files. To add the necessary information use the Resource Manager Essentials; Administration; Inventory; Change Device Attributes application. Figure 8-2 demonstrates how to update the password on a router used for telnet. This information is only for the database—it does not affect the device.

Figure 8-2 *The Change Device Attributes Dialog Box*

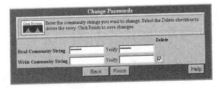

CAUTION When changing the parameters of existing devices, remember to select the delete check box to remove prior settings. After the older information is deleted the new information will be added. If delete is not selected, the changes are added to the database and do not replace the original information. This activity could cause Resource Manager to still use the older, incorrect information.

Importing Configurations from CiscoWorks UNIX

You can import the latest device configurations from the CiscoWorks Sybase database into the configuration archive. You do not need to know the Sybase password or be a member of the CiscoWorks group to do so. You can import configurations from CiscoWorks for UNIX 4.0 as follows (CiscoWorks for UNIX 4.0 has been replaced by CiscoWorks 2000):

Step 1 Select Resource Manager Essentials; Administration; Configuration Management; Import from CiscoWorks. The Import from CiscoWorks dialog box appears.

Step 2 Enter the hostname of the CiscoWorks machine in the Host Name field.

Step 3 Enter the username of the CiscoWorks administrator in the User Name field.

Step 4 Enter the number of configuration versions for each device to import.

Step 5 Click Finish. The Import from CiscoWorks Status page displays the import status.

Step 6 Click Update to refresh the Import from CiscoWorks Status window and view the latest import status.

The requirements to set up the import are the same as detailed in the Importing from a Remote Network Management Station in Chapter 6, "Resource Manager Essentials System Administration." Figure 8-3 shows the Import from CiscoWorks dialog box when an import process is started.

Figure 8-3   *The Import from CiscoWorks Dialog Box*

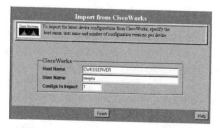

Configuration File Management General Setup

The next series of steps are all performed from the Resource Manager Essentials; Administration; Configuration Management; General Setup application and can set a number of configuration file management options from this page:

- Archive Purging Policy
- Archive Directory

- Change Probe Setup
- Transport Setup
- NetSys Setup

Archive Purging Policy

In a network with thousands of devices, the configuration files can grow to consume large amounts of space. Left unchecked, each copy of a configuration file consumes approximately 2 KB or more of space. If the configuration is copied to the archive every time the device is updated, it will create a new file each time. The new file will contain the differences between the two versions of the configuration file. Combining the space from updated files with regular polled updates, the server could quickly give up hundreds of MB of space. Figure 8-4 (in the next section) shows the Archive Setup dialog box used to control the age of the files in the Archive. The solution to this problem is to combine a good strategy of performing backups and purging old information. The configuration files can be purged based on age. A maximum number of prior configurations can also be configured. The ConfigPurge process, which runs nightly, purges configuration files that match the purge criteria.

Archive Directory

The default configuration of Resource Manager stores all of the server information in one place. The directory where the application is installed contains a directory called Files. In the Files directory, all configuration and software image files are maintained. By default this directory is *%NMSROOT%\files\archive\config\%device number%*.

CAUTION   The configuration archive directory contains a number of pieces of information that should not be open for public consumption. When configuration files are displayed in RME, the passwords are usually not displayed. The password and community-strings are stored in the config files in the archive directory. For this reason, never share this directory or allow it to be mounted as a remote drive. If the application is installed on Windows NT on an NTFS partition, only Administrators and the CiscoWorks user bin have access permissions. Do not change these permissions as this could open a security hole.

Moving the configuration files to a different directory enables an administrator to remove the program files without fear of removing the information also. To move the directory, implement the following steps:

Step 1   Stop the ChangeAudit service.

Select CiscoWorks2000 Server; Administration; Process Management; Stop Process. The Stop Process dialog box appears.

Click the Process radio button.

Select ChangeAudit from the Process Name drop-down list box.

Click Finish.

Step 2 Move the Configuration Archive.

Select Resource Manager Essentials; Administration; Configuration Management; General Setup. The Configuration Manager Admin dialog box appears.

Click the Archive Setup tab.

To move the archive directory, enter the new location in the Archive Directory field, or click Browse to select a directory on your system.

The file path is case sensitive. You cannot enter a new location that differs from the current location, in case only. For example, you cannot change the location from

`/var/adm/CSCOpx/``files``/archive/config`

to

`/var/adm/CSCOpx/Files/archive/config.`

Figure 8-4 shows the Archive Setup dialog box used to relocate the archive.

Figure 8-4 *The Archive Setup Dialog Box*

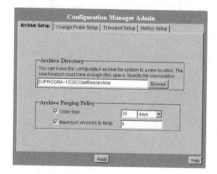

Step 3 Click Apply. A message shows that the archive directory was moved.

Step 4 Start the ChangeAudit process.

Select CiscoWorks2000 Server; Administration; Process Management; Start Process. The Start Process dialog box appears.

Click the Process radio button.

Select ChangeAudit from the Process Name drop-down list box.

Click Finish.

Change Probe Setup

The Configuration Archive automatically detects network changes. The detection process uses the Syslog messages generated by devices to monitor for changes. Each time an IOS-based device is modified, it generates a config message. The config message is sent to the Syslog Server, which is the Resource Manager Essentials Server. The Change Probe Setup dialog box from the General Setup of Configuration Management is where the Change Probe options are set. Figure 8-5 shows the Change Probe Setup dialog box.

Figure 8-5 *The Change Probe Setup Dialog Box*

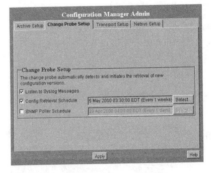

Listen to Syslog Messages

By default, the Change Probe Agent is configured to listen to Syslog messages. This configuration can be disabled if the Agent causes too many configuration files to be maintained on the server. If too many config messages go to the server too quickly, this can cause excessive server overhead, SNMP traffic, and overhead on the devices. If the network has devices generating too many configuration messages, disable the listening process. This action will restrict updates on all devices to the periodic configuration file collection.

Configuration Retrieval Schedule

The Change Probe Agent is configured to retrieve configuration files once a week by default. This option can also be configured to a more acceptable daily, weekly, or hourly schedule. For example, if the Syslog feature is turned off, then schedule the configuration retrieval more often. If the network contains many switches, then having the scheduled collection happen more frequently might be a good idea. Switches do not generate config messages like the router does, and many changes can go undetected. If the switch environment is very fluid, then increase the schedule to keep the archive more up to date.

SNMP Poller Schedule

The Change Probe Agent can also be configured for SNMP polling to monitor for device changes. This feature is turned off by default. The feature is disabled to alleviate the overhead of additional SNMP traffic. The Resource Manager Server should be able to gather all configuration changes through the Syslog or Scheduled Retrieval options. It is not recommended to have both the Syslog and SNMP options turned on. This activity would generate significantly more network traffic and consume more space on the server.

NOTE	The Config MIB is the SNMP MIB that defines the objects used in polling the device for configuration changes. Only Cisco IOS Software-based devices 11.1 or higher contain this MIB. The MIB is not present in Catalyst Operating System-based devices.

Transport Setup

The Configuration Archive has three methods for transporting the configuration file for each device across the network: Telnet, TFTP (Trivial File Transfer Protocol), and RCP (Remote Copy). The Transport Setup tab in the Configuration Manager General Setup dialog box is where the transport order is configured. Figure 8-6 shows the Transport Setup tab.

Figure 8-6 *Transport Setup*

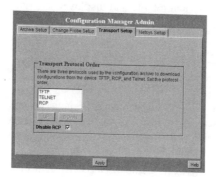

The order in which the transports are listed in the Transport Setup tab is the order they will be tried. If the first method fails, then the second will be used. If the second method fails, then Resource Manager will try the third configured method. The default order is Telnet,

TFTP, and RCP. Telnet is always used on a Catalyst Operating System device. If TACACS, RADIUS, or local login is in use, then the information must be provided to Resource Manager. TFTP can only be used to obtain the running-configuration information. RCP is only supported on IOS-based devices and support must be configured on the router as well as the server.

NetSys Integration

The NetSys Enterprise/Solver family of simulation-based network planning and problem-solving products consists of a set of connectivity and performance analysis tools. NetSys is available for Windows NT and Solaris. The integration features are only supported on the Solaris version. Connectivity tools assist network planners in designing and planning network connectivity. NetSys does the following:

- Uses Cisco Router configuration files to create a baseline network model.

- Performs syntax and semantic checks on router configuration files.

- Generates diagnostic reports based on syntax and semantic checks on router configuration files.

You can integrate configuration files stored in the Essentials configuration archive into NetSys and create a network baseline model. The configuration files are stored in a "Shadow Directory" where copies of the latest configuration files are copied. The Shadow directory is located on the server in the *%NMSROOT%\files\archive\shadow* folder. This directory only contains the latest configuration for all devices. Device class breaks down the subfolders. The files are named after the name of the device in Resource Manager Essentials. NetSys reports can be generated periodically to reflect any changes in the configuration archive. First, you need to set up NetSys Configuration Integration.

The configuration dialog box located in the General Setup of Configuration Management is explained in the following table and displayed in Figure 8-7.

Table 8-1   *NetSys Integration*

Field	Description
Disable NetSys	Select to disable NetSys integration on CiscoWorks 2000 Server. Generation of NetSys reports is suspended.
	When selected, all other fields in the dialog box become unavailable. All your settings are saved. If you re-enable NetSys by deselecting this field, previous settings are restored and NetSys report generation resumes on the previous schedule.
	If a baseline has not been generated, this field is not available.
Create Baseline	You must select this to re-create existing baseline or create new baseline.

Table 8-1   *NetSys Integration (Continued)*

Field	Description
Installation	Click correct option for type of NetSys Server System with which you are integrating:
	Click Local if NetSys is installed on your local machine.
	Click Remote (NT) if NetSys is installed on a remote Windows NT machine.
	Click Remote (Unix) if NetSys is installed on a remote UNIX machine.
Hostname	Enter name of remote NetSys host. If you selected Local in the installation field, this field is not available.
User Name	Enter NetSys host login name. If you selected Local in the installation field, this field is not available.
Password	Enter NetSys host password. Available only for integration with NetSys on a Unix System (local or remote).
Install Directory	Enter path to directory on NetSys server where NetSys is installed.
	Do not include name of any subdirectories created by NetSys (for example, NetSys) in path.
	Directory location should contain help files, executable files, and other NetSys-related files.
Baseline Name	Fully qualified pathname of baseline configuration, which is created on NetSys host using Essentials configurations. This baseline model is used for future configuration and report updates.
	To re-create existing baseline, select the Create Baseline check box. To create new baseline, change baseline name and select Create Baseline check box.
Schedule	By default, NetSys reports run daily at 3:00 a.m. You can change reschedule by clicking Select, then entering new schedule.

Figure 8-7   *The NetSys Setup Dialog Box*

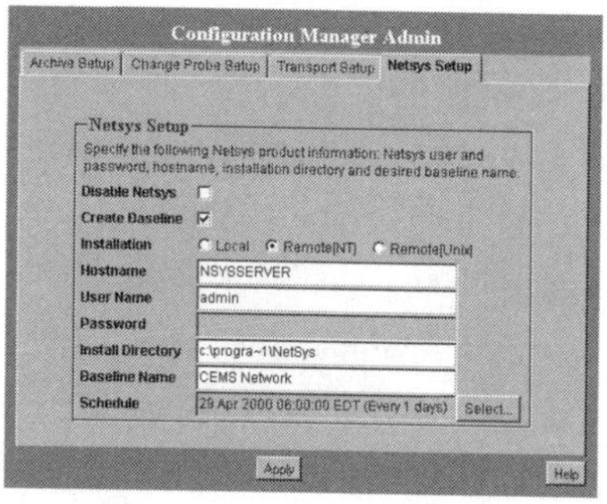

The NetConfig Tool

In any network not using TACACS or RADIUS to authenticate users logging in to the routers or switches, password management can be difficult if not impossible. In any network using a network management platform, SNMP community-string modification can be difficult if not administratively impossible.

The lack of tools to make mass changes in a consistent manner is to blame. The NetConfig tool fills that void. The NetConfig tool allows an administrator to make almost any change to any number of devices in the network through a controlled job-oriented environment. For many repetitive tasks NetConfig already has predefined templates; for anything else, custom templates can be created. NetConfig is a Java-based web applet that downloads to the client when it is run. Figure 8-8 shows the operating system of the client installing the Java applet when NetConfig is launched.

Figure 8-8   *Installing the NetConfig Java Applet*

Changes from the command line can be tedious and dangerous to carry out. Changing devices in a controlled manner is always preferable to individual changes. NetConfig provides many advantages over configuring devices from the CLI. For example, you can:

- Schedule jobs for future execution.
- Use configuration templates to make configuration changes more easily and more reliably.
- Run multiple commands during a job.
- Run commands on multiple devices during a job.
- Use the Job Approval application to require approval before a job can run.
- Roll back configuration changes made to devices when a job fails.
- Automatically copy configuration files to the archive after the changes are made.

NetConfig can configure all Cisco devices that SNMP can configure. For security reasons the PIX firewall is an unsupported device.

NetConfig Templates

NetConfig uses templates to make changes to configuration files. This allows an administrator to only have to provide information such as passwords, community-strings, and a banner to use the tool. In addition, the tool does not require any knowledge of the command-line syntax when using the predefined templates. Administrators with advanced knowledge of the command-line interface can also create their own templates for use with the tool. This tool can be used to roll out any configuration change on one or more devices.

Predefined Templates

System-defined configuration templates are supplied with NetConfig, allowing administrators to create configuration commands from the NetConfig GUI.

When you enter information in the fields of a system-defined configuration template and click Add, the commands you create are added to the job's command list. You can add multiple instances of a configuration template to a job by entering *different* information in the same template and clicking Add multiple times.

You can delete an instance of a configuration template (and its configuration commands) from a job or modify the information that you entered in a configuration template during the initial job definition or any time before the job runs.

Each system-defined configuration template also creates rollback commands that you can use to roll back the changes to devices if the job fails.

Table 8-2 presents the system-defined configuration templates that are supplied with NetConfig:

Table 8-2   *Predefined NetConfig Templates*

Template	Description
Adhoc System-Defined Template	Enter any configuration commands.
Banner System-Defined Template	Add, remove, and edit banners.
CDP System-Defined Template	Configure Cisco Discover Protocol (CDP).
DNS System-Defined Template	Configure DNS.
Enable Password System-Defined Template	Configure enable password authentication.
Local Username System-Defined Template	Configure local username authentication.
NTP Server System-Defined Template	Configure Network Time Protocol (NTP).
RADIUS Server System-Defined Template	Configure RADIUS server and key.
RCP System-Defined Template	Configure RCP.
SNMP Community-String System-Defined Template	Add, remove, and edit SNMP community-strings.

continues

Table 8-2 *Predefined NetConfig Templates (Continued)*

Template	Description
SNMP Traps System-Defined Template	Configure SNMP traps.
Syslog System-Defined Template	Configure Syslog message logging.
TACACS System-Defined Template	Configure TACACS authentication.
TACACS+ System-Defined Template	Configure TACACS+ authentication.
TACACS Server System-Defined Template	Configure TACACS server and key.
Telnet Password System-Defined Template	Add, remove, and edit Telnet passwords.

The Adhoc Template

The *Adhoc system template* allows any command to be executed during the job. The command can be executed in configuration or enable mode (not applicable on Catalyst Operating System Devices, which does not have a config mode). Job execution commands run exactly as you type them. The adhoc commands are not saved and are only designed for single use. To add permanent commands, create a new template.

CAUTION   The NetConfig tool cannot validate commands used in the Adhoc template. The commands should be checked before the job runs and the commands are executed. Incorrect commands could render a device unreachable. If the commands are run untested, the results could be catastrophic as so many devices can be affected at one time. A good idea would be to try any changes first in a lab environment.

Creating User-Defined Templates

One of the most powerful features of the NetConfig tool is the ability to create user-defined templates. *User-defined templates* allow an administrator to facilitate any network change. User-defined templates can also have rollback commands defined to undo any changes in the event of a job failure or some other administratively configured condition. *The User-defined template name is limited to 35 characters in length.*

The NetConfig tool does not have the ability to check the syntax of the template. Be certain to validate any commands before they are used in a job. User-defined templates can only affect one type of operating system at a time.

To create a user-defined template, launch the NetConfig tool from the CiscoWorks 2000 Server console. From the NetConfig tool choose Admin; Create/Edit User defined templates. Table 8-3 explains the dialog box that appears.

Table 8-3   *The Create/Edit User Defined Template Dialog Box*

Area/Field/Button	Description	Usage Notes
Templates	Select the user-defined template to modify.	Select New to create a new template that is not based on an existing template.
Name	Enter a name when creating a new template.	To create a new template from a copy of an existing template, select a name from the Templates List, then enter a new name.
		To modify a template, select it from the Templates List but do not modify the name.
Description	Enter a description of the template.	None.
Device Type	Select the device category that the template will configure.	Each user-defined template can configure devices of one type only.
Command Mode	Select the mode (config or enable) in which the template's configuration commands will run.	Each user-defined template can run commands in one mode only.
		If you selected Catalyst as job device category, enable is pre-selected, and you cannot edit the field. Catalyst devices do not have a config mode. Therefore, their configuration commands run in enable mode.
		If you select enable, Enter CLI Commands area is disabled because only config commands can be rolled back.
Enter CLI Commands	Enter configuration commands for the template to run.	You can enter configuration and rollback commands in two ways:
		Type the commands in the larger text box, one command per line.
		Enter the path(s) of one or more command list files in the Import from File text box. You can click Browse to browse for files, or type the paths to files, separating pathnames with a comma.

continues

Table 8-3 *The Create/Edit User Defined Template Dialog Box (Continued)*

Area/Field/Button	Description	Usage Notes
Enter Rollback Commands	Enter configuration commands that the template will run when a configuration job using the template fails and the failure policy is set to one of the rollback options.	You can enter configuration and rollback commands in two ways: Type the commands in the larger text box, one command per line. Enter the path(s) of one or more command list files in the Import from File text box. You can click Browse to browse for files, or type the paths to files, separating pathnames with a comma.
Assign Users	Displays the user logins that have permission to use the current template. Click Select to assign different access privileges to the template. The Assign Users Dialog box appears, and template definition is saved with current information.	None.

After configuring the template, choose the save button to save the new template or any modifications, and choose the delete button to delete the template from the system. Figure 8-9 shows a template used to deploy EIGRP into a network with redistribution into the RIP routing protocol. In the template rollback, commands have also been entered to undo the job in the event of a failure.

Figure 8-9 *Creating a User-Defined Template*

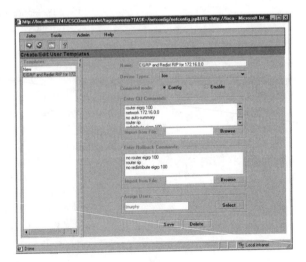

Creating a NetConfig Job

After deciding to create a new template or to use a system-defined template, the next step is to create the job. To create a job, launch the NetConfig tool from the CiscoWorks 2000 Server console. Then choose the Job; New Job menu item. This launches the Job creation wizard.

The new job wizard has two panes. The left pane is to present the high-level overview of the steps necessary to complete the job. On the right side of the window is the button or dialog box used to choose the necessary options to create the job. The bottom of the left-hand pane contains a key to explain how the steps are completed.

The necessary steps are detailed as follows, with figures to demonstrate the steps. Two 2600 Series routers are having banners added, and also are adding the EIGRP routing protocol from the user-defined template from Figure 8-9.

Step 1   From the Select a Device Category dialog box, select IOS, Catalyst, or FastSwitch. A job can only affect one device type at a time.

Figure 8-10 *The Select a Device Category Dialog Box*

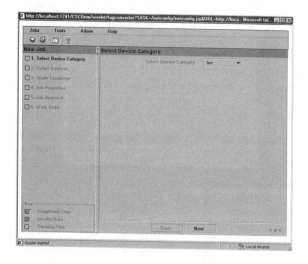

Step 2   The Select Device window appears (see Figure 8-11). Only devices that match the device category will be available from the Select Device window. This window can use views to allow an administrator to easily select the devices to receive the job. Two 2600 routers were selected using a filter on the All Devices View. The View Configurations button will launch a new browser window containing the configuration files for the selected devices. This feature can be useful to validate whether the device should receive the job based upon its current configuration.

Figure 8-11 *The Select a Device Window*

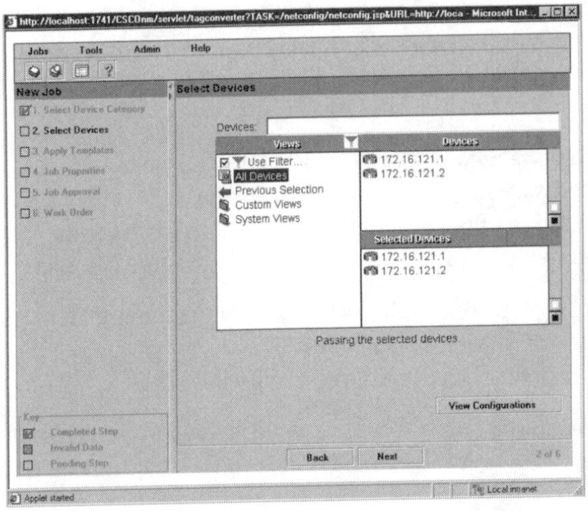

Step 3 After selecting the devices, choose Next to launch the Apply Templates window. From the Apply Templates window, choose a template from the template list. In the Setup dialog box, enter any additional information required by the template. For example, in the enable password template the enable password is entered in the Setup dialog box. In Figure 8-12 the banner template has been selected to add a banner to both devices.

Figure 8-12 *The Apply Templates Dialog Box*

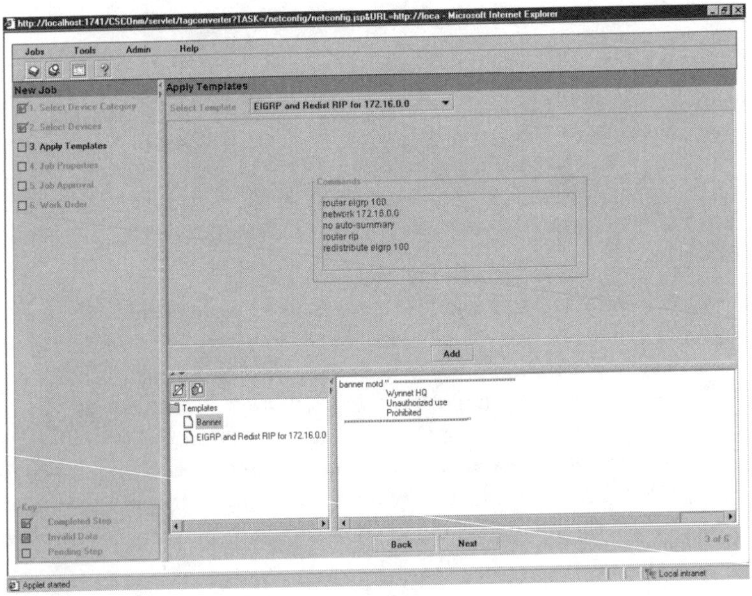

Step 4   After selecting a template, choose Add to add the template to the job. Multiple templates can be added to the job to make multiple changes in one job. Figure 8-12 shows that both the banner template and the user-defined template created in Figure 8-9 have been added to the job.

Step 5   In the bottom of the Apply Templates window, the templates added are listed on the left side. Choosing a template displays the commands in the right side. This can allow validation of the commands before they are carried out. Figure 8-12 shows the commands that will be carried out to add a banner to the devices. Choose the edit button to modify the commands in any of the templates added. Choose the delete button to remove a template from the current job. Click Next to continue.

Step 6   The Job Details window appears. Table 8-4 explains the Job Details window. In Figure 8-13, a job is created to deploy the changes to the two 2600 series routers.

Table 8-4   *The Job Details Window*

Area	Field	Description	Usage Notes
Job Comments	Description	Enter a job description.	Make each job description unique so you can more easily identify jobs.
	Text box	Enter job comments.	Comments appear in job work order, and are stored in configuration archive.
Job Schedule	Schedule Type	Select to run job immediately or once in the future.	If you select Once, Starting Date and Starting Time fields become available. If Job Approval is enabled, the Immediately option is not available.
	Starting Date	Select date for job to run.	None.
	Starting Time	Select time for job to run.	None.
Job Options	Failure Policy	Select what job should do if it fails to run on a device.	You can stop or continue the job and roll back configuration changes to a failed device or all devices configured by the job.

continues

Table 8-4   *The Job Details Window (Continued)*

Area	Field	Description	Usage Notes
	E-mail Notification	Enter e-mail addresses to which the job will send status notices. Separate multiple addresses with commas.	E-mail notification is sent when the configuration job is created, started, deleted, canceled, and completed. Notification e-mails include a URL that you can enter in a browser to display the job's details. If you are not logged in, you must log in using the provided login panel to view the job details.
	Parallel Execution	Select to allow job to run on multiple devices at the same time. If parallel execution is not enabled, job runs on only one device at a time.	If you do not select parallel execution, you can click Set Device Order to set the order of the job. In the Device Ordering dialog box, select a device name, then click Move Up or Move Down to change its place in the order. Click OK to save the current order and close the dialog box or Cancel to close the dialog box without making any changes.
	Different Configuration Version Considered Failure	Select to cause job to be considered a failure when the most recent configuration version in the Configuration Archive is not identical to the configuration that was running when you created the job.	None.
	Synch Archive Before Job Execution	Select to cause job to archive running configuration before making configuration changes.	None.

Table 8-4   *The Job Details Window (Continued)*

Area	Field	Description	Usage Notes
	Write Running to Startup Configuration	Select to cause job to write the running configuration to the startup configuration on each device after configuration changes are successfully made.	Does not apply to Catalyst and Fast Switch device categories.

Figure 8-13 *The Job Properties Window*

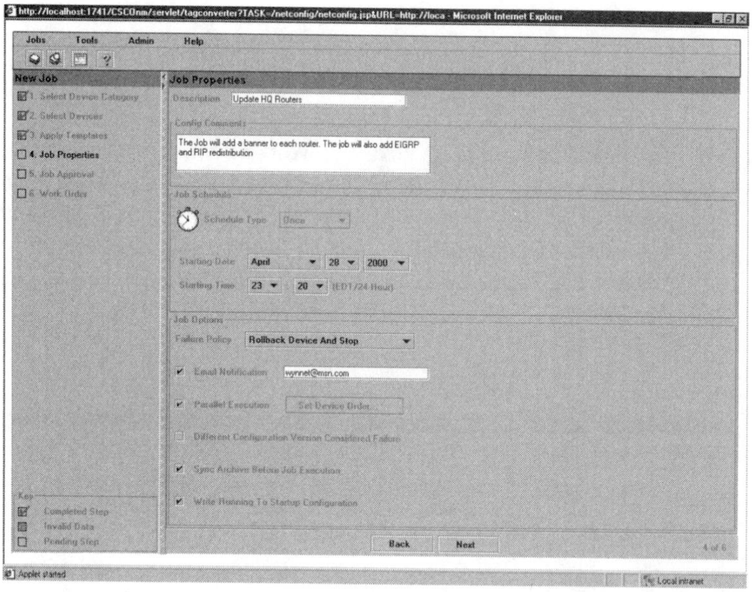

Step 7   The next window is the Job Approval window. The Job Approval window only appears if Job Approval is enabled. By default this feature is turned off. To enable this feature, navigate the browser to the Resource Manager; Administration; Job Approval; Edit Preferences. From this application window, choose the Enable Job Approval checkbox. This feature cannot be turned on until an approver list is created. The process of creating an approver list is covered in Chapter 9, "Software Image Management." In the Job Approval window select the approver list. The comments dialog box will appear in the e-mail message sent to the approvers. Figure 8-14 shows the job approval window in Resource Manager. The job is being approved for execution. Select the Next button to continue.

Figure 8-14 *The Job Approval Window*

Step 8   The Work Order appears next. The Work Order summarizes all of the selections made. This feature enables an administrator to ensure that the job will carry out the intended network changes. Figure 8-15 displays the Work Order Details window. Select Finish to complete the job creation process. Until the administrator selects Finish, the job is not actually created.

Figure 8-15 *The Work Order Detail Window*

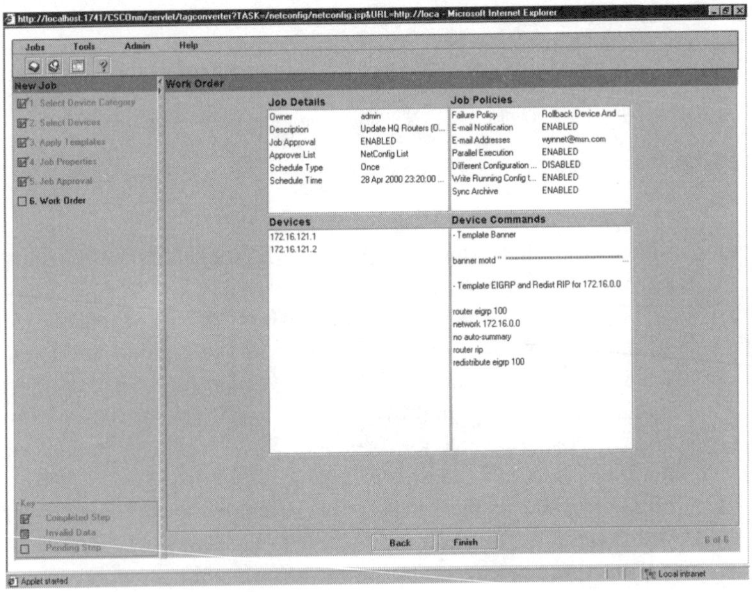

Step 9   After a job is completed, use the Job Browser in the NetConfig tool to check the status of any currently running or pending jobs. The Browse Job window also allows editing of any job not already running. If a job's execution time starts while a job is being edited, it will run without the edits. A job can also be copied, stopped, or removed from the Browse Job window. Once a job is created only the owner or an Administrator can modify the job. Figure 8-16 shows the job that was created after having been approved and is now awaiting execution.

Figure 8-16 *The Job Browser Window*

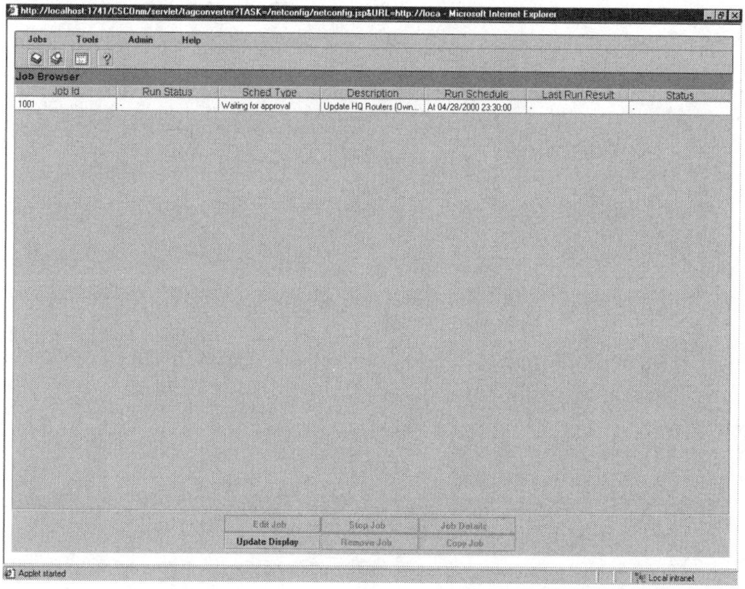

Figure 8-17 shows the job running at the scheduled time.

Figure 8-17 *The Job Running*

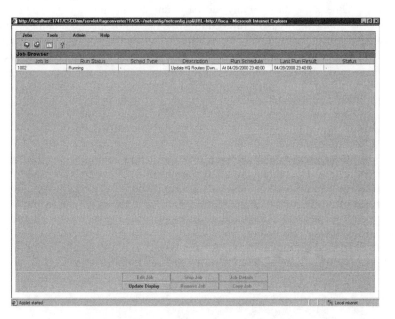

Figure 8-18 shows the job completed successfully from the Download Summary window.

Figure 8-18 *The Download Summary Window*

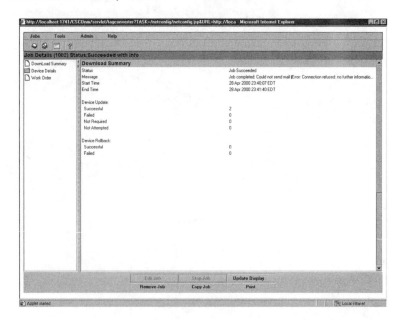

The cwconfig Command-Line Tool

The Configuration Management application is also available from a command line using **cwconfig**. The **cwconfig** tool runs on the Resource Manager Essentials' Server. The tool is different from NetConfig in that NetConfig pushes commands and **cwconfig** pushes an entire configuration file. The **cwconfig** command-line tool performs the following core functions on one or more devices, as well as the configuration archive:

- Pushes configuration files from the configuration archive to one or more devices.
- Pulls the configuration files from devices to the archive if the configuration running on a device is different from the latest archived version.
- Imports configuration files from the file system and pushes them to one or more devices, which updates the configuration archive.
- Copies the startup configuration files to the running configuration files.

In addition, **cwconfig** performs the following core functions on the configuration archive:

- Exports configurations from the archive to the file system.
- Compares the last two configuration files in the archive, specific configuration file versions, or changes based on specific dates.
- Deletes configurations older than a specified date from the configuration archive.

The **cwconfig** tool could be launched from a script that runs based on an SNMP trap or as a scheduled process that gathers the configuration files and then copies them to another location, or in any other way the administrator needs. The **cwconfig** tool has the capability to pass parameters to NetConfig for dynamic configuration file modifications This advanced capability is covered in the Using NetConfig with the **cwconfig** Tool section later in this chapter.

The **cwconfig** tool can be compared to the **nmconfig** tool used in CiscoWorks on UNIX. The **cwconfig** tool, however, has many more features that were not available with **nmconfig**.

Executing the cwconfig Tool

The **cwconfig** tool is managed through command-line switches (see Table 8-5). A minimum of two parameters is specified when **cwconfig** is run. The parameters are the command to carry out and the arguments for that command. Figure 8-19 displays the command and the log output on the router. The **start2run** command was used on router 172.16.121.1 to copy the startup-configuration file from the archive to the running-configuration on the router, having the same effect as the router command **copy tftp run**.

Table 8-5 cwconfig *Command-Line Switches*

Command Switch	Description
unlock	Removes the lock placed previously by you on the configuration.
put	Retrieves the configuration from the configuration archive.
compare	Lists the differences between versions of a device configuration.
import	Retrieves the configuration from a file and pushes it to the device.
start2run	Overwrites the running configuration of a device with its startup.
listlock	Lists the version of the configuration that is locked for a device.
export	Retrieves a configuration version for a device from the archive.
get	Retrieves the running configuration from the device
netconfig	NetConfig CLI (explained later in chapter).
delete	Deletes the specified device configuration from the archive.

Figure 8-19 cwconfig start2run *Command*

The preceding command switches affect what action **cwconfig** takes. As listed in Table 8-6, additional parameters are used to determine the affected device.

Table 8-6   *Additional* **cwconfig** *Syntax Switches*

Command Switch	Explanation
-u	Specifies the CiscoWorks2000 user name (required).
-p	Specifies the password for the CiscoWorks2000 user name (required).
-d	Specifies the debug level 1 to 5.
-m	Specifies an e-mail address to send results to.
-l	Specifies the file to log the results of the **cwconfig** command.
-device	Specifies one or more device names as a comma-separated list.
-view	Confines the device search to the specified view.
-version	Specifies the desired version.
-save	Writes the configuration as both the running configuration as well as the startup configuration.
-reboot	Reboots the device.
-input	Specifies the text file containing arguments for multiple devices.
-continue	Causes the command to proceed even if errors are encountered on one or more devices.

The **cwconfig** tool can also be used in troubleshooting the configuration file collection. If a device's configuration file does not appear in the Resource Manager environment, use the **cwconfig** tool to attempt to manually gather the configuration file. When using **cwconfig** for troubleshooting, add the –**d** parameter to include debug output to the console screen. The debug output displays the command steps and how they are interpreted. Figure 8-20 demonstrates how the debug set to level 5 displays when retrieving the configuration from device 172.16.121.2.

Figure 8-20 cwconfig *with Debug Output*

Using NetConfig with the cwconfig Tool

The combination of **cwconfig** and NetConfig enables an administrator to combine the features of configuration management with the features of configuration modification. The **cwconfig netconfig** tool uses the Adhoc system template from within the NetConfig application. Using the NetConfig tool allows command-line job creation and execution. The **cwconfig netconfig** tool uses three-part command syntax. The syntax is:

```
cwconfig netconfig subcommand common arguments command arguments
```

The subcommand determines what action is being taken with a job. The common arguments are the same for all of the subcommands. The command arguments are specific on the command level. Tables 8-7 through 8-9 list the different command-line parameters.

Table 8-7   **cwconfig netconfig** *Subcommand Arguments*

Subcommand	Description
-createjob	Creates a NetConfig job.
-listjobs	Lists the NetConfig jobs registered on the system.
-canceljob	Cancels a NetConfig job.
-deletejob	Deletes a NetConfig job.

Table 8-7   **cwconfig netconfig** *Subcommand Arguments (Continued)*

Subcommand	Description
-jobdetails	Lists the NetConfig job details.
-jobresults	Lists the job results.
-help	Displays command usage.

Table 8-8   **cwconfig netconfig** *Common Arguments*

Common Argument	Description	Usage Notes
-u *user*	Provides a valid CiscoWorks2000 username.	None.
-p *password*	Provides the password for the username.	None.
[**-d** *debug level*]	Sets the debug level	Optional.
		debug_level is a number between 1 (the least information is sent to the debug output) and 5 (the most information is sent to the debug output).
[**-l** *log_filename*]	Identifies a file to which NetConfig will write log messages.	Optional.
	If not specified, log output will appear on the screen.	
	log_filename can be a full path to the file or filename in the local directory.	

Arguments in square brackets ([]) are optional; arguments in curly braces ({}) are required. You must provide one argument from each group of arguments in curly braces ({}) to be separated by vertical bars (|).

Table 8-9 **cwconfig netconfig** *Command Arguments*

Subcommand	Command Argument	Description	Usage Notes
-createjob	[**-input** *input_filename*]	Enter some or all of the command. arguments by importing them from a file.	*input_filename* is a path to an input file. Can be a full path to file or a filename in local directory.
		You can enter other arguments on the command line in addition to **–input**, but you can specify each argument only once in a command	If you use the **-input** argument but the input file does not specify all required command arguments, you must provide the additional required arguments on the command line.
	{**-devicefile** *devicelist_filename* | **-devicelist** *device_names* | **-deviceview** *device_view_name* }	Defines devices to be configured.	Each job can run only one category of devices, IOS, Catalyst, or Fast Switch. Do not mix devices of multiple categories when entering devices.
			devicelist_filename is a path to a device list file. Can be a full path to the file or a filename in the local directory.
	{ **-commandfile** *commandlist_filename* }	Defines configuration commands to be used.	*commandlist_filename* is a path to a command file. Can be a full path to the file or a filename in the local directory.
	[**-policyfile** *policy_filename*]	Defines job policies using a job policy file.	*policy_filename* is the path to a job policy file. Can be a full path to the file or a filename in the local directory.
		You can specify job policies using a combination of the **policyfile** argument and other optional command arguments, but you can specify each argument only once in a command.	

Table 8-9   **cwconfig netconfig** *Command Arguments (Continued)*

Subcommand	Command Argument	Description	Usage Notes
	[**-schedule** *MM/dd/yyyy:HH:mm:ss*]	Defines when job will run.	*MM* is the month (01 to 12).
		It is required if Job Approval is enabled on the system.	*DD* is the day of the month (01 to 31).
			YYYY is the year (example: 2000).
		NetConfig returns a job ID when you enter a command with this option.	*HH:mm:ss* is the time in 24-hour time (*HH* is hours, *mm* is minutes, and *ss* is seconds.)
		If not specified, job will run immediately.	
	[**-description** "*job_description*"]	Enter a description of the job.	
	[**-failure** { **STOP** | **CONTINUE** }]	Configures failure property.	
		Note Rollback options in the GUI are not available because you cannot create rollback commands using the **cwconfig netconfig** command.	
	[**-sync** { **DISABLED** | **ENABLED** }]	Configures sync-archive property.	
	[**-startup** { **DISABLED** | **ON_JOB_SUCCESS** }]	Configures write-running-to-startup property.	
	[**-version** { **IGNORE_CFG_VER** | **DIFF_CFG_VER_ CONSIDERED_FAILURE** }]	Configures configuration-version property.	
	[**-execution** { **SEQUENTIAL** | **PARALLEL** }	Configures execution property.	
	[**-email** *comma_separated_email_list*]	Configures e-mail property.	

continues

Table 8-9 cwconfig netconfig *Command Arguments (Continued)*

Subcommand	Command Argument	Description	Usage Notes
	[-approverlist *list_name*]	Specifies an approver list.	
		Required if Job Approval is enabled on the system, and ignored if it is not.	
	[-mode { config | enable }]	Specifies mode in which commands will run.	
		Not valid for jobs that configure Catalyst devices, which accept configuration commands in enable mode.	
canceljob, deletejob	-id *job_id*	Cancels/deletes job, specified by the job ID.	None.
jobdetails, jobresults	[-id *job_id*]	Displays details/results of a job, specified by the job ID.	None.
listjobs	[-status {A(ll) | R(unning) | C(ompleted) | P(ending)}]	Specifies status of jobs to list.	None.
		If not specified, all registered NetConfig jobs are listed.	

Figure 8-21 uses the command syntax in Example 8-1 to create a job to update the vty (virtual telnet) and console timeout on two devices:

Example 8-1 *Creating a Job to Update the vty and Console Timeout on Two Devices*

```
D:\Program Files\CSCOpx\bin>cwconfig netconfig -u admin -p admin
[ic:ccc]-l d:\netconfig.chg -createjob -devicelist 172.16.121.1,172.16.121.2 -
    schedule 04/29/2000:09:55:00
[ic:ccc]-description "Change VTY Timeouts" -sync enabled  -execution PARALLEL
[ic:ccc]-mode config -commandfile d:\temp\vty.txtlogfile: d:\netconfig.chg
debug level=0
```

Figure 8-21 *The Job Summary Window*

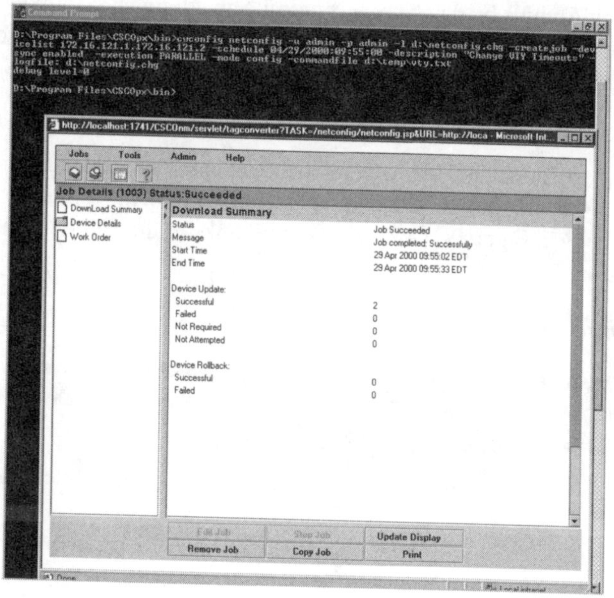

Routers 172.16.121.1 and 172.16.121.2 had their configuration changed based on a command file that used CLI commands. This ensures that the same commands were carried out on all listed devices.

Configuration File Reporting

Once configuration files are loaded into the Resource Manager Environment, reports and queries can be used to examine the information in the configuration files. There are five different types of reports/queries available:

- Search Archive by device
- Search Archive by pattern
- Startup/Running Out of Sync
- Compare Configurations
- Custom Reports

Search Archive by Device Report

The Search Archive by device report permits an administrator to query the configuration files by device. This report enables an administrator to easily examine the current or prior configuration file for any managed device or a group of devices selected through a view.

The information is displayed in three different formats: Summary, Version, and Quickview.

The Summary format lists the configuration files available, including the startup-configuration and running-configuration, the date of last update, and the three most recent versions. The report, shown in Figure 8-22, contains hyperlinks to the configuration files for easy examination.

Figure 8-22 *The Configuration Summary Report*

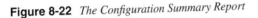

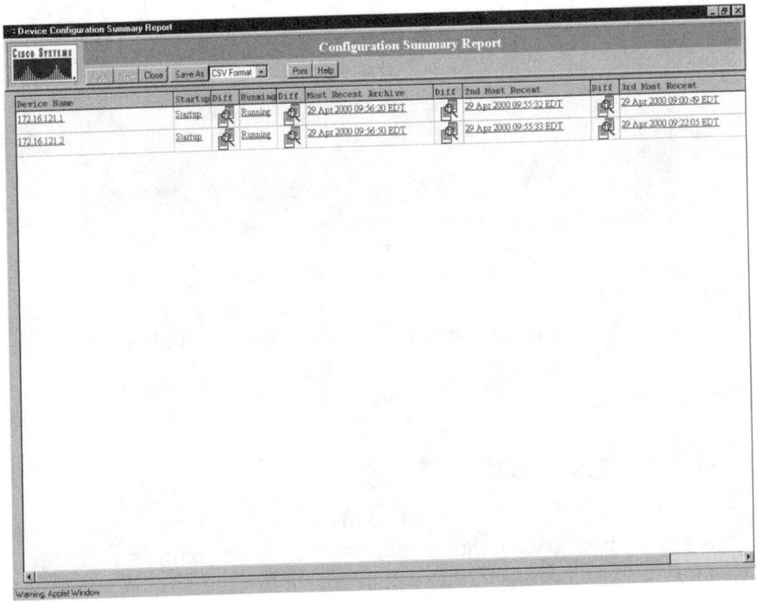

The Version format provides the option of examining the latest versions only or all versions for each device selected in the query. The report, shown in Figure 8-23, also includes a summary of the different changes between the different versions.

The QuickView format also provides an option for either the latest or all versions of the configuration files. It will display the configuration files in a three-paned window. One pane displays the selected devices. Another provides the different views of the configuration files, while the third displays the configuration information. The QuickView Window breaks the configuration file into different sections called configlets. The configlets make it easier to locate information in configuration file without having to examine the entire file. Figure 8-24 shows the QuickView Report format.

Figure 8-23 *The Configuration Version Report*

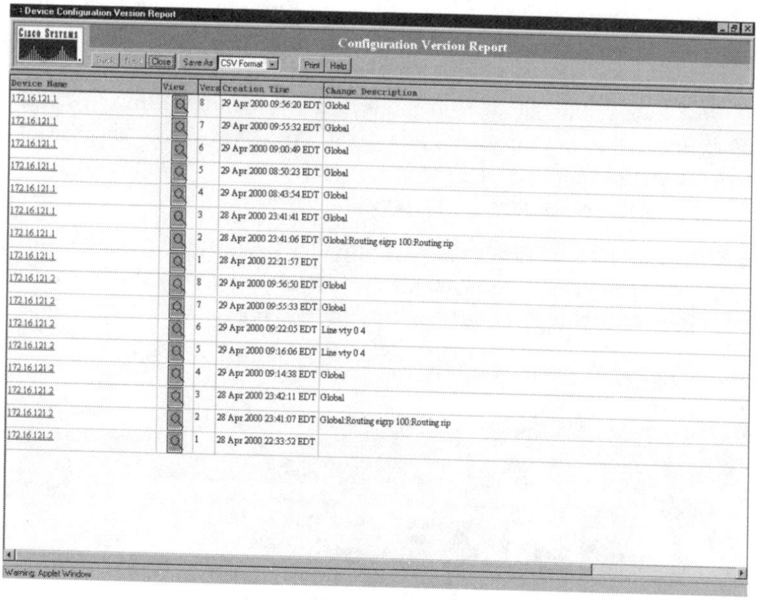

Figure 8-24 *Device Configuration QuickView Report*

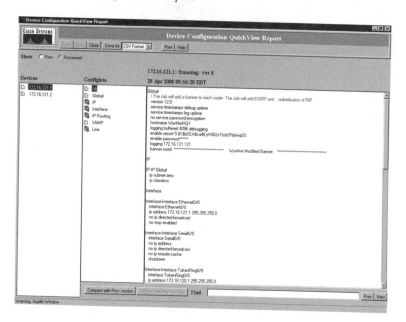

Search Archive by Pattern Report

The Search Archive by Pattern Report is very useful in finding configuration files that contain different pattern strings. This can be useful—for example, to answer questions like "Which routers are running OSPF?" or "What switches are part of VTP domain X?" This tool provides an administrator the ability to provide three strings to search for. The query can be executed as a logical operation **AND**, **OR**, **NOT AND**, and **NOT OR**. After determining the search pattern, the next option is to select which devices to search for. The device selection is done through views.

The Search Archive by Pattern Report provides two different views of the configuration information. The Version and QuickView formats are the same as in the Search Archive by Device Report. Figure 8-25 queries the database for routers running the RIP protocol.

Figure 8-25 *The Search Archive by Pattern Report*

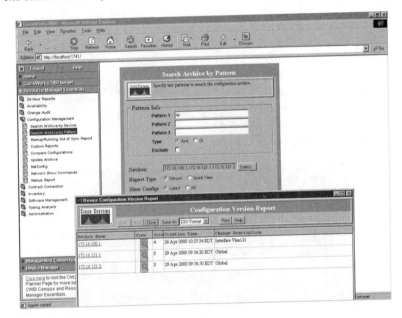

Startup/Running Out of Sync Report

The Startup/Running Out of Sync report brings up the QuickView window and displays the routers in the inventory whose current running configuration is different from the known startup configuration. Using this information, a job could then be created in NetConfig to copy the running-configuration to the startup-configuration on the reporting devices. Figure 8-26 shows the current running-configuration on 172.16.121.1 compared to the startup-configuration in the QuickView Window format. This report only applies to IOS-based devices that have both a running and startup config. Catalyst switches based on the "set" IOS only have one config file.

Figure 8-26 *The Startup/Running Out of Sync Report*

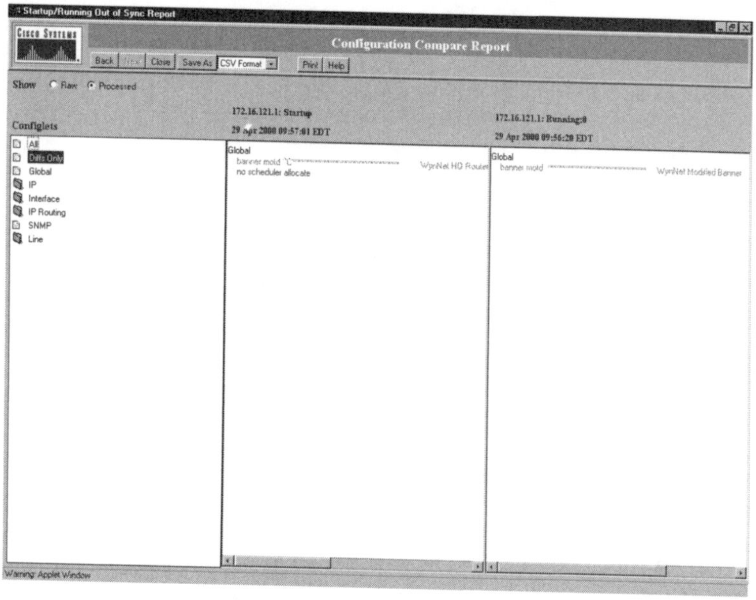

Compare Configurations Report

The Compare Configurations Report provides four different types of report options.

- Startup vs. Running
- Running vs. Latest Archived
- 2 Versions of Same Device
- 2 Versions of Different Devices

Figure 8-27 shows the Compare Configuration Report window from which you can choose the report option.

Figure 8-27 *The Compare Configurations Report Window*

Startup vs. Running

The Startup vs. Running report is only applicable to routers or IOS-based devices. It provides real-time comparison between the running-configurations and startup-configurations on the selected devices. This information is not from the configuration files on the server.

Running vs. Latest Archived

The Running vs. Latest Archived report compares the current running-configuration on a device to the last copy in the Archive. This information can be useful in determining which devices do not have their latest configuration in the archive and need to be updated.

2 Versions of Same Device

The 2 Versions of the Same Device report compares the archived copies of the configuration files from a device and then displays what changes were detected between the versions in the Summary Format. The QuickView format can then be examined to get more detail on the changes within the configuration files. Figure 8-28 shows the report 2 Versions of Same Device.

2 Versions of Different Devices

The 2 Versions of Different Devices report compares the configuration files from two devices from the archive. The comparison can be done at a configuration level or by a pattern match search. The configurations are then displayed in the QuickView format.

Figure 8-28 *2 Versions of Same Device Report*

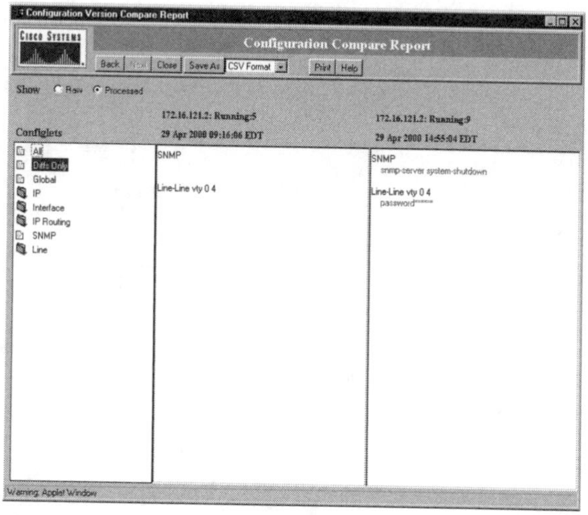

Custom Reports

Custom Reports enable an administrator to examine configuration files defined by one or two methods. A view, pattern match, or both can select the devices. The report is then displayed in Summary, Quickview, or Version format. These custom reports are saved so they can be reused.

The Custom Reports enable an administrator to combine the criteria of other reports into one reusable format. Figure 8-29 shows a report being created for all routers that have an exec-timeout of 0. The selected report format QuickView highlights the first instance of the pattern in the Configuration File.

Figure 8-29 *The Custom Report Window*

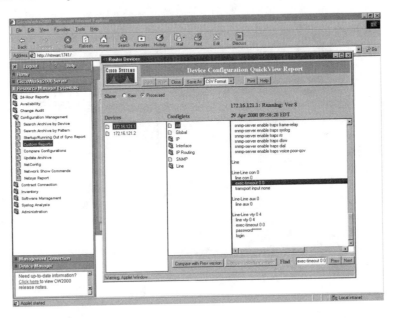

Summary

This chapter discussed Configuration Management using Resource Manager Essentials. The configuration tools in Resource Manager enable an administrator to manage the configuration files for routers, switches, and other network devices. These configuration files are updated through Syslog messages, SNMP polling, and by scheduling updates. The archive requires no manual intervention from the administrator.

The NetConfig tool permits an administrator to deploy network changes with consistency not available through normal command-line methods. Jobs can update one or more devices simultaneously. In addition, jobs can be scheduled for off-hours and can e-mail an administrator upon completion.

The **cwconfig** tool enables an administrator access to the different graphical tools from a command line. Using **cwconfig**, an administrator can gather, compare, and even push configuration files to the managed devices in the network. Combining the **cwconfig** tool with **netconfig** parameters enables an administrator to create and manage NetConfig jobs from a command line using a script.

The Configuration Management tools also have reporting options. Configuration files can be compared, searched, or displayed in a number of different formats. Reports can compare configuration files from one device or from many devices. Reports can also be generated to look for changes in the device(s) configuration files. Administrators can have the running-configuration compared to the startup-configuration on IOS-based devices to look for devices not synchronized.

Finally, custom reports enable an administrator to define criteria that generate a report and then save the criteria for reuse.

The process of monitoring for configuration changes is one of the services of Change Audit. In addition to monitoring for configuration changes, Change Audit also monitors for software and inventory modifications. The next chapter discusses the Software Management tools of Resource Manager and subsequent chapters include more details on the Change Audit process.

Topics covered in this chapter include:

- Software Image Manager Benefits
- SWIM Advanced Features
- Software Management Workflow
- SWIM Distribution Steps
- SWIM Verification

Software Image Management

In any large network with a variety of devices such as routers, switches, and access servers, the responsibility of software management can be a daunting task. Managing current versions of operating systems, checking for bugs, and upgrading software can be difficult without proper network management software. *Software Image Management (SWIM)* is the component of Resource Manager that provides operating system software management.

Software Image Manager Benefits

SWIM provides network administrators with a variety of tools for managing network operating system software. Some of the benefits of SWIM include:

- **SWIM reduces the time to deploy new images across the network**—Through job-oriented software deployment, multiple devices can have their respective operating systems upgraded at once. This function reduces the time spent using Telnet or write scripts to connect to the devices one at a time when performing upgrades.

- **SWIM reduces errors in choosing the appropriate image for target devices**—Through image analysis, SWIM ensures that devices only receive operating systems proper for the specific device platform and system image requirements.

- **SWIM enables scheduling convenience for batch upgrades**—The job scheduling tools enable an administrator to schedule upgrades at off hours when offline time is acceptable. The administrator does not need to be present to oversee the job and can even be sent an e-mail at job completion.

- **SWIM assists in selecting the correct image from CCO**—The available images for devices can be downloaded directly into the image library for network distribution through integration with the CCO (Cisco Connection Online) Software Library.

- **SWIM provides reliable auditing of upgrade job status**—Through Change Audit Services, reports can be generated to determine which devices have been upgraded and on which date.

SWIM Advanced Features

SWIM includes a number of tools that supplement basic software management. Many of these features are enhanced even further through integration directly with the CCO Software Library. The following bulleted list specifies the most important features:

- **Distribute software images to groups of devices**—Depending on the complexity of the system, you can configure upgrades for groups of devices to the same or different software images. You can specify these groups using your Resource Manager views and search criteria such as current running version.

- **Analyze a device to determine if all prerequisites have been satisfied**—The software management features maintain information about the software image file such as name, size, and memory requirements. Using this information, Resource Manager can determine for a given hardware configuration what software image can run on the hardware and whether the device has enough Flash and DRAM.

Resource Manager also keeps track of each device's image history so that if you upgrade to a new image you have a record of what has been previously installed on the device. If you encounter a situation in which the upgrade does not work well, you could easily downgrade or roll back to the previous image.

- **Reduce errors by using a recommended image**—Software Management validates an image prior to initiating a download by checking each device's Cisco IOS version, Flash device size, and DRAM memory. Software Management then notifies you if upgrades to flash memory are required and recommends appropriate images for that device.

- **Import images into the library**—Resource Manager enables you to download a software image from CCO, local file system, and devices in the network. You can then validate the image and store it in the software library.

- **Produce reports on available images and download history**—Resource Manager provides reports that summarize the status of an upgrade. When SWIM performs the tasks, it creates an audit trail of all transactions performed.

- **Maker-Checker approval for distributions**—When multiple personnel manage the network, the person that sets up the distribution is not always the same person who designs and upgrades the network. This option requires job approval before the task is carried out.

- **Image baseline library synchronization**—Baseline synchronization creates a current archive of all the software deployed in the network.

Software Management Workflow

The software management process can be broken down into a series of five steps. Following the five steps is critical to a successful deployment of network software.

Step 1   Setup

Step 2   Identification

Step 3   Planning

Step 4   Distribution

Step 5   Verification

SWIM Setup

The setup process entails four steps.

Step 1   Identifying supported devices.

Step 2   Setting SWIM preferences.

Step 3   Synchronizing the images in the software library.

Step 4   Creating one or more approver lists.

Setting SWIM Preferences

The SWIM application has administrative preferences that affect the application's behavior. To access the SWIM preferences select Resource Manager Essentials; Administration; Software Management; Edit Preferences from the CiscoWorks 2000 Console. Configurations of Maker-Checker preferences are contained in the Job Approval folder located in the same place in Resource Manager as Software Management. Figure 9-1 displays the Software Management Preferences dialog box.

Figure 9-1 *Software Management Preferences*

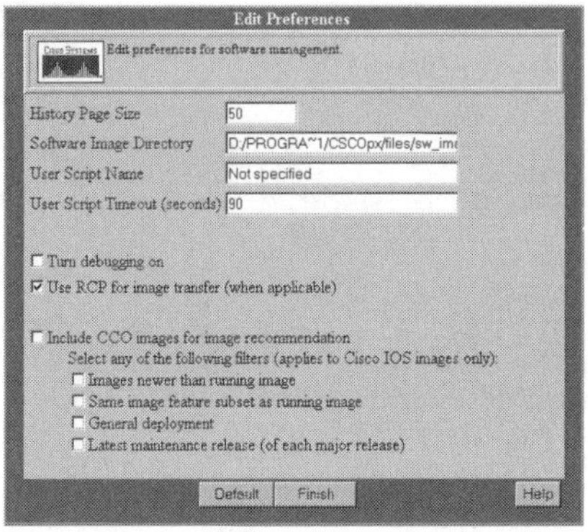

Table 9-1 explains the options for Software Preferences.

Table 9-1 *Preferences for Software Management*

Field	Description	Usage Notes
History Page Size	Maximum number of rows in a report page.	If page size is 50 and there are 500 records, history report is 10 pages. If page size is 100, report is 5 pages.
Software Image Directory	New directory to store new software images.	If you enter a new name, all existing files are moved to this directory.
		If the directory does not have enough room, the move does not take place and an error message is displayed.
User Script Name	Full pathname of user-supplied script. Scripts are explained after this table.	This script is run before and after completing each device software upgrade for all scheduled jobs.
		For UNIX, specify the full pathname.
		For Windows NT, specify the interpreter and script name (separated by a space) for all files except *.bat* and *.exe*. The interpreter runs the script. For example, if the script is in Perl, enter **%NMSROOT%\ bin\ perl.exe** *script name*.
User Script Timeout (Seconds)	Number of seconds user script may run if the script does not finish within this time (the default is 90).	Script is stopped and assumed to have failed. If "Stop on Error" is not selected in the job properties, the upgrade for the next device begins.

Table 9-1   *Preferences for Software Management (Continued)*

Field	Description	Usage Notes
Turn debugging on	Options to create debug log files.	Leaving the option on can adversely affect performance of the Software Management portion of your system.
Use RCP for image transfer (when applicable)	Remote Copy Protocol is used to copy images for Cisco IOS-based devices (if available).	None.
Include CCO images for image recommendation	During Image distribution, recommend CCO images for Cisco IOS Software, Catalyst, and 700 series devices.	For Cisco IOS Software-based devices, select one or more of the following filter options (only images that satisfy all the selected conditions will be recommended): Images newer than running image. Same image feature subset as running image. General Deployment. Latest maintenance release (of each major release).

Using scripts before and after the upgrade process can be a very powerful feature. Script-based applications can be used to test connectivity to a device before the upgrade proceeds and then test connectivity afterwards to ensure success. The same script is executed both before and after the job runs. The script could also be used to send an e-mail or page when the job begins and ends.

Resource Manager provides many environment variables that can be used during the execution of the script file. A sample Perl script is provided with Resource Manager Essentials. The sample script tests connectivity to the device both before and after the job has executed. Using Telnet, the script tests for connectivity. Make sure the device is configured to support Telnet before executing the script. The script is located in *<install_dir_path>/example/swim/userscript.pl* on both Windows NT and UNIX. Table 9-2 explains the environment variables.

Table 9-2   *SWIM Script Environment Variables*

Variable	Description
CRM_SCRIPT_CONTEXT	PRE-DOWNLOAD = Script runs before upgrade starts. POST-DOWNLOAD = Script runs after upgrade ends.
CRM_DEV_NAME	Name of device to which image will be transferred.

continues

Table 9-2 *SWIM Script Environment Variables (Continued)*

Variable	Description
CRM_SNMP_COMMUNITY	Read-write SNMP community-string.
CRM_TERMINAL_PASSWORD	Telnet password.
CRM_ENABLE_PASSWORD	Enable password.
CRM_TACACS_USERNAME	TACACS user name.
CRM_TACACS_PASSWORD	TACACS password.
CRM_ENABLE_SECRET_PASSWORD	Enable Secret password.
CRM_EX_USERNAME	ETacacs user name.
CRM_EX_PASSWORD	ETacacs password.
CRM_LOCAL_USERNAME	Local user name.
CRM_LOCAL_PASSWORD	Local password.
CRM_OUTPUT_FILENAME	Output file to which script writes its completions status. STATUS=DONE means script succeeded. If nothing is written in this file, Software Management assumes that the script has failed.
Catalyst Device Only Variables	**Description**
SWIM_NEW_SW_VER	Software version of the new image.
CRM_SUPERVISOR_SW_VER	Software version of the Supervisor engine module.

Synchronizing the Images in Your Software Library

To ensure consistency in the network, having a database of the current software images is important. If a device is upgraded outside of the Resource Manager Environment, an administrator can determine what changes were made to the device and roll back the upgrade if it was unauthorized or unnecessary. The Synchronization Job will copy a copy of all images in use on the devices that are in the management database. Then, a scheduled report can compare inventory information to determine if any devices have had their operating system software modified.

To generate the Synchronization Report a Synchronization Job must first be scheduled. The job can be scheduled to run daily, weekly, or monthly and can e-mail an administrator upon completion. To schedule the Synchronization Job use Resource Manager Essentials; Administration; Software Management; Schedule Synchronization Job.

After the Synchronization Job has run, the Synchronization Report is available from the Software Management Folder. Figure 9-2 displays the Synchronization Report.

Figure 9-2   *The Synchronization Report*

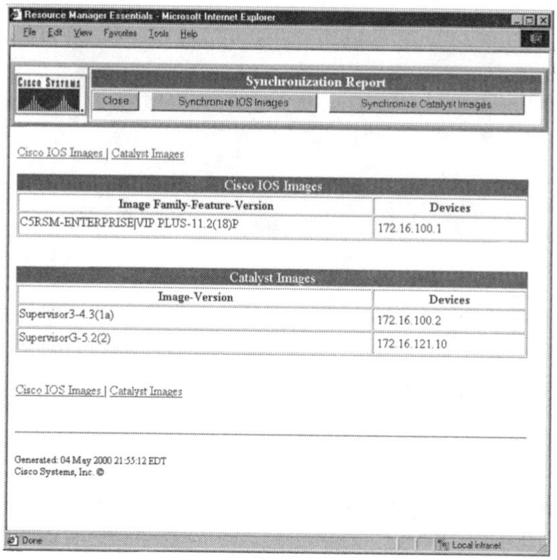

Select the report to view images that are in the network but not in the software library. If both IOS and Catalyst images are listed, they will be separated in the report output. At the top of the report a button is available to synchronize the IOS and Catalyst images. Pressing either button starts the process of creating a job to add the images to the library.

Creating One or More Approver Lists

In a large network with administrative teams the network management team might not have enough authority to approve software upgrades. The Maker-Checker feature allows job approval to ensure that the job creation process is carried out only after a member of an Approver list has approved the job. The term Maker-Checker refers to the administrator that creates the job, and who should not be the one to check it. The Resource Manager Essentials' Server will e-mail an approver about any pending jobs that await approval. Jobs will not execute unless approved, even if this means missing the scheduled execution time. If a job is not approved before execution time, the job is considered rejected and is cancelled. The members of an Approver list are chosen from the user database of the CiscoWorks 2000 server. The same Approver list created for NetConfig can be used for software distribution.

To create an Approver list in Resource Manager Essentials select the Administration; Job Approval; Create Approver list. This action lists all users who are available from the user database. A user must have the approval role or be the admin account in order to be added to an Approver list. A user may belong to more than one Approver list. Figure 9-3 shows how to create an Approver list for Software Distribution.

Figure 9-3 *Creating an Approver List*

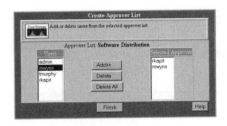

After the Approver list has been created, the Maker-Checker feature must be enabled for software distribution. To enable the Maker-Checker feature use Resource Manager Essentials and select Administration; Job Approval; Edit Preferences. Select the Software Management tab to review current settings. The options to enable include the following:

- **New Image Distribution**—Approval for distributing images to network devices.

- **Undo Image Distribution**—Using the roll-back feature to undo an upgrade to an IOS-based device.

- **Retry Image Distribution**—A failed upgrade job must be approved before the image can be distributed.

If the Maker-Checker feature is enabled, the creator of the job will be able to select which Approver list to use for the job during the creation of a distribution job.

Identification Steps

After the Software library has been synchronized and Approver lists have been created, the next step is identifying the devices that require an upgrade. A device may need an upgrade to enable new features, correct software defects, or synchronize with other devices of the same platform. The identification process entails identifying the devices and determining what software should be distributed to the devices.

With RM, upgrades can be applied to a specific group of devices that actually need the software, eliminating the possibility of wasting time and bandwidth by applying unnecessary updates across the entire network.

Identifying the Devices

To identify the devices and their respective operating system, use the Inventory; Software Report to determine which devices have the version in need of an upgrade. Figure 9-4 shows the Software Inventory Report used to identify current versions of IOS Software on devices.

Figure 9-4   *The Software Report*

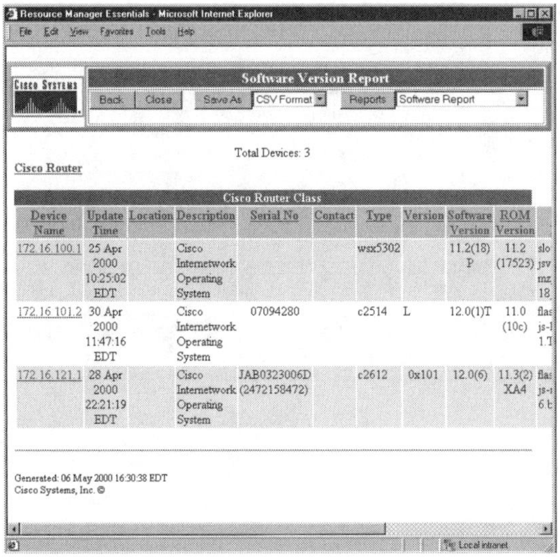

Identifying the Software

To identify the proper software, use the integration with CCO to browse the available software images. Using the CCO Upgrade Analysis helps to ensure that the correct image is selected. To access the CCO Upgrade Analysis tools select Resource Manager Essentials; Software Management; Distribution; CCO Upgrade Analysis. Figure 9-5 shows the CCO Upgrade Analysis Tool analyzing upgrade possibilities for an RSM on a Catalyst 5000.

Using the information from your inventory and CCO, an administrator can successfully identify images that have the correct feature set, memory requirements, and release type. This guarantees that the software will be able to download to the device and provide the necessary features.

CAUTION   The Upgrade Analysis tools should not be taken as a replacement for researching the best operating system to suit the needs of the network. Make sure before carrying out any upgrade to read the release notes for the software version about to be applied and also check the Bug navigator for any known bugs. Although the tool is helpful in making a proper selection, you should verify it through research.

Figure 9-5   *CCO Upgrade Analysis Tool*

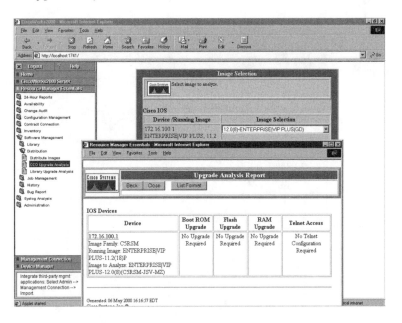

When downloading a new operating system version, understanding the different release classifications is important. The different classifications are listed and explained in the following bulleted list.

- **General Deployment (GD)**—Date at which this software release reached the "General Deployment" milestone in its lifecycle. A major release of Cisco IOS software reaches the "General Deployment" milestone when Cisco feels it is suitable for deployment anywhere in customer networks where the features and functionality of the release are required. Criteria for reaching the "General Deployment" milestone are based on, but not limited to, customer feedback surveys from production and test networks using the releases, CE bug reports, and reported field experience. Only major releases are candidates to reach the General Deployment milestone.

- **Limited Deployment (LD)**—A major release of Cisco IOS software is said to be in the "Limited Deployment" phase of its lifecycle during the period between initial First Commercial Shipment (FCS) and the General Deployment (GD) milestones.

- **ED Release Early Deployment (ED)**—Releases offer new feature, platform, or interface support. This software should only be used when the new features are absolutely necessary as the software has not been widely field-tested.

If an administrator is unsure which devices have new versions available on CCO, use the Management Connection; CCO Tools; Browse CCO IOS Images tool to see all available images on CCO. An administrator can also browse through images for switches, Microcom modems, MICA modems, 700 Series, and CIP Microcode.

Analyzing the Library Upgrade

After identifying the images and adding the images to the library, use the Library Upgrade Analysis report to verify that all prerequisite requirements have been met. This report compares an image in the library to a device to determine if it has the proper ROM version, Flash Memory, DRAM, and Telnet access. This report is done to determine the most suitable devices to upgrade. Essentially this is the same as a CCO upgrade analysis, but is done from the local library rather than CCO.

Identifying the Effects of Change

Before moving on to the planning stage, one last check should be made for software defects. Use the Bug Report tool in Resource Manager to determine if any current running images have any software defects.

Cisco is rare in the software development arena in its openness about the bugs in its operating systems. Very few other software developer companies make this amount of information available to customers. Not every bug is a major problem and affects everyone. To make this easier to understand, Cisco classifies bugs by a severity rating system of 1 through 5. Severity 1 is the most critical and 5 is the most innocuous.

Using the Browse Bugs report will utilize the Bug Navigator on CCO to list bugs related to the inventory hardware. The bugs reported will be either catastrophic (severity 1) or severe (severity 2). The impact will be determined by the configuration of the device. The bugs will be displayed for any running features on the devices such as routing protocols, interfaces, security, and so on. The report checks CCO for bugs since the report was last run. Figure 9-6 shows the report layout. This integration with CCO can ease the job of searching through the bug navigator for software defects.

Use the Browse Bugs by Device report to search for bugs based on certain devices from the inventory. Select the devices to be checked from a view and CCO Bug Navigator tool will list all bugs associated with the device and its operating system software. Figure 9-7 shows the Browse Bugs by Device for a Catalyst 5500 from January 1, 2000.

To check if a bug affects any of your network devices, use the Locating Devices by Bugs report. This report uses a Bug ID to list all affected devices and the details of the bug.

Figure 9-6 *The Browse Bugs Report*

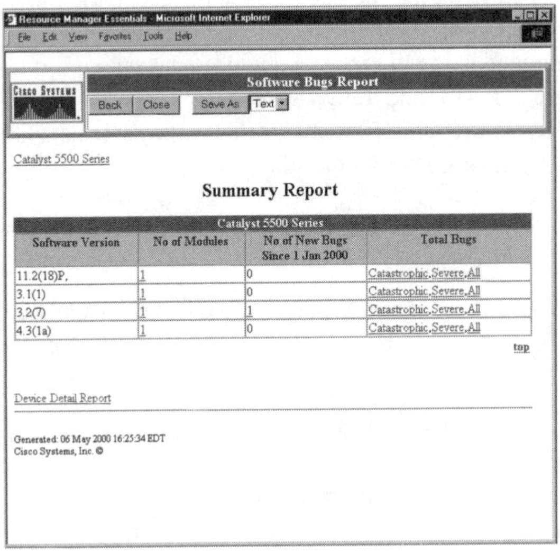

Figure 9-7 *Browse Bugs by Device*

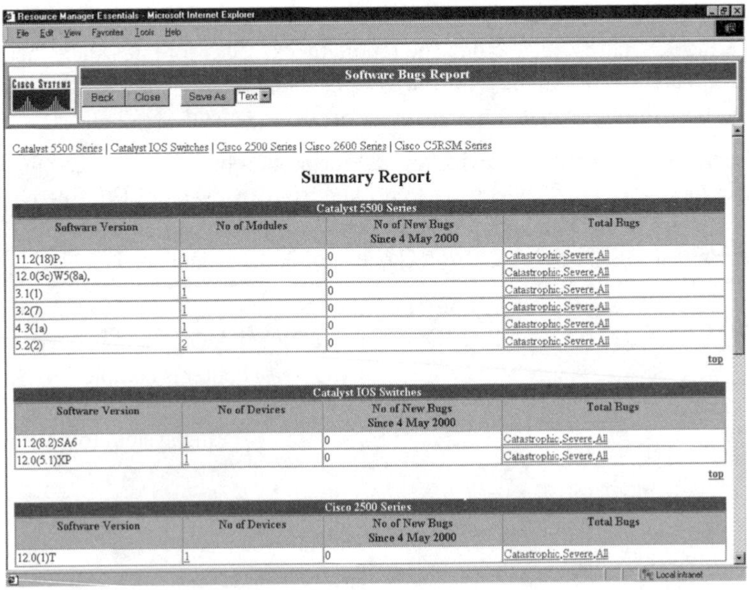

SWIM Planning Steps

Once the devices to be upgraded and versions of code to be used have been identified, the next sequence of steps prepares for the deployment of the software to the network. The deployment planning is broken down into four steps:

Step 1   Determine upgrade sequence and timing.

Step 2   Prepare a rollback option.

Step 3   Additional device requirements.

Step 4   Add images to the library.

Determine Upgrade Sequence and Timing

Although Software Management can upgrade multiple devices simultaneously, take care with the order of the upgrade process. Do not upgrade too many devices at once. Including more than 10 to 20 devices in one job is not recommended. Do not schedule more than 10 jobs concurrently. This limits the scope of a wide upgrade deployment to 100 to 200 devices at the same relative time. If the job goes badly (for example, if a power outage occurred during an upgrade), consider the impact on the affected devices.

Consider the order devices must be upgraded in before selecting any reboot options. For example, devices A, B, and C are all the same type of router and can be upgraded in one job. However, the server connects to C through B, which is connected through A. If the upgrade is done in one job and device A finishes before B and C and device A reboots in the middle of copying the IOS to B and C, this would cause the job to fail and leave B and C inaccessible. Instead, schedule multiple jobs at staggered times allowing each device to be upgraded separately.

Prepare a Rollback Option

To undo a software upgrade the current version of the operating system must be backed up before performing the upgrade. This can be done from the Synchronization Report. The rollback option is not available for Catalyst Switches. Catalyst Switches can only be upgraded, not downgraded. After the upgrade for a router is completed, open the job details report. Click the undo button to create a job to restore the device to its prior version of IOS. This new job is treated as any job to deploy an operating system to a device.

Additional Device Requirements

To guarantee a successful upgrade, be certain that the inventory contains the Telnet password, enable passwords, and SNMP community-strings. The **snmp-server system-shutdown** command must be configured on any router where the reboot system option is selected. On any SFB (Single Flash Bank) router (typically a 2500 series router), the **snmp-server system-shutdown** command must be present even if the reboot device option is not selected. The job needs to reboot the device into RxBoot mode to facilitate the upgrade. SFB devices must also meet the following requirements:

- IP routing is enabled on the device.
- The WAN interface that connects Essentials to the device has an assigned IP address and its routing IP protocol.
- If the device is configured with Frame Relay subinterfaces, the device software version is 11.1 or higher.
- The ROM monitor code version is 5.2 or higher.

Understanding the process an SFB device goes through to complete an upgrade is important for an administrator. Upgrading the operating system on a Cisco 2500 series router is a multistage process. The first step is to understand that the 2500 series router is a Run From Flash, or RFF router. This means that while the device is running, Flash memory cannot be overwritten because it is in use. The output of the **show flash** command can be used to verify that flash is read-only. The router must be booted from something other than flash memory in order to overwrite the contents of flash. The other operating system available for this process is the operating system on the ROM chips, the RXBOOT IOS.

To make the process of booting the router from the RXBOOT IOS easier, Cisco provides a process called the Flash Load Helper. Resource Manager Essentials uses the Flash Load Helper process the same way a manual TFTP upgrade does. The Flash Load Helper process automates a series of steps used to upgrade the IOS on a 2500 series router.

The RXBOOT IOS used during the upgrade process is not a full version IOS. It is designed only to provide enough functionality to upgrade the IOS. The RXBOOT IOS does not have the ability to perform any routing beyond the local interfaces. Even static routes cannot be accessed while in RXBOOT mode. The ROM chips on the 2500 series router must be greater than 9.1 in order to support the Flash Load Helper feature. To check the ROM chip RXBOOT version use the **show version** command. Resource Manager Essentials will verify the ROM version before the upgrade process.

In order for the Flash Load Helper process to function, the router must be set to boot from NVRAM configuration. In the configuration register bit, 6 must be set to off. The last four bits must also be set to either 1 or 2. When the configuration register is set to 2 in the last four bits this means boot from flash, set to 1 means boot from RXBOOT, and set to 0 means ROM Monitor mode. To verify the configuration registers use the **show version** command. If the configuration register is not correctly set, enter configuration mode and use the **config-register** *register-in-hex* command to set the register to a working value.

After ensuring that the router is properly configured for using the Flash Load Helper process, use Resource Manager Essentials to start the upgrade process. Depending on how much space is available in flash it might have to be erased to accommodate a new IOS file. The destination file name is the file name that will be created in the router to name the file in flash.

The router will reload and use the Flash Load helper process on the ROM chip. The router will attempt to access the file on the TFTP server. If flash is to be erased, then it will be erased after the router has verified access to the file on the server. The file will then be downloaded from the Server. To represent successful file access, the router will show exclamation points on the screen for every ten packets copied. To ensure the download was successful, the router will use a checksum to verify the file. After the download is complete, the router will be automatically reloaded using the new IOS.

On routers and access servers with modems, the following minimum system software versions are required to support Microcode and modem firmware upgrades. However, different versions of these image types might require different versions of system software. Software Management does not check for compatibility and dependence between each Microcode version and system software version. It merely warns the user to check this information by consulting a technical representative or the compatibility matrix published on CCO. Table 9-3 lists device class and minimum IOS version to use the MICA modem portware. Table 9-4 lists the minimum IOS version to use the Microcom modem firmware.

Table 9-3   *MICA Portware Image Types*

Device	Minimum System Software Version
AS5200	Cisco IOS version 11.3(2)T
	Bootloader version 11.2(11)P
AS5300	Cisco IOS version 11.2(9)XA
3640	Cisco IOS version11.2(12)P

Table 9-4   *Microcom Firmware Image Types*

Device	Minimum System Software Version
AS5200	Cisco IOS version 11.2(10a)P
	Bootloader version 11.2(11)P
AS5300	Cisco IOS version 11.1(14)AA

Adding Images to the Library

The last step before execution is adding images to the library. Resource Manager provides four different methods of adding software to the library. Images can be added from CCO, synchronized from the network, added from devices selected in a view, or added from the local file system.

When adding images to the library from any location but the local file system, a job will be created to add the image. The job will move the image from the source to a temporary location on the server. This directory on the server will be **%NMSROOT%\files\ sw_images\job_results***job number*, where **%NMSROOT%** refers to the directory where the application is installed. The steps to get to this point in the job are unique for each method of adding software to the library. The different methods are explained in the following sections.

At any point after creating a job, you can access the report for the job by selecting Resource Manager Essentials; Software Management; Browse Job Status.

Adding Images from CCO

Adding images from CCO requires a login to CCO that has privileges to the software library. Add the information for the CCO login to the user's profile to make the integration seamless. The procedure to download images from CCO is outlined in the following list:

Step 1 Select Resource Manager Essentials; Software Management; Library; Add Images. The Select Image Source dialog box appears.

Step 2 Click the CCO radio button and click Next. The Select Devices dialog box appears.

Step 3 Select one or more devices and click Next. Selecting devices from this list identifies a subset of device software images and helps you narrow your options on subsequent screens.

Step 4 If your CCO username and password have not been added to the database, the CCO login dialog box appears. Enter your CCO username and password and click Next.

The window is divided into several sections from which you select combinations of device platforms, software release versions, and software subset images.

Figure 9-8 shows the upgrade options for an RSM, a 2514, and a 2612. The 2514 has been selected and the software options for that device are listed in the windows.

Figure 9-8   *The Add Images Dialog Box*

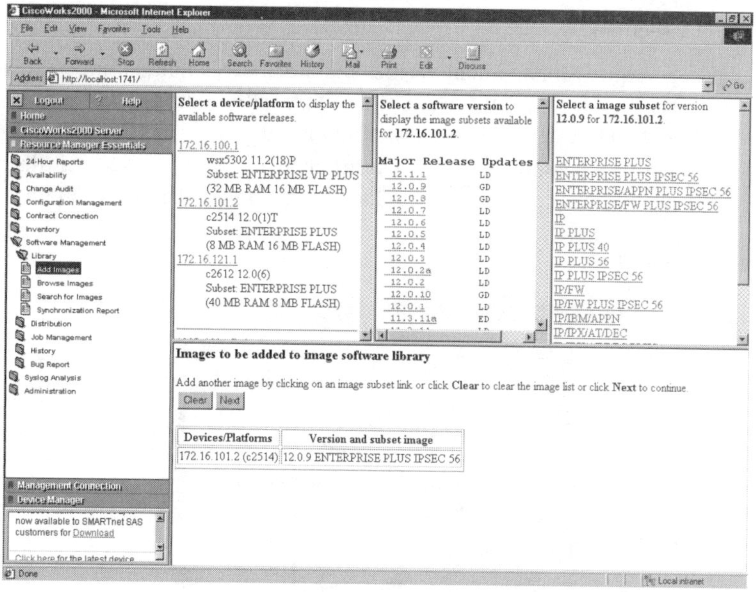

Step 5   Select the images to download. Working from left to right, top to bottom:

> **Step 5a.**   From the Select a Device/Platform section, select a device or device family.
>
> If you select an individual device, the device family, Cisco IOS release, and required Flash and RAM sizes are displayed. For 700 series devices the country of operation and feature subset also appear.
>
> A list of available software versions for that device is displayed in the top-middle section.
>
> **Step 5b.**   From the Software Versions section, select a software version.
>
> A list of available subset images for that software version is displayed in the top-right frame. If you are unsure of the subset image, you must refer to the release notes on CCO. If you select 700 series instead of an individual device, then all 700 series software versions for all countries are displayed.
>
> **Step 5c.**   From the Software Subset Images section, select a subset image.
>
> The subset image is added to the list of images to be included with the image software library list in the bottom section.

Step 6   Continue adding images to the list. When the list contains all image combinations to download, click Next. To clear the list and start over, click Clear.

Software Management verifies that the images in the image list will run on the selected devices and then displays the status in the Select Images to Add to Library dialog box. Figure 9-9 shows the IOS image for the 2514 router selected. The IOS upgrade has been verified for Flash and DRAM memory. Notice the Pass grade in the Pass/Fail column.

Figure 9-9   *The Select Images Dialog Box*

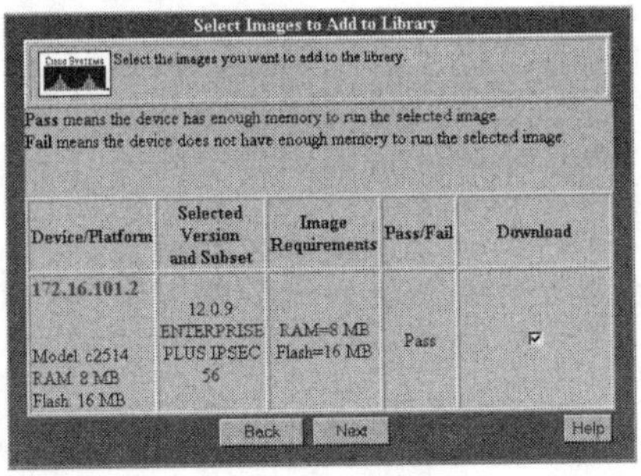

Step 7   Select the images to add to the image library, and click Next. The Verify Images to Add to Library dialog box appears. To remove images from this list, click Back.

Step 8   To copy the images immediately, click Download Now.

      Step 8a.   If you have one or more images to add, a message reminds you that the copy could take a while. Click OK to continue.

NOTE   If the download takes longer than 20 minutes, a timeout error might occur. If you have problems downloading images within that time, try downloading fewer images or use the Schedule Download option. If for some reason the file cannot be downloaded into SWIM, then download manually and import into the SWIM library.

      The images are added to the image library. When the job is complete the Add to Library Summary appears.

      Step 8b.   To view the contents of the image library, click Browse Library.

Step 9   To schedule the download for later, click Schedule Download. The Job Control Information dialog box appears.

> **Step 9a.**   Enter the job description and download time, and click Finish. If the job was scheduled successfully, the Image Import Summary shows the job information.
>
> **Step 9b.**   Note the job identification number. You will use this number to track the progress of the job that downloads the images to a temporary location.
>
> **Step 9c.**   Click Browse Job Status. The Job Status report appears.
>
> **Step 9d.**   Click the job identification number for this job. The Job Details report appears. When the report shows the status of 'ready to import,' use this report to move the images from the temporary location to the software image library.

Adding Images from the Network

Adding Images from the Network is similar to the process of synchronizing the network images. This differs from the Synchronization report, which can be scheduled as a recurring job and reviewed from time to time to verify library to network device image synchronization.

Step 1   Select Resource Manager Essentials; Software Management; Library; Add Images. Select Network as the source for the images.

Step 2   Select the device type, either Catalyst or IOS. Click Next.

Step 3   The Resource Manage Essentials' Server generates an immediate baseline of the images in the network and produces a list of the network images. Click on the Update button until the button changes to Next and the baseline is complete.

Step 4   From the list select one or more images and Resource Manager will create a job to add the requested software to the network. The device selected in the drop down list next to the image name will determine the device the image is pulled from. Figure 9-10 displays the Network Baseline dialog box with three IOS images to be added.

Click Next to see the Verify Network Baseline Report. Check Table 9-1 for device compatibility to see if the requested images are located on devices that support the synchronization and baseline process.

Figure 9-10 *The Network Baseline Dialog Box*

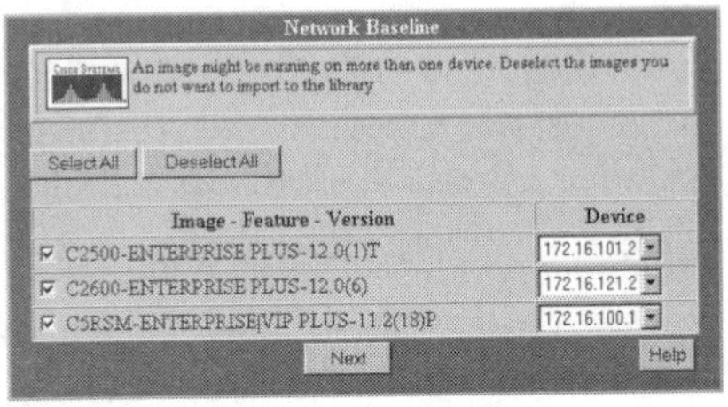

Step 5 The Verify Network Baseline report lists the selected images, the amount of hard disk space each requires, and the amount of free space on the drive where the images will be stored. If there is not enough space to hold the requested images, click the back button to remove some images from the selection.

Step 6 Click the next button from the Verify Network Baseline Report to launch the Job Control screen.

Step 7 Use the Job Control screen to provide a description and scheduled time for the job. Click Next to create the job and access the Job Summary Report.

Step 8 Select the hyperlink for the job number to access the job detail report.

Adding Images from a Device

Adding Images from a Device is similar to Adding Images From The Network. In the Adding Images from a Device application images are selected after choosing devices from a view. In the supported devices' matrix, first determine if the selected devices are supported for this feature. The steps for adding the image follow:

Step 1 Select Resource Manager Essentials; Software Management; Library; Add Images. The Select Image Source dialog box appears.

Step 2 Click the Device radio button, and click Next. The Select Devices dialog box appears.

Step 3 Select the devices that contain the images to add to the library.

Step 4 Click Next. Software Management retrieves the images, analyzes the images according to the selected image type, and then displays the Verify Image dialog box. Figure 9-11 displays the Verify Image dialog box. Deselect the images that you do not want to add.

Figure 9-11 *Verify Image Dialog Box*

Step 5 Confirm the image type selections, and select the images to add to the image library.

Step 6 Click Next. The Job Control Information dialog box appears.

Step 7 Schedule the job, and click Finish. If the job was scheduled successfully, the Image Import Summary shows the job information.

Step 8 Note the job identification number. You will use this number to track the progress of the job that downloads the images to a temporary location.

Step 9 Click Browse Job Status. The Browse Job Status report appears.

Step 10 Click the job identification number for this job. The Job Details report appears. Use this report to move the images from the temporary location to the software image library.

Adding Images from the File System

Adding Images from the File System allows an administrator to add images from the local system into the Software Library. This process enables the added images to be used in Resource Manager software deployment jobs. To add images from the file system, implement the following steps.

Step 1 Select Resource Manager Essentials; Software Management; Add Images. Select the file system as the source.

Step 2 From the Select Image Type screen select Cisco IOS, Catalyst, or 700 Series as the image type. From the Browse Dialog box, browse the server local file system for the directory where the images are located. The directory can also be typed directly into the browse dialog box.

Step 3 The Verify Image Type dialog box lists all files in the directory. Using the standard Cisco filenaming convention, Resource Manager tries to identify the file type.

Step 4 The Screen lists file name, size (MB), image type, and a check box to Add to Library. Figure 9-12 displays the Verify Image Type dialog box. The list includes several Catalyst 5000 operating system images. The last image in the list does not follow the standard naming convention and is listed as unknown.

Figure 9-12 *The Verify Image Dialog box.*

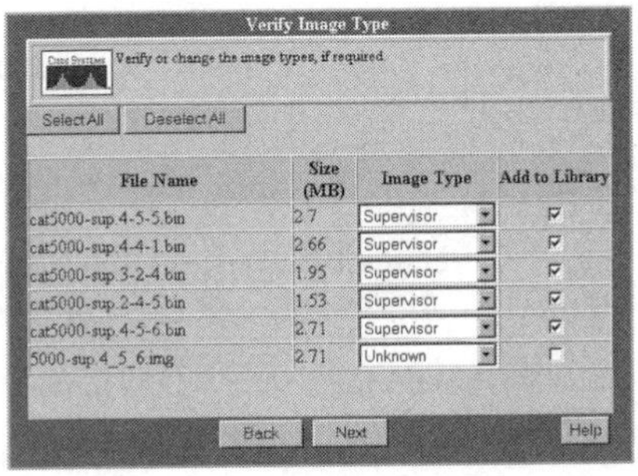

Step 5 From the Image Type dialog box, verify that the correct image type is displayed. If the file name is not the same as when the file was downloaded from CCO or pulled from a network device, the Image Type will be unknown. If the type is unknown, select the correct type from the Image Type list box. Select the Next button to proceed to the Confirm Images Screen.

Step 6 The Confirm Images Screen lists the selected images from the Verify Image Type screen. Make certain that the correct image name, version, and other requirements are listed correctly.

Step 7 If the information is incorrect, then the information can be changed in the Edit Image Attribute screen, which will follow the Confirm Image screen.

NOTE If the image is for a Catalyst Supervisor and the version is not correctly read, it must be updated. Software Image Management will not allow deploying downgrades to a Supervisor Engine. If the information is not corrected in the Edit Image Attributes screen, the image version will be blank and you will be unable to add the image to the library.

Step 8 Click Next and the image will be added to the library. No job is created and the file is immediately copied.

Moving the Image from the Temporary Location

When the job status reflects pending for import, the file has been successfully copied to the temporary location. At this point, selecting the job number hyperlink from the Job Status window brings up the job detail window. From the job detail window, select the hyperlink to add image to library. The hyperlink appears in the bottom windowpane of the job detail window. Figure 9-13 displays the job detail window with the add image to library hyperlink.

Figure 9-13 *The Job Detail Window*

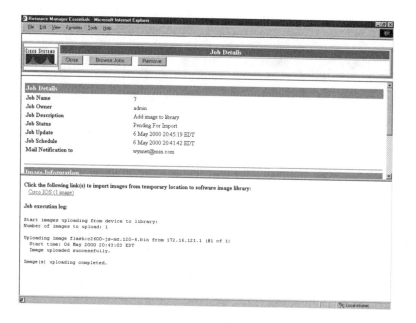

Troubleshooting Adding Images

Many variables may cause the Add Images job to fail. If the Add Image job fails, check the temporary directory for the image. The image might have been copied but failed checksum verification. The image will in this case still be in the temporary directory. If the job has ended in an error, select the hyperlink for the job number from the job status window and click remove. Figure 9-14 shows a job that is in the process of failing because a device is inaccessible. The previously mentioned procedure would remove the job from the list. Clicking remove will not remove the files from the temporary location. This must be done manually.

Figure 9-14 *A Job That Is Failing*

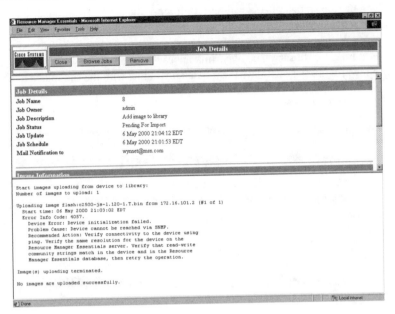

If the job does end in an error, verify that the device is supported for the requested method of adding the image. If the device is supported check the following:

- **File space on the server**—From the CiscoWorks 2000 Server channel, select Diagnostics; Collect Server Info.

- **TCP/IP connectivity from the device to the server**—From the CiscoWorks 2000 Server channel, select Diagnostics; Collect Server Info.

- **SNMP community-strings and passwords**—In Resource Manager Essentials Administration; Inventory; Check Device Attributes. This activity will verify database information against the physical device.

Once the images have been successfully added to the library, the next step is distribution of the images to the necessary devices.

SWIM Distribution Steps

Now that the images are in the library and the targeted devices have been identified, the image distribution process can be configured. Before starting the upgrade process, verify that all necessary prerequisites have been met. Make certain that setup, identification, and planning have all been completed. To begin the distribution process, select Resource

Manager Essentials; Software Management; Distribution; Distribute Images. The steps for software distribution are outlined below.

Step 1   Select Resource Manager Essentials; Software Management; Distribution; Distribute Images. The Select Device Type dialog box appears.

Step 2   Select one of the following, and click Next.

— **Cisco IOS**—Cisco IOS software

— **Catalyst**—Cisco modular switching system software

— **700 Series**—Cisco 700 Series devices

Step 3   The Select Devices dialog box appears. Use the buttons in this dialog box to add devices to the Devices list.

Step 4   After you finish adding devices, click Next.

If your CCO username and password have not been added to the database, the CCO login dialog box appears. Enter your CCO username and CCO password to update the user profile, and click Next. Click Skip if you do not want images from CCO included in the recommended images list.

The Recommended Image Upgrade summary appears.

To view the status of the selected devices (running image, Flash details, and so on), click Details. The Details report appears. Click Close to close the report.

Step 5   Select the devices to upgrade. Then, for each device, select the image you want to upgrade to. Deselect check boxes for any devices you do not want to upgrade. Figure 9-15 shows the Recommended Image Upgrade dialog box.

Figure 9-15   *The Recommended Image Upgrade*

Step 6 Click Next.

If you selected images that are located on CCO, a message tells you they will be downloaded to the software image library at the scheduled time before the device is upgraded. Click OK to continue.

Step 7 The list of devices is sent to the verification process.

The Verify Image Upgrade dialog box summarizes the results of the verification process.

The Details report includes any failure or warning messages, an explanation of the error, and any recommended action. Figure 9-16 shows the Details report and a warning about Flash memory being erased. Click Details to review this additional information. Click Close to close the report.

Figure 9-16 *The Details Report*

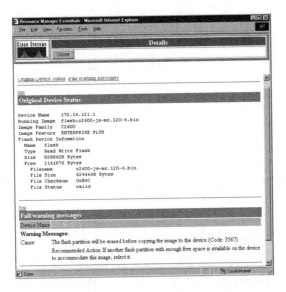

CAUTION Selecting the upgrade check box for a device for which a warning appears implies you have read the warning and understand its implications. Plus, it implies that you are giving permission to continue with the upgrade. SWIM does copy the existing running image before the current image is changed, done as a failsafe. The prior image is temporarily stored on the server and the configuration file on the device is updated to boot from the TFTP server in the event of a failed upgrade.

Step 8   To continue, click Next. The screens that appear next depend on the status of the devices you are downloading.

If none of the devices passed the verification process, resolve the problem and resubmit the list of devices.

If some devices did not pass, a message asks whether you wish to continue. Click OK to proceed or Cancel to return to the Verify Image Upgrade report.

If more than one device passed the verification process, the Distribution Sequence dialog box appears.

Step 9   To determine the upgrade order, select devices one at a time and use the Move Up and Move Down buttons.

Step 10 When the devices appear in the correct order, click Next. The Job Control Information dialog box appears.

The upgrade order is added to the Details report. Click Details to see this information. Click Close to close the report.

Step 11 From the Job Control Information dialog box, schedule the job and click Finish. The upgrade of multiple devices is carried out in serialized fashion. To upgrade devices in parallel create multiple jobs with the same scheduled time. The recommended limit is 12 jobs running at once.

If the Job Approval option is on, the Job Approval Information dialog box appears.

Step 12 Select the approver group and enter any comments, and click Next. The Work Order report appears.

If the job does require approval, then the approver must approve the job at least 5 minutes before it runs. The approval is carried out from the job detail window. Jobs that require approval cannot have their scheduled time altered.

The Details report now includes the Work Order report contents. Figure 9-17 shows the work order report for upgrading a 2600 series router. Click Details to review this additional information. Click Close to close the report.

Figure 9-17 *The Work Order Details*

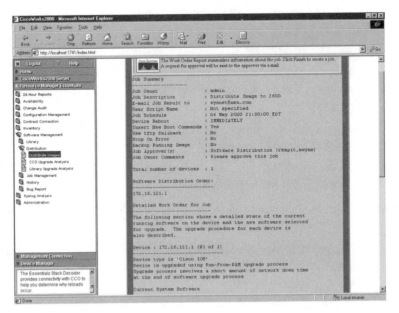

Step 13 Click Finish. If the job was scheduled successfully, the Distribute Image Summary dialog box appears.

Step 14 To change or monitor the job status, click Browse Job Status. Figure 9-18 shows the job details for an upgrade job in progress on device 172.16.121.1.

Step 15 After the job completes successfully, its status will change to complete.

Step 16 Use the job detail window to examine how the upgrade process proceeded. If the job fails for any reason, the reason for the failure will be listed in the job details. Figure 9-19 shows the job detail window after the successful completion of the upgrade job.

Figure 9-18 *The Job Details Window*

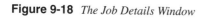

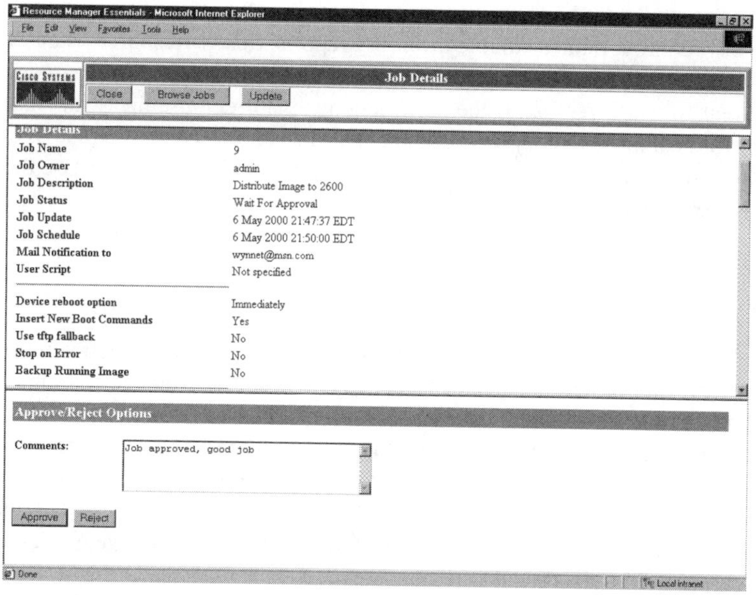

Figure 9-19 *The Job Details Window after a Successful Upgrade*

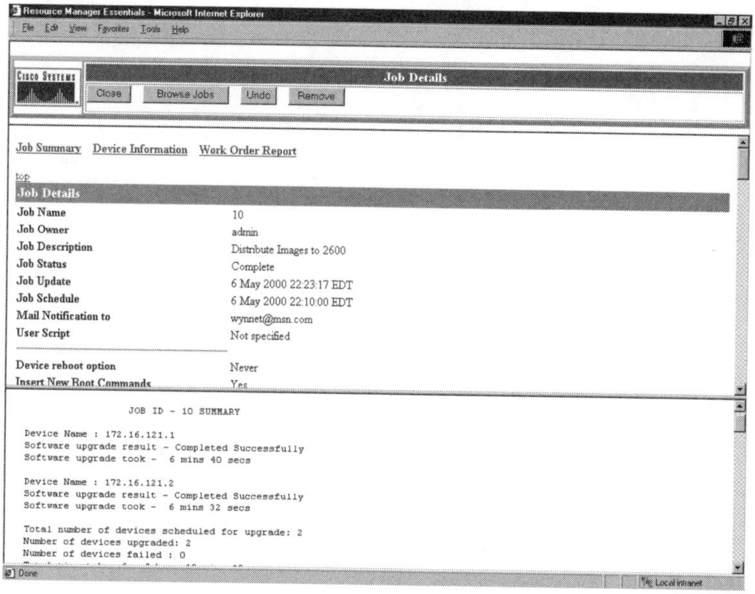

SWIM Verification

After the upgrades have been completed successfully, verify the versions of software deployed through the available inventory reports. Select Resource Manager Essentials; Inventory. From the Software Report, select the devices that were upgraded to examine the current software version. If the information is incorrect, use the Scan History Report to determine if the inventory has been updated since the software upgrade. If the inventory has not been updated, then select the Administration; Inventory folder. Use the Update Inventory application to force the inventory for the upgraded device to be updated.

Summary

Software Management in a large multi-platform network can be an administrative burden. The Software Image Management features of Resource Manager Essentials provide an administrator with a wide variety of job-oriented tools to facilitate software management. The ability to download images directly from CCO into the image library make software upgrades easier to deploy and provide the best possible image selection. The Job Approval feature allows a hierarchy to be established of technicians creating jobs and management approving the upgrades. In the next chapter, the features of Change Audit provide the ability to create audit trails of software upgrades and track changes in the network.

Topics covered in this chapter include:

- **Syslog Analyzer Features**—Provides a review of the relevant configuration commands and covers Syslog advanced features.

- **Syslog Server Administration**—Covers administrative duties including changing data storage, defining Syslog filters, creating custom URLs, and defining automated actions.

- **Syslog Distributed Architecture**—Discusses installing the SAC service under both UNIX and Windows NT and parameters for the SaenvProperties.ini file.

- **Syslog Analysis Reports**—Covers the following reports: Severity Level, Standard, Custom, Unexpected Device, and 24-Hour Reports—Syslog messages.

## CHAPTER 10

Syslog Analysis

Syslog messages provide the information needed by Resource Manager Essentials to keep track of the status or changes to devices throughout the network. Normally the IOS and Catalyst devices generate messages directed only to the administrative console. These messages that can sometimes contain critical information easily can be overlooked. Typically large networks do not have an administrator constantly monitoring the console for these messages. Syslog fills this gap. However, setting up a Syslog server allows the messages to also be stored on a server rather than just the console. On its own, a Syslog server stores the messages in a flat file. This flat file must be manually examined by an administrator to locate any important messages. Typically, the intention to examine the messages is lost due to the number of messages. Resource Manager Essentials provides a management facility for these Syslog messages. An administrator can filter messages to clean out noise generated by device messages. Automated actions can also be created to respond to messages about mission critical issues on devices.

Storing the messages on a server enables Resource Manager Essentials Change Audit Service to immediately track configuration, software, and hardware changes in the network.

Administrators can also use the reports available with Resource Manager to analyze the messages collected by a Syslog server. Resource Manager provides a Syslog Service under Windows NT and can provide additional services to the Syslog service that natively appears in UNIX.

Syslog Analyzer Features

The Syslog Service in Resource Manager Essentials provides many features beyond normal Syslog functions.

Typical Syslog services involve gathering messages from reporting devices and placing these messages into a flat file on the server. A Syslog server might also provide support for searching the Syslog messages and aging messages.

The list of enhanced Syslog Analyzer features in Resource Manager Essentials (available for managed devices and unmanaged devices) are as follows:

- Logs and tracks the Syslog messages for routers and switches, as well as for managed and unmanaged devices.

- Filters the messages from a particular device or from view occurrences of a particular message.

- Uses remote Syslog servers for message collection.

- Filters messages—removes noise.

- Applies "Action" filter scripts defined by an administrator.

- Defines custom reports important to your organization.

- Provides a default set of custom reports.

- Sets data storage size.

- Sets a user URL for system messages.

Configuration Command Review

To use the enhanced Syslog features, you need to configure devices to send their Syslog messages to the Resource Manager Essentials' Server. The process for configuring devices to send Syslog messages was covered in Chapter 3, "Configuring Devices for Network Management." A review of the commands used on IOS Software-based devices is as follows:

```
Router>enable
Router#configure terminal
Router(config)#logging on
Router(config)#logging ip-address-of-RME-Server
Router(config)#logging trap informational
```

For COS-based devices, use the following commands:

```
Switch>enable
Switch(enable)set logging server enable
Switch(enable)set logging level all 6 default
```

On a COS-based device, 6 is the same as **informational** on an IOS-based device.

Syslog Analyzer Advanced Features

Once logging has been enabled on all devices, a series of optional steps is available that takes advantage of the advanced features of the Syslog Service. The advanced features are:

- Changing data storage options

- Defining custom reports

- Changing user URLs

- Configuring remote Syslog Analyzer collectors

- Defining filters

- Defining automatic actions

Once any advanced features have been enabled, a number of reports are available to access the messages stored on the server. The available reports are as follows:

- Generate Message Log Reports
- Generate Custom Reports
- Generate Severity Level Summaries
- Generate 24-Hour Reports

Syslog Server Administration

The number and types of messages the server receives vary depending on the types of devices reporting to the Syslog Service. Firewalls tend to generate more messages than Access Servers. Access Servers generate more messages than routers. Knowing the number and type of messages devices generate is important to the administrative options that can be configured. The number of messages a device generates is directly related to the logging level configured on the device. Chapter 3 explains how to control the different logging levels. For example, level 7 debug messages should not be sent to the Syslog server, whereas level 1 and 2 messages are critical and should go to the server.

Changing Data Storage

Setting the data storage options controls the number of messages stored, how long they are stored for, and where the Syslog file is located. To set data storage options, select Resource Manager Essentials; Administration; Syslog Analysis; Change Storage Options. Figure 10-1 shows the Change Storage Options dialog box.

Figure 10-1 *The Change Storage Options Dialog Box*

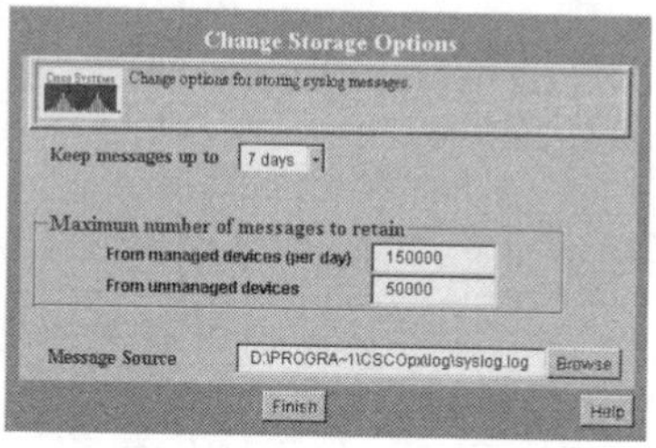

In the Change Storage Options dialog box, configure the options described in Table 10-1.

Table 10-1 *Data Storage Options*

Setting	Default Value	Usage Notes
Keep messages Up To	Seven Days	Seven days is the maximum value. Changing to less than the current setting will delete information older than the new setting.
Maximum number of messages to retain. . .from managed devices (per day)	150,000	150,000 messages can use approximately 25 MB of storage space.
Maximum number of messages to retain. . .from unmanaged devices	50,000	50,000 messages can use approximately 8 MB of storage space.
Message Source	Under UNIX, the location of *Syslog.log*, on Windows NT, *%NMSROOT%\log\Syslog*	This is the location of the Syslog.log file used for message storage. Changing this value does not move the location of the Syslog file.

Defining Syslog Filters

In a large network with many different devices, messages will be generated to the Syslog Server that are unnecessary to monitor. To reduce the disk space consumed by the messages on the server, Resource Manager Essentials allows you to define message filters. Message filters can be defined from the predefined filters based upon the predefined messages or by using custom messages created by the administrator.

To define filters, use Resource Manager Essentials; Administration; Syslog Analysis; Define Message Filter. Figure 10-2 shows the Define Message Filter dialog box. After creating a filter, do not forget to check the Enable Message Filter box in the Define Message filter window. By default, only the filter for debug messages severity level 7 is enabled.

Figure 10-2 *The Define Message Filter Dialog Box*

The message filter examines the values defined in the message and compares those values to the defined filter. The enabled filters will be the same on all collectors reporting to the Resource Manager Essentials' Server. Cisco devices generate messages using the format explained in Table 10-2.

Table 10-2   *Cisco Syslog Message Format*

Field	Description
Facility	A facility is a hardware device, a protocol, or a module of the system software. See the Cisco IOS reference manual and System Error Messages for a predefined list of system facility codes. Each code can consist of two or more uppercase letters. You can enter several facility codes, separated by commas—for example, SYS, ENV, or LINK.
Severity	The Syslog Analyzer supports all eight levels of messages that a device generates: **Code Severity** 0 emergencies 1 alerts 2 critical 3 errors 4 warnings 5 notifications 6 informational 7 debugging
Mnemonic	A code that uniquely identifies the error message.
Pattern	A text string used to describe the message.

In both predefined and custom Syslog messages, wildcards can be used to refer to multiple message strings. The wildcard for all fields except Pattern is *. For the Pattern field the wildcard is % when examining a text string, and to match any text use a *. For example, to look for the word "router," use **%router%**. To look for patterns that begin with "router," use **router%**.

Filters can also include device addresses. To add multiple addresses, use a comma as a separator in the Device Name field.

The Predefined Message Filters

Resource Manager includes four predefined message filters:

- **Link Up/Down Message Filter**—Filters link up/down messages from the managed devices. This is useful if the network contains access servers that have interfaces continually going up and down. The Syslog Server filters messages matching the following pattern:
    - Facility: Link
    - Sub Facility: *
    - Severity: 3
    - Mnemonic: UPDOWN
    - Pattern: *

- **IOS Firewall Audit Trail Messages**—Filters messages specifically generated by the Firewall features in the 2500 firewall feature set. The Syslog Server filters messages matching the following pattern:
    - Facility: FW
    - Sub Facility: *
    - Severity: 6
    - Mnemonic: SESS_AUDIT_TRAIL
    - Pattern: *

- **PIX Firewall Audit Messages**—Filters three messages generated by a PIX firewall:
    - **302001**—This is a connection-related message. This message reports that an authenticated TCP connection was started to foreign address *faddr* using the global address *gaddr* from local address *laddr*. If the connection required authentication, the user name is reported in the last field of the message.
    - **302002**—This is a connection-related message. This message is logged when a TCP connection is terminated. The duration and byte count for the session are reported. If the connection required authentication, the user name is reported in the last field of the message.
    - **304001**—This is an FTP/URL message. This message is logged when the specified host successfully accesses the specified URL.

    The Syslog server filters messages matching the following pattern:
    - Facility: PIX
    - Sub Facility: *
    - Severity: 6
    - Mnemonic: 302001, 302002, and 304001
    - Pattern: *

- **Severity 7 Message Filter**—Filters all messages generated by debugging. Enabled by default. The Syslog Server filters messages matching the following pattern:
  - — Facility: *
  - — Sub Facility: *
  - — Severity: 7
  - — Mnemonic: *
  - — Pattern: *

Using predefined message filters can cut out significant noise from the Syslog server file.

Defining Custom Filters

After examining the typical logging messages recorded at the server, an administrator will want to filter more than just the predefined filters. To define a custom filter, an administrator can use the supplied messages or define their own. Numerous predefined messages are available. Implement the following steps to define a message filter:

Step 1   To create custom filters use Resource Manager Essentials; Administration; Syslog Analysis; Define Message Filter.

Step 2   From the Define Message Filter Dialog, click Add.

Step 3   The Define Message Filter dialog box will list the available messages. Figure 10-3 shows the Define Message Filter dialog box listing the available messages. Make sure the Enable Filter checkbox is checked for the filter to take effect.

Figure 10-3   *The Define Message Filter Dialog Box*

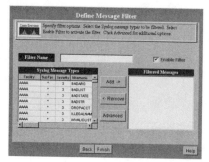

Step 4   Click any of the column headings to change the order of presentation. When a message that you want to filter is located, select the message and click Add. For example, to filter ISDN connect messages click the Facility column and scroll to ISDN. Select the CONNECT message and click Add.

Step 5   To modify any predefined message, click Add to move the message to the filtered message list.

Step 6   Click the message to select.

Step 7   Click Advanced. The message will appear in the Define Message Filter - Advanced window. Change any of the fields. For example, to filter only ISDN messages from Access Servers but not routers using the ISDN for backup connections, put the TCP/IP address of the Access Servers in the Device Names list. Separate device addresses with commas. Figure 10-4 shows how this could be done for ISDN Access Servers.

Figure 10-4   *The Define Message Filter - Advanced Dialog Box*

Step 8   To define custom messages, select Advanced and from the Advanced window click Add. This adds a new row to the Advanced window. Make sure when entering information into the fields to press Enter after each entry. Otherwise the field will be a wildcard. For example, many messages for Catalyst Switches are not defined. Figure 10-5 shows how to generate a filter to restrict Kernel messages generated by a catalyst switch.

Figure 10-5   *The Advanced Message Filter Dialog Box*

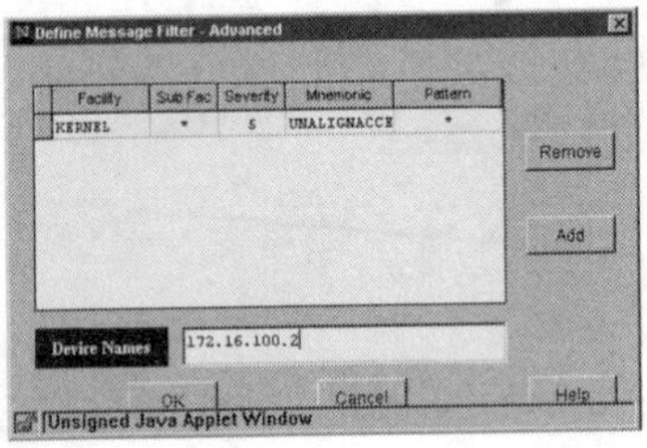

Once messages are filtered from the Syslog Server, they are no longer stored in the Syslog.log file. Older messages already in the Syslog file are not filtered; only new messages are affected.

Create Custom URLs

Message definition provided by the Syslog Server is a very helpful feature. The predefined messages included with Resource Manager Essentials have predefined explanations for the message meaning. The explanations are provided when a user views any of the Syslog reports and clicks on the message description hyperlink.

However, if the Syslog Server receives messages that are not included with Resource Manager, an administrator can define own explanations. These explanations can be used to help a user to further understand the purpose of the message or even a recommended action to take. For example, call an administrator, change a device, send a page, and so on.

If the Resource Manager Essentials does not have a definition for a message, then the message explanation window will provide a hyperlink to a User URL.

These explanations are called from a Perl script referred to as the *User URL*.

The User URL is set by default to *<%NMSROOT%>/cgi-bin/sysloga/userUrl_perl_template.pl*. This Perl script contains the scripting to separate a message into the different sections recognized by Resource Manager Essentials. These values are then placed into variables that can be used within the script. By default the script will display just the variables' values in the User URL window.

To modify the script called by an unknown message navigate to Resource Manager Essentials; Administration; Syslog Analysis; Change User URL. Figure 10-6 shows the Change User URL Dialog Box.

Figure 10-6 *The Change User URL Dialog Box*

An administrator with basic Perl and CGI knowledge can use the script to provide explanations for messages by changing the script or creating one of their own. The script passes variables for the parameters in the message. If non-Cisco devices are also sending messages to the Syslog Server, an administrator can add explanations for the messages the devices generate. If the message sent to the Syslog Server has no explanation built into the server, the message will show a hyperlink to the custom user URL. Figure 10-7 shows the default user URL that is displayed when a user selects a Spanning Tree message that has no definition.

Figure 10-7   *The Default User URL*

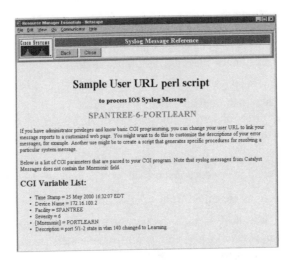

Figure 10-8 shows a URL used to direct users to additional resources available on a company intranet when the same message is generated but the URL has been customized.

Figure 10-8   *Customized User URL*

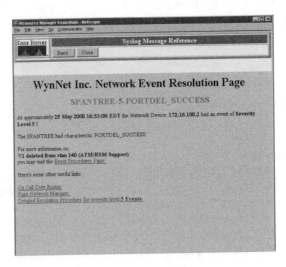

Defining Automated Actions

An administrator can define automated actions to take place when certain messages are received. The automated actions can launch any executable on the Resource Manager Essentials' Server. The only restriction is that the executable cannot generate any output to the screen on the server. The Syslog service can pass two parameters to the command—the message as **$M** and the device as **$D**. An administrator could build parsing language into the script to determine the message information or use the device name to execute some command on the device. For example, **CWConfig** could be used to retrieve the config file of the device. **SendMail** could be used to send an e-mail message to an administrator when a message is received.

To add or change Automated Actions, implement the following steps:

Step 1   Select Resource Manager Essentials; Administration; Syslog Analysis; Define Automated Action.

Step 2   Click Add or Change to access the Define Automated Action dialog box.

Step 3   In the Action Name Field, assign the action a name.

Step 4   Select the Syslog messages that will initiate the command line. Click Advanced to define a custom message or specify a particular device.

Step 5   In the command-line box, type in the full path to the command or click Browse to select from a browse window.

Step 6   Check the Enable Action check box to enable the command line. Click Finish when the command and devices have been selected. Figure 10-9 shows the Define Automated Action dialog Box configured to run an automated action on a link-up-down message on a router.

Figure 10-9 *Add Automated Action*

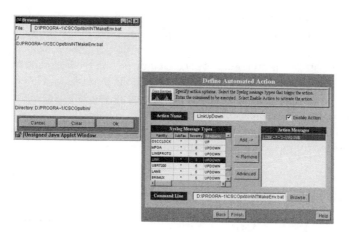

To delete an action, select Action from the list and click Delete.

If the command returns an error, check the daemons.log file in UNIX under the /var/adm/CSCOpx/log directory, and check the *SyslogAnalyzer.log* file in the <*%NMSROOT%*>*log* directory under Windows NT.

Syslog Distributed Architecture

In a large network with hundreds or thousands of devices, the number of messages a server receives a day could enter the hundreds of thousands range.

The server spends too much time processing messages to perform other functions. To alleviate this overhead, the Syslog Architecture of Resource Manager can be distributed over many devices. A distributed Syslog solution enables the administrator to lower the overhead on the Resource Manager Essentials' Server. A distributed solution will also lower the number of messages that will cross the network only to be discarded at the Resource Manager Essentials server. The distributed solution does increase the complexity of setting up a Syslog server environment. The administrator must manually configure certain devices to send to one server and others to different destinations. This can make the configurations harder to manage.

The Remote Syslog Analyzer Collector Service runs on Windows NT or Unix. The service utilizes a Java application environment that uses a CORBA (Common Object Request Broker Agent) to connect to the Resource Manager Essentials' Server.

The service can receive messages on the collector by two different methods. If the operating System already has a Syslog daemon, then the SAC (Syslog Analyzer Collector) can read the file created by the service, as is commonly the case in Unix. If the operating system does not come with a Syslog Service, as is the case with Windows NT, the service listens on UDP port 514 (the Syslog port for messages being sent to the server).

When the service starts on either platform, it connects to the Resource Manager Essentials' Server, reads the Syslog filters, and applies the filters to any messages received before the messages are passed to the Syslog service on the Resource Manager Server. This service can alleviate overhead normally generated by having the Resource Manager Essentials' Server receive the messages and also perform the filtering. In a large network with many firewalls, routers, and switches, the number of messages can easily reach 50,000 per day. Combining a distributed solution with filtering is important. Otherwise, the same number of messages are received. Without proper filters, no benefit would be realized from a distributed Syslog solution. To configure the Remote SAC Service, see the following sections.

Installing the SAC Service Under Unix

Installation under UNIX requires knowledge of the Unix operating system being used, as well as the root privileges. If you do not have root privileges on the system, contact the UNIX administrator for assistance.

Under UNIX, do the following:

Step 1   Make sure JDK or JRE is installed on the machine on which you will also install the Syslog Analyzer collector. Check the necessary version of the JRE in the release notes of Resource Manager Essentials.

Step 2   Obtain the installation file from the Essentials' Server using one of the following methods:

Through FTP from the /opt/CSCOpx/htdocs/rdist/sysloga directory of the Essentials' server.

Through a browser on the remote server, the URL is http://Essentials-server/sysloga/SAC.html. Figure 10-10 shows this file.

Figure 10-10   *The SAC.html File*

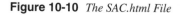

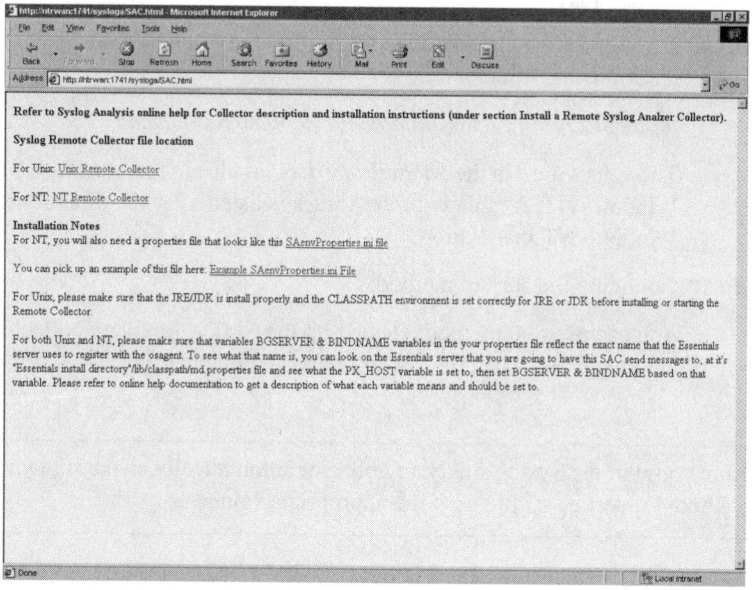

Step 3   Select the hyperlink for the Unix Remote Collector. This hyperlink will access SAC.bin and the administrator will be prompted to save it to the Unix host.

Step 4   Log in to the remote server as root.

Step 5   Set the JRE CLASSPATH variable to the appropriate directory or Jar files.

Step 6   Run the Bourne-shell shar script *SAC.bin*, for example, **sh SAC.bin**.

Step 7   When the installation script asks where to install the CSCOsac package, select a directory.

Step 8   If you do not select a directory, the product is automatically installed in the */opt* directory.

If you do select a directory, enter the fully qualified pathname to the directory so that a symbolic link can be made to it from the */opt* directory.

The installation script creates a *sacStart.sh* script and a *sacStop.sh* script in the */opt/CSCOsac/lib* directory. These scripts are used to start and stop the Syslog Analyzer collector.

The script will also ask for the location of the JRE or JDK. For example, if the JRE or JDK is installed in */usr/jdk1.1*, enter:

`/usr/jdk1.1`

Step 9   If you have not already done so, modify the *SAenvProperties.ini* file in the following directory:

/opt/CSCOsac/lib/classpath/com/cisco/nm/sysloga/sac

The values used in the *SaenvProperties.ini* file are the same in UNIX and Windows NT. A table with the values is listed after the directions for Windows NT installation.

Step 10   Configure the startup method.

You can use two methods to start up the Syslog Analyzer collector: automatically, when the server boots, and manually.

NOTE   Before you start the Syslog Analyzer collector automatically, make sure you have modified the SAenvProperties.ini file with the appropriate values.

— To start the Syslog Analyzer collector when the server boots, add the start script (sacStart.sh) to the system boot startup files.

— To start the Syslog Analyzer collector manually, do one of the following:

To start the collector manually without passing it arguments, enter: **sh /opt/CSCOsac/lib/sacStart.sh**.

To start the collector manually and pass it arguments, set your classpath to *opt/CSCOsac/classpath*. For example, enter:

```
setenv CLASSPATH

    ${classpath}:/opt/CSCOsac/lib/classpath
```

Pass the Syslog Analyzer collector arguments by entering:

```
java com.cisco.nm.sysloga.sac.TransProcess [arguments]
```

The command arguments are in Windows NT and are presented in a table after the information on the Windows NT installation procedure.

The TransProcess executable is located in the */opt/CSCOsac/lib/ classpath/com/cisco/nm/sysloga/sac* directory.

NOTE   Specify arguments only if you want parameters that differ from those in your SAenvProperties.ini file. You can specify either syslog filename or syslog port number for the Syslog Analyzer collector to read from; you cannot specify both at the same time. The first parameter in the file will be the one that will be used; the second will generate an error.

Step 11   To stop the Syslog Analyzer collector, enter **sh /opt/CSCOsac/ lib/sacstop.sh**

You also can stop the Java or JRE process if it was started manually.

Installing the SAC Service Under Windows NT

Installation under Windows NT requires knowledge of the operating system. To install the SAC Service you must have administrative privileges on the target system. If you lack the proper administrative privileges, contact your Windows NT administrator. The steps for installing the SAC Service under Windows NT are as follows:

Step 1   Make sure that Internet Explorer 4.01 or higher is installed on the remote server and Java support has been installed.

Step 2   Obtain the installation file from the Essentials' Server using one of the following methods:

Through FTP from the */opt/CSCOpx/htdocs/rdist/sysloga* directory of the Essentials' Server.

Through a browser on the remote server. The URL is *http://Essentials-server/sysloga/SAC.html*.

Step 3   Click the hyperlink for NT Remote Collector to download the SacNTService.exe.

Step 4   Obtain the *SAenvProperties.ini* file from the same location in which you obtained the *SacNTService.exe* file.

Step 5   Place the file in any directory you want.

NOTE   You will need to specify the file's location when you start the Syslog Analyzer collector. Make sure to remember the location.

Step 6   Update each variable in this file with the appropriate values from the Properties Variables Table.

Step 7   From the command line, enter **SacNTService/install** to install the SAC service.

NOTE   Do not add the *.exe* extension to the SacNTService file.

Step 8   If you have not already done so, modify the SAenvProperties.ini file.

Step 9   To start the service, select Start; Settings; Control Panel; Services. The Services window appears.

Step 10   Select Syslog Collector.

Step 11   In the Startup Parameters field, enter the location of your *SAenvProperties.ini* file, for example:

```
-pr c:\\<directory>\\SaenvProperties.ini
```

NOTE   Make sure you use two backslashes (\\) when you specify the pathname, and remember to use the -pr argument. Otherwise, the remote Syslog Analyzer collector will not run. The file and directory name are also case sensitive. Be sure to check the Windows NT event log for any error messages.

Step 12 Click Start.

Step 13 If debugging is turned on, view errors and debug messages with Microsoft Event Viewer by selecting Log Application. The Event Viewer is under the Administrative Tools folder.

Step 14 To run the Syslog Analyzer collector with different parameters, include additional arguments when you enter the full pathname of the properties file.

For example, enter:

```
-pr C:\\tmp\\SaenvProperties.ini -bsn ntrwan -bsp 42342 -bnd
ntrwan::SaReceiver
```

Step 15 To stop the Syslog Analyzer collector:

— Select Start; Settings; Control Panel; Services. The Services window appears.

— Select Syslog_Collector.

— Click Stop.

Parameters for the SaenvProperties.ini File

For the Syslog Remote Collector to operate properly, the SaenvProperties.ini file must have the proper parameters configured. A sample file is located on the Resource Manager server in the *<%NMSROOT%>\htdocs\redist\sysloga* directory. The file has sample settings for all of the parameters. Table 10-3 explains the parameters.

NOTE   It is recommended that you leave the default 4, which reports ERRORS. Setting it to any other value may result in a large number of reported debug messages.

Table 10-3 *Parameters for the SaenvProperties.ini file*

Variable	Description
FILE	File from which Syslog messages are read. Set a value if a Syslog daemon is running on the server.
	On UNIX systems, specify the file from which Syslog Analyzer collector will read Syslog messages. By default, device Syslog messages go to the file pointed to by the *local7 facility in* /etc/syslog.info.
	On Windows NT Systems without a Syslog Service, remove this parameter from the file and use the SYSPORT parameter instead.
SYSPORT	The number of the port on which Syslog messages are coming in, typically, port 514. If this parameter is in this file, then the service will start a listener on this port.
	On UNIX systems, the OS comes with a Syslog daemon. To set variable, first stop the Syslog daemon. To use the built-in Syslog daemon remove this parameter from the file.
	On Windows NT systems, specify number of port from which Syslog Analyzer collector reads Syslog messages. To verify a listener has been started, use the command **netstat –a –p udp	more_look** for the Syslog as a listener.
BGSERVER	Essentials' Server to which Syslog Analyzer collector forwards parsed and filtered messages.
BGPRT	Number of port used by RmeOrb process on Essentials' Server.
	To check port number, implement the following steps:
	1. Using a browser, log in to the Essentials' Server.
	2. Select CiscoWorks2000 Server; Administration; Process Management; Process Status. The Process Status table is displayed.
	3. Scroll down and click RmeOrb. The Process Details window is displayed.
	4. In the Flags column, note the port number (after the **-p** option). The default port is 42342.
VERSION	Syslog Analyzer collector version. Recommended version is 1.0.
BINDNAME	Name used by Syslog Analyzer collector to bind to OSAgent process. Value should be the same as value set for BGSERVER variable and followed by **::SaReceiver**. For example, if BGSERVER variable is set to **nm_bgdemo.cisco.com**, then BINDNAME variable should be set to **nm-gdemo::SaReceiver**.
	Make sure the name you enter for this variable matches the Essentials' Server name exactly.
	To find out the name under which the Essentials' Server is registered, refer to the value set for PX_HOST in the *<%NMSROOT%>/lib/classpath/md.properties* file located on the Essentials' Server.

Table 10-3   *Parameters for the SaenvProperties.ini file (Continued)*

Variable	Description
DEBUG_LEVEL	Debug level in which you run the Syslog Analyzer collector.
SA_APP_NAME	Name Syslog Analyzer collector uses for printed ERROR or DEBUG messages. Leaving the default, Syslog Analyzer, is recommended.

The settings in the *SaenvProperties.ini* file can be overridden by passing additional parameters to the script under UNIX or to the Service under Windows NT. The parameters have the same meaning as in the file. Table 10-4 lists the parameters and their corresponding file values.

Table 10-4   *Parameters Passed to the Syslog Service*

Parameters	File Variable
-pr<*properties filename*>	Properties filename
-sf<*syslog filename*>	FILE
-sp<*syslog port #*>	SYSPORT
-bsn<*bg server name*>	BGSERVER
-bsp<*bg server port*>	BGPRT
-bnd<*orb bind name*>	BINDNAME
-dbg<*debug level*>	DEBUG_LEVEL
-h	Print usage information

After the Remote SAC has been installed, use Resource Manager to verify the Remote SAC has registered with Resource Manager. In Resource Manager Essentials select Administration; Syslog Analysis; Syslog Collector Status. All Syslog servers registered with the ORB agent will be listed. Figure 10-11 shows the Syslog Collector Status screen with a remote collector called *cisco_ntserve* that has been receiving and filtering messages for the Resource Manager Essentials' Server.

Figure 10-11 *The Syslog Collector Status Window*

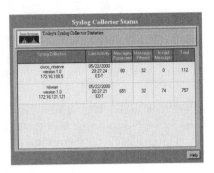

Syslog Analyzer Reports

Resource Manager Essentials provides many reports that can be used to view the Syslog information. Reports are available from the Resource Manager Essentials; Syslog Analysis Channel selection. There are five selections that can be made:

- Severity Level Summary
- Standard Reports
- Custom Reports
- Custom Report Summary
- Unexpected Device Report

Each report format provides a different method of viewing the Syslog messages on the server. The Syslog messages for the last 24 hours can also be viewed for all devices in the 24-Hour Reports folder (select Syslog messages).

Severity Level Summary

The Severity Level Summary report displays (for the devices selected) how many messages have been received at each severity. If a device has not generated messages it does not show up in the Summary Report. The summary report provides hyperlinks to the device, which brings up the device center and links to the different messages broken down by severity level. Figure 10-12 displays the Severity Level Summary report for the devices currently in the Resource Manager Essentials' database.

Figure 10-12 *The Severity Level Summary Report*

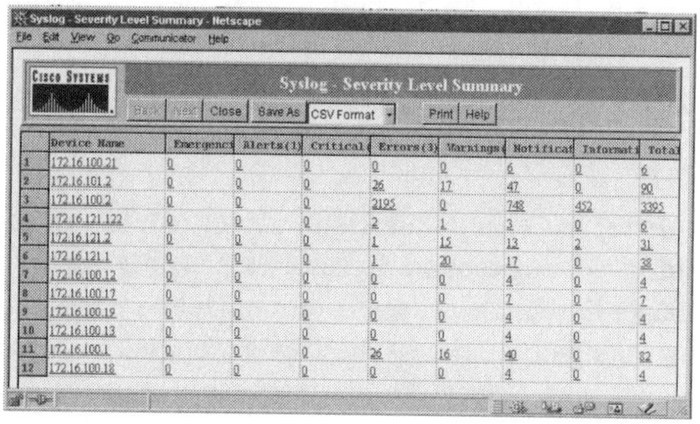

Standard Reports

Standard Reports display messages from the selected devices. Severity Level, Message Type, or All Messages can be the selected message types. The messages can be selected by a date range going back as far as the message archive, which has a maximum of seven days. The messages then are displayed in date order. Clicking any of the column headings changes the order of the listing. Figure 10-13 shows all messages for device 172.16.100.1 going back seven days.

Figure 10-13 *The Standard Report*

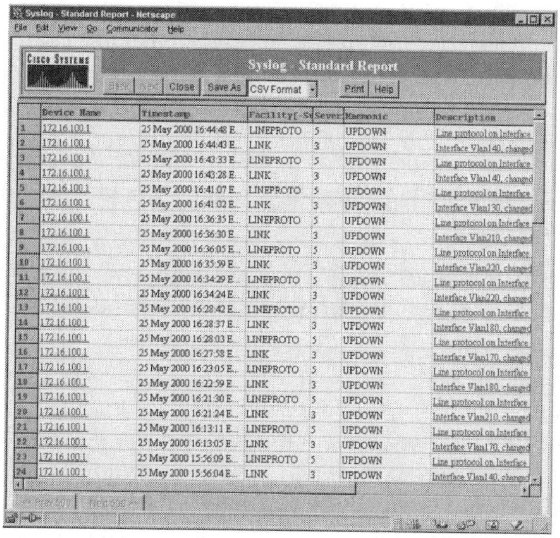

Custom Reports

Custom Reports enables an administrator to view messages of interest by creating their own report filter. The report must be defined before it can be used.

Defining Custom Reports

Defining custom reports enables an administrator to add new reports, modify existing reports, and delete existing reports. To access the Define Custom Reports application select Resource Manager Essentials; Administration; Define Custom Report. From the Define Custom Report dialog box, select Add, Change, or Delete. Select Add to start the process of creating a new report. Select Change to access an existing report's definition in order to change it. Select delete to remove an existing report.

The process of creating a new report is explained in the following steps.

Step 1   Click Add. The Define Custom Report dialog box is refreshed.

Step 2   Enter a unique name for the report.

Step 3   Select the types of messages to be reported on from the Syslog Message Types list and click Add. To exclude messages from the report, select a message from the Reported Messages list and click Remove.

Step 4   Select the 24-Hour Report check box if you want to include it in the 24-Hour Reports; Syslog Messages report.

Step 5   To set custom message options, click Advanced. This step is optional. The Define Custom Report - Advanced dialog box appears. The dialog box contains five columns: Facility, Sub Facility, Severity, Mnemonic, and Pattern. To locate values to put into these fields, locate the message in any of the reports and the report will break down the fields as applicable.

To change a field in a message type, double-click in the field and enter the new text.

You can use an asterisk (*) as a wildcard, and you can use the Pattern attribute to specify the string pattern the message should match.

Press Enter.

NOTE   If you do not press Enter, the new text will not be retained. The text will be replaced with the wildcard if it is not required information

After you finish, click OK.

Figure 10-14 shows a custom report that looks for management messages that report logins to a Catalyst Switch.

Figure 10-14 *The Define Custom Report Dialog Box*

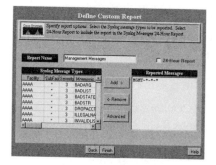

Step 6   Click Finish. A confirmation message appears.

Generating Custom Reports

After a Custom Report has been defined, the report can be run from the Custom Report option in the Syslog Analysis folder in Resource Manager Essentials. The steps for generating a Custom Report are as follows:

Step 1   Click the Custom Report application in the channel window under Syslog Analysis in Resource Manager Essentials.

Step 2   Select the devices to be included in the report from the Device Selection window.

Step 3   Choose the report from the list. The available default reports are as follows:

— Configuration Changes

— CPU Hog Report

— Duplicate IP Address Report

— Environmental Monitor Report

— Flash Memory Error Report

— IOS Firewall Application Level Intrusion

— IOS Firewall Denial of Service

— Memory Allocation Failure Report

— PIX Denial of Service Report Incoming TCP or UDP Connections

— PIX Denial of Service Report Outgoing TCP or UDP Connections

— Reload Report

— Severity Level 0 & 1 (Emergency/Alert Messages) Report

— Severity Level 2 (Critical Messages) Report

Step 4   Select the dates for which to view the messages.

Step 5   Click Finish to generate the report.

Figure 10-15 shows a Custom Report defined in Figure 10-14 that looks for management messages from a Catalyst Switch capturing login attempts.

Figure 10-15 *A Custom Report*

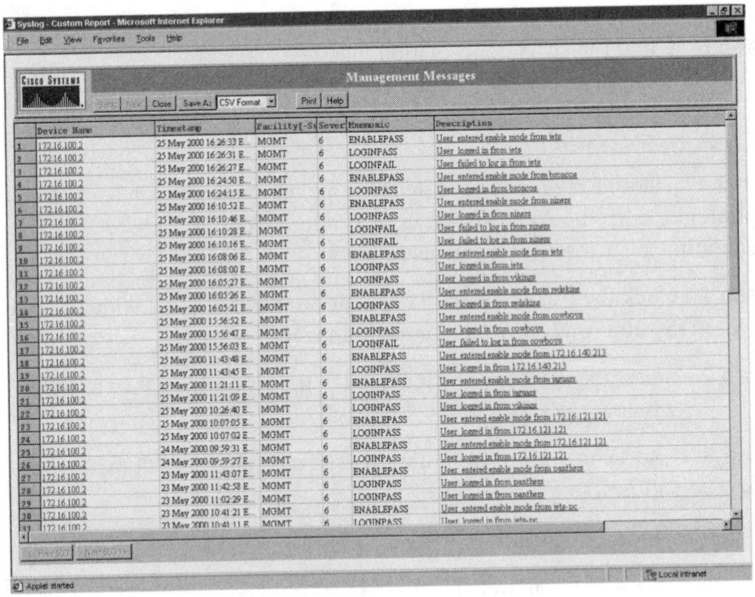

The Custom Report Summary

The Custom Report Summary (see Figure 10-16) generates a report of how many messages would be present in each custom report. Using the Custom Report Summary, an administrator could quickly gauge the reports that need to be run. To run the Custom Report Summary, implement the following steps:

Step 1   In Resource Manager Essentials, select Syslog Analysis; Custom Report Summary.

Step 2 Select the devices to be included in the report from the Device Selection window, click next.

Step 3 Select the date range and click Finish.

Step 4 Click any of the Custom Report names in the report to view the Custom Report that includes the messages.

Step 5 Reports with zero message counts have no records for the custom report.

Figure 10-16 *The Custom Report Summary*

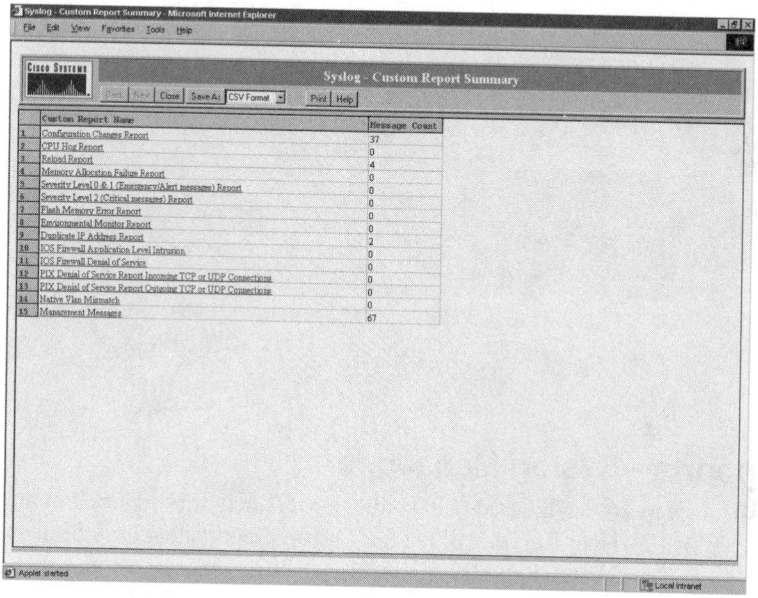

The Unexpected Device Report

If an administrator changes the IP address or name by which a device is known to Resource Manager, then Resource Manager will not recognize the device messages in the Syslog reports. If a device is sending messages to Resource Manager, but not in the inventory database, then the device is considered an unexpected device by Syslog Analyzer.

The Unexpected Device Report can be used to detect devices that have changed addresses or devices that are not in the inventory. Use the Unexpected Device Report to determine if either condition has occurred. The Unexpected Device Report in Figure 10-17 shows Syslog messages generated by network devices before being added to the inventory.

Figure 10-17 *The Unexpected Device Report*

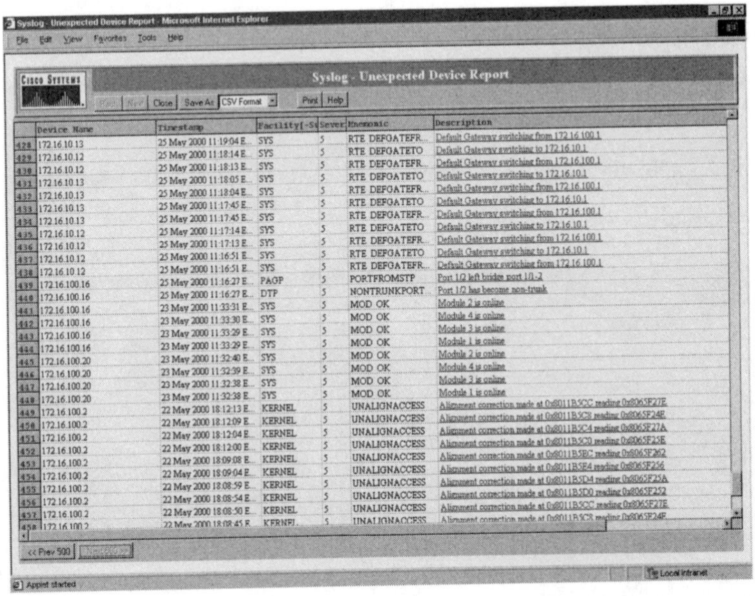

24-Hour Reports—Syslog Messages

24-Hour Reports can be used to examine network activities reported in the last 24 hours. The Syslog 24-Hour Report will list the Custom Reports that have been enabled to track 24 hours. The Custom Reports will be listed with any message counts generated in the last 24 hours. Figure 10-18 shows the 24-Hour Report that looks for configuration changes from the custom report Configuration Changes.

Figure 10-18 *The Syslog 24-Hour Report*

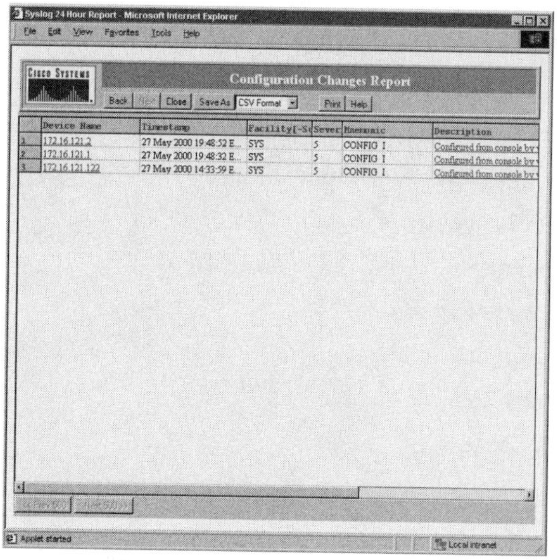

Summary

Notification messages are generated by Cisco devices and normally sent to the router console or stored in the router buffer. Using a Syslog server enables these messages to be stored for reporting and troubleshooting purposes. Resource Manager provides a full-featured Syslog management environment on both the UNIX and Windows NT platforms.

In a large internetwork, thousands of messages can be generated on a daily basis. Using a complex set of filters, Resource Manager controls message storage space. In networks where the number of messages could overwhelm a server, or to allow filtering closer to the message source, Resource Manager uses a Remote Syslog Analyzer and Collector. The Remote Analyzer and Collector provide remote message storage and filtering. Once messages are stored in the server, numerous reports are predefined for examining the messages. Custom reports can also be created on almost any criteria.

The Syslog Services in Resource Manager support both managed and unmanaged devices to provide a centralized reporting and logging location in the network. The centralized location for message logging provides the Resource Manager environment a method for monitoring device status without the need for constant polling. The ENCASE processes discussed in this chapter are expanded in Chapter 11, "Change Audit Services." The messages received by Resource Manager allow Change Audit Services to be aware of inventory, hardware, software, and configuration modifications. The Change Audit Services will then facilitate the inventory, hardware, software, and configuration updates in the Resource Manager Database.

Topics covered in this chapter include:

- The Change Audit Processes
- Managing The Change Audit Process
  - Defining Exception Time(s)/Date(s)
- Deleting Change History
  - Administration of Change Audit Traps
- Change Audit Reports
  - Exceptions Summary
  - Search Change Audit
  - All Changes

## CHAPTER 11

Change Audit Services

At the center of all the reporting and change services of Resource Manager is Change Audit Services. Change Audit is an internal service in Resource Manager that provides other services (such as Configuration Management, NetConfig, Software Image Management, and Syslog Services) with the ability to interact with each other. CAS acts like a job foreman and reporter. CAS provides administrators with a centralized reporting process and helps to raise the level of accountability for network changes. CAS also ensures that changes in one area of the Resource Manager Essentials Database are properly reflected by the other applications. An administrator can configure Change Audit to monitor changes, issue traps, generate reports on changes, and track what changes were made to managed devices and how those changes were made.

The Change Audit Processes

When a change is made to a device through NetConfig, Software Image Management (SWIM), console connection, or even Telnet, understanding when the change was made, who made the change, and what impact the change had on the device are important. Here are some examples of how Change Audit works:

Example: A Device Change Through Telnet

The list that follows outlines the steps that occur during a device change through Telnet.

Step 1 A technician telnets to a router and logs in using TACACS or Local Login.

Step 2 A change is made to a device.

Step 3 Some record of this change must be made to verify the change was approved and what impact it had.

Step 4 The router automatically generates a message to the Syslog Service in Resource Manager containing the time of the change, who made the change, and the TCP/IP address used to connect to the device.

Step 5 The Syslog Service passes this Syslog message to the CAS.

Step 6   The CAS notifies the Configuration Agent.

Step 7   The Configuration Agent issues an SNMP request to the device
requesting the configuration file.

A record of the change now exists on the Resource Manager Essentials' Server. The record
contains the login used to make the change and a copy of the configuration file that includes
the changes. The CAS notifies the Configuration Management process to retrieve the
modified configuration file.

Example: A Change to the Operating System Through SWIM

The list that follows outlines the steps that occur during a change to the operating system
through SWIM.

Step 1   An administrator creates a job to upgrade the software on a Catalyst
Switch.

Step 2   The SWIM registers the job with Change Audit.

Step 3   The job runs successfully or unsuccessfully.

Step 4   The SWIM registers the job results with the Change Audit process.

A record of the job in Change Audit now contains the job number, the owner of the job, and
a link to the job details. The process is the same for any other job-oriented process, such as
NetConfig.

The ENCASE Process

The previous two examples have utilized the ENCASE (Enterprise Network Change Audit
Services Environment) process, which is diagramed in Figure 11-1.

After the ENCASE process is completed, the CAS stores the change information in two
tables, Change Audit Summary and Change Audit Details. The Change Audit Summary
table provides an overview of the changes. The Change Audit Detail table itemizes all the
information about the changes.

Figure 11-1 *The ENCASE Process*

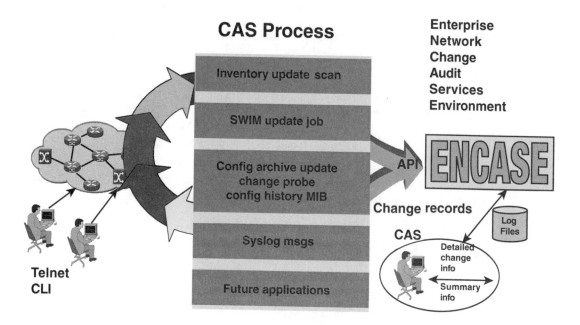

Change Audit gets the information it presents from a number of different sources:

- **The Inventory Process:**

  — If the inventory has a new device added, then the Inventory Process notifies CAS. The CAS then notifies the Configuration Archive process, which collects the new devices configuration file. This action creates the baseline for future comparisons.

  — If the inventory polling detects an inventory change, the change is reported to CAS. The CAS then creates a change history record and links the record to any Syslog messages in the same time frame.

- **The Configuration Management Process:**

  — If the configuration polling process detects a change, this process collects the configuration file and records a change with the CAS.

  — If the Syslog process records a configuration change message, the CAS records the Syslog message in the CAS tables and then notifies the Configuration Management process to collect the new configuration file.

— If NetConfig is used to create a job, the job then is recorded with the user who created it. When the job is run, the configuration file is collected and linked to the NetConfig job. This process creates a complete record of the change from start to finish. This ensures accountability for network changes.

- **The Software Image Management Application:**

  — When a job is created to change the software on a device, a record is created in the CAS tables. When the job runs, the record is updated to reflect whether the outcome was successful or not. If Maker Checker is used, the approval process is also recorded.

The CAS provides an administrator with the centralized repository for tracking changes, such as who made the changes, what the changes were, and when the changes were made. This provision can help to enforce a corporate change control process.

Managing the Change Audit Process

The Change Audit Process is always running. Only three administrative tasks are associated with CAS. These tasks are as follows:

- Defining Exception Time(s)/Date(s)
- Deleting Change History
- Administration of Change Audit Traps

Defining Exception Time(s)/Date(s)

A network in a production environment must always be available to the users. If network services become unavailable to the users during business hours, the outage could cause reduced revenue, reduced productivity, and so on. If an administrator who made a change caused the outage, the pressure on the administrator to resolve the problem is immense. To prevent downtime many companies have set change windows, which designate what time of day changes are acceptable and to what degree of change can be made without prior approval. In the age of our global economy and 24-hour networks, the change window gets smaller by the day.

Change Audit provides a tool for tracking changes made during the hours when changes should not be made. The Exceptions Summary Time defines when changes should not be made to the devices managed by Resource Manager.

NOTE	The Exceptions Summary does not have the capability to prevent changes during exception times. The purpose of the tool is to record changes during blackout periods. To control changes during these blackout periods, draft and enforce a strict change and security policy through TACACS, RADIUS, and physical security. These options are the most effective in restricting and recording changes.

Using the CiscoWorks 2000 Console, select Resource Manager Essentials; Administration; Change Audit; Define Exceptions Summary. The Exceptions times are set on a 24-hour clock Monday through Sunday. In Figure 11-2, the Define Exceptions Summary dialog box is configured to report changes Monday through Saturday 5:00 a.m. to 12:00 a.m. This leaves a 5-hour change window Monday through Saturday and all day Sunday.

Figure 11-2 *The Define Exceptions Summary Dialog Box*

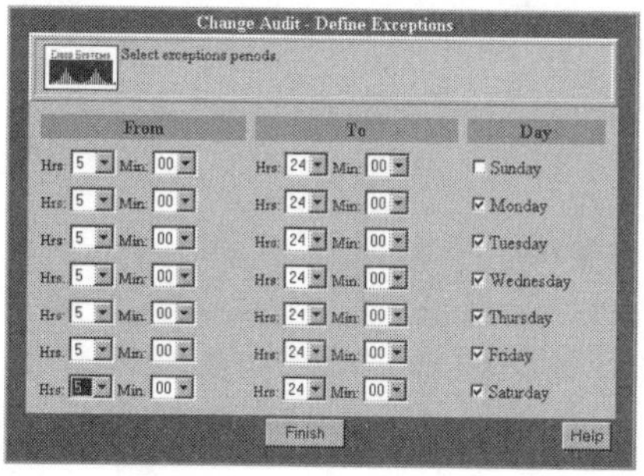

Deleting Change History

Over a period of time the information on the Change Audit log can grow significantly depending on the volatility of the network. This information can be deleted from the Change Audit log using the Delete Change History Tool. The Delete Change History Tool allows granular control over what information is removed and how often. A recurring job can be created to control the size the change audit tables grow to. The steps to manage the Change Audit records are as follows:

Step 1 Select Resource Manager Essentials; Administration; Change Audit; Delete Change History.

Step 2 The Change Audit Filter Options dialog box appears. Select the view or devices to have their change records deleted.

Step 3 The Change Audit – Delete Change History dialog box appears. The dialog box is explained in Table 11-1. Figure 11-3 shows the Delete Change History dialog box set to remove messages from the Change Summary table that are Configuration Messages from the prior month. Table 11-1 explains the different sections of the Delete Change History dialog box.

Figure 11-3 *The Delete Change History Dialog Box*

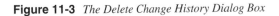

Table 11-1 *Delete Change History*

Field	Description
Application	Essentials' applications that log change records are Configuration Management, Inventory, and Software Management.
Category	Categories are config, inventory, and SWIM.
User	User name passed by application that registered a change record. If the change was made through Resource Manager Essentials, the user who was logged in and created the change will be recorded. To record changes through Telnet or a console connection some other method of authentication needs to be used. The authentication process could be managed through TACACS or local login user names. The user name is then passed in the Syslog message. There will not be user names recorded during an operation that does not require login, such as a hardware swap.
Mode	Connection mode through which the change was made—for example, Telnet, console, or Essentials application.
Date Range	You can delete records ignoring date range or select the date range for the records to be deleted.[1]

1 The date and time are based upon the Resource Manager Server time and date, which might not be the same time as the administrator's station.

Step 4 Click Next to access the Change Audit – Schedule Jobs window.

Step 5   The job can be scheduled immediately, once at the scheduled time, daily, weekly, or monthly. If any choice is made other than immediate, a calendar appears to select the date and time for the job(s) to be scheduled. Figure 11-4 shows the schedule set to the 14th of every month at 3:00 a.m. Click Finish to confirm the choices.

Figure 11-4   *Change Audit – Schedule Jobs Dialog Box*

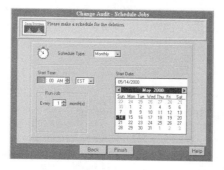

Step 6   The Change Audit – Delete Change Records window appears. The deletion created a job, the ID for which will be displayed. To verify the job or check the job status use CiscoWorks2000 Server; Administration; Job Management. Figure 11-5 shows the job has been scheduled with an ID of 1005.

Figure 11-5   *The Job Management Application*

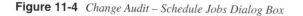

The capability to control the method that selects the records to be deleted allows an administrator to create different deletion schedules for different devices and for the changes made to those devices. For example, an administrator can set mission-critical devices to have their change record maintained for longer periods than access layer devices.

Administration of Change Audit Traps

Change Audit generates SNMP traps for the change messages it receives from the reporting client. By default, these SNMP traps are generated for all categories that Change Audit supports, which includes:

- Software Image Management
- Configuration Management
- Inventory Management
- NetConfig

This method of ENCASE operation allows Cisco and third-party vendors to create additional applications that can report to the CAS in order to take advantage of the trap generation feature of Change Audit. The file that lists the client applications is located at **%NMSROOT%\objects\share\mibs\CISCO-ENCASE-APP-NAME-MIB.my**. This file can be opened in a text editor. The file contains comments on the ENCASE process and how it operates. In the same directory, another file, **CISCO-ENCASE-MIB.my**, contains the format used by the trap when it is reported to the Network Management Station. An example of this extension is the Access Control List Manager application. This application is an add-on to Resource Manager and uses the CAS to monitor for changes to access-lists in the Network.

The generated traps are sent to the local host of Resource Manager on SNMP Trap UDP port 162. An additional destination for the traps can be added to send the traps to another management station. This feature relieves the burden of continually checking the network for changes. Some of the messages are going to be redundant. If traps are enabled on the router, then it has already generated traps form the config and Syslog MIB. This can be useful if the router does not report to the trap management station on its own.

To configure Trap Generation, use Resource Manager Essentials; Administration; Change Audit; Administer Trap Generator. Table 11-2 explains the different parts of the dialog box. Figure 11-6 shows the Administer Traps dialog box with the default settings. The Reset button at the bottom of the dialog box sets the application back to its defaults.

Table 11-2   *The Administer Trap Generator Dialog Box Options*

Option	Description	Default
Start/Stop Trap Generation	Starts or stops trap generation for every change record logged.	On
Filter Trap Generation	Allows you to set conditional trap generation based on the list of Change Audit client applications.	ALL
Customize port/ hostname of the trap receiving system	Enables configuration of single or dual destination port numbers and hostnames for the traps generated by Change Audit.	Port 162 and hostname to localhost

Figure 11-6   *The Administer Traps Dialog Box*

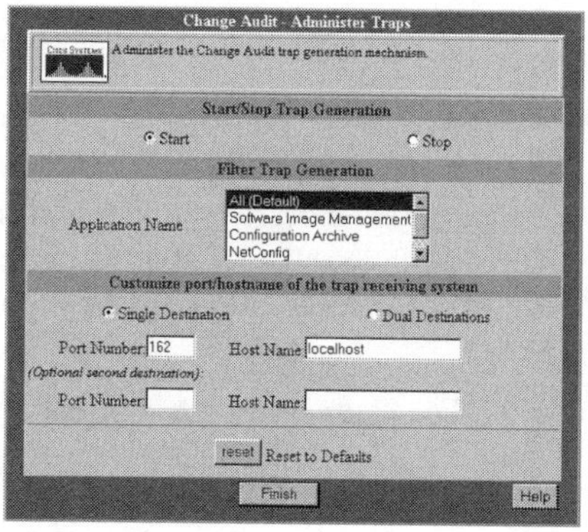

Change Audit Reports

The information in the Change Audit Summary and detail table is accessible through three reports:

- Exceptions Summary
- Search Change Audit
- All Changes

All the displayed reports follow the same layout. The selections process simply determines the records displayed in the output. The fields for the report are explained in the following bulleted list:

- **Device Name**—The name used in Resource Manager to refer to the device.

- **User Name**—The value in this field depends on the mode used to make the change:
  - **Telnet**—If TACACS or Local Login is used, it will be the user who connected to the router.
  - **Inventory Manager**—Shows up as root.
  - **Configuration Archive**—Displays as Unknown if Local Login or TACACS was not used to make the connection to the device.
  - **NetConfig** or **SWIM Job**—The Resource Manager user name that owned the job.
- **Application Name**—The Resource Manager application that caused or recorded the change.
- **Creation Time**—The time the change was recorded on the Resource Manager Essentials' Server.
- **Connection Mode**—The detected mode used to make the change on the device.
- **Category**—The client application that recorded the change.
- **Message**—A brief description of the change that was detected.
- **View Details**—This will initiate the client application that registered the change to provide more details. For example, a configuration change will launch the Compare Configurations Report with the affected configuration and a prior version. Figure 11-7 displays the Show All Changes Report with the accompanying details for a configuration change.
- **More Records**—This displays in a window at the bottom of the report any additional records related to the selected record. For example, a software update creates many affiliated records for the upgrade process. So, these records are displayed as part of a group. Figure 11-8 displays a software upgrade to a 2600 series router and the additional change records associated with the one record selected.

Figure 11-7 *The Show All Changes Report; Configuration Change*

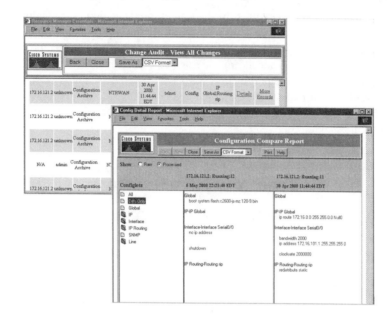

Figure 11-8 *The Show All Changes Report; Software Change*

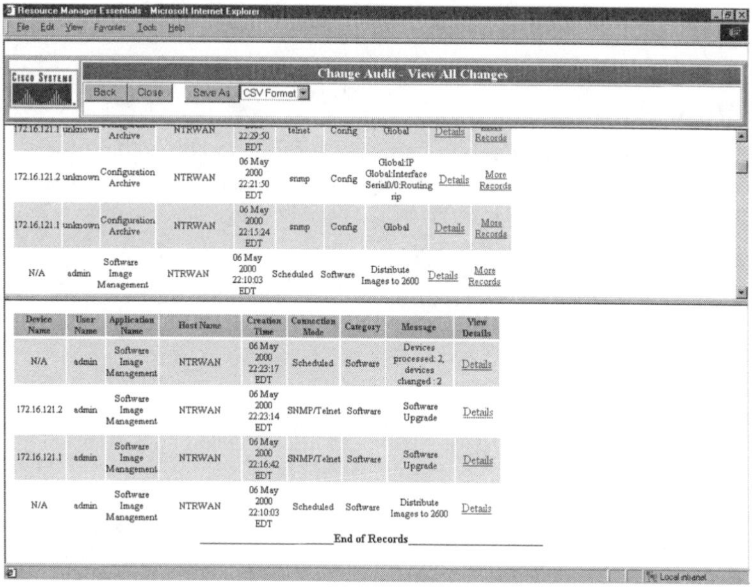

Exceptions Summary

The Exceptions Summary uses the days and times specified in the Define Exceptions Summary to report on any changes made during the exception period. From the View Exceptions Summary dialog box, select the days to include in the report. The report then displays any changes made during the selected exception periods. The days selected reflect the current week. The report always starts from Sunday of the week the report is run. To access older information, use either the Search Change Audit report or All Changes report. Figure 11-9 displays the Exceptions Summary report with changes made during the selected exception time.

Figure 11-9   *The Exceptions Summary Report*

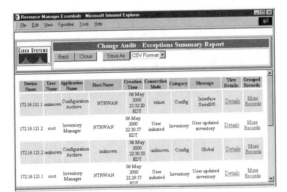

Search Change Audit

The Search Change Audit report generates information based on devices selected from a view or any group of devices. All changes from all dates that affect the selected devices are displayed in the report. Figure 11-10 shows all changes recorded for device 172.16.100.1.

Figure 11-10 *The Search Change Audit Report*

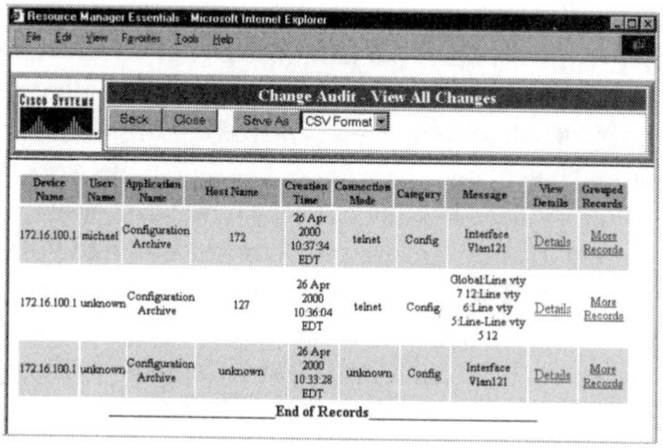

All Changes

The All Changes report displays all change records in the Change Audit Summary table. The records are displayed in descending date order. Figure 11-11 displays the Show All Changes report.

Figure 11-11 *The Show All Changes Report*

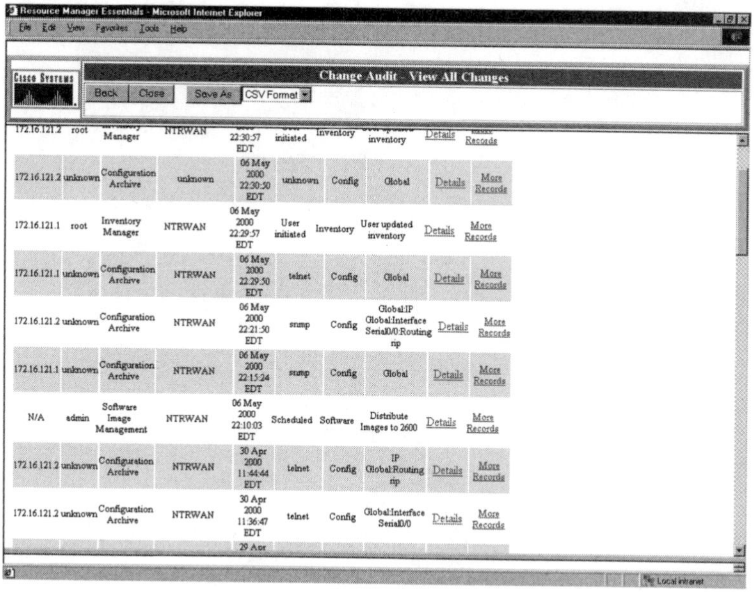

Looking Ahead

Change Audit is the central repository used by many other Resource Manager applications to track changes in the network. An administrator can view reports from the change audit tables to track changes made to devices either though configuration modifications, hardware changes, or software updates. The Exceptions Summary enables an administrator to define periods when changes should not be made to network devices. Change Audit also generates SNMP traps based on the changes it tracks. These traps are sent to a network management station to allow an administrator to be notified of any changes immediately after they are recorded. The next chapter covers an application of the Resource Manager Essentials frameworks, the Access-Control List manager. The ACLM manages the access lists of the routers in the Resource Manager Essentials inventory.

Topics covered in this chapter include the following:

- ACL Terms and Definitions
- Benefits of ACL Manager
- ACLM Functionality
- Getting Started with ACL Manager
- Creating an ACL
- Components of ACL Manager
- Creating an ACE
- Applying Templates to Devices
- Applying ACLs to Interfaces
- ACL Downloader Tool
- ACL Optimizer Tools

## CHAPTER 12

Access-Control List Management

Access-Control List Manager (ACLM) is included with the RWAN bundle of CiscoWorks 2000. The ACLM is an add-on program that runs in Resource Manager Essentials. ACLM assists with managing network security by building and maintaining ACLs (Access-Control Lists) through templates. ACLM enables an administrator to concentrate on security management rather than micromanagement of individual access lists.

ACLM is designed for the administrator already comfortable with creating ACLs in the Cisco Router IOS. ACLM supports access lists for both the TCP/IP and IPX protocol suite for Cisco IOS 10.3 and higher. With ACLM, an administrator can create access lists to manage network security. The ACLM can also track modifications of access lists even if the access lists use Access-Control elements currently not supported by ACL Manager.

ACL Terms and Definitions

To understand and make full use of the ACLM, an administrator must become familiar with some terms to utilize the tools for maximum benefit, as documented in Table 12-1.

Table 12-1 *ACL Terms and Definitions*

Term	Definition
Access-Control List (ACL, ACL Definition) and Access-Control Entry (ACE)	Consists of one or more ACEs that collectively define the network traffic profile. This profile can then be referenced by IOS features such as traffic filtering, priority or custom queuing, dynamic access-Control, encryption, Telnet access, and so on. Each ACE includes an action element, permit or deny, and a filter element based upon criteria such as source address, destination address, protocol, protocol-specific parameters, and so on.
ACL Template	A named set of ACEs. Templates can be inserted into ACLs (see Template Include ACE). Templates can include other templates.

continues

Table 12-1 *ACL Terms and Definitions (Continued)*

Term	Definition
ACL Use	In a device configuration, utilizes or references an ACL for a specific purpose. There are over 50 possible purposes, which include, IP packet filtering, line access, traffic shaping, IP multicast rate limiting, SNMP server, IPX input SAP filtering, and IPX router filtering.
ACL Use Modes and Contexts	Can be used in various IOS configuration modes: global, router, route-map, crypto-map, line, and interface. Except for global, the configuration modes have named contexts within which ACL use statements can be created in IOS. The contexts for line mode are the actual vtys (for example, console, vty 0, and vty 1); the contexts for interface mode are interface names (for example, Serial 0, Ethernet 0, and TokenRing 0). ACLM allows use statements to be created only for line and interface modes. ACLM enables you to apply these statements only for line access and packet filtering.
Logical View	An abstract or high-level view of ACE statements in an ACL. The logical view could show ACEs using service and network class definition templates that include statements and comments.
Network	A named IP address and mask combination. It is a subnet specification used in the source and destination fields of ACE statements.
Network Class	A named set of IP addresses, hostnames, IP address ranges, networks, or (recursively) other network classes that ACLM allows you to use in ACE source or destination fields.
Physical View	A low-level view of ACE statements in an ACL. The physical view maps one-to-one with the IOS commands corresponding to the ACE statements.
Scenario	The set of devices whose ACLs and ACL Use statements you are currently editing. You can name a scenario and save it for future use. Note that you can edit devices in multiple scenarios simultaneously.
Service	Named TCP or UDP ports that can be used in individual ACEs to provide a specification of the network traffic to be matched by filter criteria.

Table 12-1   *ACL Terms and Definitions (Continued)*

Term	Definition
Service Class	Consists of named port range specifications that ACLM enables you to use in ACE port specification fields. Service Class definitions are recursive and can use other service or service class definitions.
Template	Refers to ACL Template.
Template Include ACE	A special ACE that proxies for, or represents, the set of ACEs corresponding to the template.

Benefits of ACL Manager

Access-Control lists can be long and complex to configure. They are necessary in every network to control the flow of traffic from one device or subnet to another. Access lists have many different uses in the routed environment. Access lists are used whenever the administrator needs the router to compare a packet and make a determination based upon the packet's header. For example in routing, update packets are used to filter updates, in queuing they are used to determine packet importance, and in dial-on-demand they control line activation, among many other uses.

The same access list is not commonly used in the same fashion on every device in the network. Routers are interdependent devices. In order for information to reach the intended destination, all the routers along the way must be willing to pass the traffic. Long access lists can become so complex that one incorrect entry could cut off entire sections of the network. In a long access list, statements can be entered that are redundant. Redundant statements in an access list waste processing power and also can be dangerous. Once an access list is applied to an interface, any changes made to the list take effect immediately. This means that changes to the access list must be made carefully with the consideration of their importance.

To help alleviate the previously mentioned problems, Access-Control List Manager provides the following benefits:

- Provides a uniform interface that insulates the user from differences in ACL features for the supported IOS versions.
- Is easy to use and ensures high productivity for the user.
- Is integrated with Essentials and uses the Config Archive, Inventory, Change Audit Service, and Transport facilities.
- Acts as a browser-based GUI and integrates the task flow with the Essentials' GUI.
- Enables a novice operator to safely deploy complex ACLs previously set up through templates.

- Enables the enterprise to establish policies and to standardize ACLs through the use of templates.

- Avoids the drudgery of entering ACL configurations repeatedly on multiple devices by providing point-and-click, copy-and-paste functionality.

- Minimizes human error in ACL creation by reducing the necessity of establishing multiple ACEs. This is done through the use of classes.

- Improves network throughput by enabling ACL optimization.

- Permits the use of Domain Name System (DNS) names in ACE source and destination fields. ACLM will automatically perform a DNS lookup and convert these fields to the appropriate IP addresses.

ACLM Functionality

ACLM is a set of applications designed to address all aspects of ACLM:

- Class Manager enables you to create and edit services, service classes, networks, and network classes. You can then use these definitions in ACE source and destination fields, saving you the trouble of entering multiple IOS commands covering all possible combinations of source and destination field components.

- Template Manager enables you to create and edit ACL templates.

- Template Use Wizard and its variants enable you to apply access lists to a series of interfaces and devices, and perform downloads through step-by-step processes.

- Job Browser displays the status of a download job.

- Downloader provides for scheduling and downloading the modified ACL and ACL use statements. In addition, changes can be downloaded, such as comments and new template-include statements.

- Optimizer enables examining an ACL to see if optimization is possible after an ACL has been created or edited.

- Hits Optimizer provides for reordering ACEs within an ACL in accordance with the hit-rate.

- Diff Viewer displays the configuration changes you have made since creating the scenario.

Getting Started with ACL Manager

Before using the ACLM, the administrator must know what type of security policy is going to be created. This requires knowledge of how the resources in the network are used and how any in-house applications operate. A good suggestion would be to determine where the security policy is to be implemented and then determine how the affected network resources are used. Using a protocol analyzer, an administrator can examine traffic at the frame level. Using this information an administrator can make the correct policy decisions.

NOTE   When deciding on the security policies for the network, involving the users who will be affected is important. If the user population understands why certain traffic types are to be restricted, it will make their acceptance of policies proceed much faster.

ACLM was written to enable administrators to focus more on policy and less on syntax. It is important to properly assess network security risks and see where improvements can be made. Many organizations hire outside auditing companies such as Netigy, KPMG, and other Cisco strategic partners to provide them with a security risk assessment. This assessment includes evaluating external and internal risks.

Another reason to create access lists is bandwidth management. Bandwidth on WAN links can be very expensive. Making proper use of WAN bandwidth on connections between sites and connections to the Internet is paramount to managing traffic flows. Using analysis tools, an administrator can determine who is using links in the WAN and the traffic types being generated.

An important aspect of network policies implemented by Access lists is consistency. Focusing efforts on securing links and restricting link use is important when creating a consistent policy. If network policies are not consistent, some resources could be utilized in ways they should not be by users or outsiders who locate inconsistent holes in a policy. Using ACLM, an administrator can ensure the policies are the same on all managed devices. ACLM also makes it easier to manage any deviations from the policy by providing easy access to all access lists on managed devices. The ability to manage multiple access list types such as routing filters, security access lists, queuing filters, and dialer lists, provides an administrator with a centralized application for maintaining a consistent security policy networkwide.

CAUTION   It is important to understand an administrator already familiar with the command-line syntax used to create access lists can only correctly use the power of ACLM. If a novice unfamiliar with access list syntax uses this tool, then this could be disastrous and multiple devices could be rendered inaccessible.

Creating a Scenario

To use the ACL Manager, follow a series of steps that revolve around scenarios. The scenario allows an administrator to create rules for many devices at once. Access-Control Lists can be applied to all the devices in the scenario. This ensures a common security policy across the network. The first step is therefore to create a scenario.

Step 1 From the Resource Manager Essentials' Application select ACL Management; Edit ACLs.

Step 2 If this is the first time using ACLM, then the list of scenarios will be empty. The Edit Scenario dialog box will open. Figure 12-1 shows the Edit ACLM dialog box.

Figure 12-1 *The Edit ACLs Dialog Box*

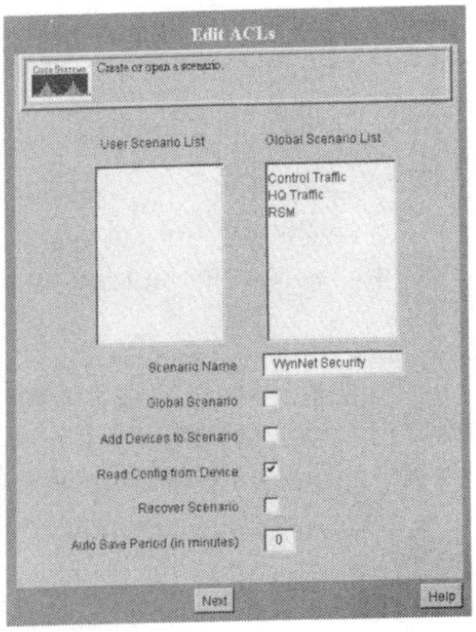

The Edit ACL dialog is explained in Table 12-2.

Step 3 Click Next. If this is a new scenario or the Add Devices to Scenario check box was previously selected, the select device or view dialog will appear. Select the devices to add to the scenario.

Step 4 Select Finish. The main ACLM application will appear.

Table 12-2   *The Edit ACL Dialog Box*

Field	Description
User Scenario List	List of non-global scenarios available to this user.
Global Scenario List (list box)	List of scenarios that all users have at least read access to.
Scenario Name	Name of the scenario selected for modification or creation.
Global Scenario (check box)	Check box that makes the scenario available for read-only access by all Essentials' users. If unchecked, your scenario will not be visible to other Essentials' users.
Add Devices to Scenario	Check box that enables devices to be added to an already existing scenario.
Read Config From Device	Check box that synchronizes the Config Archive with the devices in the scenario to get the configuration file before starting ACL Manager.
Recover Scenario	Check box that opens the auto-saved version of the scenario instead of the last saved version; a tilde (~) is then appended to the end of the scenario name in the ACLM main window. This check box is available only if ACLM exited abnormally and detected an auto-save version of the scenario you are attempting to open.
Auto Save Period (in minutes)	Option defines how often changes to the scenario are saved. Use the Auto Save option for a scenario to guard against browser crashes.

NOTE   If the ACLM has not been used before or forms have not been installed, the CAM Manager asks if the forms should be installed. Selecting Yes will install local copies of the Java Classes used by the ACLM. Installing the classes locally can dramatically improve the Java client performance on some browsers. The application will take a few minutes to load. Leaving the browser open after using the application will keep the classes loaded. Subsequent uses of the application will be significantly faster. Not all browsers benefit from the CAM. Internet Explorer will create its own cache of Java classes and does not need the CAM. For more information see Chapter 4, "CiscoWorks 2000 Server and Resource Manager Essentials Installation."

Navigating the ACLM Application

The ACLM will start as its own application environment. The application consists of three main elements: the main window (see Table 12-3), a menu bar, and an icon toolbar. Figure 12-2 shows the ACLM Application open to a scenario called HQ Traffic.

Figure 12-2 *The ACLM Application*

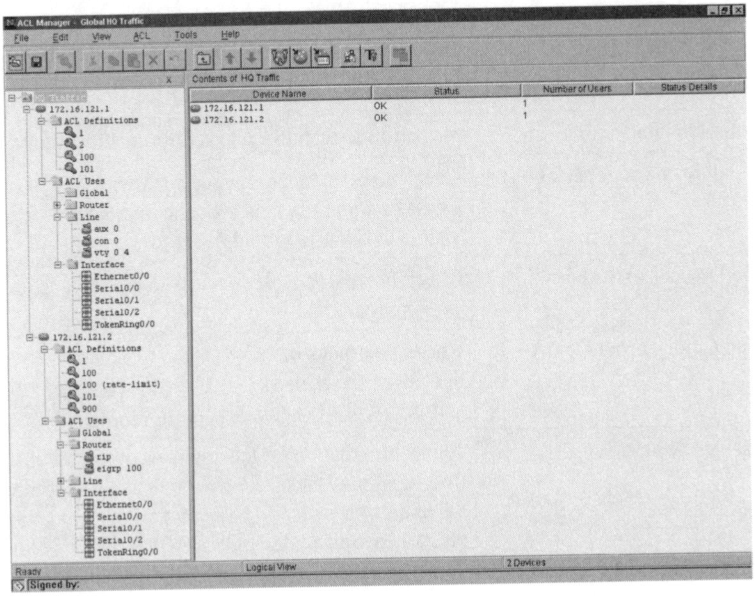

Table 12-3 *The ACLM Main Window*

Item	Description
Folder (left pane)	Shows a hierarchy of items starting with the scenario, the routers in the scenario, and ACLs and ACL; uses contexts in expanding and collapsing folders.
	To expand or collapse a folder, click the + or - icon next to the folder, or double-click the folder.
Contents (right pane)	Shows the attributes of any item selected in the folder pane. The contents are empty if there are no attributes associated with the selected item.
Status area (bottom left)	Indicates the status of the application. The following status is displayed in this area:
	Loading—when ACLM is reading the device config files and preparing to display the tree hierarchy for each device in the scenario.
	Ready—when loading is completed.

Table 12-3   *The ACLM Main Window (Continued)*

Item	Description
Item count area (bottom right)	Shows the number of items contained in the currently selected object.
	When a scenario is selected, shows the number of devices in the current scenario.
	When the label "ACL Definitions" on a device is selected, shows the number of ACLs for that device.
	When an ACL is selected, shows the number of ACEs in that ACL.
View mode area (bottom center)	Shows the view mode for viewing ACEs. If you are in an ACL context and in physical view mode, the contents pane has a gray background. No editing operations are permitted in physical view mode, except for reordering ACEs.

Creating an ACL

Once a scenario is created, the next step is to start creating and applying access lists. The following steps go through the process of creating an ACL to apply to a device in a scenario.

Step 1   Select the scenario folder from the folder pane.

Step 2   Expand the folder and select a device to create the list for.

Step 3   Expand the device and open the ACL Definitions folder to view any existing access lists on the device. The ACL Uses folder lists the interfaces on the device and the interfaces' current status. Any Access-Control List applied to the interfaces will also be listed.

Step 4   To create any new Access-Control Lists, select the device's ACL Definitions folder and from the toolbar select either the ACL; New ACL menu option or New ACL icon. The icon looks like a key.

Step 5   The ACL Editor dialog box will appear. Figure 12-3 pictures the ACL Editor dialog box.

Figure 12-3 *The ACL Editor dialog box.*

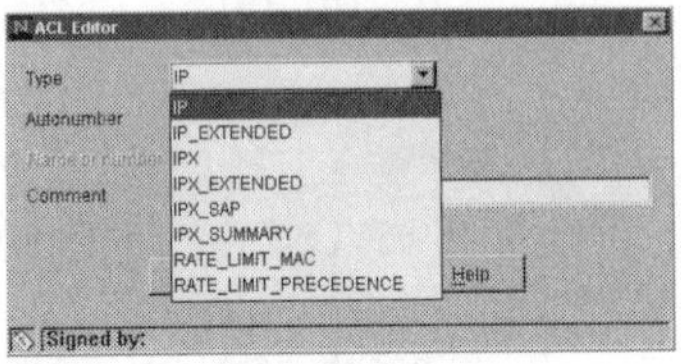

Step 6   Choose the ACL Type from the drop-down list. For an explanation of the different ACL types, consult the IOS release notes for the device. The types are:

— IP (Standard)

— IP_Extended

— IPX (Standard)

— IPX_Extended

— IPX_SAP

— IPX_Summary

— Rate_Limit_MAC

— Rate_Limit_Precedence

Step 7   After selecting the type, select Autonumber to assign an automatic number from the range of the list type or deselect Autonumber. If Autonumber is deselected then a name or number can be chosen. Add a comment that will appear in the configuration of the device.

Step 8   After the ACL is created, the next step is to assign ACEs to the ACL.

The Components of ACL Manager

The ACLM is designed to make access list management easier and more efficient. This complex task is tackled by breaking access lists into separate components. The different components are each managed by a separate application. The ACLM, the main application, is where the ACL is first defined in a scenario. Once the ACL has been defined, the next step is to assign ACEs to the ACL. ACEs are the entries in the ACL that define the traffic that is permitted or denied. For example, an ACE to permit Telnet might say **permit tcp any eq telnet**.

The real power of the ACLM is in how an ACE is defined. An ACE can be broken down into two different components, each with its own management application:

- **Template Manager**—Multiple ACE statements can be grouped to define a template. Multiple templates can be combined into one ACL. The Template Manager is used for joining ACEs into templates.

- **Class Manager**—In an ACE, the different traffic types that are known to the ACLM are called services. The services are defined in the Class Manager application. The administrator can also create custom services and group services to make a class. The networks that are defined in an Access list can also be defined in the Class Manager to make them easier to select and recognize. Networks can be grouped into classes.

In order to make better use of all of the features of ACLM, understanding the relationship between the components managed through ACLM to build an access list is important. Figure 12-4 shows a graphic to explain the relationships between the different components of an access list created in ACLM. Each access list can use one or more templates, which in turn can use one or more ACE entries, which can include one or more classes that include one or more networks and services.

Figure 12-4 *ACLM Object Relationships*

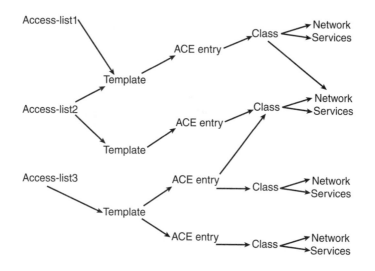

Creating an ACE

To create an ACE to be applied to the newly created ACL, select the ACL in the folder pane under the ACL Definition folder. From the menu choose New ACE to add an individual ACE or select New Include Template to apply a template that contains ACEs. Templates are covered later in this chapter. So for now select New ACE. The steps for creating an ACE for TCP/IP extended access lists follow:

Step 1 The ACE Editor window appears. The ACE Editor window contains three tabs: General, Advanced, and Other. The ACE Editor in its default state is pictured in Figure 12-5.

Figure 12-5 *The ACE Editor Window*

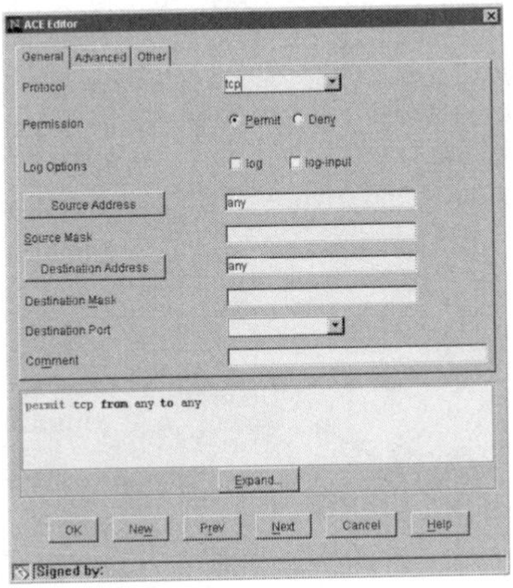

Step 2 In the General tab first select a protocol from the list of IP protocols. The list currently contains:

— **IP**—The entire IP protocol suite

— **TCP**—The Transmission Control Protocol

— **UDP**—The User Datagram Protocol

— **ICMP**—The Internet Control Message Protocol

— **IGMP**—The Internet Gateway Message Protocol, also known as Internet Group Management Protocol used for controlling multicast traffic

— **EIGRP**—The Enhanced Interior Gateway Routing Protocol

— **GRE**—The Generic Routing Encapsulation protocol

— **IGRP**—The Interior Gateway Routing Protocol

— **IPINIP**—IP in IP Tunneling

— **NOS**—KA9Q NOS-compatible IP over IP Tunneling Protocol

— **OSPF**—The Open Shortest Path First Protocol

— **AHP**—The Authentication Header Protocol

— **ESP**—The Encapsulation Security Protocol

— **PCP**—The Payload Compression Protocol

If the protocol does not show up in the list, the protocol number can be typed in.

Step 3   The dialog box will then display the appropriate options based on the protocol selected.

Step 4   Select if the statement is a permit or a deny statement.

Step 5   Choose whether to log hits to this line in the list. Log messages contain information about the packet that causes the hit. It can be helpful to send these messages back to the Resource Manager Syslog Server and define automated actions or custom reports on the hits. On the router use the **logging** *ip-address-of-syslog-server* command to set the logging destination as discussed in Chapter 3, "Configuring Devices for Network Management."

Step 6   The Source Address is next. If the source can be any source, then use the keyword **any**. If the address is a host, then type the address and leave the source mask empty. The word "host" will appear in the preview box at the bottom. Clicking Source Address will bring up the Network/Class Selector dialog box. Networks and Classes are covered in the Class Manager section later in this chapter.

Step 7   The Source Mask dialog box is next. The mask is the standard wildcard mask used when writing an access list in the IOS command line. Leave a blank for the **any** or **host** keywords to be used. See your version of IOS documentation on how to determine the wildcard mask.

Step 8   In the Destination Address and Destination Mask boxes use the same format as the Source Address and Source Mask boxes.

Step 9   If TCP or UDP were the selected protocols, then a destination port can also be specified by selecting a port from the drop-down list or typing it in the port number.

Step 10 The comment field provides a place for any comments to be added to the line. This provision can be helpful in remembering the purpose of the line at a later time. The comments are transferred to the router with the access list. These comments are stored in the router config and can be invaluable to documenting the use of an access list.

Figure 12-6 shows an ACE used to permit telnet to the router from the management station.

Figure 12-6   *A Telnet ACE*

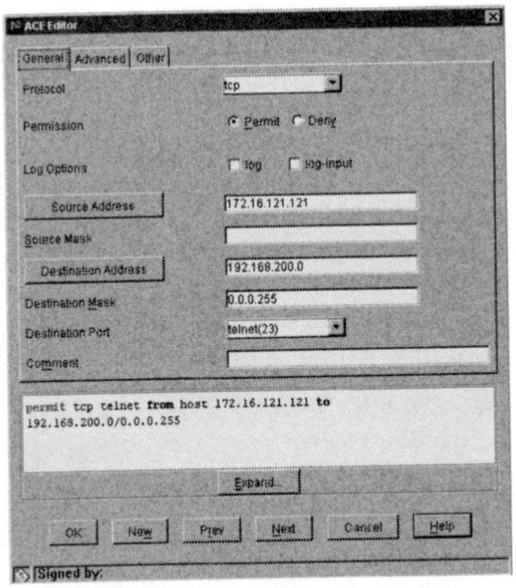

The ACE editor dialog box in Figure 12-6 shows the following information on the ACE that was created:

— **Source Address**—The source address for the traffic. In this case, the NMS.

— **Destination Address**—The destination for the traffic on the target device. In this case, the router.

— **Protocol**—TCP used to control what application is controlled in the statement.

— **Permission**—Whether the traffic is permitted (allowed) or denied (dropped).

— **Destination Port**—Telnet(23) is the destination port being accessed on the device.

— **Summary window**—Shows the syntax that will be used on the router to create the list statement.

Step 11 If only one line is being added, then click OK. To add another line click New and choose to save the current ACE when prompted.

Step 12 The Advanced tab is used to specify additional protocol parameters.

— For TCP, TCP flags can be examined. For example, choose established to only allow established traffic flows to be affected by the line, or just to look for the reset flag.

— For TCP and UDP, select a source and/or destination port by a range or mathematical operator such as less than, greater than, equal to, not equal to, or range.

— For ICMP, select the message or specify the type and code.

— For IGMP, select any of the following special IGMP multicast messages: dvmrp, host-query, host-report, pim, and trace.

If the desired message does not appear, then type the message into the dialog box space.

Figure 12-7 shows the advanced tab used to check the ICMP message ping.

Figure 12-7 *ACE Editor: Advanced Tab*

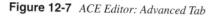

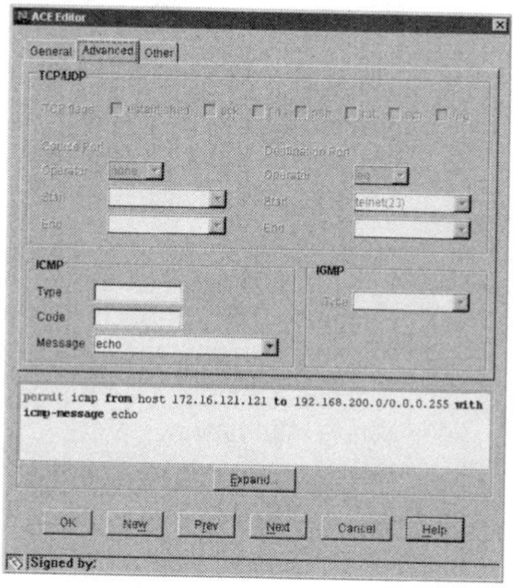

Step 13 The other tab displayed in Figure 12-8 is used for protocol-independent options, as explained in Table 12-4.

Figure 12-8 *ACE Editor: Other Tab*

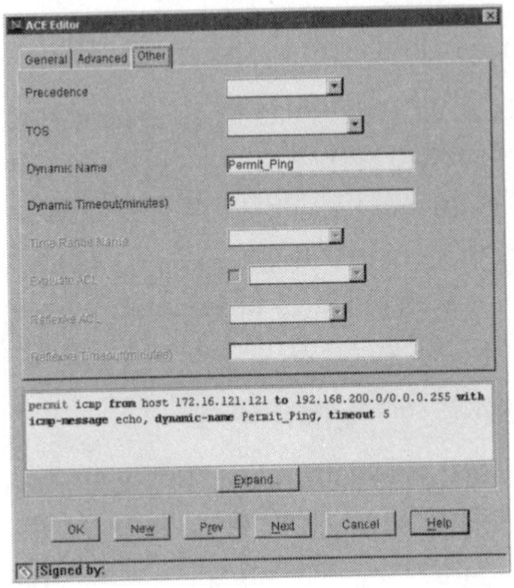

Table 12-4 *Edit ACL Other Options*

Field	Description
Precedence	Packets can be filtered by precedence level, as specified by a number in the range 0 to 7 or by name. You can select a name from the drop-down list box.
TOS	Packets can be filtered by type of service level, as specified by a number in the range 0 to 15 or by name. You can select a name from the drop-down list box.
Dynamic Name	Specifies the name of a dynamic access list. This field is optional.
Dynamic Timeout (minutes)	Specifies a maximum time limit (in minutes) that a temporary access list entry can remain within the dynamic access list. The default is infinite and allows an entry to remain permanently. This field is optional.
Time Range Name	Specifies a named time range, which combines at most one fixed interval and zero, or more, periodic intervals during which this ACL entry is in effect. This range must have been already set up on the device (available only on IOS releases later than 12.0(1)T).
Evaluate ACL	Select this check box to nest a reflexive access list within an ACL. Enter the name of a reflexive ACL. This field is optional.

Table 12-4   *Edit ACL Other Options (Continued)*

Field	Description
Reflexive ACL	Select this check box if this entry should create and insert dynamic entries into a reflexive ACL. This feature is used to filter IP traffic so that TCP or UDP session traffic is permitted through the firewall only if the session originated from within the internal network. This field is optional.
Reflexive Timeout (minutes)	Reflexive access list entries expire after no packets in the session have been detected for a certain length of time (the timeout period in minutes). If you do not specify a timeout for the reflexive list, the list uses the global timeout value. This field is optional.

The steps for creating an ACE for IPX are similar to creating an ACE for TCP/IP, except that the protocol options are specific to IPX. The ACLM can make the normally confusing job of building IPX Extended access lists simple. For example, on a dial-up connection an administrator normally wants to stop IPX RIP and IPX SAP but permit all else. This task can be easily completed with ACL Manager. Figure 12-9 shows an IPX SAP filter that denies the server NWSERVER on network A0.

Figure 12-9   *IPX SAP Filter*

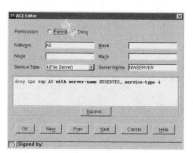

Once an ACE is created, it can be moved through the list either upward or downward. This advancement is huge compared to the normal access list manipulation through the IOS command line. Normally, newly inserted lines only go to the bottom of the list in an IOS configuration and cannot be moved without excessive use of copy and paste. When an access list grows to hundreds of lines, this can substantially save time when changing an access list's structure. To move an ACE in an access list, select the ACE in the Contents windowpane. From the Edit menu, select either Move ACE Up or Move ACE Down, depending on the location of the ACE. From the toolbar, select the blue up or down arrow to have the same effect.

Advanced ACE Options

One important feature of the ACL Manager is the capability to have consistent security policies through the use of Templates and Class Services. The Template Manager can create templates containing frequently used ACEs. The templates can be combined into one ACL or used independently. The Class Manager allows an administrator to define custom TCP and UDP port applications and define frequently used devices and networks by name. These Classes can then be used in the template to define ACEs by names easily recognizable.

Template Manager

The Template Manager Application is a hierarchical application organized by folders. The folder window contains the Template Root Directory folder. To use Template Manager, templates are created and then ACEs are added to those templates. To make the application easier to use, additional folders under the root can be created to organize templates by an administrator's preference.

An administrator may create folders to represent different sections of the network, folders based on different levels of control initiated by the templates, or folders based on ACE type. An example is separating IP and IPX templates. To avoid a crowded look at the root, create folders and subfolders to organize the templates. Figure 12-10 shows the Template Manager with a folder hierarchy. The Template Root Directory has a subfolder called IP Extended Lists. A template in that folder, Permit Telnet, has been selected. The right-hand side of the screen shows the template has been used on device 172.16.121.1 in access list 101.

Figure 12-10 *The Template Manager*

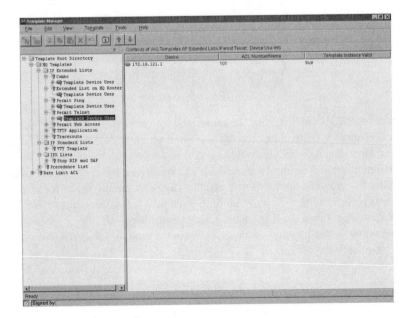

The most powerful feature of the Template Manager is that after a template has been created, the ACLM application keeps track of which ACLs use which templates. If a template is ever modified, the users of the template can also be updated. This situation creates a consistent environment where an additional line might be needed on all devices using an ACL and the update can be done through the template. For example, in Figure 12-11 the Template Combo was modified to include a permit statement for EIGRP. Right-clicking on the device 172.16.121.1 where the Combo Template was used brings up the secondary menu option, Synch template on devices.

Figure 12-11 *Synchronizing Templates*

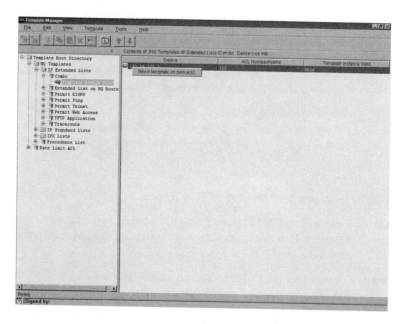

A temporary scenario is then created that contains the devices along with their updated information. This information has not yet been downloaded to the device. In Figure 12-12 the modified template and the old template have been synchronized into a temporary scenario. This scenario can now be downloaded to the devices. This setup will synchronize the devices in the scenario with the actual devices.

Figure 12-12 *The Temporary Scenario*

This scenario is then synchronized with the device through a job created in Figure 12-13. Only device 172.16.121.1 was using the template. However, many more routers could have been using the template and would have been updated accordingly. The synchronization job will run immediately in order to ensure the synchronization process is successful. All the parameters for the synch job are automatically filled in by the application.

Figure 12-13 *The Synchronization Job*

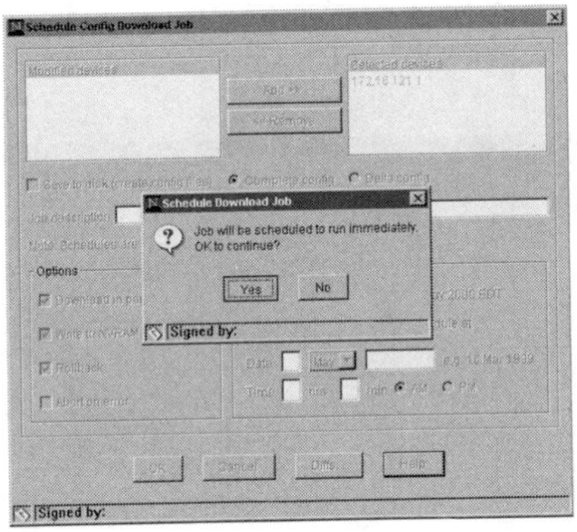

To create templates, implement the following steps:

Step 1 Launch Template Manager from any of the ACLM Applications or from Resource Manager Essentials; Administration ACL Management; Edit ACL Templates.

Step 2 Create a new subfolder under Template Root Directory to start creating and organizing templates.

Step 3 In the folder where the template is going to be stored click New Template on the toolbar or select the menu option New Template.

Step 4 The Template editor appears. Choose the Template Type from the list. This is the same as the ACL types. Specify a name for the template and any comments, and click OK to create. Figure 12-14 shows a new template being created to permit SNMP traffic.

Figure 12-14 *Creating a Template*

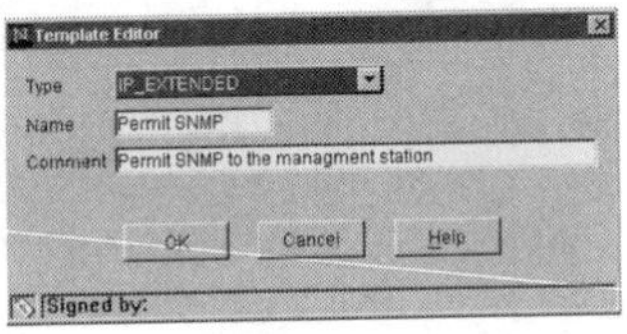

Step 5   Once the template is created the template will appear under the folder where it was created. A list of devices using the template will also appear.

Step 6   To use the template, begin by adding ACEs to the template. This is the same as the process explained earlier in adding ACEs to an access list. Choosing Include Template from the template menu will embed one template into another. Choose Template New ACE to begin adding ACEs.

Step 7   Once the ACEs have been applied to the template use the ACLM to apply the template to an access list.

Class Manager

The Class Manager application enables an administrator to define variables such as application ports and networks, which can be referenced by name when defining ACEs. Do this by defining TCP and UDP ports as services, devices, and Networks into groups called Network Classes.

Defining Services

Custom applications are deployed in many large TCP/IP networks. These applications must also be protected through access lists. The Cisco IOS comes with knowledge of many of the well-known ports used in the TCP and UDP protocols. When defining an access list to control custom or proprietary applications, however, the administrator must always remember the port numbers used by the application. The Class Manager allows an administrator to define an application port for TCP or UDP. This application will now show up in the list of available ports in the Edit ACE dialog box. Figure 12-15 displays how to create a UDP service for port 666 used by a video game.

To create a new Service, start by following the steps outlined as follows:

Step 1   Start Class Manager by using either selecting Resource Manager Essentials; Administration; ACL Management; Edit Class Definition application, or from ACLM selecting Class Manager using the Tools menu.

Step 2   The Class Manager is a two-window-paned application containing a folder and a content window. Select the Services folder from the Class Root folder.

Step 3   Click New Service from the toolbar or select New Service from the Class menu.

Step 4   The Service Editor window will appear. Select either TCP or UDP as the protocol. Enter a name for the new service and the port the service uses to connect.

Figure 12-15 *Creating a New Service*

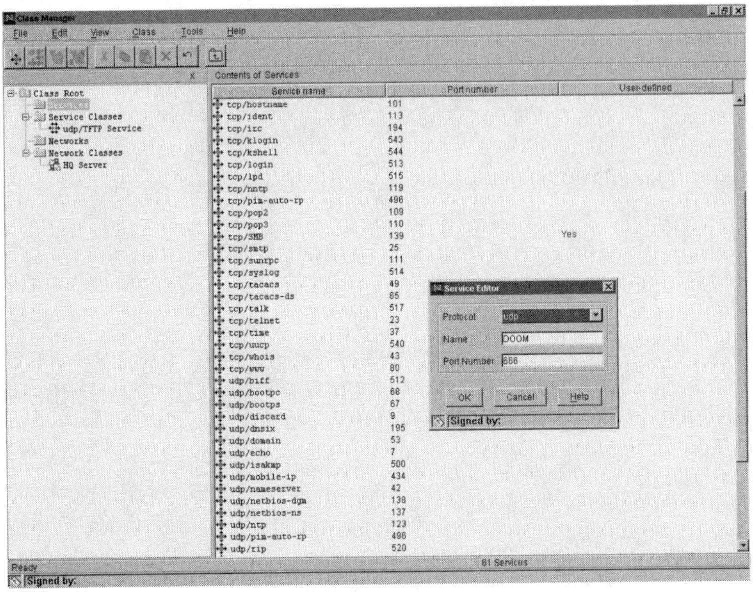

Services can be combined to define a Service Class. A Service Class can be used when multiple applications from one protocol type are used in tandem. For example, SNMP uses two ports—one for traps and one for messages. Services can be combined into a Service Class to make multiple services easier to use together. Therefore, if the Service Class is used to permit or deny traffic, it affects all the ports in the defined class. Service Classes can be embedded into each other to create larger, more modular classes. Figure 12-16 shows a new Service Class to permit SNMP and SNMP Traps.

Figure 12-16 *Creating a New Service Class*

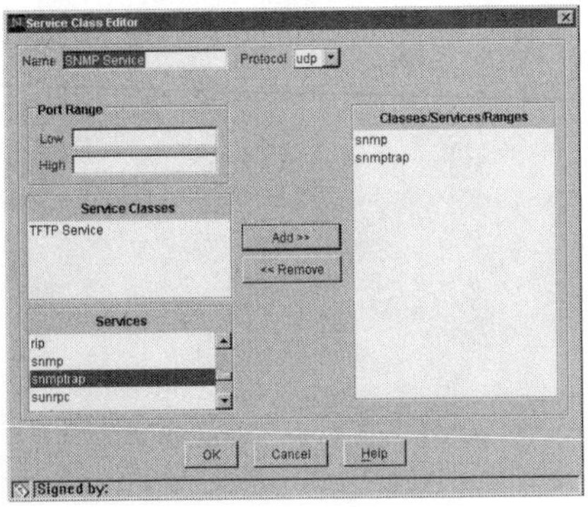

To create a Service Class, implement the following steps:

Step 1   Launch the Class Manager application.

Step 2   Select the Service Classes folder.

Step 3   Under the Class menu, select New Service Class.

Step 4   The Service Class Editor will appear. The Service Class Editor is explained in Table 12-5.

Table 12-5   *The Service Class Editor Dialog Box*

Field	Description
Name	Is the name of the Service Class.
Protocol	Is the protocol for the service—either TCP or UDP.
Port Range	Defines a range (lowest and highest) of port addresses to be added to the service class.
Service Classes	Lists all defined service classes that can be added to this service class.
Services	Lists all defined services that can be added to this service class.
Classes/Services/Ranges	Shows the classes, services, and port ranges belonging to this service class.
	Click Add to add an item from a left pane into Classes/Services/Ranges.
	Click Remove to remove an item from Classes/Services/Ranges.

Defining Network Classes

Administrators commonly define security policies for the same devices or subnets in the network. By using a network map the administrator can define which subnets refer to which network. However, looking at an access list without the network map and knowing which devices are being controlled through the list is difficult. The Class Manager tool enables an administrator to create networks and Network Classes. Networks can define one subnet. Network Classes group networks and define hosts in the subnet.

To create a network, select the New Network option from the Class menu or click New Networks from the toolbar. When the Network Editor dialog box appears, type in a Network Name, subnet address, and subnet mask. Figure 12-17 demonstrates creating a new network for the Headquarters subnet.

Figure 12-17 *Creating a New Network*

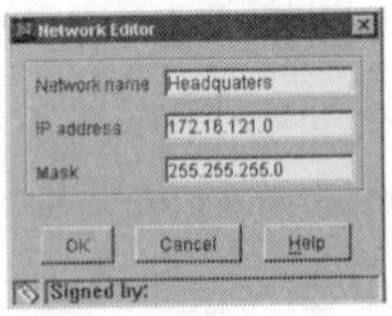

To create a Network Class, select the New Network Class option from the Class menu or the New Network Class icon from the toolbar. The Network Class Editor dialog box will appear as illustrated in Figure 12-18.

Figure 12-18 *The Network Class Editor Dialog box*

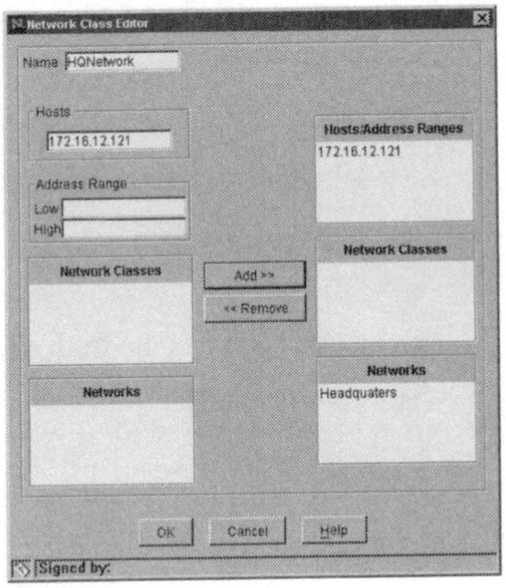

Table 12-6 explains the fields in the Network Class Editor dialog box.

Table 12-6 *The Network Class Dialog Box*

Field	Description
Name	Is the network class name.
Hosts	Is the name of a host to be added to the network class.
Address Range	Defines a range of IP addresses to be added to the Network Class.
Network Classes	Lists all defined network classes that can be added to this Network Class.
Networks	Lists all defined networks that can be added to this network class.
Hosts/Address Ranges	Shows the hosts and address ranges defined so far in this network class.

Once classes have been defined for both services and networks, the classes can be used in the definition of an ACE and can be used in templates. In Figure 12-19, the Service Class SNMP Service and the Network Class HQNetwork are used in the template Permit SNMP to enable SNMP to get to the management station in the HQNetwork.

Figure 12-19 *Putting Classes and Networks Together into a Template*

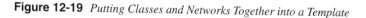

In the ACE Editor dialog box, click the Expand button to determine what statements the service class and network class will appear as in the access list in Figure 12-20.

Figure 12-20 *The ACE Editor Expand button*

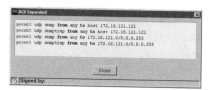

Applying Templates to Devices

Once you have defined templates, the templates can be applied to a device (or devices) through the wizards in the ACLM application. The ACL Use Wizard is a step-by-step tool for applying templates to a device's interfaces or terminal lines for traffic control. To start the ACL Use Wizard, start the ACLM by opening a scenario. Or, in Resource Manager

Essentials, choose ACL Management; Use ACL Templates. The steps for using the ACL Use Wizard are as follows:

Step 1 The ACL Use Wizard will first present an ACL Use Selection Box. From this box choose either Packet Filtering or Line Access.

Step 2 The next selection option is the Template Selection window. Select a Template to apply. Multiple Templates cannot be selected. However, use the Template Manager to group templates before using the wizard. Figure 12-21 shows a template called Combo, which includes multiple IP Extended templates being applied to device 172.16.121.1.

Figure 12-21 *The ACL Template Use Wizard*

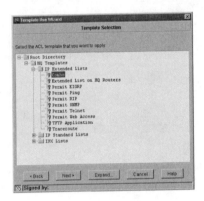

Step 3 The Router Selection screen is next. The routers in the scenario will be in the selection box. Select one or more routers.

Step 4 The interface selection screen is next. Select one or more interfaces for either in or out or both directions. If multiple devices were chosen and the template will be applied the same way, select the "Treat all subsequent devices exactly like this device?" check box. Figure 12-22 shows the ACL Template Use Wizard interface selection screen. Interface e0/0 has been selected on device 172.16.121.1.

Figure 12-22 *The ACL Use Wizard*

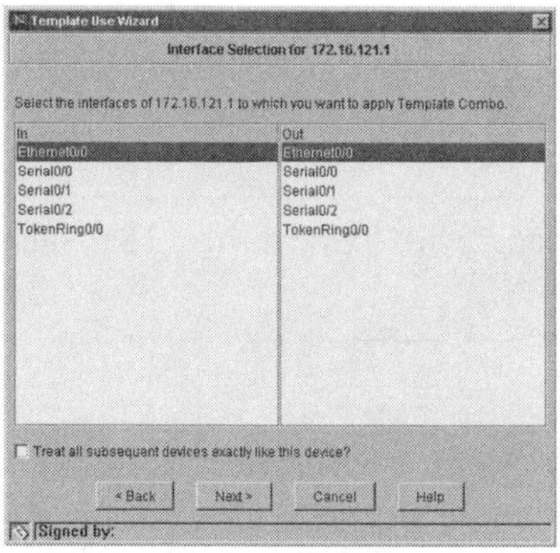

Step 5   The Summary window will appear next. The Summary window will list the devices and interfaces to be modified and the template to be applied. Two check boxes are available. The "Overwrite exiting ACLs and uses?" check box will overwrite any existing access lists on the interfaces with the new lists. The "Auto number the new ACL?" check box will assign the next available number to the list on each device. Auto numbering could lead to different devices using different numbers for the same template. If the Auto Number option is not selected, you can specify a name in the ACL Name box. Figure 12-23 shows the ACL Template Use Wizard Summary window for the changes on 172.16.121.1.

Figure 12-23 *The Template Use Wizard Summary Window*

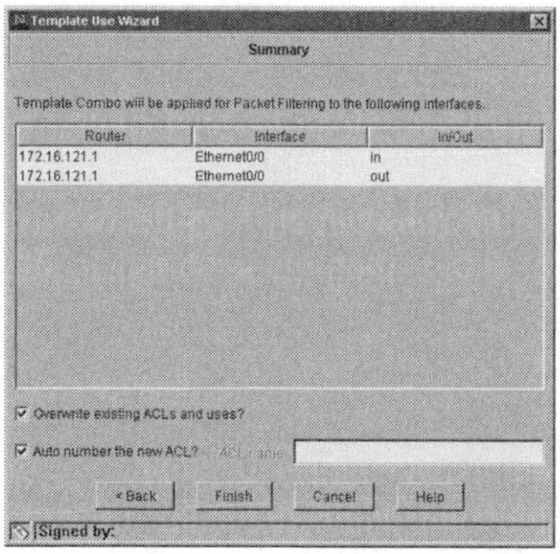

Step 6 Click Finish to see the Results window. The Results window will display the same information as the Summary window. The number selected by Auto Number will also be displayed if the result was okay or if an error was encountered.

NOTE   This does not download the list to the device. That must be done through the ACL Downloader tool.

To apply templates to a single device, select the device in the folder pane. Then right-click on the device and choose the Apply Template menu option. The Apply Template tool will work just like the ACL Use Wizard except that the device selection window will not appear.

To apply templates to existing ACLs, select ACL in the ACL Definitions folder under the device to be modified. Select the ACL; New Include Template to add the template to the existing ACLs.

Applying ACLs to Interfaces

If an ACL is created outside of the ACL Use Wizard, the ACL is not applied to any interfaces. The ACL can be applied to interfaces through ACL Manager with the following steps:

Step 1 In ACLM, select an ACL in the folder window under the device in the ACL Definitions folder.

Step 2 To apply the ACL to interfaces, choose Use ACL from the Edit menu, or right-click on the ACL and choose Use ACL.

Step 3 The ACL Use Selection dialog box will appear. If the ACL supports both packet filtering and line access, select a use. Click Next to continue.

Step 4 The Line Selection or Interface Selection window will now appear. Select the lines or interfaces for the list to be applied in each direction (in and out).

Step 5 The Summary window will appear, listing the device, interfaces, and direction.

Step 6 Choose whether to overwrite existing ACLs and uses.

Step 7 Click Finish. The Results window will display the same information as the Summary window and will display the status of the update. Click Close to return to the ACL Manager.

NOTE	The update will not be applied to the physical device until the ACL Downloader tool is used to download changes.

The ACL Downloader Tool

The last step in applying access lists to a device is to download the changes to the device using the ACL Downloader tool. Until this tool is run, nothing is actually done to the device.

If the device is modified while the scenario is loaded, the device will become stale and its icon will turn gray.

Before performing a download, the ACLM first verifies that the selected device is the same as when the tool was opened. Choosing Refresh Device from the View menu will manually do this. If the device has changed, you will be warned that changes made in the scenario could possibly be lost. To determine what changes were made, use the Resource Manager Configuration Management tools to report on the differences between the current configuration and archived copies. If the changes on the device will not affect the ACLM, then refresh the device.

The Refresh Device option will remove changes made in the ACL Use portion of the program—it does not affect any templates or classes. If changes have been lost, reapply the changes before proceeding with the download. In Figure 12-24, device 172.16.121.1 has been modified while the ACLM was open and therefore is now stale.

Figure 12-24 *Stale Devices*

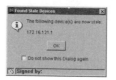

In Figure 12-25, the device 172.16.121.1 is going to be refreshed. Access list 100 has been applied through the ACL Use Wizard and will not be in the refreshed configuration of device 172.16.121.1. If a job were created for download to a device before it showed up as stale in the ACL Manager, the job would therefore fail.

Figure 12-25 *The Refresh Device Dialog Box*

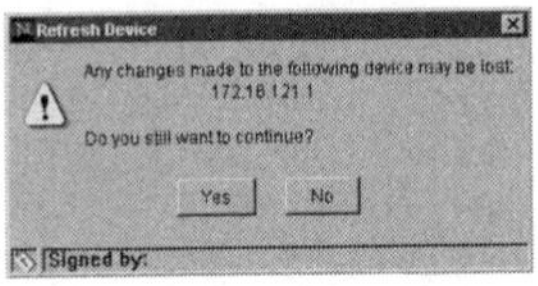

Figure 12-26 shows the access lists after the refresh has removed access list 100 from device 172.16.121.1, reflecting the updated configuration.

Figure 12-26 *The Refreshed Configuration*

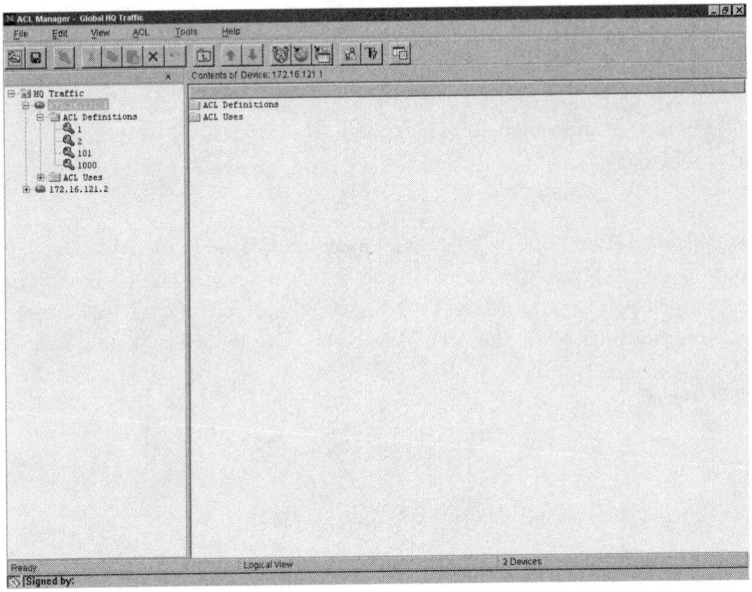

The download process starts with the ACL Downloader Tool. Click the icon on the toolbar or choose ACL Downloader from the Tools menu. The Downloader can also be started from Resource Manager Essentials by selecting ACL Management; Schedule Downloads. The Schedule Downloads dialog box will first require selecting a scenario from the Scenario list.

The steps for the ACL Downloader are as follows:

Step 1   The Schedule Config Download Job window will appear. The dialog box is explained in Table 12-7 (at the end of this list). Figure 12-27 shows the Schedule Config Download Job dialog box.

Figure 12-27 *The ACL Downloader Tool*

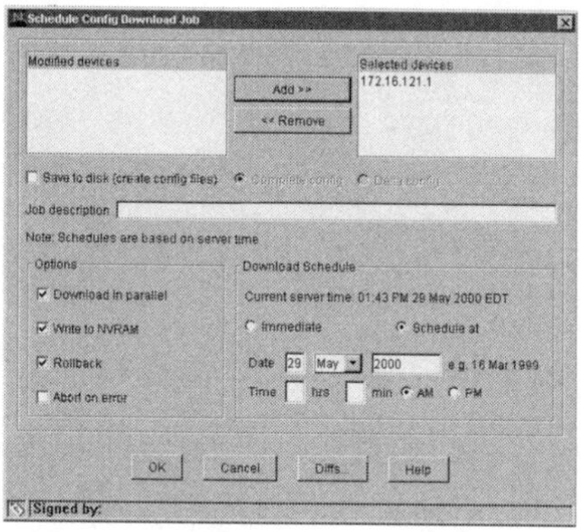

Step 2   Click the Diffs button to view the differences between the original configuration and the changes to be made by the access lists.

Step 3   In the Config Diff View window, select the config button to view the complete configuration for a device. Click the Delta button to view the commands to be sent to the device. Figure 12-28 shows the Config Diff View dialog box and the commands that will be sent to device 172.16.121.1.

Figure 12-28 *Displaying the IOS Commands to be Downloaded for a Given Device*

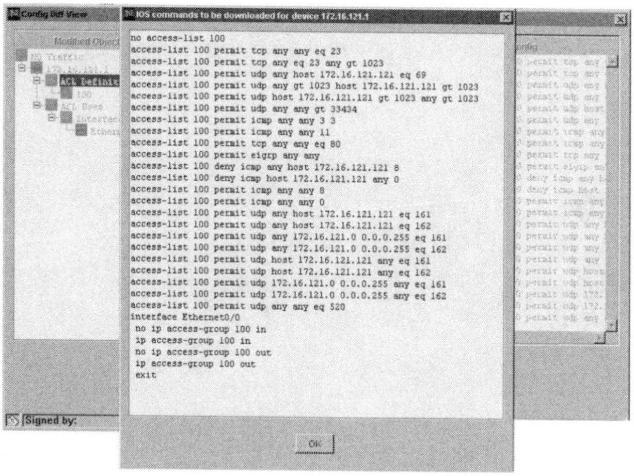

Step 4   Click OK to create the job. If the scenario has not been saved, the program will prompt to save the scenario. Click Yes to proceed.

Step 5 If the scheduled job was selected to start immediately, a prompt to start the job will appear.

Step 6 The job number will be displayed and created.

Step 7 After the job is created use the Job Browser tool to view the job status. To access the job outside of ACL Manager, use Resource Manager Essentials; ACL Management; Browse Download Jobs. Figure 12-29 shows the Job Browser window with Job 1015 as the job created to update device 172.16.121.1.

Figure 12-29 *The Job Browser Window*

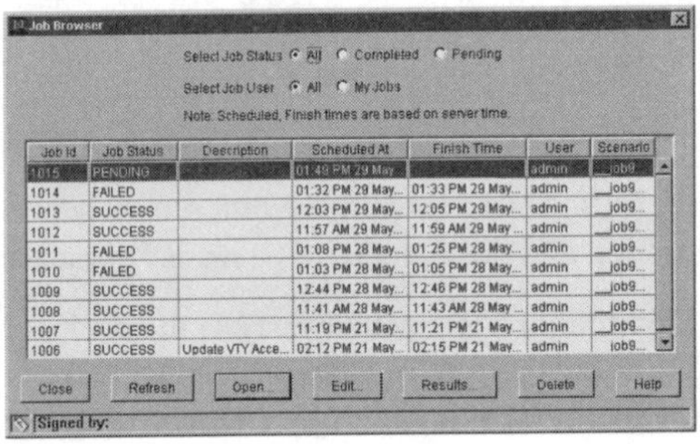

Step 8 Upon Successful completion of the job, the job status will change to Success in the Browse Download Jobs window. Click Results to view the job options selected, when the job ran, and the affected devices. Figure 12-30 shows that job 1015 has completed successfully, as well as the time and the device updated by examining the job results window.

Figure 12-30 *The Job Results Window*

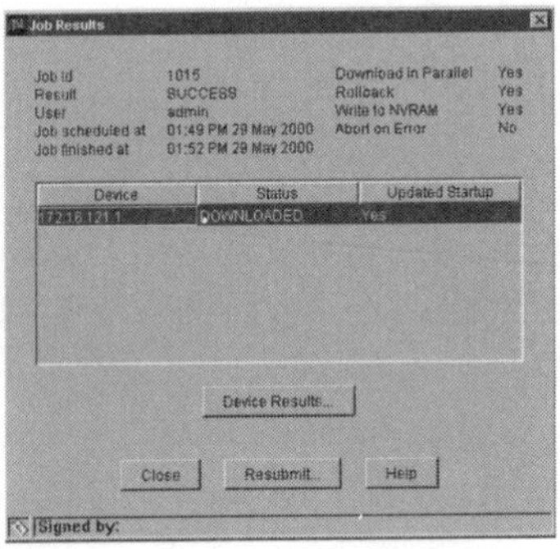

Table 12-7   *The Schedule Config Download Dialog Box*

Field	Description
Modified devices/Selected devices	Lists the modified devices. Click Add to move the devices to the Selected Devices window.
Save to disk (create config files)	Saves either the complete config or delta config to the disk without making changes to the device. The files will be created under *%NMSROOT%\objects\aclm\aclmTest\ __GlobalScenarios__* as the device name for the file name. Select Complete config to save the complete config or Delta config to just see the changes.
Job description	Shows a job description to appear in the job report.
Download in parallel	Downloads all devices at once if selected. If not selected, the download occurs in order of how the devices are listed in the Selected Devices box. The order in which the devices are added dictates how they are listed.
Write to NVRAM	Copies the router's Running Configuration to the Startup Configuration upon successful job completion.
Rollback	Makes an effort to restore the device to its original state if an error occurs. The job download will continue on other devices.
Abort on error	Aborts on an error and will stop the job on all devices. It will also restore all devices back to their original state if an error occurs.
Download Schedule	Will perform the download immediately if selected (five minutes after job creation), or select a date and time to run the job.

The ACL Optimizer Tools

An access list can be more than 100 lines in length and affect hundreds of devices in one statement. An access list processes the statements in the list in the order each was entered. Any access lists outbound on that interface affect every packet that leaves an interface. On the inbound, the same processing happens for these lists. If the access list is long and the statement that either permits or denies the packet is at the end of the list, the packet will be delayed.

In TCP/IP and IPX access lists, a single statement can affect hundreds or even thousands of hosts. This is accomplished through wildcard masks in the list. In a live environment, access lists are always changing by adding statements and removing statements. The new statements could affect traffic from devices already affected in other statements. The statements are either redundant, which will make the list longer than necessary, or just incorrect.

ACLM includes two tools to improve the performance of access lists—the ACL Optimizer and the ACL Hits Optimizer. The ACL Optimizer will remove redundant and unnecessary statements, aggregates statements with masks, and merges port ranges. The ACL Hits Optimizer will examine the hit count on an extended access list and rearrange statements based on the highest hit count without affecting semantics.

The ACL Optimizer

The ACL Optimizer can be used on IP standard and extended access lists. The ACL Optimizer does not require any user intervention to determine how to reduce the number of statements in an access list. To use the ACL Optimizer, read the following steps:

Step 1 Create a Scenario that includes the devices that will have their access lists optimized. If one already exists then open the scenario.

Step 2 Select the access list to be optimized from the ACL Definitions window under the device.

Step 3 From the Tools menu, select Optimizer.

Step 4 The Optimized ACL Statements will appear in a window. At the bottom of the window, the Optimization Summary will list the number of entries before optimization, number of entries after optimization, and the percentage in improvement after optimization. Figure 12-31 shows how the access list created for device 172.16.121.1 could be optimized to provide better performance with fewer statements.

Figure 12-31 *The ACL Optimizer*

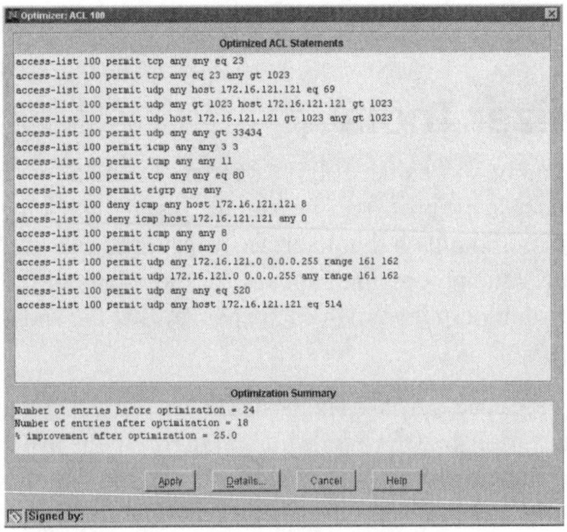

Step 5 Select Details to verify the changes made from the original list to the new list. The display is broken into three panes. One contains the old list, another the new list, and the third details the changes made to the list. Lines that were deleted will be colored blue in the old list window, lines that are changed will be colored red, and any lines inserted will be colored green. Click Done to continue. Figure 12-32 shows the Details window for the suggested changes to device 172.16.121.1.

Figure 12-32 *Optimization Details for a Given Access List*

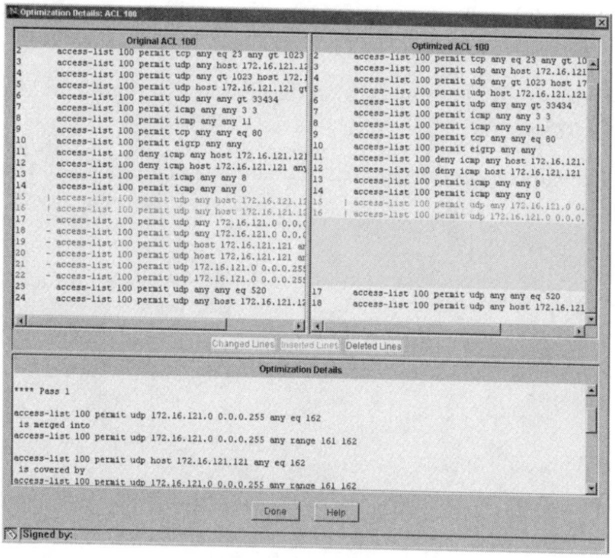

Step 6 If the changes are satisfactory, click Apply to make the changes.

Step 7 After the changes are applied you must download the changes through the ACL Downloader. The ACL Downloader will delete the current version of the access list and apply the new one. This action is important because removing the old list will lose any hit counts.

If an existing ACL is going to be saved as a template, first use the ACL Optimizer to improve the list before creating the list as a template.

Before using the Hits Optimizer, run the ACL Optimizer to consolidate the statements. The ACL Optimizer will make changes that will affect the hit count on all the access list lines. After the changes have been made and the device has used the list and successfully generated new hit counts, run the Hits Optimizer.

The ACL Hit Optimizer

IP and IPX extended access lists maintain counts of each time a line on an access list affects the packet. If a line causes a packet to be permitted or denied, then this constitutes a hit. The ACL Optimizer will rearrange the statements in an access list to move the ones with the most hits towards the top of the list without changing how the list works. The steps to use the ACL Hits Optimizer are as follows:

Step 1 Open a Scenario that contains the devices that will have their ACLs modified.

Step 2 Select the ACL in the ACL Definitions folder under the appropriate device.

Step 3 From the Tools menu or by right-clicking on the list, select the Hits Optimizer.

Step 4 The Hits Optimizer will examine the list and display the hit count for each line. Figure 12-33 displays an access list on device 172.16.121.2 being optimized for hits.

Figure 12-33 *The ACL Hits Optimizer*

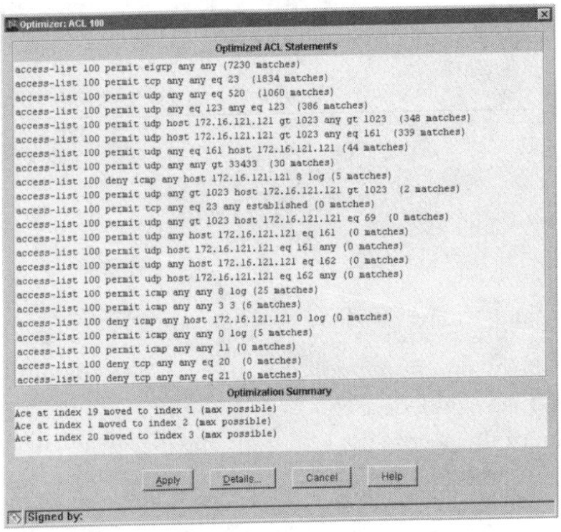

Step 5 When the Hits Optimizer has decided on the optimization, it will display the newly modified list. Click Details to view the differences between the old and new lists.

The Details window will display information on the same format as the ACL Optimizer. The Optimization Details window will display how the statements were rearranged and any conflicts that occurred between permit and deny statements. Figure 12-34 displays the details produced by the optimization of access list 100 on device 172.16.121.2.

Figure 12-34 *The Optimization Details Window Displays Changes Made to Access Lists*

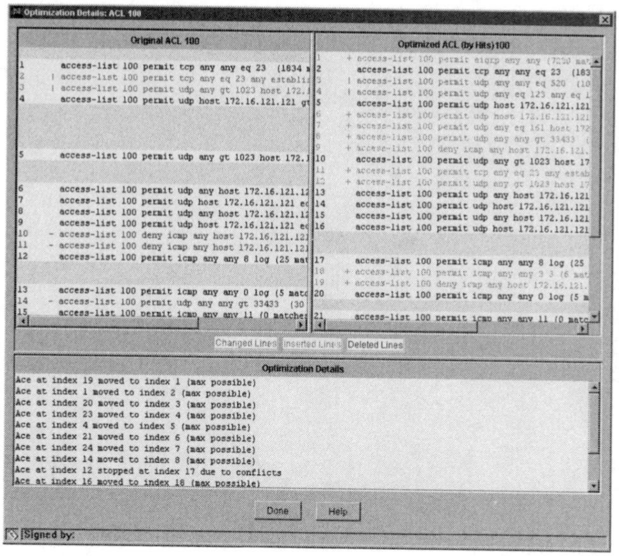

Step 6   Click Done to proceed.

Step 7   If the changes are acceptable, click Apply to apply the list changes.

Step 8   After the changes have been applied, they must be downloaded using the ACL Downloader tool.

Resetting Counters

The counters used to make decisions by the ACL Hits Optimizer are stored on the router. If substantial changes happen to the traffic patterns passing through the router or for trouble-shooting purposes, clearing these counters might be beneficiary. The hits can be cleared on the router using the **clear access-list counters** command. The counters may be removed device by device using this command. The counters can also be reset from Resource Manager Essentials. To reset counters in Resource Manager Essentials, select Administration; ACL Management; Reset Hit Counter. Select the devices' counters you wish to reset from either a view or list, and then click Finish. The ACLM will telnet to the devices and execute the command to clear the access list counters. A message will be displayed upon successful completion. Figure 12-35 shows the counters cleared on two devices: 172.16.121.1 and 172.16.121.2.

Figure 12-35 *Reset Hit Counters*

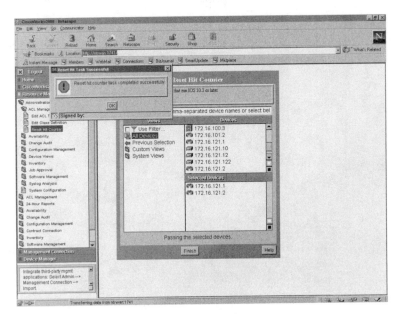

Summary

This chapter discussed how to use ACLM to create and manage Access-Control Lists. Access list configuration is normally performed at the command line and can be quite a complex task in a large internetwork. ACLM eases a lot of the administrative burden of creating access lists by providing easy-to-use graphical interfaces. Templates allow an administrator to build access lists through modules that can serve as building blocks for a secure environment. Changing access lists through the ACLM is much more efficient than command-line modification. Making changes through templates can affect multiple devices with one modification. Using the ACL Optimizer tool and the Hits Optimizer tool, an access list can be modified to perform more efficiently and even help to correct errors in the list.

ACLM creates access lists in devices maintained by the Resource Manager environment. Previously discussed Essentials' tools provide the information necessary for the ACLM to function. The Inventory Manager provides the information to access the device, and the Configuration Management provides the ability to change configurations and maintain access list information. Without these tools, the ACLM would not operate.

Chapter 13, "Availability and Connectivity Tools," demonstrates how to further use the inventory information to monitor device availability.

Topics covered in this chapter include the following:

- Availability Tool Features
- Configuring Polling Features
- Availability Reports
- Troubleshooting Availability Tools
- Connectivity Tools

Availability and Connectivity Tools

Previous chapters detailed the numerous tools and reports that Resource Manager Essentials offers. Tools, such as Inventory Management, Configuration Management, and Software Image Management, provide proactive detailed device management. This chapter discusses additional reporting tools—the Availability Tools and the Connectivity Tools.

The Availability Tools aid in reactive network management for mission-critical devices. The Availability Tools are not intended to replace a full Network Monitoring tool, such as IPSwitch's "What's Up Gold" or HP Openview Network Node Manager.

Rather the Availability Tools are intended to monitor critical devices to record device availability statistics into the Resource Manager Essentials' Database. The Availability Tools depend on views, which are created by using the information generated by the Inventory Manager. By using views, an administrator can dictate devices polled and the devices' polling intervals. The polling process can be resource-intensive on the server and the network. Keep the number of devices polled to a minimum to restrict the overhead incurred by the polling process. The frequency of polling also impacts the overhead created. The more frequent the polling, the greater the overhead on the server and network.

CiscoWorks 2000 Server provides other tools for testing network connectivity in real-time. These tools can be used on any device in the network.

Availability Tool Features

The Availability Tools are HTML-based tools for monitoring device availability in the network. Availability is verified using the ICMP ping application. By using the Availability Tools, an administrator can track network status through the following reports:

- **The Reachability Dashboard Report**—Can provide a quick overview of devices in the selected views and the device's last reporting time.

- **The Availability Monitor Report**—Can provide more detailed information about a device's response percentage the last time the device was polled. The average response time is also presented for the same polling period.

- **The Reloads Report**—Displays information about the previous five reloads of the selected devices and the respective reload reason. If the device experienced a software crash, the Stack Decoder Trace can help determine the reason for the Stack Dump.

- **The Offline Device Report**—Lists any devices that have been determined to be offline by being nonresponsive to polling requests during the last polling interval.

- **The Protocol Distribution Graph**—Displays a graphical breakdown of Layer 3 protocol traffic including IP, IPX, AppleTalk, DECnet, and XNS. This application is applicable to devices that process traffic at Layer 3. Layer 2 switches do not report these statistics.

Before the Availability Tools can be used, you must configure polling intervals.

Configuring Polling Features

Polling intervals are applied to the Availability Tools based upon views. The status of the devices contained in the view(s) will be verified at every polling interval. Multiple views can be used for setting polling options. However, all views use the same polling settings. Figure 13-1 shows the Select Polled View screen.

Figure 13-1 *The Select Polled Views Screen*

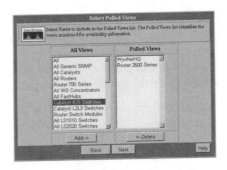

Devices can overlap more than one view because all views get the same polling intervals. To set polling options, select Resource Manager Essentials; Administration; Availability; Change Polling Options.

Table 13-1 explains the fields in the Polling Options dialog box pictured in Figure 13-2, as well as what options are available.

Table 13-1 *Polling Interval Options*

Option	Description	Default	Minimum/Maximum
Poll Reload and Protocol Distribution Every	Interval at which protocol distribution and reload statistics are collected. To improve system performance, increase this value.	2 Hours	1 Hour/4 Hours
Verify Interface Status Every	Interval at which interface status data is collected. To improve system performance, increase this value.	60 min	15 min/120 min
Verify Device Reachability Every	Interval at which the ICMP poller collects data. To improve system performance, increase this value.	30 min	5 min/60 min
Remove Data Older Than	Number of days of data to be saved. This value is determined in part by the amount of available disk space.	3 days	3 days/9 days
Number of Ping Packets	Number of ICMP probe packets sent to each device to determine availability.	4 times	2 times/5 times
Initial SNMP Timeout	Initial SNMP response timeout.	10 sec	10 sec/90 sec
Number of SNMP Retries	Number of times SNMP will retry the device	2 times	2 times/6 times

Figure 13-2 *The Change Polling Options Dialog Box*

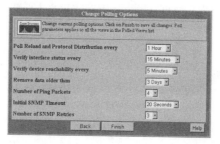

The Availability Monitor and Reachability Dashboard Reports use ICMP Pings to test connectivity to network devices. Make sure that the Resource Manager Essentials' Server has the ability to ping all of the devices being polled. If access-lists have been configured to prevent the routers or switches from receiving ICMP, modify the list to allow the Resource Manager Essentials to ping the polled devices. The response time reading is also dependent on ICMP having the same priority in the network as other traffic. If any queuing has been implemented it will impact the response time reading.

After at least one polling interval has passed, the Availability Monitor's reports will be populated with data, which can be used to examine the Availability Statistics.

Availability Reports

The Availability reports can provide an administrator a quick overall view of the health of mission-critical devices. The information is presented based on the last polling process. Understanding the polling process is not constant so the information is not live information. A device could have experienced a momentary outage at the polling time and therefore will be reported as unresponsive.

Other tools are available in CiscoWorks 2000 to test real-time connectivity. The tools Ping, Traceroute, NSLookup, and Management Station to Device will be discussed later in this chapter.

Reachability Dashboard Report

The Reachability Dashboard report can be used to obtain a quick overview of the status of the polled devices. The simple display makes it quick to recognize any device experiencing a connectivity problem. The Reachability Dashboard Report also provides easy access to the Device Center. As well, other tools can be launched from the Device Center to examine the status of the device.

To access the Reachability Dashboard report, use Resource Manager Essentials; Availability; Reachability. Polling must be configured before any information will be available.

The Reachability Dashboard report lists the different views currently selected for polling and the devices contained in those views. The devices are listed as unreachable if a red arrow pointing down appears next to the device name. If a device is reachable, a green arrow pointing up appears next to the device name. The last time the device was responsive is listed next to the device name. The Reachability Dashboard report in Figure 13-3 is polling three different views. The views are broken into separate windowpanes. To view more detailed device information, select the hyperlink of the device name. The Device Center will be launched. To get more detailed information about the group of devices in the view, select the hyperlink of the view name and the Availability Monitor report will be launched.

Figure 13-3 *The Reachability Dashboard*

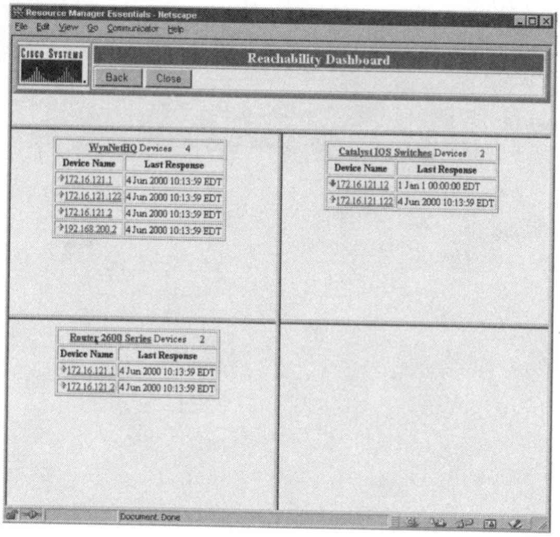

The Device Center

The Device Center is a powerful tool enabling an administrator to view all available information about a device in one report. The Device Center provides access to over 15 different tools and reports within Resource Manager. The tool could be used, for example, if a device is reported as unavailable—an administrator could obtain hardware information about the device, Syslog messages, or even view the configuration file. If the device supports a web interface such as the 2900XL Catalyst Switch, the interface can be accessed from the Device Center. Figure 13-4 shows the Device Center accessing the Visual Switch Manager Home application on a 2900XL Catalyst Switch.

Figure 13-4 *The Device Center*

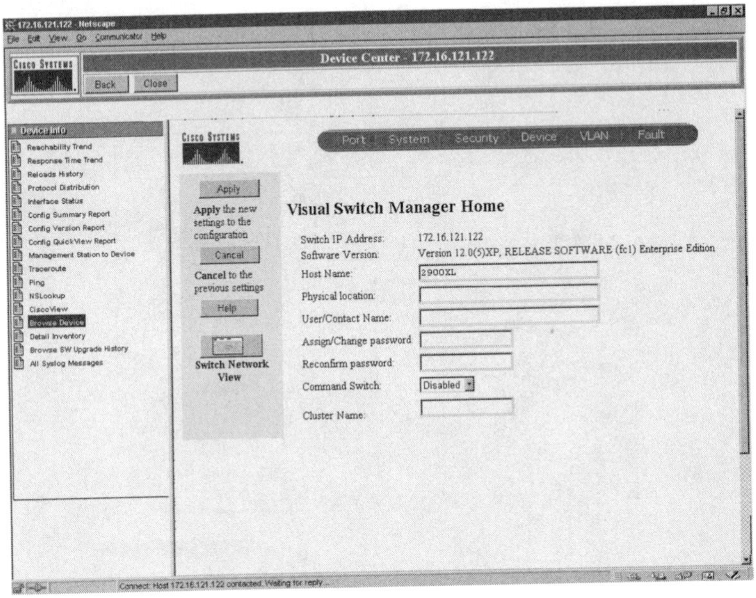

Availability Monitor Report

The Availability Monitor report provides all of the statistics of the Reachability Dashboard report along with a response time in MS and in percentage of the response. The Reachability Percentage and Response Time are based upon the last polled response. The devices interface status is also included. This tool is useful for light trend analysis. For example, if users complain that a device is slow or traffic becomes congested, use the Availability Monitor report to view current and past information on a device's response time and availability.

The interface polled is based upon the device's name, so this might not reflect the true overall health of the device. The device's name only corresponds to one TCP/IP address. This scenario could give the impression that a device is available when only one interface remains up, or the opposite and show a device is down if only one interface fails.

Figure 13-5 shows the Availability Monitor report launched from the Reachability Dashboard report.

Figure 13-5 *The Availability Monitor*

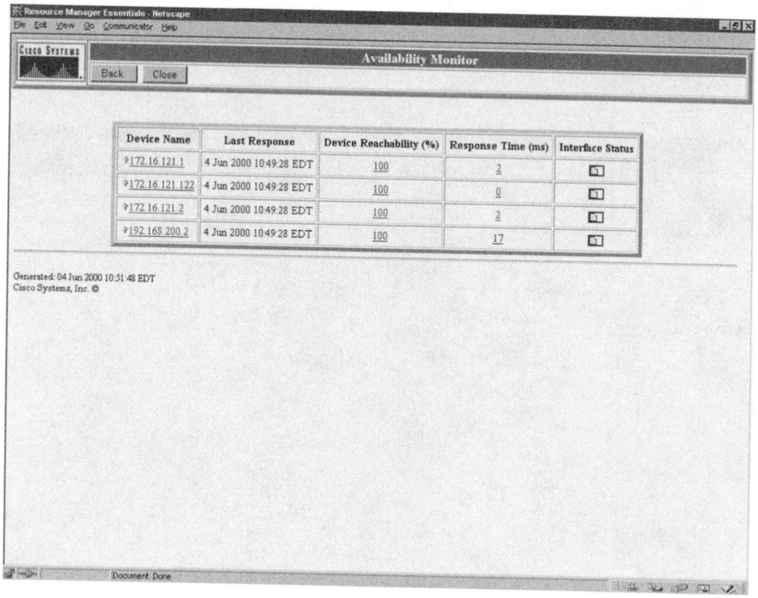

The columns in the Availability Monitor are described as follows:

- **Device Name**—The name or TCP/IP address of the device that was polled.
- **Device Reachability (%)**—The percentage of reachability during the last polling process. This is not cumulative over polling periods. For example, if the polling sends four pings each polling interval and during one interval two pings time out due to congestion, then the percentage will reflect only 50% reachability. This is only on the last polling process, not a trend over time.
- **Response Time (ms)**—The average response time in the last polling interval, not a trend over time.
- **Interface Status**—Shows the status of the interfaces on the device. Used on routers to determine interface status.

The Back button at the top of the window returns to the Reachability Dashboard report.

The device name, response time, and reachability percentage are all hyperlinks that will launch more detailed reports. Selecting the hyperlink for the device name will launch the Device Center. The response time hyperlink will launch a report of the available polling information for response time trend analysis.

Figure 13-6 shows the response time trends for device 192.168.200.2. Device 192.168.200.2 is connected to a serial interface on 172.16.121.2. The device had 0 response time overnight of June 3, 2000 to June 4, 2000. This could indicate the link was down or the device was off during that period of time. It is important to recognize that the response time of 0 is not an indication of good performance. This could be misleading to an administrator not aware it could in fact indicate the device was offline.

Figure 13-6 *Device Response Time*

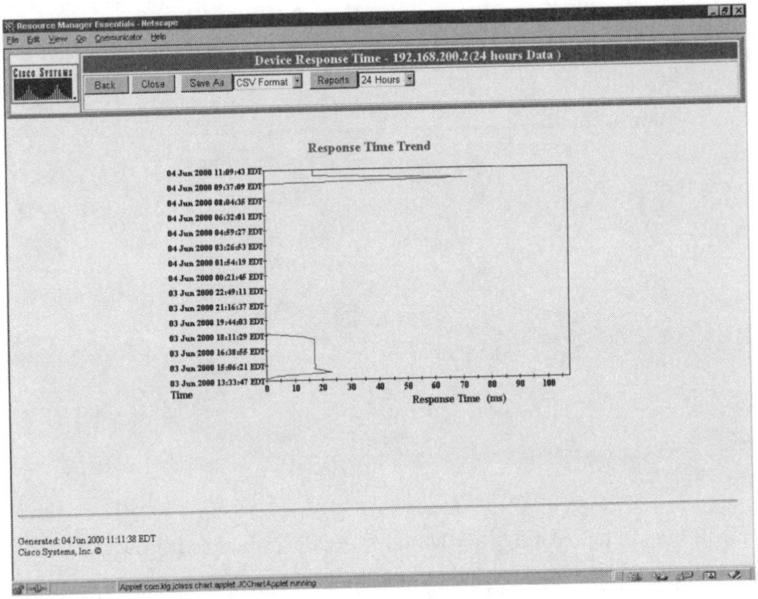

By viewing just the last 24 hours, more detailed information can be determined about response time. Launch the Device Center to determine if any Syslog messages were recorded. The Reload Report can also be used to determine if the device was reloaded during that time.

The reachability percentage launches a report listing reachability trends from the polled data on the server for that device. This information can be used to perform trend analysis. This is a very simple form of trend analysis because only the ping application is used to verify reachability. Do not use this as a definitive tool for trend analysis. The reachability percentage can provide a quick overview.

Figure 13-7 shows the reachability for device 192.168.200.2. Notice the device had a period of being unreachable over the past 24 hours.

Figure 13-7 *The Device Reachability Percentage*

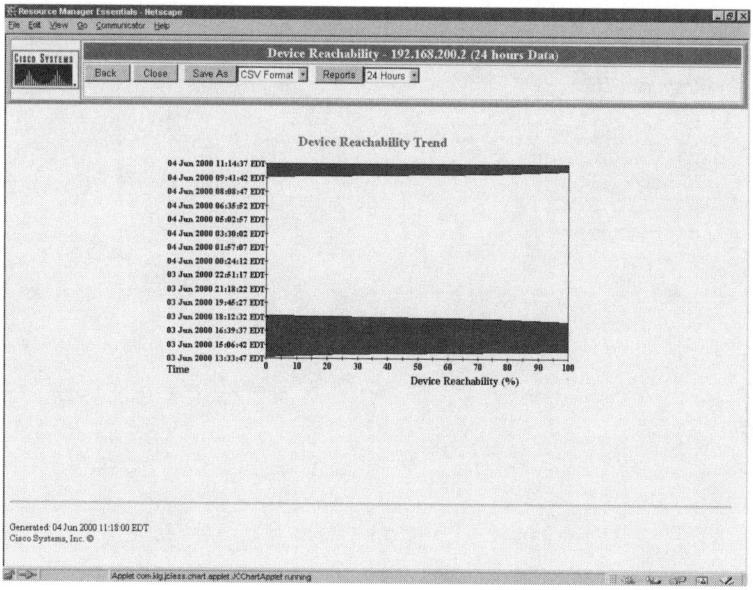

From the top of either of the report windows, select 24 hours from the reports drop-down dialog box to view just the last 24 hours. Select All Data to view all recorded data stored in the availability tables.

Selecting interface status from the Availability Monitor report lists the status of the individual interfaces on the device. The update time, operational status, admin status, speed in bps, physical address, and TCP/IP network address are displayed in the report. Figure 13-8 shows the status of the serial interface on 172.16.121.2, which is connected to the serial interface on 192.168.200.2.

Figure 13-8 *The Interface Status*

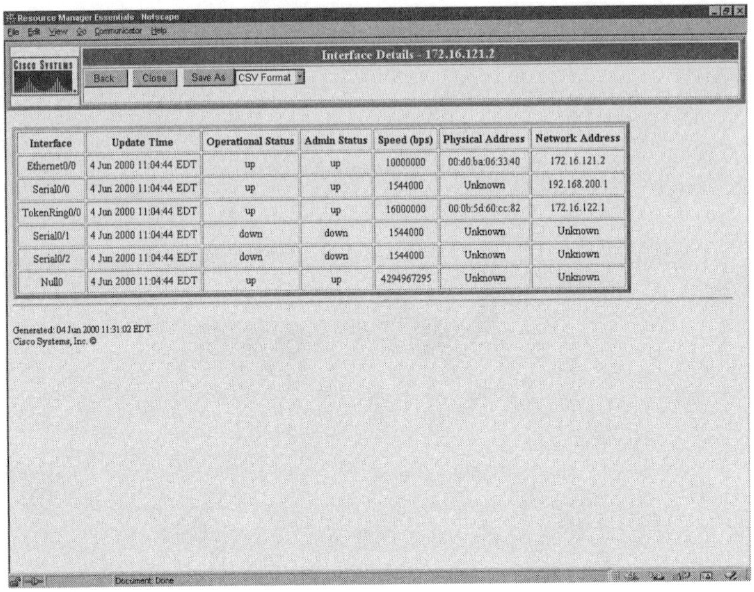

The Reloads Report

The Reloads Report uses the reloadReason MIB to report on the reloads of a device and the reload cause.

The Reloads Report is useful to determine if a device has a software defect that causes the device to reload. The reload report displays information about the last five reloads and the reason for the reload. If the device experienced an unexpected reload that caused a stack dump, the built-in stack decoder and trace tool will automatically try to determine the cause of the reload.

An unexpected reload is a reload for any reason other than power-on or user initiated. When the reload report appears, click on the reload reason. The Reload Report can also be used to determine if a device was powered on and off in the last five polling intervals.

In Figure 13-9, the Reloads Report is used to determine if 192.168.200.2 powered down over the last 24 hours. This helps to detect device failures. The Reloads Report for device 192.168.200.2 was launched from Resource Manager Essentials; Availability; Reloads Report. In the Reloads Report, select the device(s) to view their reload history.

Figure 13-9 *The Reloads Report*

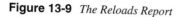

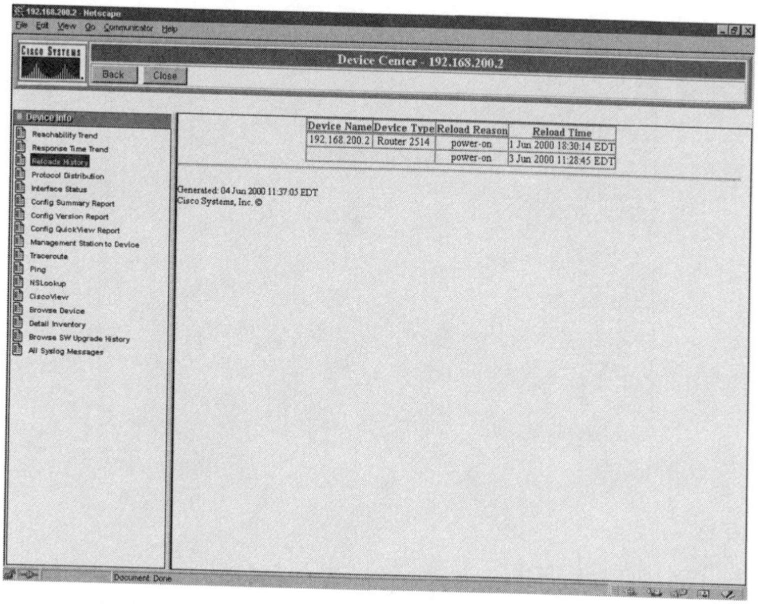

The Reloads Report is also available in the Device Center by selecting Reloads History. Figure 13-9 does not reflect any change in status for device 192.168.200.2 from June 3, 2000. Possibly this is because a reload poll has not happened yet. Wait at least one polling interval past the prior interval to see if the status changes.

To determine when the last poll for reload took place, open the RELOADS.PROT_DIST file and view the time of the last poll of the devices listed. Figure 13-10 shows the RELOADS.PROT_DIST file. This file is located on the Resource Manager Essentials server in %NMSROOT%\objects\availability\data\RELOAD.PROT_DIST. Notice that the last poll was at 11:04 a.m. The current time on the server is 11:58 a.m.

In the Reloads Report, click the hyperlink under the name of the device to launch the Device Center.

Figure 13-10 *The RELOAD.PROT_DIST File*

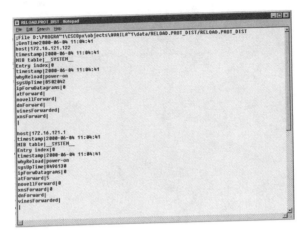

The Offline Device Report

The Offline Device Report lists devices that have been unresponsive to polling. The devices listed must have been set up for availability polling to be monitored. The report can display devices that have not responded to polls in the last 3, 6, 12, 24, 48, or 72 hours. If a device has been unresponsive, the device name and last time of response will be listed in the report. This information can be useful if the Availability Monitor shows a device as not available. The report can help to determine for how long the device has been offline.

The Offline Device Report is also useful to determine any devices in the inventory that might have been removed from the network but not the Resource Manager Essentials database. Figure 13-11 shows the offline device report. Device 172.16.121.12 has been offline since January 1. This could indicate that the device is no longer in the network or its name has been changed.

Figure 13-11 *The Devices OffLine Report*

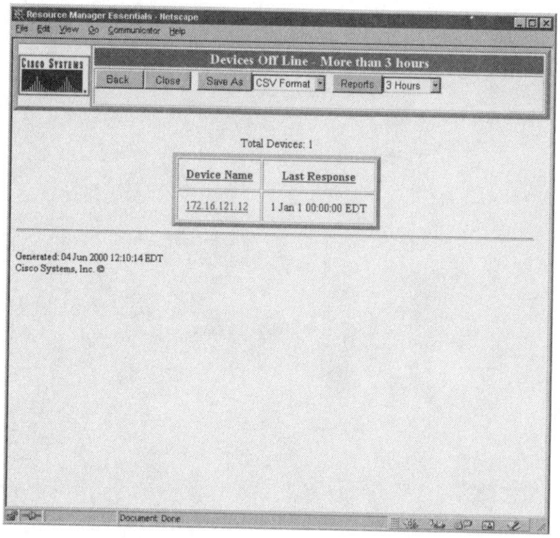

The Protocol Distribution Graph
=====================

The Protocol Distribution Graph

The Protocol Distribution Graph displays Layer 3 protocol distribution in a bar graph or pie chart. The TCP/IP, IPX, AppleTalk, DECnet, and XNS protocols can be monitored by the graph. The graph reads information from the database gathered by the polling process. This information is not produced in real-time. All devices have their statistics aggregated in the report. For individual statistics, run each device separately. Figure 13-12 shows the protocol distribution graph for the WynNetHQ view. This information is available only from Layer 3 devices.

Figure 13-12 *The Protocol Distribution Graph*

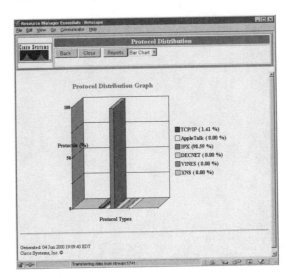

Troubleshooting Availability Tools

The Availability Tools generate CPU overhead on the server based on how many devices are polled and how often. If too many devices are polled too often, overhead is generated on the server and on the network.

The overhead generated can cause network congestion and performance degradation. Therefore, poll mission-critical devices using intervals only occur when absolutely necessary.

Table 13-2 explains the different processes that are used.

Table 13-2 *Availability Processes*

Process	What It Does
AvInputGen	Creates two input files, icmpinput.txt and pollerinput.txt, that store the list of devices to poll, polling options, and so on. The files are located in *%NMSROOT%\Objects\availability\data*.

continues

Table 13-2 *Availability Processes (Continued)*

Process	What It Does
AvSnmpPoller/AvIcmpPoller	Collects data such as interface status, device reloads, and so on. After each polling cycle, the poller process creates or updates the output file. The files generated are located in *%NMSROOT%\Objects\ availability\data*. There are three subdirectories that contain the raw data: *AVAIL_ICMP*, *AVAIL_STATUS*, and *RELOAD.PROT_DIST*. Each contains a text file with the same name as the directory. This text file has the raw data.
AvLoader	Loads the data from the poller into the respective database tables.
AvTrimmer	Deletes Availability data older than the specified settings in the Availability Polling Options.

The processes also generate log files. The log files are located in *%NMSROOT%\log* where *%NMSROOT%* is the directory the software is installed into. The files are the same name as the processes. The logs contain information about errors loading data into tables, accessing devices, process startup, and other useful pieces of information. To verify that the processes are running, use CiscoWorks2000 Server; Administration; Process Management; Process Status. Figure 13-13 shows the Process Status Window. The process information is also available using **PDSHOW** from a command line. For information on troubleshooting processes using **PDSHOW**, see Chapter 15, "Troubleshooting Resource Manager Essentials."

Figure 13-13 *The Process Status Window*

Connectivity Tools

CiscoWorks 2000 Server provides other tools for testing connectivity to managed devices. These tools test connectivity and availability in real-time. The tools consist of Ping, Traceroute, NSLookup, and Management Station to Device. To access the tools, select CiscoWorks 2000 Server; Diagnostics; Connectivity Tools. The tools and how they operate are described in the list that follows:

- **Ping**—Provides a TCP/IP address or DNS name to test layer-3 ICMP connectivity to the selected device. The device does not have to be a managed device. Figure 13-14 shows the Ping application.

Figure 13-14 *The Ping Application*

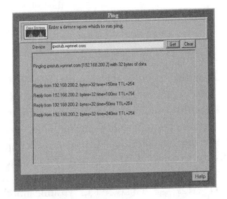

- **Traceroute**—If ping does not work, try using Traceroute, which can help to find the location in the network where the traffic is being stopped from its intended destination. Traceroute accepts a TCP/IP address or DNS name. Figure 13-15 shows the Traceroute application.

Figure 13-15 *The Traceroute Application*

- **NSLookup**—Will submit a DNS query to the first DNS server in the list on the CiscoWorks 2000 Server. The fully qualified domain name and TCP/IP address will be queried for resolution. The DNS Server name, address, and resolved information will be displayed. Figure 13-16 displays the NSLookup Application.

Figure 13-16 *The NSLookup Application*

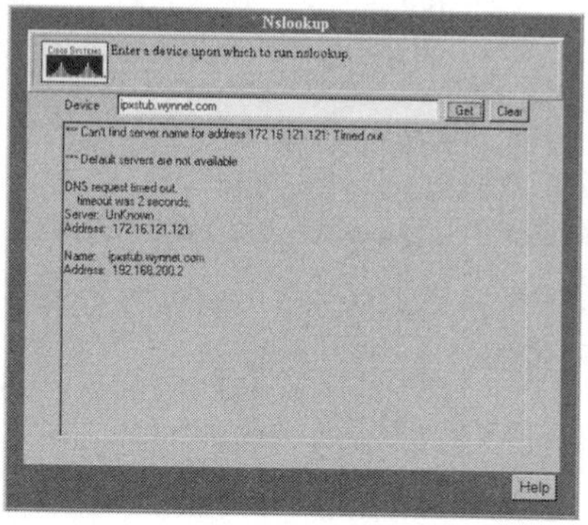

- **Management Station to Device**—If a device responds to Ping and Traceroute but does not appear to support SNMP or other layer-4 applications, this tool can be used to test application problems. This tool will test for connectivity for UDP, TCP, HTTP, TFTP, Telnet, and SNMP. For UDP and TCP, the application tests port 7, and for other protocols the server side ports are tested. The application acts like a client for the respective applications. In order for the tests to succeed, the device must be running the previously mentioned protocols as a server. For example, in order for the HTTP test to succeed, allow the **ip http server** command to enable the web interface on a router. If a host name is used instead of a TCP/IP address, the host name will be resolved and displayed before the test is run. Figure 13-17 shows the Management Station to Device application testing Telnet, HTTP, and TFTP to the router IPXStub.

Figure 13-17 *The Management Station To Device*

Summary

Resource Manager provides two different sets of monitoring tools: the Availability Tools, which are based upon a polling process, and the Connectivity Tools, which provide real-time information.

The Availability Tools are used to monitor various aspects of the network. By analyzing the information gathered by the polling process, reports are generated. The reports can contain information about device availability trends, response time, reloads, and Layer 3 protocol distribution. An administrator configures views to determine which devices are polled during the polling process. The reports are useful tools in troubleshooting device connectivity. Due to the limitations of devices polled and polling intervals, however, the amount of devices polled and the polling intervals are limited.

The Connectivity Tools provide quick information about a device's status through the Ping and Traceroute applications. The information is not as detailed as the Availability tools and cannot provide trend analysis. However, Connectivity tools do not generate any significant overhead on the server or on the network.

Chapter 14, "Resource Manager Tools," covers **network show** commands that can be used in combination with the Availability and Connectivity tools to examine specific information about a device's status using **show** commands, available only from the command-line interface.

Topics covered in this chapter include the following:

- Network Show Commands Application
- Management Connection
- CCO Tools
- Device Navigator

Additional CiscoWorks 2000 Tools

Previous chapters have discussed how Resource Manager integrates with the Cisco web site through Software Image Management, Bug Toolkits, Stack Decoder, and the Tech Tip window. This chapter focuses on how Resource Manager integrates with additional web-based applications to further extend management functionality. Resource Manager can add connection documents to external web-based applications to provide a centralized management gateway for all network devices. Inventory integration tools allow for contract management and case management. Tools are also provided to simplify gathering information from devices using Network Show Commands. The Network Show Commands tool can be useful when using the CCO integrated troubleshooting engine, which is also accessible through Resource Manager Essentials.

Network Show Commands Application

The Network Show Commands application is a Java-based tool enabling administrators to define lists of **show** commands that users can run against their Cisco devices. The Network Show Commands application also provides an optional Remote Console option for entering **show** commands not defined in the **show** command list.

The problem is that this can be a complex series of permissions that might unintentionally limit a user's ability to perform their job or conversely allow them to do more than they should be allowed.

The Network Show Command application allows users to execute **show** commands on network devices without having the passwords used to telnet to the device. The Network Show Command tool uses Telnet information provided in the database to connect to the device. This eliminates the need for users to have telnet access on their own. The roles users are assigned will control which network **show** commands they can use.

This setup helps restrict the commands a user can execute without limiting functionality. When using the Network Show Command application in combination with the NetConfig tool, a user may have limited privileges. The user can configure only certain settings on network devices. The user can only modify settings of a device based upon templates in the NetConfig application. An administrator creates these templates. A user can verify the outcome of the NetConfig job through the Network Show Commands tool. Another advantage to the Network Show and NetConfig tools is that many devices can be affected at once in a more efficient manner.

The Network Show Command application uses Telnet to connect to the destination devices and execute the requested commands. The capability to Telnet to the device is crucial to the application's operation. The information used to Telnet, such as passwords or user names, comes from the Resource Manager Essentials' database.

The Network Show Commands application shown in Figure 14-1 is divided into five different areas. The device selection area enables an administrator to use a view to select the target devices. The command set area provides up to six different grouped command sets to choose from or allows you to type a command into the Remote Console dialog box. As the devices are processed, the Device Result Status area shows the number of devices pending execution, as well as the number of successful and failed devices. The Navigation Control selection area is used to report on which commands are being executed on the different devices and to navigate the command results for each device. The Command Output window displays the results of the different applications.

Figure 14-1 *The Network Show Commands Application*

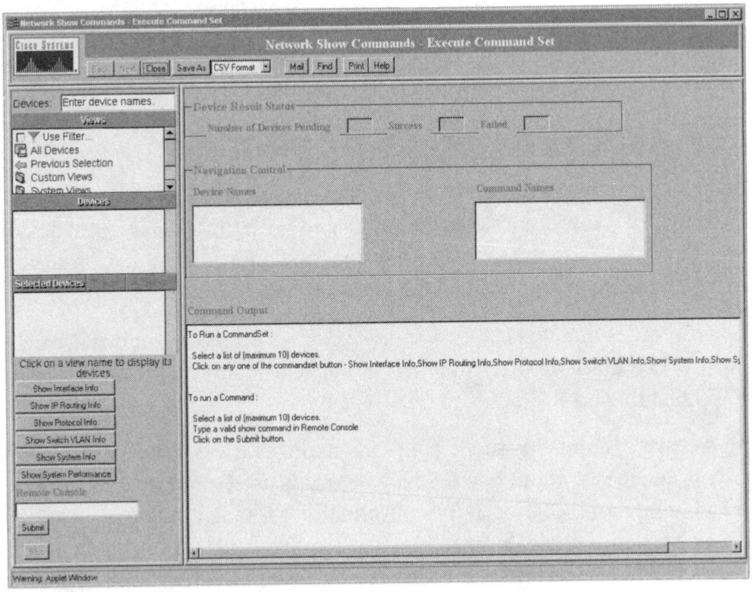

Network Show Commands Administration

An administrator can add additional commands by creating new command sets to display to specific users. The command sets can also be assigned to users by their CiscoWorks user name. Command sets enable an administrator to define certain commands that examine sensitive information, such as access lists, to only users who should be able to view the commands. Enabling the Remote Console allows the user to execute any **show** command. Administration of the command sets is the first job in configuring the Network Show Commands application.

Administration of Command Sets

To administer the command sets, navigate in CiscoWorks 2000 to the Resource Manager Essentials; Administration; Configuration Management; Network Show; Define Command Set. From the Define Command Set dialog box, create, edit, or delete any of the existing command sets. The Define Command Set dialog box displays all the defined command sets and their respective commands. Only user-defined command sets may by edited or deleted. Figure 14-2 shows the Define Command Set Dialog box.

Figure 14-2   *The Define Command Set Dialog Box*

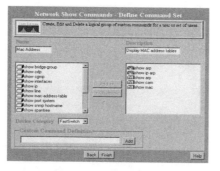

To create a new command set, implement the following steps.

Step 1   Click Create in the Define Command Set dialog box.

Step 2   In the Name field, provide a name for the new command set.

Step 3   In the Description field put in a brief description that explains the purpose of the command set.

Step 4   In the Device Category drop-down list select from FastSwitch, Catalyst, or Router to see a predefined list of commands for each platform. A FastSwitch is an IOS-based, not COS-based, Catalyst Switch such as the 2900XL series.

Step 5   If the command does not appear in the list of available commands, type the command into the Custom Command Definition dialog box. The command is added for the currently selected device platform. The application does not check the command syntax, so make certain all necessary syntax is added correctly.

Step 6   Click Add to add commands to the command set and Remove to take commands out. When the command set is selected in the Network Show application, all the commands are always run. Each command set can have a maximum of six commands. Keep in mind the more commands in a set, the longer it will take to run. This impact is even greater over multiple devices.

Step 7   Click Finish to create the command set.

Once a command set is defined, it must be assigned to users before it will appear in the Network Show Command application.

Controlling Access to Command Sets

To assign users permissions to a command set, select the Resource Manager Essentials; Administration; Configuration Management; Network Show; Assign Users hyperlink. Figure 14-3 shows the Assign Users Dialog box. The Mac Address command set has been added for user mwyns. The Show Protocol Info command set had to be removed in order to add the Mac Address command set.

Figure 14-3 *The Assign Users Dialog Box*

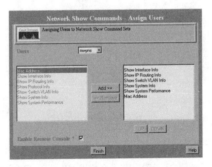

In the Assign Users dialog box, select the CiscoWorks 2000 user name from the drop-down list. Then click Add to add a new command set for that user. Each user may only have six command sets assigned. If a user already has six command sets assigned, one must be removed before adding another. To enable a user to run commands other than those defined in the command sets, add the Remote Console option for the user. This permits the user to run any **show** command as well as **ping** and **traceroute** from each of the devices selected. This option should be selected with caution due to the possible information it can provide. If the Remote Console is used freely, a user who should not be able to use such commands as **show running-config** would be able to do so through the Remote Console. There is no way to control commands used through the Remote Console.

Once the command sets have been configured, users can begin to use the application.

Using the Network Show Commands Application

All users with valid logins can launch the Network Show application and access the default command sets. To limit access to the various command sets, follow the instructions described in the previous section. Once in the Network Show Commands application, perform the following:

Step 1 In the Device Selection window, add devices from either a view or from the quick device window. Multiple platform types can be selected at once, and the appropriate commands will then be used. A maximum of ten devices can be selected at once.

Step 2 Select the command set to execute. All commands will then be executed on the selected device. Keep in mind that all commands for the appropriate platform will be executed on each device. The commands are executed in parallel and results are displayed listed by the order the devices are listed.

Figure 14-4 shows the Network Show Commands application running the **show ip route** on two routers. The commands are still running. Notice that the icon next to the router address imitates a person running.

Figure 14-4 *Using the Network Show Commands Application*

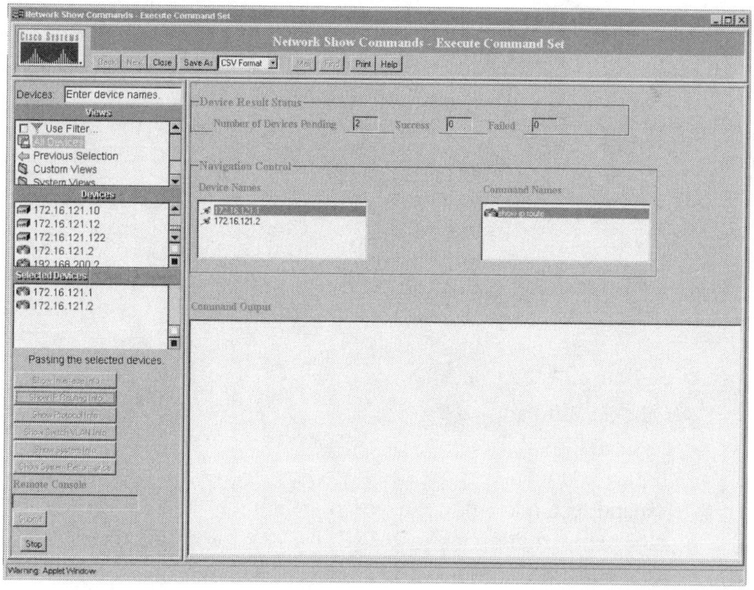

Step 3 Click Stop to end the command execution.

Step 4 If no command sets contain the necessary commands or you want to run only one command, use the Remote Console dialog box. The Remote Console dialog box is enabled on a user-by-user basis. The Remote Console can also be used to execute the **ping** and **traceroute** commands. The commands are executed on the devices, not from the management station. This action can be used to test connectivity from the device. In the Remote Console window, shorthand command strings such as **sh** can be used as normally used through Telnet. The **?** can also be used to obtain **show** command help. If an unsupported command is executed in the Remote Console dialog box, an error will appear. In Figure 14-5, the Remote Console is used to execute the **ping** command on a remote router, testing connectivity to a server in the network. Click the Submit button to issue the command.

Figure 14-5 *The Remote Console*

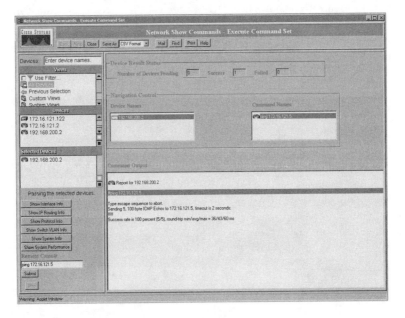

Step 5 The results are listed in the Command Output window. Figure 14-6 displays the routing tables for 172.16.121.1 and 172.16.121.2 from the **show** commands executed in Figure 14-4.

Figure 14-6 *The Network Show Command Results*

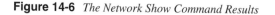

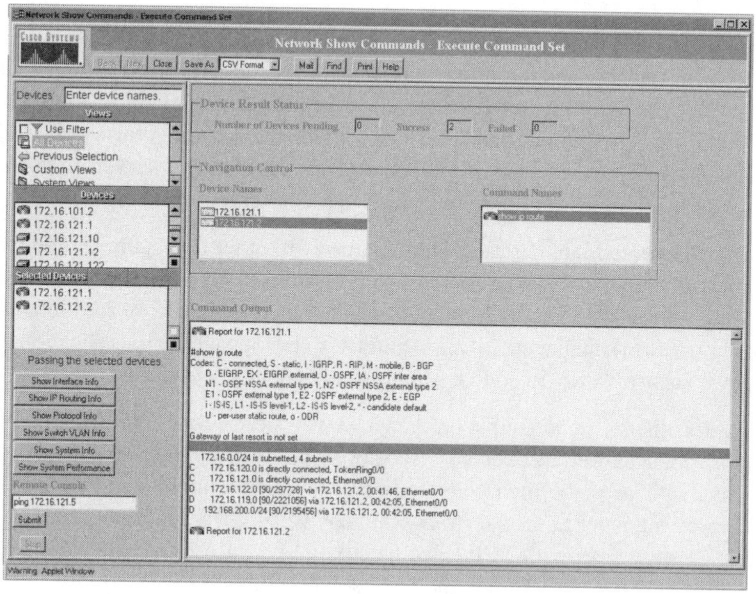

Step 6   Navigate the Command Output from the scrollbar in the output window or select the device in the Device Navigation Control Window.

Step 7   The results can be saved in CSV format, printed, or e-mailed. Use the Find button to search the command output for any text string.

Step 8   When done using the Network Show Commands application, click Close to end the application.

The Network Show Commands tool saves time by executing **show** commands on many devices at once. This tool eliminates the need to Telnet to each device to execute commands. Users no longer need to have logins to network devices. Limiting the device access enhances the security of the device. In order for the application to work, the device must be accessible through Telnet. Therefore, giving some users individual logins to the device might be prudent in the event the user needs to bypass the Network Show Commands tool. If, for example, the interface used for Telnet goes down, the user might need console port access.

Management Connection

As management systems become more complicated, more servers in the network are dedicated to management functions. An administrator must remember which server manages which devices and remember how to access each application. No central repository is available for accessing all the management applications without knowing where the application resides.

All Resource Manager's applications are web-based. The applications are launched from within Resource Manager by navigating a folder and hyperlink structure. Importing link documents that provide a folder and a hyperlink to external applications can extend this architecture. These link documents can provide the central gateway into all the web-based network management applications. Connections to the other servers in the network are then sourced from the Resource Manager Essentials' Server.

Using Resource Manager as a central gateway to other management applications can have several advantages. Permissions can be given to users based upon their Resource Manager Essentials' login. Resource Manager link documents can add an additional level of security to other network management applications. If the management application does not provide its own security, then Resource Manager adds that functionality.

Link documents are available on the CCO web site for over 30 different third-party applications, as well as over 10 Cisco applications. If applications used in the network are not available as predefined link documents, a link document can be easily created within Resource Manager Essentials to point to any web-based application. These links point to a URL on any server with TCP/IP connectivity to the Resource Manager Server. Link documents can be exported to the local server and then imported into another system.

Importing a Connection Document

The import process uses either an administrator's custom connection document created through the export process or connection documents imported from CCO. Connection documents are available on the CCO web site for both third-party applications and for Cisco applications. The list of available connection documents grows as new vendors create applications that can integrate into the CiscoWorks 2000 environment. The connection document allows a central location for users to connect to launch a variety of network management applications.

The CVSM, Cisco Visual Switch Manager, is an example of an importable application from CCO. The CVSM application is a web-based console for Catalyst 1900, 2820, 2900XL, and 3500 series switches. The CVSM connection document creates a link to quickly launch the application. The following numbered list details how to import a document from CCO.

Step 1 Select Management Connection; Administration; Import.

Step 2 Select Certified Management Connections on CCO and click Next.

Step 3 If the application is a Cisco product, select Cisco Products. If the application is a third-party application, select Cisco Network Management Partner Products and click Next. For CVSM, select Cisco Products. Figure 14-7 shows the list of Cisco applications currently available as connection documents on CCO.

Figure 14-7 *The CCO Connection Import*

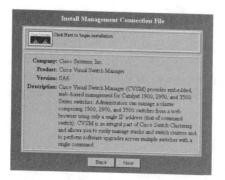

Step 4 In the Select Management Connection File window, select the Cisco Visual Switch Manager connection document.

Step 5 The Install Management Connection File window appears and explains the application's version and purpose. Click Next to proceed. The download of the connection document will be started. Figure 14-8 shows the information provided about CVSM.

Figure 14-8 *The CVSM Import*

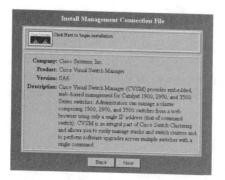

Step 6   The Verify Connection window appears with information about the folder that will be created and the Item Name of the application to be installed. The users that will have access to the connection document will also be displayed. Click Next to proceed. This action is similar to creating a connection document already described.

Step 7   Next, put in the address of where the application resides. In the case of CVSM, this would be the command switch of the cluster. Click Next to proceed.

Step 8   Figure 14-9 shows the CVSM application after it has been installed and connected to a Catalyst 2912XL.

Figure 14-9   *The CVSM Application*

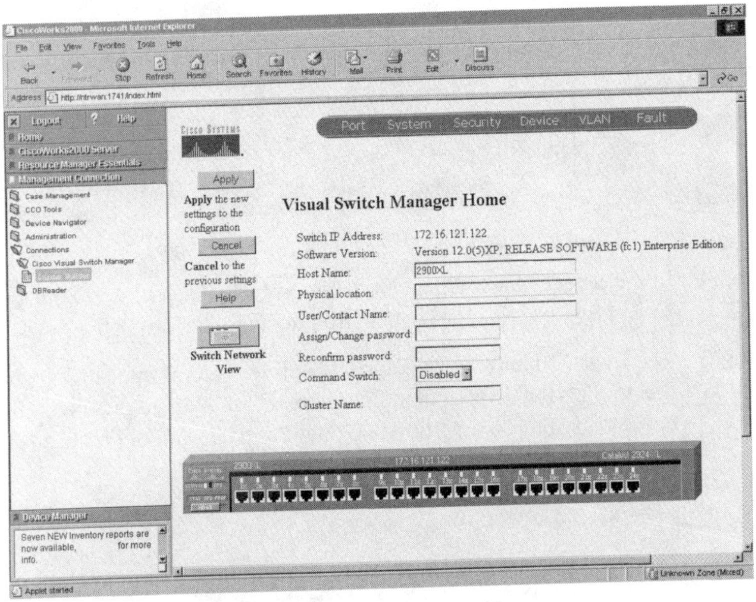

The process for importing a connection document from the local file system is the same as importing a document from CCO, except for the option to browse the server file system to find the connection document. In the initial Import a Connection dialog, select Local File System.

If a connection document no longer points to an existing application, the connection document should be deleted.

Deleting a Connection Document

Once a connection document is no longer needed it can be removed from the system. To remove a connection document, implement the following steps.

Step 1   Select Management Connection; Administration; Delete. The Delete a Connection window will appear.

Step 2   From the drop-down list, select the connection document to remove from the system.

Step 3   Click Next to remove. A warning message will appear confirming the delete process. Click OK to confirm the deletion.

Step 4   Once the Connection is deleted, click Update Menu to finish and update the environment.

Third-party developers can create applications that integrate into the CiscoWorks management framework. Therefore, the connection documents for these applications can be posted on CCO.

Certifying A Management Connection

Developing applications that integrate into the CiscoWorks 2000 environment can be very beneficial to third-party developers. Applications, which have been certified to integrate into the CiscoWorks 2000 Server framework, can be advertised with the Cisco Management Connection logo. The logo entices customers to purchase a product, which integrates with the CiscoWorks Management Framework.

Third-party developers need to have new applications tested against a set of Cisco compliance rules to certify an application as compliant with the CiscoWorks 2000 server environment. This testing process is handled by Keylabs, Inc. Keylabs is a respected independent lab-testing facility that certifies applications for many companies such as Cisco, Sun Microsystems, Microsoft, and Novell. The testing process costs between $1,200 and $2,000 for a one-day-long test. Keylabs, Inc. is available on the Internet at www.keylabs.com. Once it certifies an application connection document, it is posted on CCO for customers to access. Figure 14-10 shows the Keylabs web site page describing the certification process.

The integrated applications are just one method of expanding the features of CiscoWorks 2000. Other applications on the CCO web site are already integrated with the Management connections.

Figure 14-10 *The Keylabs Web Site*

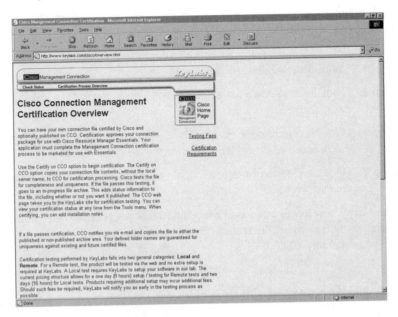

CCO Tools

A number of tools are available on the Cisco CCO web site. These tools have been integrated into the CiscoWorks 2000 server framework. The advantage of the integration is that the administrators do not have to spend time navigating the CCO web site to access the tools. These tools provide hyperlinks to helpful pages on the CCO web site.

Integrated tools provide links to the Troubleshooting Engine, Case Management, Open Q&A Forum, Browse CCO Software, and the Bug toolkit. The tools are located in the Management Connection channel under CCO Tools. The Browse CCO Software and Bug Toolkit were discussed in Chapter 9, "Software Image Management."

The Open Q&A Forum

The Open Q&A Forum is an excellent tool for asking implementation questions. The Open Q&A forum allows CCO users to post questions or search previously asked questions. New questions are answered by any logged in CCIE. The Open Q&A Forum is an excellent place to ask for technology explanations or implementation recommendations.

The Troubleshooting Engine

The Troubleshooting Engine is a step-by-step tool for troubleshooting basic configuration problems. The tool can answer questions on almost any topic from TCP/IP routing to DSL and WAN switching. The tool gives commands to type and output to look for in order to determine what problems are being encountered. Figure 14-11 shows the Troubleshooting home page.

Figure 14-11 *The Troubleshooting Engine*

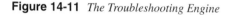

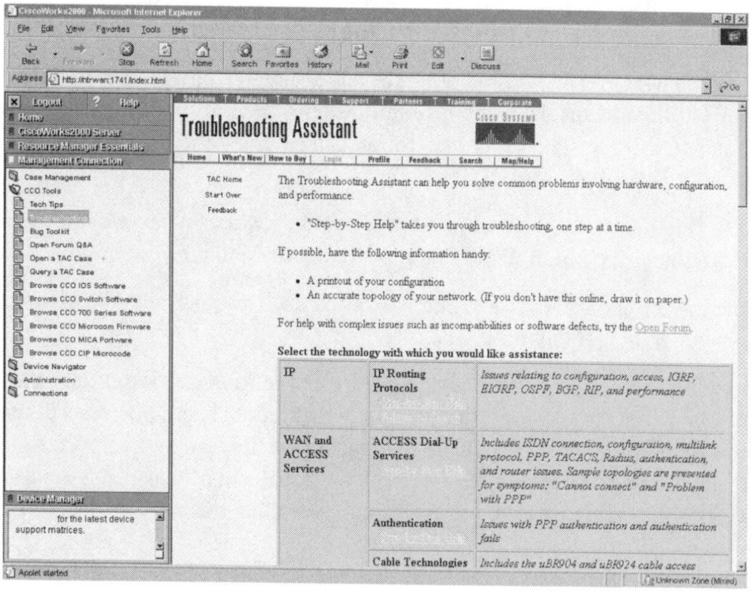

Case Management

If a problem cannot be resolved through the Open Q&A Forum or the Troubleshooting Engine, then a case can be opened with the TAC. Cases opened through CiscoWorks are opened with a priority of 3. To change the priority call the TAC after the case has been opened. The Case Open tool will use the CCO Login contact information as the point of contact for the case.

After a case has been opened it will be assigned a case number. The case number can then be referenced in the Query or Update Case tool. The Query or Update Case tool enables an administrator to add additional information to an open case or check the progress of the case's resolution.

Many of the CCO tools are not inventory-aware. One tool that can provide additional inventory management features is the Contract Management tool.

Contract Management

All new hardware purchased must be accompanied by a service contract. Keeping the service contracts up to date is very important. If the contract on a device expires, the device is unsupported. In a network with hundreds of devices, managing these contracts can be a full-time job. One problem with contract management is that the serial number internal to the device is not always the serial number that is under contract. This inconsistency makes matching up devices to contracts even harder without some management system to track the serial numbers to the inventory. The serial number typically associated with the service contract is the external serial number on the chassis exterior. Typically, the serial number retrieved during internal checks is not the external serial number.

Resource Manager Essentials provides a tool called Contract Connection. The Contract Connection tool correlates the inventory to the external serial numbers and then integrates with the CCO site. The CCO integration can examine the inventory for devices that are currently under contract.

Collecting the external serial numbers from the devices is the most difficult part of the integration in the initial deployment of Resource Manager.

Once the serial numbers have been recorded each number must be entered into the Resource Manager database, one at a time.

To update the inventory of a device use Resource Manager Essentials; Administration; Inventory; Change Device Attributes. One method that could be used to update the devices is to export the inventory to a CSV file, update the file, and then import the information back into the database. To export the inventory use Resource Manager Essentials; Administration; Inventory; Export to a File. Figure 14-12 shows the inventory export screen configured to export a CSV file.

Figure 14-12 *The Inventory Export Application*

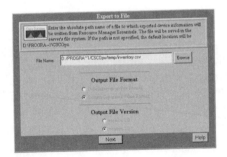

Once the device has had the inventory information updated, use Resource Manager Essentials; Contract Connection; Check Contract Status. The CCO login used to access the Check Contract Status report must be the same login registration as on CCO. The customer name and e-mail address are displayed. Figure 14-13 shows the contract connection for a single contract on a 2600 series router.

Figure 14-13 *The Contract Connection*

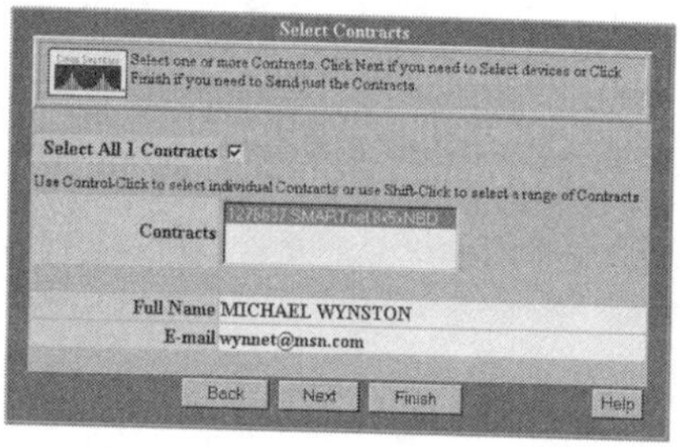

In the Contract Connection window, click the next button to check the contract status of a particular device. The select device window appears. Select one or more devices to check their contract status. This is based upon the serial number of the device in the database compared to the information on CCO. This information is sent in encrypted format to Cisco. Click Finish to transfer the information. The Device Type Summary Report is displayed. Figure 14-14 shows the Device Type Summary Report.

Figure 14-14 *The Device Type Summary Report*

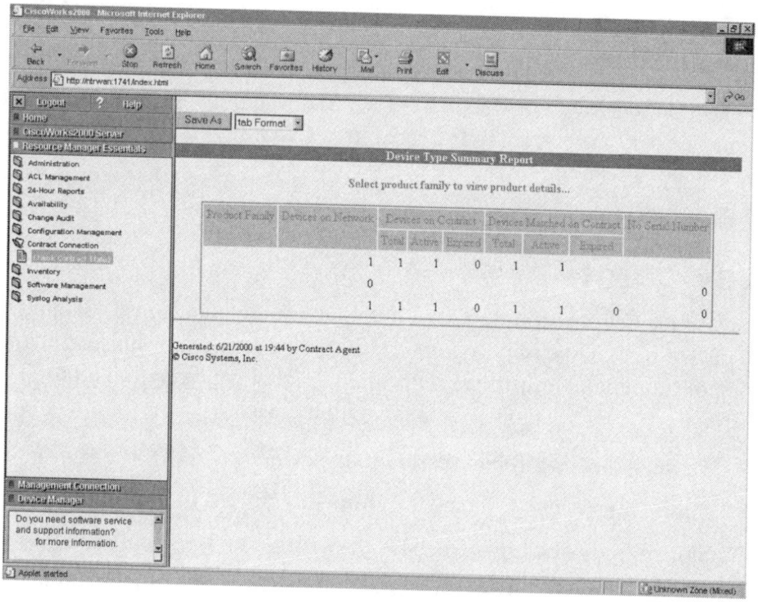

Click the hyperlink for any device family to view details for all devices in that family. Figure 14-15 shows the details about the contract on the 2600 series router.

Figure 14-15 *The Device Contract Status Report*

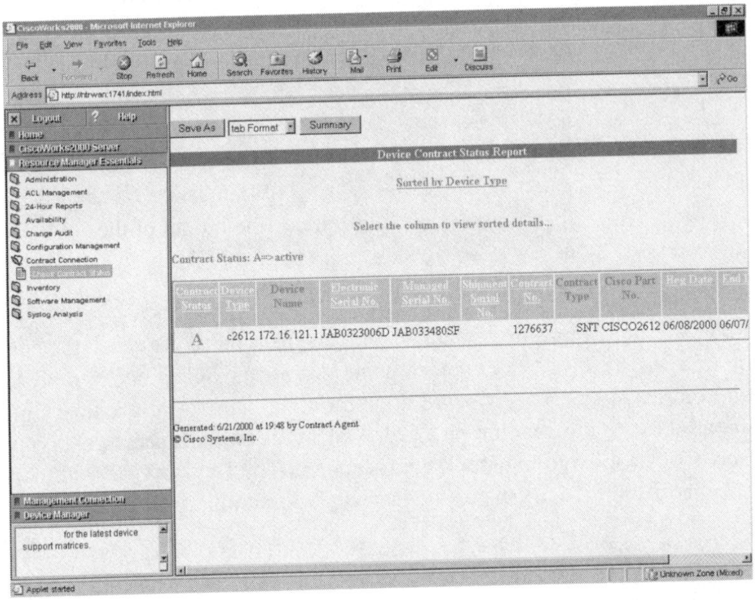

To check the contract status on all devices in inventory, click Finish from the Contract Connection window. The Check Contract Status application will list all contracts that can be managed by the current user logged in to CCO. It will also display an inventory of all devices along with the respective contract status.

Device Navigator

Many of the new versions of Cisco IOS Software include an HTTP interface to configure the device from. On Cisco Routers and IOS-based switches this interface can be enabled using the command **ip http server** while in global configuration mode. This HTTP interface provides six tools for managing the device.

- **Telnet**—Opens a Telnet session to the device.
- **Show interfaces**—Execute the **show interfaces** command on the router or switch.
- **Show diagnostic log**—Displays the console message buffer.
- **Monitor the router**—Provides HTML access to the router command line. Many commands can be entered from both privileged mode and configuration mode.

- **Connectivity Test**—Pings the DNS server the device is configured to use.
- **Show tech-support**—Combines the output of over 10 different commands. The commands displayed are based on the device's abilities. Commands that are always included are **show running-config**, **show controllers**, **show interfaces**, **show process cpu**, **show process memory**, **show stacks**, and **show version**. The show tech-support tool can be useful to the TAC for information on how a device is configured and what type of hardware is on the device.

Once the HTTP server has been enabled it can be accessed form CiscoWorks 2000 by opening Management Connection; Device Navigator; Browse Device. This will launch another browser window that contains the IP HTTP interface for the device. Figure 14-16 is the Device Navigator for a 2600 series router. The output of the **show tech-support** command is displayed.

Figure 14-16 *The Device Navigator*

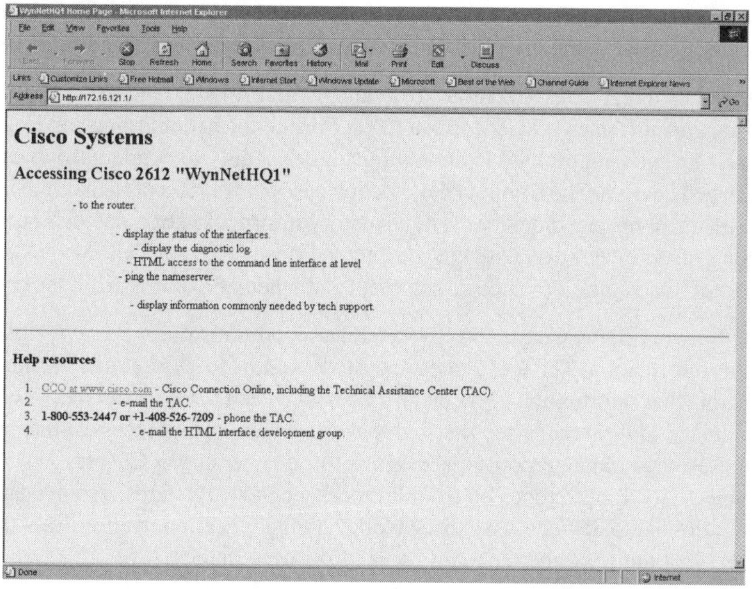

Opening the HTTP for a router or a switch could be considered a security hole in the network. To lower the security risk of opening the HTTP port on the router, an administrator can change the port that the HTTP server listens on. To change the port HTTP uses, execute the command **ip http port** *number* while in global configuration mode.

If the port number is changed and an administrator wants to access the HTTP server from CiscoWorks 2000, the port number must also be updated on the CiscoWorks 2000 Server. Unfortunately, the fallback port number must be the same on all devices accessed from the server. To change the fallback port use Management Connection; Device Navigator; Configure Fallback Port. If a fallback port is configured, 80 will still be tried first and then the fallback port will be used next. Only one fallback port can be set.

The advantage to the HTML interface is that it runs inside a browser and provides easy access to a few **show** commands. The interface, however, is not extensible so the use is limiting. Resource Manager provides a much more robust tool for executing **show** commands. The Network Show Commands tool provides access to all **show** commands on any device in the network, not just devices that support the HTTP server.

Summary

This chapter discussed the usefulness of CCO for accessing link documents to integrate applications into the CiscoWorks management framework. Furthermore, third-party vendors are able to have their applications integrated with this framework through custom link documents. Link documents provide a central gateway to multiple management platforms, thereby creating an organizational paradigm for easy administration.

Numerous integrated CCO tools are available to further extend the CiscoWorks 2000 management framework. The Open Q&A Forum, the Troubleshooting Engine, and the Case Management tool aid in an administrator's ability to conduct troubleshooting of managed devices. The Contract Connection eases the burden of managing hardware service contracts on managed devices. The inventory information of a device's serial number allows direct integration with the contract database on CCO. This enables an administrator to check the expiration dates of contracts and whether a device is under contract or not.

The Network Show Commands tool enables an administrator to provide users with device status information. The tool can have custom command sets defined for individual users to control what information users can access about each network device. The Network Show Command tool eases the security burden of providing users access to the network devices. The Resource Manager tools discussed in this chapter and in Chapter 13, "Availability and Connectivity Tools," focus on troubleshooting a device's status. Troubleshooting however is not limited to devices. The CiscoWorks 2000 application itself utilizes troubleshooting tools. That topic will be the main focus of the next chapter.

Topics covered in this chapter include the following:

- Troubleshooting General Connectivity
- Troubleshooting Server Administration
- Troubleshooting General Device
- Validating Inventory Records
- Troubleshooting Inventory Importing
- Troubleshooting Device Update Processes
- Troubleshooting Software Image Management
- Troubleshooting Access-Control List Manager

Troubleshooting Resource Manager Essentials

Previous chapters have focused on using the different applications of Resource Manager Essentials. During and after deployment of Resource Manager, situations will occur where different applications do not operate properly. The troubleshooting tools of Resource Manager require a complex series of processes both on the server and on the device. The tools need constant connectivity to the agents on the managed devices and numerous resources on the server in order for everything to function correctly. The different processes, installation, inventory, configuration management, and other tools require a certain chain of events and settings to operate properly. This chapter covers how to troubleshoot the different processes and their connectivity within the Resource Manager environment. It separates troubleshooting into a series of steps for each tool.

Troubleshooting General Connectivity

All the Resource Manager applications require connectivity to the devices to function and keep information up to date. Connectivity problems can occur in a number of areas. The best method of connectivity troubleshooting is to try to troubleshoot based upon the seven-layer OSI model. This model involves starting at the Physical layer and working up to the Application layer. Troubleshooting connectivity must be done from the perspective of both the client to the server and the server to the devices.

The first rule of troubleshooting is to never assume that any aspect of connectivity or configuration is done correctly until it is verified. Never trust any information until it has been investigated. This is not a question of competence but of connectivity.

Troubleshooting Client and Server Connectivity

The different levels of the OSI model can help to cover all different types of communication problems. This section will address issues such as client to server IP connectivity, client to RME Java problems, and client to server browser problems. The first series of steps involve troubleshooting client to server connectivity. The tools under the local operating system

must be used to test the connectivity from the client to the server. The method of troubleshooting that traces the OSI model use the steps outlined in the following list:

Step 1   The first steps on both the client and the server are to check the TCP/IP
address and default gateway.

If the operating system is either Windows NT or Windows 98, use the
command **ipconfig /all**. Figure 15-1 shows the ipconfig application.
The DNS server, TCP/IP address, and default gateway are listed.

Figure 15-1   *The ipconfig Application on Windows NT*

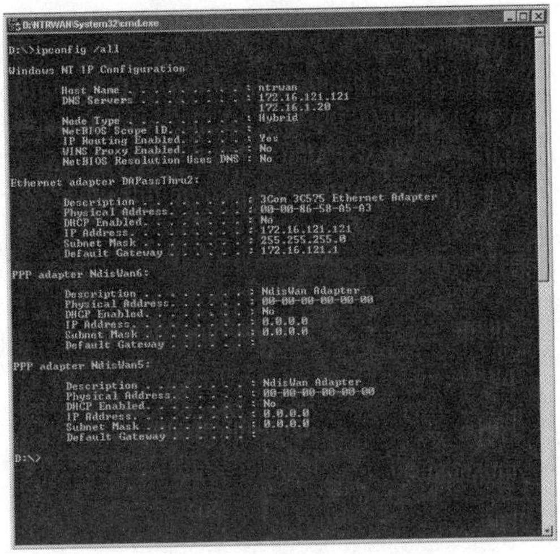

If the operating system is Windows 95, use **winipcfg**.

If the operating system is a UNIX-based system, use **ifconfig** or check
the operating system documentation for the appropriate command.

The following example shows a sample output of the **ifconfig**, netstat
routing table, and the *resolv.conf* file used to resolve host names.

```
# ifconfig -a
lo0: flags=849<UP,LOOPBACK,RUNNING,MULTICAST> mtu 8232
        inet 127.0.0.1 netmask ff000000
hme0: flags=863<UP,BROADCAST,NOTRAILERS,RUNNING,MULTICAST> mtu 1500
        inet 172.16.96.31 netmask ffffff00 broadcast 172.16.96.255
        ether 8:0:20:cf:dc:ad
hme1: flags=863<UP,BROADCAST,NOTRAILERS,RUNNING,MULTICAST> mtu 1500
        inet 10.16.96.31 netmask ff000000 broadcast 10.255.255.255
        ether 8:0:20:cf:dc:ad
# netstat -r
```

```
Routing Table:
  Destination            Gateway             Flags  Ref  Use    Interface
  ------------------     ------------------   ----   ----  ------  ---------
  172.16.96.0            lully                 U      3    3113    hme0
  arpanet                lully-1               U      2      32    hme1
  224.0.0.0              lully                 U      3       0    hme0
  default                nms-7010-1.cisco.com  UG     0   13804
  localhost              localhost             UH       01063216   lo0
# cat /etc/resolv.conf
domain  cisco.com
nameserver    171.68.10.70
nameserver    171.68.10.140
# cat /etc/nsswitch.conf
#
# /etc/nsswitch.files:
#
# An example file that could be copied over to /etc/nsswitch.conf; it
# does not use any naming service.
#
# "hosts:" and "services:" in this file are used only if the
# /etc/netconfig file has a "-" for nametoaddr_libs of "inet"
transports.

passwd:       files
group:        files
hosts:        files        dns
networks:     files
protocols:    files
rpc:          files
ethers:       files
netmasks:     files
bootparams:   files
publickey:    files
# At present there isn't a 'files' backend for netgroup; the system will
#  figure it out pretty quickly, and won't use netgroups at all.
netgroup:     files
automount:    files
aliases:      files
services:     files
sendmailvars:    files
#
```

Step 2   Verify that the client and server can ping their configured default gateway.

Step 3   Verify that the client can ping the server by both TCP/IP address and host name.

Step 4 If pinging by address works but pinging by name fails, verify the client and server name resolution process. Verify the name resolution by using NSLookup with the device name as the target. A nslookup application is built into CiscoWorks2000. This tool only works if name resolution uses DNS and not exclusively a host file. This tool was covered in Chapter 13, "Availability and Connectivity Tools." Figure 15-2 shows the CiscoWorks 2000 Server NSLookup Connectivity Tool.

Figure 15-2 *The NSLookup Tool*

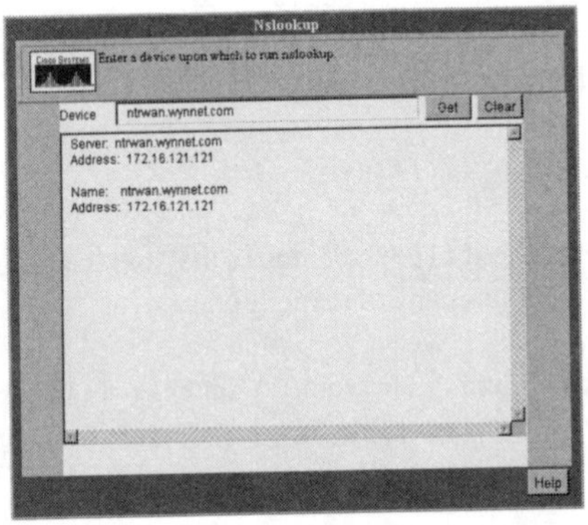

Step 5 If the client can ping the server but cannot connect to the CiscoWorks 2000 application, the problem might be that the client browser does not support the necessary Java environment or that the services on the server have failed. For troubleshooting the processes on the server, refer to the Server Administration Troubleshooting section later in the chapter. For instructions on how to verify the client minimum requirements such as memory, hard drive space, and so on, check local operating documentation. The supported browser versions change with different releases of the CiscoWorks 2000 software, so check the release notes for supported browser versions. To verify Java support, use browser tools.

Java problems occur when the page loads on the client but the browser reports errors. These errors are usually visible by examining the Java Console. The Java problems would occur if the communication at layer 3 is available with the server and if the CiscoWorks 2000 server page displays but does not show either the complete page or seems to hang.

In Netscape Navigator 4.6.1, check the Java version by selecting Communicator; Tools; Java Console. The supported version is Java 1.1.5. Figure 15-3 shows the Java Console. The Java version is in the top of the Console window.

Figure 15-3 *The Java Console*

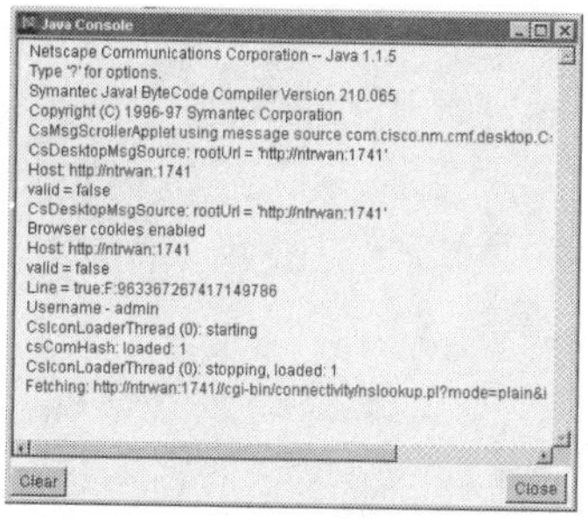

In Internet Explorer, the Java Console is not enabled by default. To enable the Java Console select Tools; Internet Options; Advanced Tab; Microsoft VM. Verify Java console enabled is selected. If it is not checked, check the box and restart Windows. Once Windows is restarted under the View menu, select Java Console. The supported Java VM versions are 5.0.0.3167 through 5.0.0.3186.

Step 6 If the CiscoWorks 2000 page comes up with errors, try clearing the client cache of temporary Internet files. Temporary Internet files can sometimes be the cause of pages that do not display properly. After clearing the caches, restart the browser. If a change is made to an application setting, such as a collection schedule, but the page does not indicate the changes were made, this problem could be with the browser cache.

In Netscape Communicator select Edit; Preferences from the toolbar. In the preferences dialog box, select the Advanced section of the dialog box. Click Clear Disk Cache and Clear Memory Cache to be sure the pages displayed are the current pages on the server.

In Internet Explorer select Tools; Internet Options from the menu bar. Select the General tab and click Delete Files in the Temporary Internet Files section of the tab page. Figure 15-4 displays the Internet Options dialog box in Internet Explorer 5.01.

Figure 15-4 *The Internet Options Dialog Box*

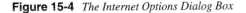

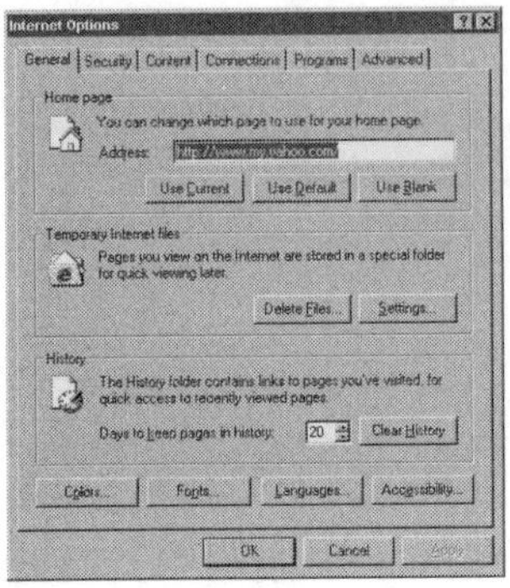

Another problem is how Internet Explorer uses cache pages when a page is revisited. IE does not always display the most current page. To ensure it does, make the following change—Tools; Internet Options, then under Temporary Internet Files section, click Settings. When that window opens, the setting for "Check for newer versions of stored pages" should be "Every visit to the page."

Once connectivity from the client to the server has been verified, troubleshooting can move to the server. The first step in troubleshooting the server application is verification of the server processes.

Troubleshooting Server Administration

Once connectivity between the server and client is verified, the next step is troubleshooting the server. Some symptoms that would point to the server are:

- Multiple clients experience the same problems when communicating with the server and client connectivity has been verified. Router configuration is correct. To ensure that the connectivity is valid, try to establish a connection to the server from the same IP segment and bypass any routers.

- Errors in the Windows NT Event log, messages in the UNIX Syslog file.

- Services or daemons fail to start on the server platform.

- Inventory information fails to update even though changes were made.

- Polling processes are not gathering correct information.

- Syslog messages are not showing up in the reports.

- Availability Monitor shows that a device is offline when the device is not experiencing any problems.
- Multiple server records report inconsistent information with the actual device information.

This section covers the following five main areas:

- Verifying the server processes
- Changing the server Computer Name under Windows NT
- Changing the TCP/IP address in Solaris
- Managing server log files
- Moving the database

Subsequent sections will focus on the individual application processes. This section assumes that the client can connect to the server but cannot access the CiscoWorks 2000 Console or certain applications once connected to the console.

If this is not the case, see the prior section on troubleshooting connectivity between client and server.

Verifying Server Processes

The CiscoWorks 2000 server runs a number of processes to support the Resource Manager Essentials environment. This section presents a series of steps to verify that the server processes are properly started and presents issues that could cause services to stop working properly.

Step 1   If the client can ping the server but cannot open the CiscoWorks 2000 Console, first check that any routers in between the client and server do not have an access-control list preventing the communication. This reason could be why some contact from client to server is available but not contact to the CiscoWorks 2000 console. Verify that the access list enables TCP port 1741 or the port the server was installed on (if not on 1741). Check the Apache httpd.conf file for information on what port the server is listening on. If access lists are not present, verify that the Apache Web Server is started. If the server is running a Telnet daemon, then telnet and use the command **pdshow** to verify the Apache Server process is started. Figure 15-5 shows the output of the command **pdshow | more**. Notice the process WebServer at the top of the display. The status for the process is Program Started.

Figure 15-5 *The* **pdshow** *Command*

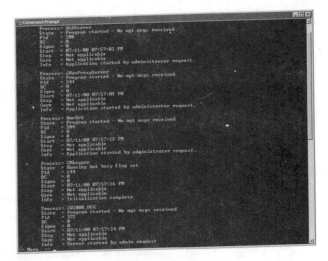

Step 2 The daemon manager process is the main system process for the CiscoWorks 2000 application. The daemon manager will attempt to start the other processes once it is started. It will start the database engines, TCP/IP servers like tftp and Syslog, the CORBA agent, the Java Run time environment, and the web server. If the daemon manager does not start, then the entire application is in a down state. If the daemon manager is not started, start it.

Under Solaris start the process by typing the following command as the root:

```
# /etc/init.d/dmgtd start
```

In the Windows NT operating system, start the Apache Web service by using the Control Panel; Services. Select the Apache WebServer service and click Start.

Step 3 If the Apache Service is started but does not respond, verify the port number the server is configured to listen on. Open the *httpd.conf* file. Figure 15-6 shows the *httpd.conf* file.

Figure 15-6 *The httpd.conf File*

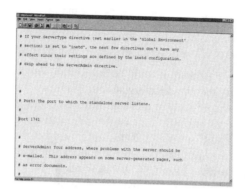

In the Solaris installation, the httpd.conf file is located in the */opt/CSCOpx/objects/web/conf* directory.

In Windows NT, the httpd.conf file is located in the *Program Files\ CSCOpx\lib\web\conf* directory. Verify the port number in the Port section of the document.

The default port number is 80, or if that port is already in use by another web server, 1741. Verify that the port is not already in use by another application. To verify the ports the server is listening on use the **netstat –a –p tcp** command.

Step 4   If the Apache Web Service is started but the client still gets no response from the server, verify that the following other services are started:

— JRUN Proxy Server for CW2000

— CW2000 Daemon Manager

— CW2000 cmf Database Engine

— CW2000 Essentials Database Engine

— CW2000 VisiBroker Smart Agent

If any of the services are not started, use the Control Panel; Services under Windows NT to stop and then restart the services. Make sure to start the daemon manager first. To start the daemon manager from a command prompt, use the **net start crmdmgtd** command to start the service and **net stop crmdmgtd** to stop the service.

Under Solaris, type the following command as root:

```
# /etc/init.d/dmgtd stop
# /etc/init.d/dmgtd start
```

System Verification

If the processes failed to start, try to verify that the following information is correct:

- The administrator logged in to start the services or daemons has administrator rights under Windows NT and has superuser or root privileges under UNIX.

- If services will not start, it could be that certain directories have been moved or deleted. Verify that the directory structure is intact. This is the directory structure to Resource Manager 3.1. For more information check the current release notes. Directory names in UNIX are case sensitive and are usually all lowercase in the application. The CiscoWorks 2000 directory structure is intact. If the defaults were followed during installation, then the application is installed under *opt/CSCOpx* in UNIX and *Program Files\CSCOpx* in Windows NT. Table 15-1 contains the directories of the application and a brief description of their purpose:

Table 15-1   *System Directory Structures*

Solaris	Windows NT	Description
Backup	Backup	N/A
Bin	Bin	Executables and Perl scripts
cam-repository	cam-repository	Client CAM files
cgi-bin	cgi-bin	Web site cgi and Perl scripts
Collect	Collect	Scripts used in collect server info report
Conf	Conf	Scripts used to configure the server and databases during installation
Databases	Databases	System databases Ani, RME, and CMF
Dbupdate	Dbupdate	N/A
Etc	Etc	Legacy CWSI system files
Files	Files	Files collected by the system IOS, config, jobs, etc
Htdocs	Htdocs	Web-server files
Lib	Lib	System library files
	Log	System log files
Man	Man	N/A
Nmim	Nmim	N/A
	Proxy	JRUN Proxy configuration
Selftest	Selftest	Scripts used in the Self-Test report
Setup	Setup	Setup files and information
	Shared	Microsoft VC run-time files
	Temp	temporary files

Table 15-1 *System Directory Structures (Continued)*

Solaris	Windows NT	Description
	Tftpboot	Tftp directory
Users	Users	N/A
www	www	Web-server Java files
Objects	Objects	Subsystems
Ani	Ani	
Data	Data	
Dmgt	Dmgt	
Eds	Eds	
Jrm	Jrm	
Jrun		
Util		
Cmf	Cmf	
Db	Db	
Mngconnection	mngconnect	
perl5	perl5	Perl subsystem
Proxy	Proxy	
Share	Share	Shared subsystem files
web		

Under Windows NT, verify the registry contains the keys for the CiscoWorks 2000 Server. The key *HKEY_LOCAL_MACHINE\SOFTWARE\Cisco\ Resource Manager* must be present for the system to start. Use *regedt32.exe* to verify the registry key. Figure 15-7 shows the Resource Manager\ Environment registry key.

Figure 15-7 *The Resource Manager Registry Keys*

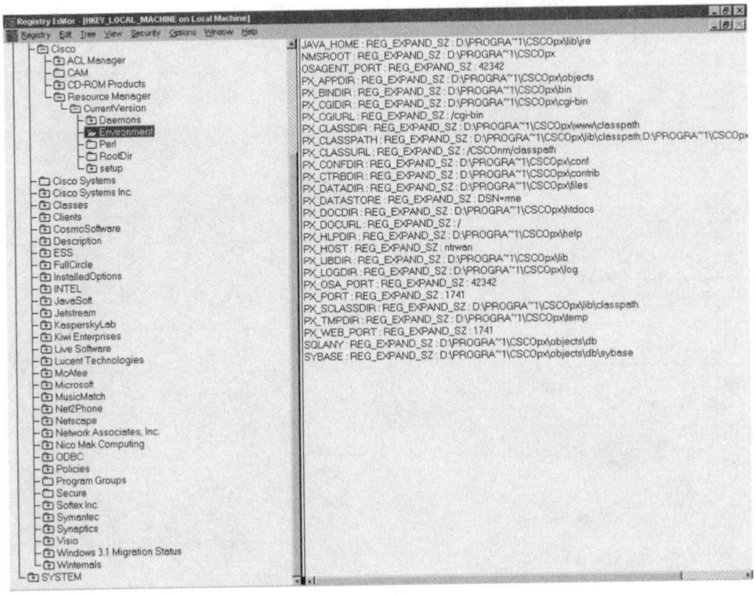

- At a minimum, the CiscoWorks 2000 daemon manager, Apache Web Server, and JRUN Proxy Server must be started to get into the CiscoWorks 2000 Server web site.

- If the services will not start, verify that the server has hard drive space available on the partition where the application is installed. The server creates many temporary files and updates log files, all of which require disk space.

- If there is available drive space, verify that the environment variables point to the proper directories where the files are installed. If the partition structure has changed on the server, then the application process will not be able to locate the necessary files. At a command prompt use the **set** command to verify that the PX environment variables are set. Verify that the temp directory setting exists.

- After verification is made, the necessary services are installed and directories exist. If the services cannot be started, contact Cisco TAC. Reinstalling the application could also be an option.

- Once the services are started, the troubleshooting process can move into the CiscoWorks 2000 Server application.

  To verify process status, use the CiscoWorks 2000 Server console. Select CiscoWorks2000 Server; Administration; Process Status. The Process Status Report can be used to verify any of the processes running on the CiscoWorks 2000 Server. The Process Status window displays the Process Name, ID, start time, stop time, and any messages about the process status. Figure 15-8 shows the Process Status report. This output is the same output presented by the **pdshow** command.

Figure 15-8 *The Process Status Report*

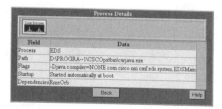

If a process has failed to start due to an error, it will be displayed here. Click the process name to verify the command string used to execute the process. Using the operating system tools verifies that the necessary files exist on the server. Figure 15-8 showed that the EDS process has failed to start. Clicking on the link resulted in the information displayed in Figure 15-9.

Figure 15-9 *The EDS Process Detail*

Field	Data
Process	EDS
Path	D:\PROGRA~1\CSCOpx\bin\cwjava.exe
Flags	-Djava.compiler=NONE com.cisco.nm.cmf.eds.system.EDSMain
Startup	Started automatically at boot.
Dependencies	RmeOrb

If the process is dependent on any other process to start, then that information is also displayed.

- If a process has failed or stopped, use the CiscoWorks 2000 server console to attempt to start the process again. To try to start the processes select the CiscoWorks2000 Server; Start Process application. Choose the process from the list and click Start. If the process starts successfully, the process information will be displayed. If the process fails to start, an explanation will be given as to why the process failed. Figure 15-10 shows how the JRM process has failed to start. Clicking on the link "Failed To Run" will display log messages about the application and what the process did. On July 11, 2000 at 22:44:14, the application terminated resulting in a warning in the log.

Figure 15-10 *The JRM Process Log*

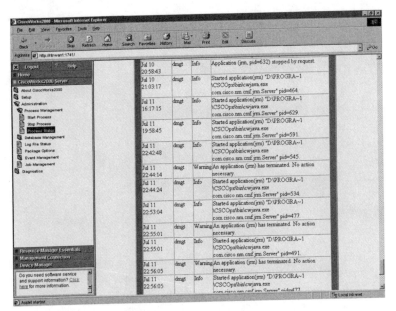

- If a process has failed, use the SelfTest or Collect Server Info tools to verify the server configuration.

The Self Test Tool

To create reports with the Self-Test Tool use the CiscoWorks 2000 Server; Diagnostics; Self Test application. The Server can store multiple copies of the report for historical analysis. This feature is useful if any other applications are installed on the server. Figure 15-11 shows the Self Test Report tool run on the server that has encountered the failed processes. All the tests in the SelfTest passed.

Figure 15-11 *The Self Test Report*

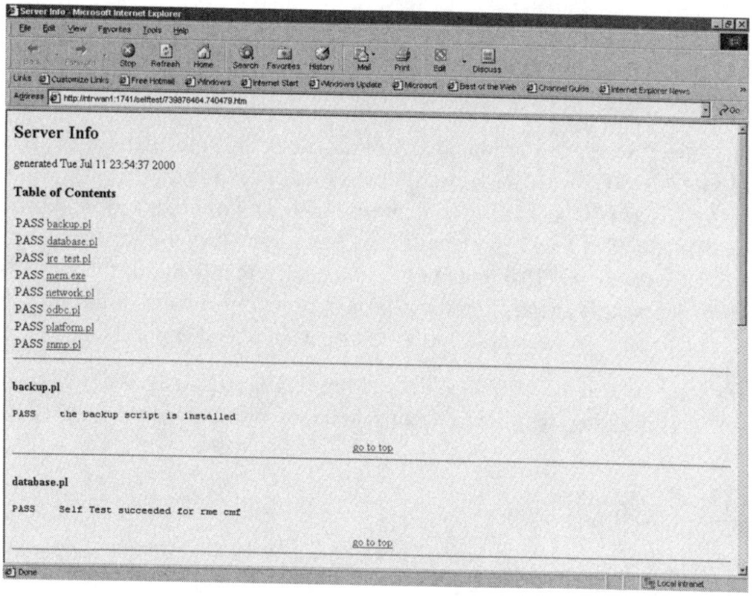

The Self Test tool will verify the following information:

- **Backup.pl**—The script to backup the database.

- **Database.pl**—Database sanity self test. Tests each data source to see if each is installed.

- **Jre_test.pl**—Verifies the Java runtime environment version and JRE Home location are set to <NMSROOT>\lib\jre.

- **Mem.exe**—Tests how much memory is on the system and how much is available.

- **Network.pl**—Tests name resolution of the server local host name.

- **Odbc.pl**—Verifies the version number of the ODBC DLL files.

- **Platform.pl**—Checks that the server product type is supported.

- **Snmp.pl**—Checks that the SNMP DLL files exist in the CSCOpx\bin directory.

WARNING   Many manufacturers that provide SNMP support on the Windows NT platform use the *wsnmp.dll* file. However, not all versions of the file are the same. If the *wsnmp.dll* file exists in the *WINNT\System32* or *WINNT\System32\drivers* directory and is a different version, CiscoWorks 2000 will encounter SNMP problems. The version can be verified by checking the file's properties. The CiscoWorks 2000 version of the file is 2.32.19981012. For example, Sniffer Pro uses version 2.32.19980608, which is not compatible.

The Collect Server Info Tool

To create a report with the Collect Server Info tool use CiscoWorks2000 Server; Diagnostics; Collect Server Info. The report will take up to five minutes to run. The server can store multiple copies of the report for historical analysis. The size and number of log files will determine the report size and how long it takes to display.

The Collect Server Info tool is really designed as the equivalent of the IOS **show tech-support**—in other words, a way to gather, with one command, a large amount of diagnostic info for Cisco TAC and DE to look at for debug and troubleshooting purposes. Customers are not intended to read it, which is to say that it isn't very user-friendly. Still, a lot of useful information is there. Note that not every message that contains the word "warning" or "error" necessarily means that there is any defect or problem in the system. This report is intended to be submitted to Cisco TAC as part of a tech support call.

If for some reason the web server is not running or it is not possible to run this function from the web server, the function can also be run by hand from a DOS command line using the following syntax:

```
cd <cw2k home>\bin
perl collect.info > <output file>
```

where *<cw2k home>* is the home directory where RME is installed (for example, **c:\progra~1\cscopx**) and *<output file>* is a destination to send the output of the Perl script collect.info (for example, **c:\info.html**).

Note that the size of that output file can be very large, as all the CW2K error log files are copied into it, including the Syslog file. If your NT system is low on disk space, you may wish to check how much space the log files occupy before running this script.

In a Solaris environment, the syntax would be:

```
# /opt/CSCOpx/bin/collect.info > <output file>
```

where *<output file>* is the destination (for example, **/var/tmp/info.html**).

The Collect Server Info Tool is very useful in obtaining information about the server's overall health and the contents of CiscoWorks 2000 log files. Figure 15-12 shows the Collect Server Info Report on the server encountering process errors. The Environment section helps to recognize what the problem on the system is. The Computer Name is set to *NTRWAN1* but the PX_HOST variable is set to *ntrwan*. This indicates the Computer Name has been changed since the installation.

Figure 15-12 *The Collect Server Info Report*

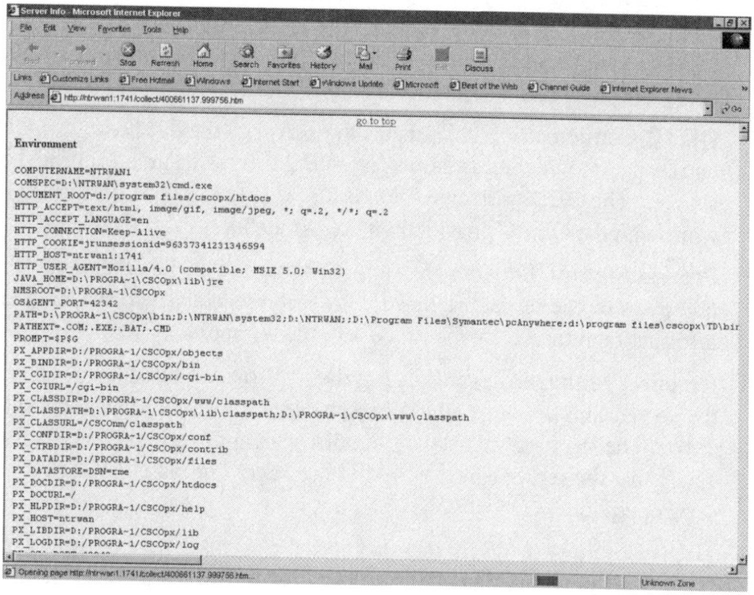

The Collect Server Info Tool will display the following information:

- **System Info**—Displays server version information. This includes operating system version, service pack information, and system root.

- **Environment**—Includes all system environment variables such as the Java Run-Time Home, NMSROOT, and other CiscoWorks 2000 system directory paths. For the different applications to operate, each must be able to locate the executables. The information in the system path and environment variables must be correct for the critical system files to be located.

- **Memory and System Drive**—Includes the amount of system memory and hard drive space on the install drive. The system processes take memory and could cause a low memory condition. The log files, databases, operating system images, and other system files can quickly consume large amounts of disk space. If the server runs low on disk space, the system could be prevented from collecting information or updating files.

- **Network Configuration**—Includes network adapter addressing, local routing table, and IP protocol statistics for IP, TCP, UDP, and ICMP. This information can be useful in trying to diagnose how much information the server is sending and receiving from the network. This can help to troubleshoot server network problems.

- **Event logs**—Diplays the local system error logs. This can be helpful if services do not start. The log entries might provide some possible reason. Status for system services for database and daemon management will be displayed.

- **Resource Manager Registry**—Displays the local server system registry entries used by Resource Manager and CiscoWorks 2000 server. When CiscoWorks 2000 backs up the database, it does not back up the local system registry. This information is necessary for the applications to operate properly. The information in the report could be used to re-create information that becomes corrupt.

- **ODBC Configuration**—Connects the server to the database. The ODBC registry entries can provide information on ODBC drivers installed for the different data sources. The ODBC driver version is also displayed. CiscoWorks 2000 is designed to work with the ODBC provided on the Windows NT 4.0 CD-ROM.

- **Process Status**—Provides the same information as the command **pdshow**. The processes on the server are listed with each respective process number and any information returned by the process to the operating system.

- **Resource Manager Essentials log files**—Provides a display of all of the log files on the server. This contains all log files used by Resource Manager and the CiscoWorks server. The log files are used by the different applications to log event messages. To verify that the server is receiving log messages compare the log entries with current server activities.

- **JRUN Log files**—Logs service start and stop events in the Java Run-Time environment. If a new application is installed that uses a Java Run-Time server, it might conflict with the Java environment of CiscoWorks 2000 server. The log file can be useful when looking for changes in the environment.

- **JRE Registry**—Creates entries in the Registry that record the version and home location. Another Java-based application might change this. Use this information to compare any changes after a new application has been installed.

When the reports are created each is stored on the server. If the server cannot be started, use prior reports to obtain information about the server and state when the report was last run. The reports are stored in the *CSCOpx\htdocs\collect* directory. The files are html documents and can be opened in any browser.

Troubleshooting Server Name and TCP/IP Address

If connectivity issues or server problems are related to a name or TCP/IP address change, then the following problems might show up. This bulleted list assumes all of the connectivity requirements have been met.

- Server does not respond to ping by name but does by IP address.

- Nslookup is not able to resolve the server name to a TCP/IP address.

- Errors within applications such as ACLM report "cannot connect to server" problems.

- Solaris reports the following error, "Display: applet cannot start: class browserServer not found."

- Services fail to start and error logs report problems locating the server or daemon manager.

Changing the server name in Windows NT and changing the TCP/IP address under Solaris can also cause server process to fail. The server should not be a DHCP or BOOTP client to prevent the TCP/IP address from changing. It is recommended that you not change the server Computer Name under Windows NT if it can be avoided. If the Computer Name needs to be changed in Windows NT or the TCP/IP address needs to be changed under Solaris, follow the respective directions. Under Windows NT, the TCP/IP address can be changed without causing any known problem. Under Solaris, the host name is used for DNS purposes only and can be changed.

Changing the TCP/IP Address on Solaris

In the installation on UNIX platforms, the server's TCP/IP address is used in many of the configuration files as a system identifier. Changing the TCP/IP address after installation can produce numerous problems. If the address needs to be changed, implement the steps that follow. Be sure to do a full system and CiscoWorks 2000 backup before making any changes.

Step 1   Edit file /opt/CSCOpx/objects/web/conf/httpd.conf.

Step 2   Change the two lines containing occurrences of ServerName to the new IP address. For example, change line:

ServerName 123.45.67.14

to

ServerName 123.45.67.72

123.45.67.14 is the old IP address and 123.45.67.72 is the new IP address of the server that has RME installed on it.

Step 3   Run the **kill -HUP** [*main web server process id*] command on X-window using the process ID that is shown in **PS** command.

Step 4   Look at **pkgparam -v CSCOmd** and scan for the old IP address and host name. Any variable that includes it would need to be modified. The variable to be most concerned about is PX_HOST.

Step 5   Change the two files containing PX_HOST.

These files will have the following paths:

/var/sadm/pkg/CSCOmd/pkginfo

/opt/CSCOpx/lib/classpath/md.property

Step 6 Shut down and restart the entire RME/CiscoWorks 2000 environment.

After the TCP/IP address has been changed, launch the CiscoWorks 2000 server console. Run the Self Test Report and the Collect Server Info Report to verify that the server is functioning properly.

Changing the Computer Name Under Windows NT

Under Windows NT, the server Computer Name is written to many of the configuration files as a server identifier. The TCP/IP address is bound to the name. The TCP/IP address can be changed without any repercussions. Changing the Computer Name can be dangerous. Before changing the Computer Name, perform a full system and CiscoWorks 2000 Server backup. Implement the following steps to change the name in the necessary locations. The Resource Manager Server in Figures 15-9 through 15-12 has had its Computer Name changed from NTRWAN to NTRWAN1. Fix the server by following these steps:

Step 1 Modify the registry key HKEY_LOCAL_MACHINE/SOFTWARE/ cisco/Resource Manager/Current Version/Environment/PX_Host to reflect the new server name. Figure 15-13 shows the registry on the server modified to reflect the new Computer Name NTRWAN1.

Figure 15-13 *The Resource Manager Registry*

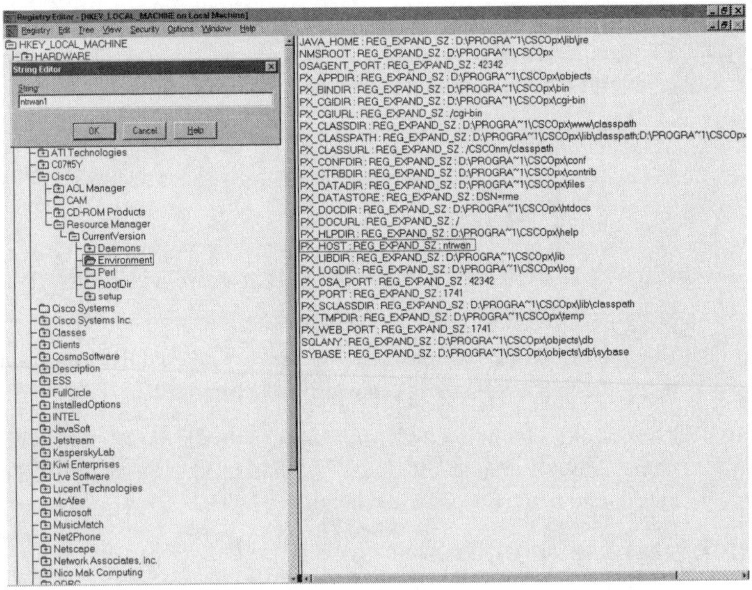

Step 2   Modify PX_HOST in md.properties to reflect the new server name, PX_HOST= *new_server_nam*e. For md.properties, the path is *installation_dir*\CSCOpx\lib\classpath\md.properties.

Figure 15-14 shows the *md.properties* file where the PX_HOST name is changed to match the new Computer Name NTRWAN1.

Figure 15-14 *The md.properties File*

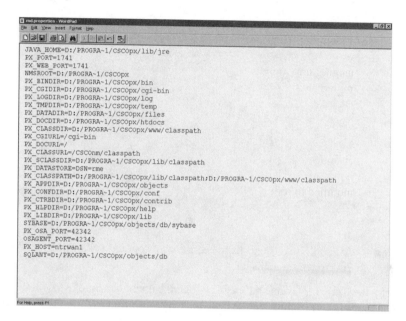

Step 3   Modify ORBagentAddr in aclm.properties to reflect the new Computer Name and reboot the server. For aclm.properties, the path is *installation_dir*\CSCOpx\objects\aclm\etc\aclm\aclm.properties.

Figure 15-15 shows that the *aclm.properties* file has been modified to match the new Computer Name NTRWAN1 at the ORBagentAddr parameter.

Figure 15-15 *The aclm.properties File*

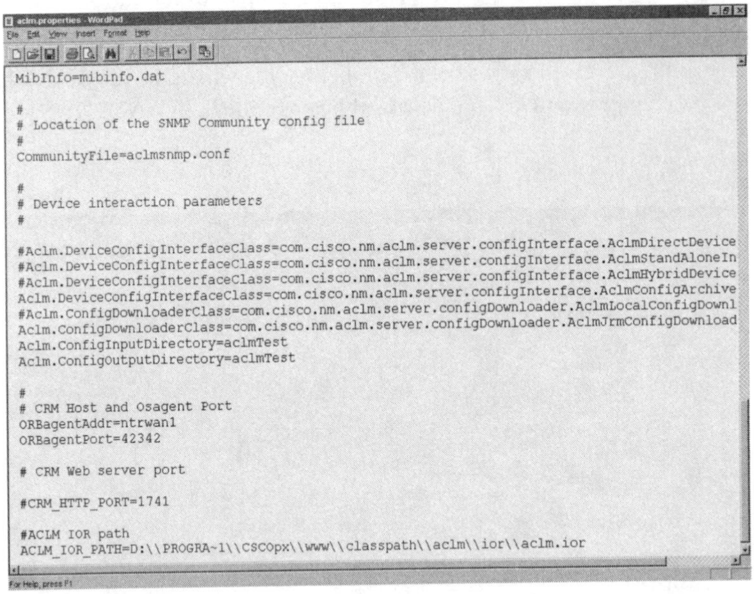

```
MibInfo=mibinfo.dat

#
# Location of the SNMP Community config file
#
CommunityFile=aclmsnmp.conf

#
# Device interaction parameters
#

#Aclm.DeviceConfigInterfaceClass=com.cisco.nm.aclm.server.configInterface.AclmDirectDevice
#Aclm.DeviceConfigInterfaceClass=com.cisco.nm.aclm.server.configInterface.AclmStandAloneIn
#Aclm.DeviceConfigInterfaceClass=com.cisco.nm.aclm.server.configInterface.AclmHybridDevice
Aclm.DeviceConfigInterfaceClass=com.cisco.nm.aclm.server.configInterface.AclmConfigArchive
#Aclm.ConfigDownloaderClass=com.cisco.nm.aclm.server.configDownloader.AclmLocalConfigDownl
Aclm.ConfigDownloaderClass=com.cisco.nm.aclm.server.configDownloader.AclmJrmConfigDownload
Aclm.ConfigInputDirectory=aclmTest
Aclm.ConfigOutputDirectory=aclmTest

#
# CRM Host and Osagent Port
ORBagentAddr=ntrwan1
ORBagentPort=42342

# CRM Web server port

#CRM_HTTP_PORT=1741

#ACLM IOR path
ACLM_IOR_PATH=D:\\PROGRA~1\\CSCOpx\\www\\classpath\\aclm\\ior\\aclm.ior
```

Step 4 After all the changes have been made, stop and restart the CiscoWorks 2000 daemon manager.

After the Computer Name has been changed, launch the CiscoWorks 2000 server console. Run the Self Test Report and the Collect Server Info Report to verify the server is functioning properly.

Managing Server Log Files

On a server that has been running for a period of many months, log files can quickly grow and consume large amounts of disk space. Resource Manager requires free disk space to create database log files, server log files, temporary software images, config files, and so on. The log space for Change Audit Services and the Syslog messages are managed from the Resource Manager Essentials application. Log files not managed by Resource Manager such as error.log, stdout.log, as well as many others, can quickly grow to multiple megabits in size. These log files must have their information manually squeezed to the maximum allowed size—30,000 bytes or a little under 30 Kb. To change the maximum allowed log file size, use the *logconfigure.pl* script. This script allows an administrator to expand or reduce the maximum log file size. The *logconfigure.pl* script is located in the *%NMSROOT%\ cgi-bin\admin* directory. To execute the script, follow the syntax:

```
%NMSROOT%\cgi-bin\admin\perl logconfigure.pl -ADD¦REMOVE < log file path> -SIZE
<size in bytes>
```

%NMSROOT% represents the directory where the application is installed. This directory is typically *opt/CSCOpx* in UNIX and *Program Files\CSCOpx* in Windows NT.

Figure 15-16 shows an example of the *logconfigure.pl* script. The *ChangeAudit.log* file has had the size changed to 100,000 bytes from 30,000 bytes. The new size is reflected in Figure 15-17.

Figure 15-16 *The logconfigure.pl Script*

Use CiscoWorks2000 Server; Administration; Log File Status to check which log files are over the maximum size. Figure 15-17 shows the Log File Status Report. Many of the log files have grown beyond the maximum allowed size.

Two methods can be used to clear out the log files. An administrator can manually stop all system processes and then open the log files and delete contents that are out of date. A script is also provided to clear out log files and back up their contents. The script file is much safer than manually deleting the file contents. The necessary steps for clearing out log files on UNIX and Windows NT are detailed in the sections that follow.

Figure 15-17 *The Log File Status Reports*

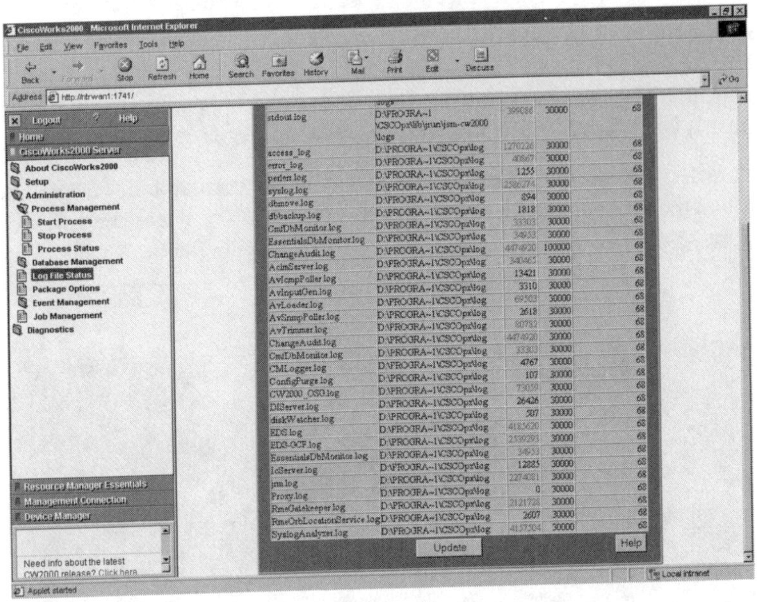

Clear Out Log Files Under UNIX

Before clearing out the log files with the provided script, all daemons must be stopped. Ensure that no jobs are running when the processes are shut down or the jobs will fail. The steps are outlined as follows:

Step 1 Log in as the superuser and enter the root password.

Step 2 Stop all processes:

On Solaris: **/etc/init.d/dmgtd stop**

On AIX: **/etc/rc.dmgtd stop**

On HP-UX: **/sbin/init.d/dmgtd stop**

Step 3 Perform log maintenance:

```
$NMSROOT/bin/perl $NMSROOT/cgi-bin/admin/logBackup.pl [-force] [-dir
destination directory]
```

where **$NMSROOT** is the CiscoWorks2000 installation directory.

-force enables backup regardless of the log file size. Without **-force**, only log files that reach 90 percent of their size limits are backed up and the original log file is emptied.

-dir specifies the full path of the backup destination directory.

NOTE   The target directory must be owned by user bin and group bin. The user must have read, write, and execute permissions, and the group must have at least read permission. Otherwise, the program will terminate with an error message and the log files will not be updated.

Step 4   Without any options, the script backs up the log files to their default directory, $PX_LOGDIR/backup.

Step 5   Verify the procedure was successful by examining the contents of the log files in this location: */var/adm/CSCOpx/log/*.log*.

Step 6   Restart the system:

On Solaris: **/etc/init.d/dmgtd start**

On AIX: **/etc/rc.dmgtd start**

On HP-UX: **/sbin/init.d/dmgtd start**

Clearing Out Log Files on Windows NT

Before clearing out the log files with the provided script, all daemons must be stopped. Ensure that no jobs are running when the processes are shut down or the jobs will fail. The necessary steps are as follows:

Step 1   Log in as Administrator or Server Operator.

Step 2   Open an MSDOS Command Prompt window. Stop all processes by entering:

```
net stop crmdmgtd
```

Step 3   Change to the directory where the Perl script is located. If CiscoWorks2000 has been installed on the C: drive, use:

```
C:\>cd    \Program Files\CSCOpx\cgi-bin\admin
```

Step 4   Perform log maintenance:

```
C:\Program Files\CSCOpx\cgi-bin\admin>perl logBackup.pl [-force]
[-dir destination directory]
```

-force enables backup regardless of log file size. Without **-force**, only log files that reach 90 percent of their size limits are backed up and the original log file is emptied.

-dir specifies the full path of the backup destination directory. Without **-dir**, the default backup directory is: *C:\Program Files\CSCOpx\log\ backup*.

NOTE   If there is a problem, the program will terminate with an error message and the log files will not be updated.

Figure 15-18 shows that the *logbackup.pl* has been run with the Force parameter and has backed up the log files to the backup directory. The script tries to back up a default list of log files. If a log file is not found, an error message will be reported but the script will continue to run.

Figure 15-18 *The logbackup.pl Script*

Step 5 Verify that the procedure was successful by examining the contents of the log files in the following location: *C:\Program Files\CSCOpx\log*.log*.

Step 6 Restart the system and run the Log File Status Report to verify the log files have been cleared out. Figure 15-19 shows the Log File Status Report. To restart the systems, use the **net start crmdmgtd** statement.

Figure 15-19 *Log File Status Report*

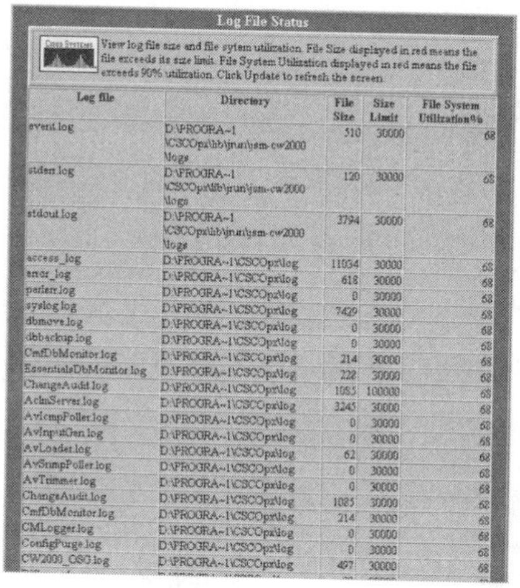

Log File Status

View log file size and file sytem utilization. File Size displayed in red means the file exceeds its size limit. File System Utilization displayed in red means the file exceeds 90% utilization. Click Update to refresh the screen.

Log file	Directory	File Size	Size Limit	File System Utilization%
event.log	D:\PROGRA~1\CSCOpx\lib\jrun\jsm-cw2000\logs	510	30000	68
stderr.log	D:\PROGRA~1\CSCOpx\lib\jrun\jsm-cw2000\logs	120	30000	68
stdout.log	D:\PROGRA~1\CSCOpx\lib\jrun\jsm-cw2000\logs	3794	30000	68
access_log	D:\PROGRA~1\CSCOpx\log	11034	30000	68
error_log	D:\PROGRA~1\CSCOpx\log	618	30000	68
perlerr.log	D:\PROGRA~1\CSCOpx\log	0	30000	68
syslog.log	D:\PROGRA~1\CSCOpx\log	7429	30000	68
dbmove.log	D:\PROGRA~1\CSCOpx\log	0	30000	68
dbbackup.log	D:\PROGRA~1\CSCOpx\log	0	30000	68
CmfDbMonitor.log	D:\PROGRA~1\CSCOpx\log	214	30000	68
EssentialsDbMonitor.log	D:\PROGRA~1\CSCOpx\log	222	30000	68
ChangeAudit.log	D:\PROGRA~1\CSCOpx\log	1085	100000	68
AclmServer.log	D:\PROGRA~1\CSCOpx\log	3245	30000	68
AvIcmpPoller.log	D:\PROGRA~1\CSCOpx\log	0	30000	68
AvInputGen.log	D:\PROGRA~1\CSCOpx\log	0	30000	68
AvLoader.log	D:\PROGRA~1\CSCOpx\log	62	30000	68
AvSnmpPoller.log	D:\PROGRA~1\CSCOpx\log	0	30000	68
AvTrimmer.log	D:\PROGRA~1\CSCOpx\log	0	30000	68
ChangeAudit.log	D:\PROGRA~1\CSCOpx\log	1085	30000	68
CmfDbMonitor.log	D:\PROGRA~1\CSCOpx\log	214	30000	68
CMLogger.log	D:\PROGRA~1\CSCOpx\log	0	30000	68
ConfigPurge.log	D:\PROGRA~1\CSCOpx\log	0	30000	68
CW2000_OSG.log	D:\PROGRA~1\CSCOpx\log	497	30000	68

If the problem is that the server is running out of disk space, a possible solution is to move the databases to another location on the server.

Moving the Databases

Moving the databases on the server should be attempted only when the disk (where the databases are located) is near full and the disk cannot be cleaned out. Moving the databases is done from a command prompt using the *dbmove.pl* script. To move either the Resource Manager Essentials database or CiscoWorks 2000 Server database, use the steps shown in the list that follows:

Step 1 To run the script first shut down the CiscoWorks 2000 Server Daemon Manager.

On UNIX, stop all processes:

— On Solaris: **/etc/init.d/dmgtd stop**

— On AIX: **/etc/rc.dmgtd stop**

— On HP-UX: **/sbin/init.d/dmgtd stop**

On Windows NT, stop all processes: **net stop crmdmgtd**

Step 2 Make sure the target directory for moving the database is already created and has enough space for the database files.

Step 3   Execute the *dbmove.pl* script using the following command line:

```
%NMSROOT%\bin\perl %NMSROOT%\bin\dbmove.pl -s [rme ¦ cmf] -dir
destination directory
```

Step 4   After the script completes, check the *dbmove.log* file to verify the script executed properly.

Step 5   Check that the destination directory contains the files for the RME or CMF database.

Step 6   Restart the CiscoWorks 2000 daemons.

Once the process of troubleshooting the server is complete and you have verification that the server processes are running, the next area of troubleshooting is general device troubleshooting.

General Device Troubleshooting

To troubleshoot most application processes, there are two different areas of problems with inventory information. Troubleshooting these two different areas follows a series of steps. The first area is device connectivity. This involves SNMP connectivity and IP connectivity. The second area is validating if information in the database is still correct. Information such as TCP/IP address, community-strings, and passwords can be changed without updating device information in the inventory. These two areas affect all processes and should be the starting areas for troubleshooting almost any application.

Troubleshooting Device SNMP Connectivity

Connectivity from the management station to the device should be tested first. The inventory collection process is run from the management station, not necessarily from the same location as where the administrator is configuring the process.

Step 1   From the CiscoWorks 2000 Server console select CiscoWorks2000 Server; Diagnostics; Connectivity Tools. These tools were covered in detail in Chapter 14, "Additional CiscoWorks 2000 Tools."

Step 2   Use the Ping tool to test connectivity from the server to the device.

Step 3   Use the Traceroute tool to test the path to a device.

Step 4   Use the NSLOOKUP tool to test DNS name resolution.

Step 5   Use Management Station to Device tool to test UDP, SNMP, HTTP, TFTP, Telnet, and TCP.

If a device responds to the tests in the connectivity tools but does not update in the inventory, use the checkaddr.pl tool. The checkaddr.pl tool can be used to validate the

SNMP connectivity and retrieve a device's object ID. The checkaddr.pl tool can use a comma-separated value file, device list, or all managed devices to check for SNMP connectivity.

The Checkaddr.pl Tool

The *checkaddr.pl* script is located in the *%NMSROOT\bin* directory. The syntax for the command is explained in Figure 15-20; it shows the tool used to detect all devices on the 172.16.121.0 subnet. Notice that it returns the device's SNMP object ID.

Figure 15-20 *The checkaddr.pl Tool*

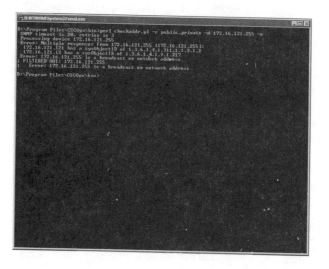

```
%NMSROOT%\bin\perl checkaddr.pl [-c <community_strings>] [-f] [-o <output_file>]
[-e <error_file>] [-r <retry_count>] [-t <timeout_in_secs] <device_file> ¦ -d
<device_list> [-v]
```

The command is typed on one line and the parameters are described in Table 15-3.

Table 15-2 *Parameters for* **checkaddr** *Command*

Parameter	Use
-c	Specifies a comma-separated list of community strings to use if not specified in *<device_file>*.
-f	Disables testing by subnet broadcast address.
-o	Writes input devices to an output file instead of STDOUT (console prompt).
-e	Writes errors to an output file instead of STDERR (console prompt).

continues

Table 15-2 *Parameters for* **checkaddr** *Command (Continued)*

Parameter	Use
-r	Retries count.
-t	Specifies timeout in seconds for SNMP. If none specified, then values from database are used.
<device file>	Can be one device per line or in Resource Manager import format.
-d	Separates devices by commas if no filename specified. Use a '-' to check all managed devices.

If a device responds to the *checkaddr.pl* script but still has problems in the inventory, the next step is to try changing SNMP timeouts. If a device fails to get populated into inventory even though simple SNMP tests are successful, this can be an SNMP timeout issue particularly for devices with a large number of interfaces. What happens is this: When RME makes the SNMP queries necessary to populate the inventory, it sends up to 13 SNMP requests all at once. (It does not send one, wait for a response, send the next, and so forth.) This action is necessary to get the data back as quickly as possible. There can be an SNMP timeout due to how long it may take to get the data of all 13 requests back. Increasing the SNMP timeout usually rectifies this. This issue is not of network performance but rather the response time issue of the SNMP agent on a device. Typically, the device can only process one get request at a time. This causes the larger devices to generate an SNMP timeout. For example, a Catalyst 5500 with modules in all 13 slots would time out because separate SNMP requests would be created for each module and then some.

To increase the SNMP timeout setting, use Resource Manager Essentials; Administration; System Configuration; SNMP. Refer to Chapter 6, " Resource Manager Essentials System Administration," for more information on the configuration of SNMP timeout values.

Validating Inventory Records

Troubleshooting inventory records involves using a combination of tools in Resource Manager Essentials and command-line tools. The Check Device Attributes and Change Device Attributes tools can be used to verify the inventory and update the inventory.

Most often if connectivity is not the cause of the problem in Resource Manager, the problem is that information in the inventory has become unsynchronized with the target device. Three pieces of critical information are required to keep Resource Manager in touch with the devices it manages.

- The device's DNS name or TCP/IP address.
- The device's SNMP community-strings.
- The device's passwords.

Troubleshooting each area will help to resolve connectivity issues with Resource Manager Essentials.

To first verify that the device cannot have its inventory updated, try to force an inventory update to happen. To force a device to update in the inventory and verify the device has updated, implement the following steps:

Step 1 Use Resource Manager Essentials; Inventory; Detailed Device Report.

Step 2 Select the device in question in the Select Device window.

Step 3 Click Finish.

Step 4 The Detailed Device Report will appear. Document the update time information in the top-left corner of the report. Figure 15-21 shows the Detailed Device Report for device wynnethq1.wynnet.com. The last update time is July 11, 2000 at 20:07:02 EDT.

Figure 15-21 *The Detailed Device Report*

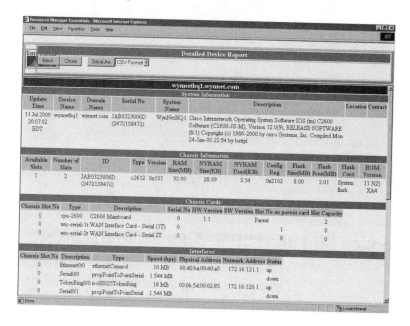

Step 5 Use Resource Manager Essentials; Administration; Inventory; Update Inventory.

Step 6 Select the device from the Select Device dialog box.

Step 7 Click Finish.

Step 8 If the device successfully updated, then the Update Inventory window will list the devices that were processed.

Step 9 If the device is not successfully updated, a System Error will appear. The error will state the device could not be contacted.

Step 10 If the update did work, run the Detailed Device Report again and the Update time should reflect a new date and time. Figure 15-22 shows the Detailed Device Report with the updated time for wynnethq1.wynnet.com. The device is able to have its inventory updated.

Figure 15-22 *The Updated Time on the Detailed Device Report*

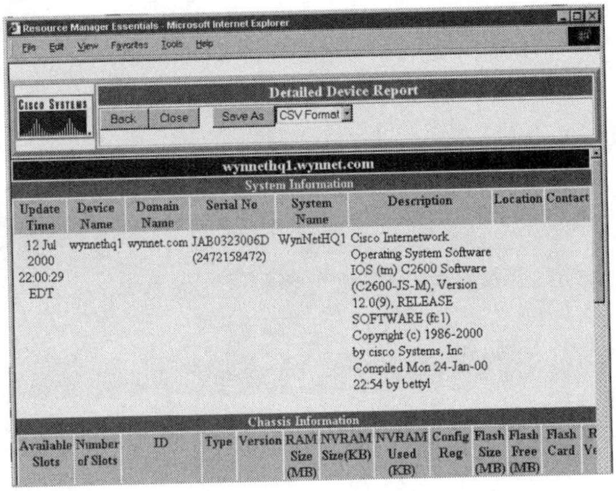

If the update failed, proceed with the troubleshooting steps outlined in the following sections.

Troubleshooting DNS and TCP/IP Address Problems

If the TCP/IP address or DNS host name for a device has changed since the device was added to Resource Manager Essentials, the device would stop responding to Resource Manager requests. The first question is, "How was the device first added?" The second is, "Was the device added by DNS host name or by TCP/IP address?" Each method has specific issues that need to be addressed.

Troubleshooting a Device's DNS Host Name

Recognizing devices in the inventory by DNS host name is easier than having to remember TCP/IP addresses. If the name changes or TCP/IP address resolution changes, the inventory will need to be updated.

If the device's TCP/IP address in DNS changes but is still correct in the DNS server, then Resource Manager does not need to be updated manually.

The inventory will dynamically change at the scheduled polling interval. The inventory can also be manually updated to reflect the new address. To manually update the inventory use Resource Manager Essentials; Administration; Inventory; Update Inventory. Select the device in a view and then update the inventory to reflect the TCP/IP address change. Device wynnethq3.wynnet.com has had the IP address on its Ethernet 0/0 interface changed from 172.16.121.3 to 172.16.121.2. This interface address was used in DNS resolution. The information has been updated in DNS but not in Resource Manager. Figure 15-23 shows the Detailed Device Report for device wynnethq3.wynnet.com.

Figure 15-23 *The Detailed Device Report*

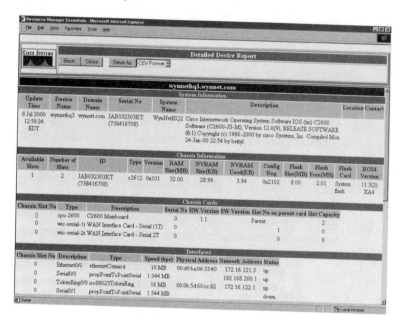

After the report is generated, a manual inventory update is run on wynnethq3.wynnet.com to update the record. The name resolution still works because the DNS server has been updated with the new IP address of the Ethernet 0/0. Figure 15-24 shows the Detailed Device Report after the DNS update.

Changing a device's DNS host name changes how the device is accessed. Resource Manager will no longer be able to access the device because the name change cannot be reflected in the database. Device wynnethq3.wynnet.com has had its host name changed to wynnethq2.wynnet.com to reflect the new IP address on the Ethernet 0/0 interface.

Figure 15-24 *The Updated TCP/IP address in the Detailed Device Report*

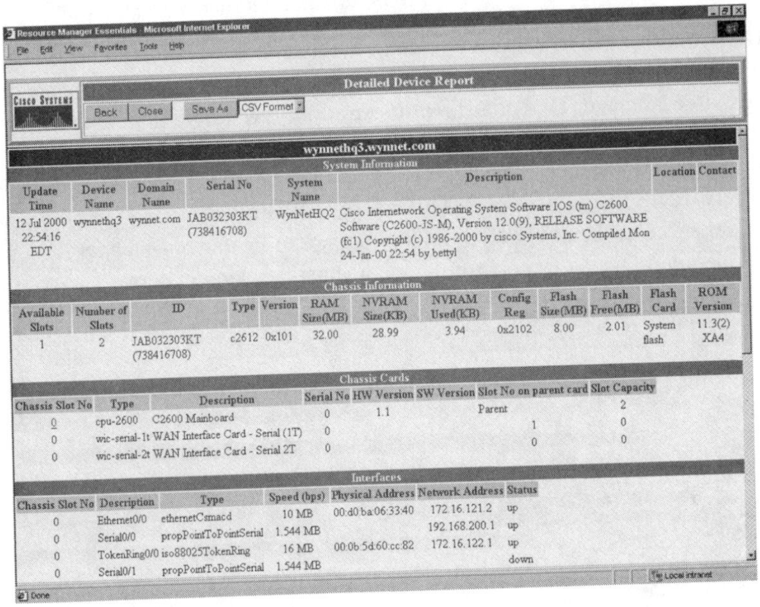

To resolve this problem, a new inventory record will have to be created to reflect the device's new name. A new record had been added manually in Resource Manager Essentials. Figure 15-25 displays the information the server discovered as a duplicate.

Figure 15-25 *The Aliases for Managed Devices Dialog Box*

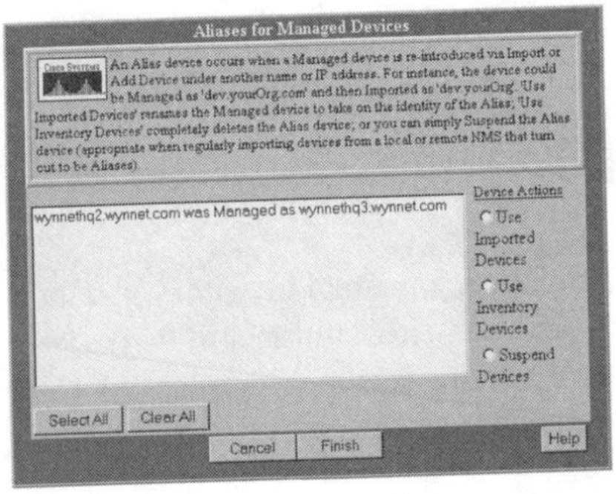

Resource Manager will recognize the device is a duplicate and will list it as Alias in the import status dialog box. Alias problems can be resolved in three different ways:

- **Use Imported Devices**—Renames the managed device to match the new alias.

- **Use Inventory Devices**—Deletes the new alias device. Do not use this selection if the device's host name has changed. This choice should be made if importing from different NMSs and these NMSs contain duplicate records.

- **Suspend Devices**—Moves both the original and new device to a suspended state to be resolved later.

If the device's name has changed, use the option to Use Imported Devices. This option preserves the newly imported device name and matches it to the old name history information. The old configuration, Syslog, and software management information remain intact.

If the DNS server goes down, the host name to TCP/IP address resolution will fail. This action can create a single point of failure. To avoid DNS problems, set up a secondary DNS server with the same Zone information. If the server has multiple DNS servers, it can resolve the host names in more than one place.

Troubleshooting a Device's TCP/IP Address

If a device is added to the database by a TCP/IP address on the system, that address needs to remain constant. In DNS, a device can have multiple address points to the same name on one device. The advantage of DNS is that addresses can change without negative impact on the CiscoWorks 2000 server.

If the TCP/IP address that a device was added under is changed, the device will become unmanageable in the CiscoWorks 2000 Server. To rectify this problem, the device must be added again by the new address. Resource Manager will not recognize the device as a duplicate or Alias (as is the case) with DNS name changes. Therefore, the original device will need to be deleted from the database manually.

If the device has not had the TCP/IP address changed or the DNS host name changed, the next step is to use tools in Resource Manager to try to validate the device information on passwords and community-strings.

Verifying Device Attributes

Resource Manager Essentials comes with a powerful tool for validating a device's passwords and community-strings. The Check Device Attributes Report runs a real-time report to compare the device information with the information in the database. To access the Check Device Attributes report, use Resource Manager Essentials; Administration; Inventory; Check Device Attributes. When a new record is added to the inventory, select the Check Device Attributes box to run the Check Device Attributes report on the new device as the information is added. This can help to ensure the information is correct. Figure 15-26 shows the output of the Check Device Attributes report on the newly updated device wynnethq2.wynnet.com. The write-community string is incorrect and needs to be fixed.

Figure 15-26 *The Check Device Attributes Report*

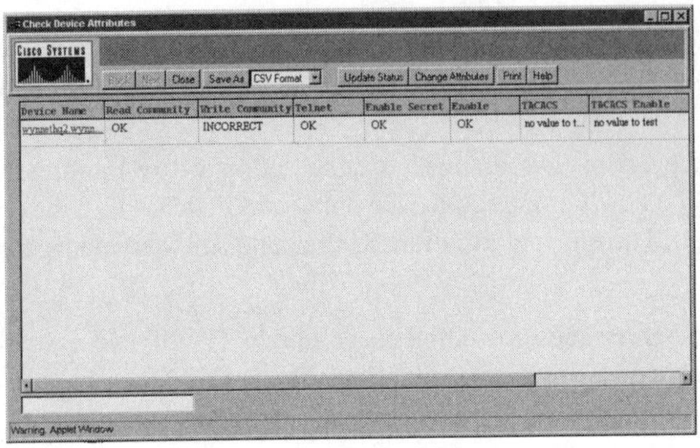

The Check Device Attributes Report can be used to verify the following information. For explanation of the fields see Chapter 7, "Resource Manager Essentials Inventory Management."

- Read-community
- Write-community
- Telnet
- Enable Secret
- Enable
- TACACS
- TACACS Enable
- Local User

The device must be online and responsive for the test to work. If the information is correct, the test will report OK. If the information is incorrect, then the information will report as Incorrect. If the test failed completely because the Telnet password, read-community, or TACACS password were incorrect, the test will show Failed. To change information after the report is run, click on Change Attributes at the top of the report. The Change Device Attributes application will launch in a separate window.

In the Change Device Attributes application, understanding that information is not always replaced when the Change Device Attributes application is used is important. Certain attributes must be deleted before they are changed. Figure 15-27 shows the Change Device Attributes application used to correct the information about the write-community on wynnethq2.wynnet.com. First, the information for the write-community was deleted before the new information was added.

Figure 15-27 *Changing Device Attributes*

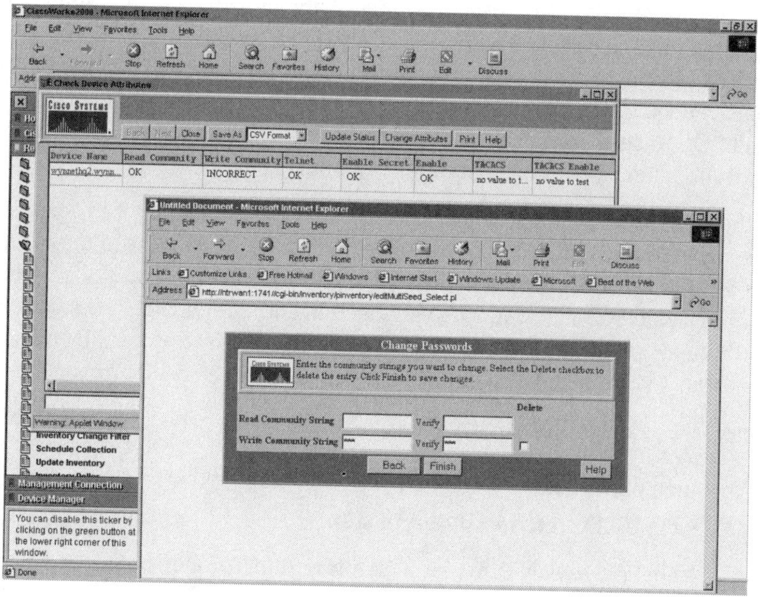

The following attributes should be deleted before they are changed:

- Write-community string
- TACACS user name
- TACACS password
- Enable TACACS user name
- Enable TACACS password
- Local user name
- Local password
- Telnet password
- Enable secret password
- Enable password
- All user fields
- Serial number

After the information is updated, the Check Device Attributes report should be reviewed to verify that the information is correct. If the attributes are verified as correct or the update does not seem to work and the device is still not responding, the record or database may be corrupt. The first step is to try removing the record completely for the device. Then add the device back. If this fails, then the database may indeed be corrupt.

Recovering a Corrupt Database

The Sybase SQL Anywhere engine comes with built-in tools for validating database information. Some of these tools are accessible from the command line of the server. The DBReader.html tool can be used to verify records in the different tables of both Resource Manager and CiscoWorks 2000 Server. This tool allows an administrator who is familiar with SQL to enter select statements to query the table of the Resource Manager Database for information about the device that will not respond or update.

If the database is completely inaccessible, the only option may be to replace the Resource Manager database with the blank database created during the installation. Depending on the degree of corruption, the database engine may or may not start. For certain corruptions, such as bad indexes, the database can function until the corrupt index is accessed. Database corruptions, such as index corruption, can be detected by the dbvalid utility, which requires the database engine to be running. To detect a database corruption use the following steps:

Step 1   Log on as root (UNIX) or with administrator privileges (Windows NT).

Step 2   Stop the daemon manager if it is already running.

On UNIX: **/etc/init.d/dmgtd stop**

On Windows NT: **net stop crmdmgtd** (at a command prompt)

Step 3   Make sure no database (dbeng50) processes are running and there is no database log file. For example, if the database file is */opt/CSCOpx/databases/rme/rme.db*, the database log file is */opt/CSCOpx/databases/rme/rme.log*. This file is not present if the database shuts down cleanly.

Step 4   (UNIX only) Check if the database file(s) and the transaction log file (*.log) are owned by user bin. If not, change the ownership of these files to user bin and group bin.

Step 5   (UNIX only) Set the environment variables (K-Shell syntax):

```
export SATMP=/tmp/.SQLAnywhere
export LD_LIBRARY_PATH=/opt/
CSCOpx/lib (Solaris only)
Export SQLANY=/opt/CSCOpx/objects/db
```

Step 6   Start the database engine

On UNIX, start in the foreground:

```
$SQLANY/bin/dbeng50 -c 16M -m -n validateEng (database file name) -n
validateDb
```

On Windows NT, start at a Windows NT command prompt in the directory where CiscoWorks 2000 is installed, for example *d:\program files\CSCOpx*:

```
1 D:\Program Files\CSCOpx\objects\db\win32\dbeng50 -c 16M -n testing
[ic:ccc](database file name) -n testDb
```

If the database engine starts, it displays a message like this:

```
16364K of memory used for caching
Transaction log: XXX.log
Starting checkpoint
Finished checkpoint
Database: XXX.db started
Press 'q' to quit
```

Step 7 If this message does not appear, the database has fatal corruption, but can sometimes be recovered.

(UNIX only) If there was no error in Step 5, restart the engine as a daemon.

```
$SQLANY/bin/dbeng50 -ud -c 16M -m -n validateEng (database file name) -n
validateDb
```

Step 8 Run dbvalid to detect any other errors such as corrupt indexes:

On UNIX:

```
$SQLANY/bin/dbvalid -c "uid={dba user id for the database},
[ic:ccc]pwd={dba password for the database},
eng=validateEng;dbn=validateDb"
```

On Windows NT:

```
D:\Program Files\CSCOpx\objects\db\win32\dbvalid -c
[ic:ccc]"uid={dba user id of the database};
[ic:ccc]pwd={dba password for the database};eng=validateEng;
dbn=validateDb"
```

The login is either **cmfdba** for the CiscoWorks 2000 database, or **dba** for the Resource Manager Essentials database. The password **c2kY2k** is the same for both. The database name is either *rme.db* for Resource Manager or *cmf.db* for CiscoWorks 2000 Server.

The **dbvalid** command displays a list of tables being validated. The Validation utility scans the entire table, and looks up each record in every index and key defined on the table. If there are no errors, the utility displays something like:

```
Validating DBA.XXX
run time SQL error - Foreign key parent_ has invalid or duplicate
[ic:ccc]index entries 1 error reported
```

On UNIX, the command also returns a non-zero return code, that is $?=1.

If errors are detected in the indexes, then they can be dropped and re-created. If errors are detected in the log files, then the database engine can be forced to create new log files at the expense of a few transactions. Next, the process for both rebuilding indexes and restarting the engine to create log files is explained. The process continues from the preceding steps after an error has been encountered.

WARNING   Before attempting any recovery procedures call the TAC. If the recovery procedure is not done correctly, then the problem could be made worse. Make copies of the necessary database files before performing any recovery steps. Although these steps are documented they are only intended for customers with prior database experience.

Step 1   To forcibly start the engine without a transaction log use the following command:

For UNIX:

```
$SQLANY/bin/dbeng50 -f -n rmeTst /opt/CSCOpx/databases/rme/rme.db
```

For Windows NT:

```
D:\program files\CSCOpx\objects\db\win32\dbeng50 -f -n rmeTst
"D:\program files\CSCOpx\db\rme\rme.db"
```

This starts the database in recovery mode, recovers the database, and immediately terminates the engine. Messages similar to the following appear during the recovery process:

```
2648K of memory used for caching
Database recovery in progress
    Last checkpoint on Mon Dec 06 1999 03:06 pm
    Checkpoint log...
    Transaction log: rme.log
    Forcing recovery without transaction log
    Rollback log...
    Checkpointing...
Starting checkpoint
Finished checkpoint
Recovery complete
Recovered to last checkpoint
```

If the corruption was due to bad indexes, then implement the following steps to drop and rebuild the indexes.

Step 2   Start the database engine as described earlier in the section.

Step 3   Run the isql utility to fix the bad indexes:

For UNIX:

```
$SQLANY/bin/isql -c "uid={dba user id};pwd={dba password};
[ic:ccc]eng=validateEng;dba=validateDb"
```

For Windows NT:

```
D:\program files\CSCOpx\objects\db\win32\isql -c
[ic:ccc]"uid={dba user id};pwd={dba password};eng=validateEng;
dba=validateDb"
```

Step 4   Run the following **isql** commands to delete and add the indexes.
Depending on the size of the table this could take some time to run.

Delete an index with the following SQL statement:

```
DROP INDEX {the index name}
```

Add an index with the SQL statement:

```
CREATE INDEX [UNIQUE] INDEX {index name} on {table name} {column_name}
{ASC|DESC}
```

If the database is corrupted, the preceding steps cannot correct the problems, and there is
no valid backup, then it is possible to start with the database that existed during the
installation process.

WARNING   Do not do this process before performing a full backup of the database and the server. This
will completely remove all objects from the inventory. The managed devices will have to
be added again. The only reason to perform this function is to avoid a complete reinstall to
correct a corrupt database.

Step 1   Exit All CiscoWorks applications.

Step 2   Use the Who is logged on application in the CiscoWorks2000 Server
console to verify no one is using the databases. Send a message to any
users connected to the server to disconnect.

Step 3   Stop all CiscoWorks 2000 Services by stopping the daemon manager:

For Solaris: **/etc/init.d/dmgtd stop**

For Windows NT: **net stop crmdmgtd**

Step 4   In the *%NMSROOT%\databases* directory is a folder for each database
RME, CMF, and ANI. In each folder for the database is a folder named
orig. The orig folder contains the blank databases used at install. They are
named *rme.dborig*, *cmf.dborig*, and *ani.dborig*. In the RME directory is
another file *Syslog.dborig*. This is a template for the database used to
store Syslog messages.

Step 5   Rename the current database and any log files in the directory to something other than their current name. Using .old can make the file easier to recognize. Renaming the file safeguards against replacing a database that is not the cause of a system failure. Figure 15-28 displays the command prompt used to progress to the point to stop the CiscoWorks 2000 services and rename the old database files.

Figure 15-28   *Renaming the Original Databases*

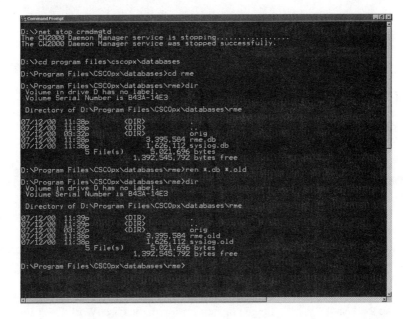

Step 6   To replace a corrupt database with the new one, copy the .dborig file to the directory where the actual database is located. For RME copy both rme.dborig and Syslog.dborig.

Step 7   Rename the *.dborig* file to just *.db*. Figure 15-29 shows the files have been copied to the RME directory. The files have then been renamed.

Step 8   Restart the CiscoWorks 2000 Daemon Manager.

Step 9   Verify that the database has been replaced and the service has started successfully. Figure 15-30 shows the CiscoWorks 2000 services and the RME database service has started after the new databases have been added back.

Figure 15-29 *Renaming the Files*

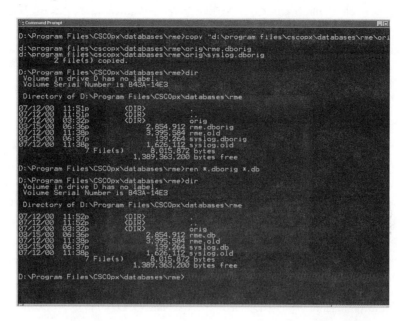

Figure 15-30 *Starting the Services*

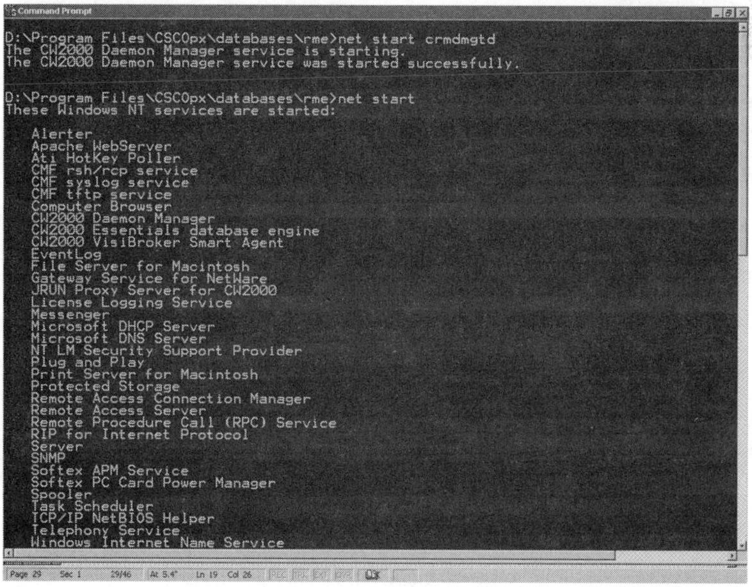

Step 10 To verify the service, connect to the CiscoWorks 2000 server console and check under CiscoWorks2000 Server; Administration; Process Status. Look for the process associated with the databases.

Step 11 The steps for verifying that the information is no longer present depend on the database.

To verify the Resource Manager database has been replaced use the Resource Manager Essentials; Administration; Inventory; List Devices. No devices should be listed.

To verify the CiscoWorks 2000 Server database has been replaced use CiscoWorks2000 Server; Setup; Security; Modify/Delete Users. Only Admin and guest should be listed.

Step 12 Once the new databases have been verified the old files can be deleted or moved to another location.

So far troubleshooting has focused on device connectivity, server processes, server health, inventory information, and database inventory record troubleshooting. The previous sections will assist in solving most day-to-day problems an administrator encounters. The remainder of this chapter will focus on application troubleshooting. If at any point an administrator's comfort threshold is passed, consult the TAC and CCO.

Troubleshooting Inventory Importing

In the initial process of adding devices to the inventory there can be issues that prevent a successful import. There are different types of inventory import that can be done.

- Remote NMS Import
- Local NMS Import
- CSV and DIF file import

Troubleshooting Remote Import

To troubleshoot a remote inventory import, follow these steps:

Step 1 First, verify TCP/IP connectivity to the remote network management System.

Step 2 Verify the remote NMS has the appropriate services and daemons loaded. This is different for each application.

Step 3 Verify the remote NMS is supported for Remote Import. The following are supported:

— CiscoWorks for Switched Internetworks (CWSI)

— HP OpenView

— Tivoli NetView (AIX remote hosts only)

— CiscoWorks

— Cisco WAN Manager (CWM)

Step 4 Windows NT is not supported on any platform application as a source for a remote import.

Step 5 Check to see that user bin can log in to the UNIX Server. Use the following process to check login and directory permissions:

On UNIX:

```
%su bin
%remsh <host name> -l <remote login> ls <directory name>
```

On Windows NT (must be logged on as user bin):

```
%SystemRoot%\system32\rsh.exe <host name> -l <remote login>
ls <directory name>
```

Step 6 A *.rhosts* file is in the remote user's home directory and contains an entry for the Essentials server. The username entry should be bin.

Step 7 The */etc/hosts. equiv* file on the remote server does not contain any statements that disallow access by the Essentials server.

Step 8 For CiscoWorks, the remote user is a member of the CiscoWorks group. On UNIX, the remote user ID is part of cscworks (or the group entered when CiscoWorks was installed) in */etc/group*.

Step 9 For CiscoWorks, the Sybase server is running on the remote host and the Sybase database uses the default query server name CW_SYBASE.

Step 10 For CWSI, the remote user is a member of the group bin and a member of the CWSI Known Network database group. This database group must have write access to the Known Network database.

Step 11 For HP OpenView, HP OpenView is running on the remote host.

Step 12 For Tivoli NetView, Tivoli NetView is running on the remote host.

Step 13 For Cisco WAN Manager, the default user name is svplus.

If the user bin can execute RSH to the remote server, but the import still fails, use the Dataperp.pl script to verify the import process.

The Dataprep.pl Tool

The dataprep.pl tool is located in the *%NMSROOT%\cgi-bin\import\pimport* directory. It must be executed with the **Perl** command. The command directory location must be specified because the script is not in the same directory as the Perl executable. The syntax is displayed along with an explanation for the command's parameters. If the command is run on a remote database, it must be located on a UNIX host. The script will try to open a console connection to the host using the information provided in the command.

```
dataprep.pl [-a] [-p] [-x][ [-d <src>] [-H<host>] [-D<sysdir>]
[ic:ccc][-S[<host>:]<inqep>] [-A<admin>] [-b<db>] [-u<user>]
[ic:ccc][-K[<host>:]<knet>] [-r<cty>] [-w<cty>]
[ic:ccc][-c<ctyfile>]                [-U<ruser>] [-E<ani>] ¦ [-f<importfile>]
[ic:ccc][-s<sep>] [-N<NIL>] [-L<file>] [-l<level>]            [+¦-F]
[ic:ccc] [-V<result>] [-P<pwd>] [<target>]
```

The command is typed on one line and the parameters are described in Table 15-4. Default settings are in brackets [].

Table 15-3   *Parameters for* **dataprep.pl** *Command*

Parameter	Description
-a	Deselect administrative domains from CiscoWorks database (CWDB).
-p	Deselect telnet and console (enable) passwords from CWDB.
-x	Use DB column information and produce extended output.
+F	Turn device import filter on [default].
-F	Turn device import filter off.
-V *<result>*	Validate command-line arguments & write results to file *<result>*.
-d *<src>*	DB source is *<src>* = {**cw** | **ov** | **cwsi** | **cwsi2** | **snmpc** | **cr** | **cwm**}.
-H*<host>*	DB host is *<host>*; [*localhost*].
-D*<sysdir>*	System directory *<sysdir>*; [**computed**].
-U*<ruser>*	Remote user ID for *<host>* is *<ruser>*; [*current user id*].
-S[*<host>***:]***<inqep>*	CWDB inquiry engine path is *<inqep>* (on *<host>*).
-A*<admin>*	CWDB administrator is *<admin>*.
-b*<db>*	CWDB name is *<db>*.
-u*<user>*	CWDB user is *<user>*.
-K[*<host>***:]***<knet>*	CWSI 1.3 known network is *<knet>* on *<host>*.
-f*<importfile>*	Use prepared *<importfile>* as DB source [STDIN].
-s*<sep>*	Set one-character field delimiter to *<sep>* ['|'].
-N*<NIL>*	Set one character SQL NULL replacement to *<NIL>* ['-'].
-L*<file>*	Message logging in file *<file>* [STDERR].

Table 15-3   *Parameters for* **dataprep.pl** *Command (Continued)*

Parameter	Description
-**l**<*level*>	Logging level of details is <*level*>, ranges from 0–7 [0].
-**E**<*ani*>	CWSI 2.x AniServer to contact for import [*AniServer*].
-**r**<*cty*>	CWSI 1.3 read-community <*cty*> [**public**].
-**w**<*cty*>	CWSI 1.3 write-community <*cty*> [**private**].
-**c**<*ctyfile*>	CWSI 1.3 community file <*ctyfile*>.
-**P**<*pwd*>	CWDB password <*pwd*> to grant admin access.
<*output*>	Generated output file <*target*> [**STDOUT**].

If the dataprep.pl script fails to successfully execute the remote import, contact the Cisco TAC for additional assistance, or check the CCO web site for the remote NMS specifics.

Troubleshooting a Local Import

A local import is a less complex process than remotely importing data. The database and services for the other NMS reside on the same machine as CiscoWorks 2000, so there is no need for an RSH to the remote server. Therefore, troubleshooting is also simpler.

There are really only a few things to do to troubleshoot a local import. First, remember that local imports do not happen from older versions of CiscoWorks. The older versions are removed prior to installation and the install process upgrades the data.

- Verify the correct application services are running for the NMS that is the data source.
- Verify the correct user name and permissions to be used by RME to log in to the NMS.
- Use the dataprep.pl script. The script uses the same parameters locally as it does remotely. The host defaults to local host if no host is specified.

Once information is added successfully to the inventory, troubleshooting moves to the process of managing the devices themselves.

Troubleshooting Device Update Processes

Almost all device information revolves around Change Audit Services. Rather than troubleshoot the Configuration Management and Syslog Server applications separately, it is better to perform troubleshooting by remembering how the process works.

1 All applications depend on connectivity and a device's attributes, so use prior steps to validate the device's connectivity and attributes.

2 Configuration files are updated when CAS receives a Syslog message indicating a change.

3 If the Syslog message and change should constitute a change but the Archive does not update, verify that the Configuration Agent is monitoring the Syslog messages. In Resource Manager Essentials; Administration; Configuration Management; General Setup, verify on the Change Probe Setup tab that "Listen to Syslog Messages" is selected. Figure 15-31 shows the Change Probe Setup tab. Notice that "Listen to Syslog Messages" is selected.

Figure 15-31 *The Change Probe Setup Dialog Box*

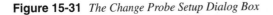

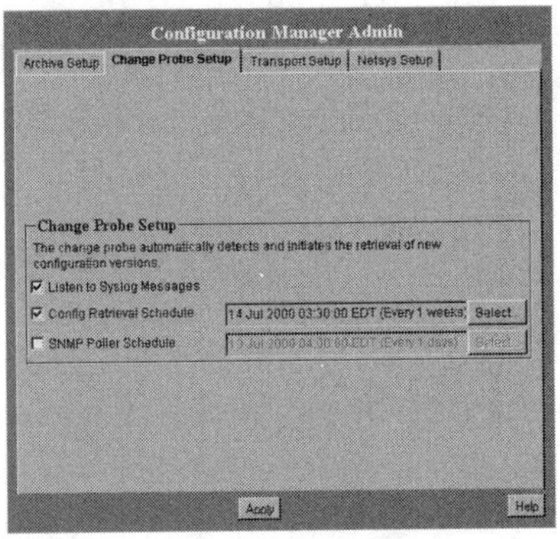

4 If listen to Syslog messages is selected, troubleshooting should focus on Syslog Management.

Troubleshooting Syslog Management

Cisco devices generate Syslog messages for many occurrences, such as on configuration changes, link states, system errors, and so on. Troubleshoot Syslog Messages using the following steps:

Step 1 Verify the devices' logging level. The logging level configuration is covered in Chapter 3, "Configuring Devices for Network Management." The messages must be at the level that logging is set to, or lower, for the message to be sent to the server.

Step 2 Verify that the logging destination is set to the Resource Manager Server or Remote SAC Collector. The steps for configuration of logging destination are covered in Chapter 3. Most platforms can have the logging process validated using the command **show logging** or **show log**. On Cisco IOS-based devices, the number of messages sent to the management station is also listed. Figure 15-32 is a Telnet session to WynNetHQ1.wynnet.com router. The router has sent 300 logging messages to the Syslog server.

Figure 15-32 *The* **show logging** *Command*

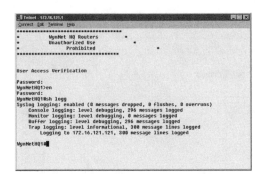

Step 3   If the logging messages are being sent to the correct destination, verify that the messages are reaching the server. Verify that there is not a router blocking the Syslog UDP port 514. Also verify the device connectivity as described earlier in the chapter.

Step 4   If the Syslog messages should be reaching the server, then verification of the server process is next.

Step 5   Verify the Syslog daemon is running on the server. Use CiscoWorks2000 Server; Administration; Process Management; Process Status. Verify the CMLogger, Syslog Analyzer, RMEOrb, EssentialsDBMonitor, and EDS processes are running. If any of these processes are not started, select Start Process in the Process Management folder and start the appropriate process.

NOTE   The daemon manager does not control Syslog. In a UNIX environment, Syslogd is a standard background daemon, and is generally the responsibility of the UNIX sysadmin. In NT, the CW2k Install installs a Syslogd, which is started independently as an NT service.

Step 6   If all processes are started, verify the Inventory Change Filter settings. In Resource Manager Essentials; Administration; Inventory; Inventory Change Filter. This filter controls which messages are filtered so as not to cause an inventory update. Figure 15-33 shows the Inventory Change Filter configuration on the WynNet Resource Manager Essentials server. The figure shows that on the Cisco Chassis table the Config-Reg attribute is not being monitored for changes.

Figure 15-33 *The Inventory Change Filter*

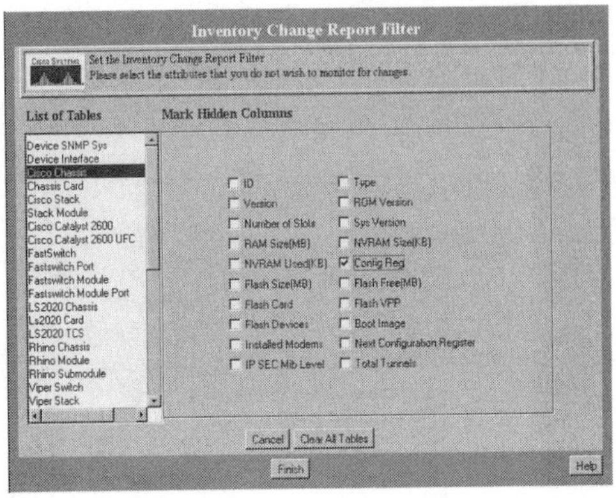

Step 7 Verify the Syslog Process is not filtering the message. Use Resource Manager Essentials; Administration; Syslog Analysis; Define Message Filter. Verify that any filters in place do not affect the missing messages. Syslog message filters were covered in Chapter 10, "Syslog Analysis." A filter is discovered in Figure 15-34 that drops all messages from the 172.16.121.0 subnet. This filter could stop all messages from any devices in that subnet. The filter is disabled.

Figure 15-34 *The Syslog Message Filter*

If there are no filters, the next step is to verify the registered Syslog Analyzers, in Resource Manager Essentials; Administration; Syslog Analysis; Syslog collector Status. If all the Syslog Analyzers are not listed, go back to process verification for each Syslog Analyzer and start the Syslogd daemon (UNIX) or Syslog service (Windows NT). Figure 15-35 shows the Syslog Collector Status report.

Figure 15-35 *The Syslog Collector Status*

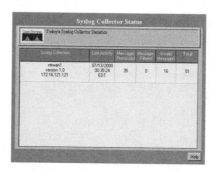

Step 8 If a Remote SAC is being used, follow the steps that come after the following bullet list.

Step 9 If a Remote Syslog Analyzer and Collector is being used, verify the following:

— Verify the Resource Manager Essentials server can contact the remote SAC.

— Verify the SAC Service is running on the remote server.

— If the remote server is UNIX, verify the Syslog daemon is running and the Syslog.log file contains messages.

— If the remote server is Windows NT, use the Windows NT Event Viewer Application log to verify any messages received and filters applied to the messages.

— Verify the SaenvProperties.ini file is correctly configured to point to the Resource Manager Essentials server.

— Examine Chapter 10 for steps to verify the server is correctly installed.

Step 10 Check the Syslog Analysis Storage Options. Open Resource Manager Essentials; Administration; Syslog Analysis; Change Storage Options, and verify the storage maximum age, and message number. Keep in mind messages are never kept more than seven days.

Step 11 Examine the contents of the Syslog.log file for any messages. If the location of the file is different for the UNIX platforms, check the platform's documentation. Under Windows NT the Syslog.log file is located in the %NMSROOT%\log directory. As long as RME is not writing to the file it can be open in any text editor. Figure 15-36 shows the log file is receiving messages from the wynnethq1.wynnet.com device. This verifies the server is working and that the device wynnethq1.wynnet.com is able to send messages to the server.

Figure 15-36 *The Syslog.log File*

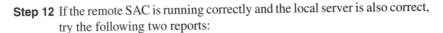

Step 12 If the remote SAC is running correctly and the local server is also correct, try the following two reports:

Resource Manager Essentials; Syslog Analysis; Standard Reports: Select the all messages option for all days. If there are no messages at all and all other steps have been exhausted, try restarting the server. If this does not correct the situation, contact the TAC. If messages are received for some devices but not others, verify the device settings and check the Software Bug Navigator for any software bugs. If there are no known bugs, try resetting the device. If resetting the device does not help, contact the TAC.

Resource Manager Essentials; Syslog Analysis; Unexpected Device Report: Select All day messages. This can be used to see if the device is showing up as Unmanaged. If this is the case, verify the inventory record is correct. If a device sent messages before it was added to the inventory, the messages will still appear here even after the device is added. In Figure 15-37, the Unexpected Device shows the devices wynnethq1 and wynnethq3 had sent messages at some point before each was added to the inventory.

Figure 15-37 *The Unexpected Device Report*

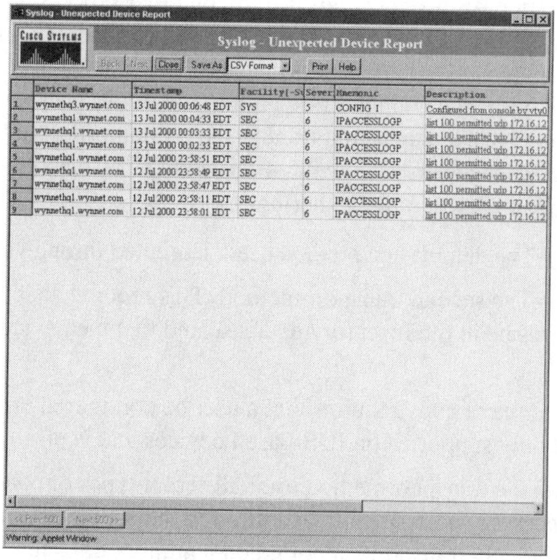

Name Resolution causes some other problems that might be encountered with the Syslog Analyzer. Syslogd starts each record in a Syslog file with a timestamp (when the message was received on the workstation) and either the IP address of the sender or (if a reverse name lookup is successful) the host name of the sender. RME Syslog Analyzer compares that (either the IP address or host name) with the inventory to see if it can match that to a managed device. If the device has been entered into inventory by the host name (and host name to address resolution works), but if there is no reverse name resolution (address to name), then SA marks the record as from an unmanaged device.

The performance capacity of the Syslog Analyzer must also be taken into account. RME Syslog Analyzer can handle up to 150K Syslog messages per day. This is a reasonable number for a fairly large network. If the user is directing Syslog output from one or more PIX firewalls to the same Syslog file, however, a single PIX is capable of generating 4 million Syslog records per day. Exceeding the recommended rate may cause Syslog Analyzer to stop functioning and even may cause the database tables used by the Syslog analyzer to become corrupted.

If Syslog Messages are being received but the Configuration Archive does not update, move on to configuration archive troubleshooting.

Configuration Archive Troubleshooting

The Configuration Archive depends heavily on other processes to operate properly. Primarily the method of updates is that when a Syslog message is received at the server, an SNMP write net request to the device is initiated. The other method for gathering configuration files after updates is the configuration poller. The poller is disabled by default. Catalyst switches do not have a config-mib used in the polling process. Another issue with configuration management is how the file is gathered. There are three different transports available for configuration file gathering:

- **TFTP**—The default first method used. Executed through an SNMP write net request.

- **Telnet**—The second transport method. This requires that the Telnet and enable passwords be in the Inventory database and that the device be capable of supporting Telnet.

- **RCP**—Remote copy requires that a user be configured on the device to be executed. RCP is only supported on IOS-based devices and is disabled by default.

Depending on the transport method used, different types of connectivity are necessary. Verify the necessary ports are allowed through the access lists on the routers. The Telnet transport is the only transport supported on a number of Catalyst switches and is the only way to retrieve startup configuration files from an IOS-based device like a router.

The Archive Setup tab for Configuration Management is used to configure how the server maintains the configuration files. Verify the archiving policy on how many days to keep the files and the number of versions to hold.

On the Archive Setup tab verify the directory where the files are being stored. On the server verify the directory exists and has not been moved or deleted. The default directory is *%NMSROOT%/CSCOpx/files/archive*. In the archive directory look in the config folder, which contains separate subfolders for each device. The folder names represent the device's ID number in the Resource Manager Database.

In the device subfolders verify there are configuration files. Open the files in any text editor to verify what device each represents. The filename contains the date the file was collected. The naming convention for configuration files is *YYYYMMDDHHMMSS<configtype>.cfg*. By examining the filename an administrator can tell the date and time the file was created.

The Archive Status Report can also be helpful in troubleshooting device configuration management. In Resource Manager Essentials select Administration; Configuration Management; Archive Status. The Archive Status report will list how many configuration files can be successfully uploaded. For any devices that failed, the report will list a reason. Figure 15-38 shows the Archive Status Report. There were 26 successful, 1 not supported, and 3 partial failures.

Figure 15-38 *The Archive Status Summary Report*

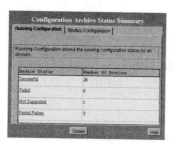

Select the hyperlink for the status in the report to see each device individually and any additional information relevant to the device. After selecting the Partial Failure link, a report displays why the partial failures occurred. For the system reports on the devices 10.1.5.2, 10.1.1.2, and 10.1.2.2, the system did not have the correct Telnet passwords to collect the configuration files. Figure 15-39 shows the detailed information on Configuration Archive.

Figure 15-39 *The Archive Status Details*

Another method of troubleshooting Configuration Management is **cwconfig**. The **cwconfig** can be used from a command line to try to manually force a configuration update (the command is typed on a single line):

```
D:\program files\cscopx\bin\cwconfig -u admin -p admin -d 5 -l d:\temp\
    cwconfig.log -view "Router 2600 Series"
```

The command-line tool reports errors immediately upon the attempt to pull the config file. This can provide a clear path the troubleshooting process should take. Figure 15-40 shows how **cwconfig** is used to pull the configurations from all the 2600 series routers using the system view "Router 2600 Series." Make sure to put quotation marks around the view name, otherwise the system will return an error. Not all the 2600 devices running configurations are updated because the archive has the latest information. Increasing the debug level expands the output. Figure 15-40 displays the log file generated by the following **cwconfig** command. For more details on **cwconfig** command switches see Chapter 8, "Device Configuration Management."

Figure 15-40 *cwconfig Log File*

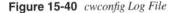

The Change Audit Services also become aware of changes through jobs. Jobs are created in a number of different applications—SWIM, NetConfig, and ACLM.

Troubleshooting Change Audit Services

Change Audit Services are used to keep track of any changes made to manage devices. Change Audit Services trigger the configuration agent based upon changes it has received. To verify the Change Audit Services implement the following steps:

Step 1 First, verify connectivity as described earlier in the chapter.

Step 2 In the CiscoWorks 2000 Server console verify the following Change Audit services are started: Change Audit, Syslog Analyzer, EssentialsDbMonitor, EDS, and CMLogger.

Step 3   If the services are running and the device has connectivity, verify Syslog services as described earlier in the chapter.

Step 4   Delete the Change Audit Service logs using Resource Manager Essentials; Administration; Change Audit; Delete Records. After deleting records, generate a change that should be recorded in the CAS log.

Step 5   If the Syslog services are running, verify that any change messages are being recorded. Use Resource Manager Essentials; Change Audit; All Changes. Figure 15-41 shows the All Changes report.

Figure 15-41   *The All Changes Report*

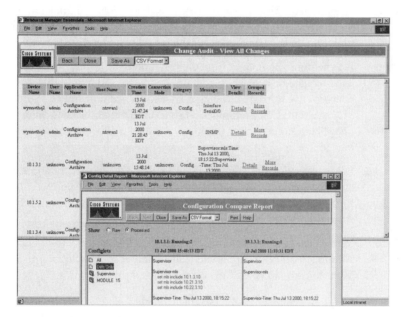

After all the update management and inventory applications have been verified troubleshooting other applications can begin.

Troubleshooting Software Image Management

Software Image Management (SWIM) involves four different areas—setup, identification, planning, and distribution. Each area has specific issues that can cause problems in Software Distribution. This section breaks down the troubleshooting for each area.

Troubleshooting SWIM Setup

SWIM setup prepares Resource Manager for the process of image distribution. This involves analyzing images in the library, creating approver lists, and identifying supported devices. The following steps outline areas where the setup process can encounter problems:

Step 1 Identifying whether the device is supported can save a lot of angst if software management does not work on that device. To verify if the device is support check on CCO.

Step 2 Verify device connectivity to the server as described earlier in the chapter.

Step 3 A Synchronization Report must be created before images can be synchronized. User Resource Manager Essentials; Administration; Software Management; Schedule Synchronization Job. After the job runs wait up to five minutes for the report to be ready for review.

Step 4 In synchronizing images from the network to the library verify the server has adequate disk space to contain the images. To relieve disk space concerns use Resource Manager Essentials; Administration; Software Management; Edit Preferences. From this dialog box the location where images are stored can be modified. All files will be moved to the new location.

Step 5 If Approver lists are going to be used, then any users to be added must have the approver role. Verify the users added to the Approval List in Resource Manager Essentials; Administration; Job Approval; Edit Approval List.

Step 6 Verify the approval preferences in Resource Manager Essentials; Administration; Job Approval; Edit preferences. The Software Management tab is used to control Job Approval Options.

Step 7 Verify Resource Manager has a valid SMTP server setup to be able to e-mail notifications to the approvers. An approver must approve a job at least five minutes before the scheduled execution time.

Once SWIM has been successfully set up the next area is identification. Identification involves identifying which devices are upgrading candidates.

Troubleshooting Software Identification

Software Identification involves analyzing devices and possible images to be used for the distribution process. The identification process can run into problems in identifying possible candidate images and connecting to CCO. To troubleshoot these problems implement the following steps:

Step 1   The library upgrade analysis does not support Catalyst Switches with Supervisor Engines. To verify a catalyst switch's requirements, use the release notes for the software image.

Step 2   If an image came out after Resource Manager, the Resource Manager library analysis will not work. To update the Upgrade Path information use Resource Manager Essentials; Administration; Software Management; Update Upgrade Info. Figure 15-42 displays the Update Upgrade Info dialog box.

Figure 15-42 *The Update Upgrade Info Dialog Box*

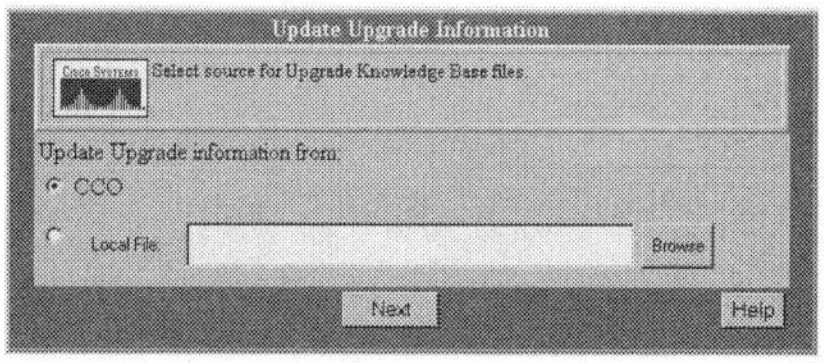

Step 3   If the CCO upgrade analysis does not work, verify the users' CCO login information is correct and that the user has CCO rights to the software library. Use CiscoWorks2000 Server; Setup; Security; Modify My Profile. Verify the CCO login and password are correct. Figure 15-43 is the Modify My Profile dialog box. Change the CCO login from here.

Figure 15-43 *Modify My Profile Dialog Box*

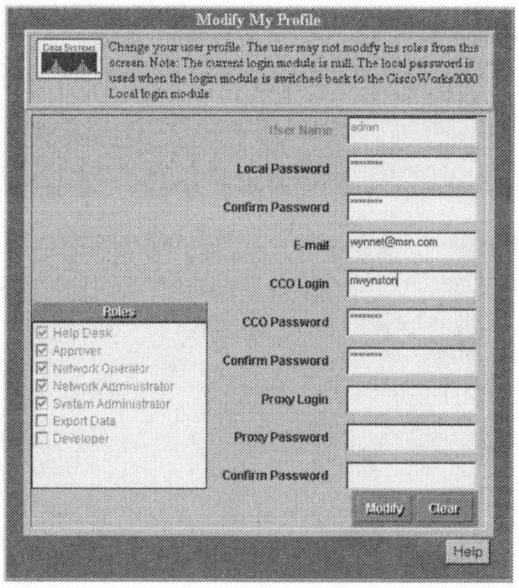

Step 4   If the CiscoWorks 2000 Server is using integrated logins with a network operating system such as Windows NT, then the CiscoWorks user name is being taken from the NOS. The CCO user name and password must still be added to the profile.

Step 5   If the login information for CCO is correct, verify any proxy server settings. The connection to CCO is being made from the Resource Manager Essentials server. If a Proxy server is needed, use Resource Manager Essentials; Administration; System Configuration. On the Proxy tab put in the address of the Proxy Server. Figure 15-44 shows the Proxy Server configuration dialog box.

Figure 15-44 *The Proxy Server Configuration*

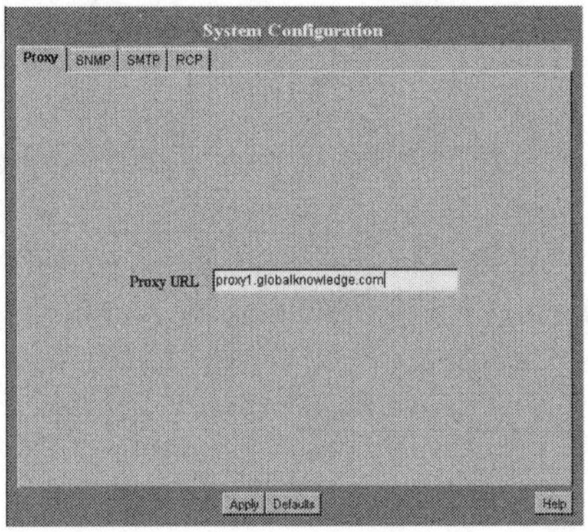

Step 6   If the Proxy Server is a secure Proxy Server verify that the Proxy login information is in the users profile. Use CiscoWorks2000 Server; Setup; Security; Modify My Profile. Verify the proxy user name and password are correct. Figure 15-43 has the Modify My Profile dialog box open.

Step 7   Verify DNS is properly configured on the server to resolve the Cisco Web site. Use CiscoWorks2000 Server; Diagnostics; Connectivity Tools; NSLookup. Type **www.cisco.com** to test DNS resolution.

Once the Software Identification process is complete the next area is Distribution Planning. Distribution Planning involves adding images, determining the device upgrade order, and preparing for a rollback.

Troubleshooting Distribution Planning

Software Distribution Planning can encounter a lot of the same problems as the steps already examined. To troubleshoot the planning processes follow the steps outlined below:

Step 1   Awareness of the order in which devices will be upgraded is very important. If device X provides device Y connectivity to the server, be sure to upgrade device Y before upgrading device X. The order of the process is controlled in the software distribution job detailed in Chapter 9, "Software Image Management."

Step 2   When adding images to the system through a job the files are always stored first in a temporary location. For each job, the administrator must manually click the "add image to library" hyperlink for the image to get into the library.

Step 3   Adding images from CCO can encounter the same problems in CCO access as the Identification process described. Use those steps to troubleshoot adding images from CCO.

Step 4   If images are added from the local file system and the filename is not the same as when the file was downloaded from CCO, the hardware requirements will not be available. The system defaults to version 0. This file cannot be used to upgrade a Catalyst switch as it will show as an older software version and downgrades are not possible to a Catalyst switch through SWIM.

Step 5   When images are added to the system verify that there is adequate disk space for the image to be stored. To change the file storage location, refer to the troubleshooting setup section previously.

Step 6   Do not reset the server while a job is in progress. This does not cancel the job. When the server restarts so will the job. If the server is in process of copying an IOS to a device, this could leave the device inaccessible.

Step 7   Schedule the job at off hours. Be sure to synchronize the clocks on the server with the devices. The job starts based upon the time on the server.

Step 8   If a job is scheduled at off hours and approval is necessary, be sure the job is approved or it will not run at the scheduled time.

Step 9   Run from Flash Routers, such as 2500 series routers, require both an enable secret and enable password. This is to ensure that if the boot ROM cannot read the encryption of the secret password, the enable password is used.

Step 10 Run From Flash Routers will not be able to write to flash while it is in use. Therefore, these devices will reboot into RXBoot mode and erase flash and then download the file. If the download fails, the device will be unreachable. This is different from other platforms, which Run the IOS from RAM and can do in-place upgrades.

Step 11 Run From Flash Based Devices require the IOS command **snmp-server system-shutdown** to successfully reboot the router to RXBoot mode.

Step 12 If the job fails, use CiscoWorks2000 Server Administration; Job Management to determine the cause by clicking the job and then examining the job details.

Step 13 If a job fails, telnet to the device to examine flash and verify the current contents before resubmitting the job. If the file is in flash, use show version to see the current IOS file used. Reload the device if necessary to use any new file in flash.

Step 14 If a job fails, go to the Device Connectivity section in this chapter to verify the connectivity and inventory information for SNMP community-strings and passwords.

Step 15 Debugging can also be enabled for the Software Image Management process. The debugging option is on the Resource Manager Essentials; Administration; Software Management; Preferences. Click the check box labeled Turn debugging on.

Step 16 After the job is complete or an error is encountered, view the log file by selecting Resource Manager Essentials; Software Management; Job Management; Mail or copy Log File. The log file can be copied to any destination. It will be compressed in .tar format. This can be opened by almost any decompression utility including WinZip. Figure 15-45 is the log file created during an upgrade that encountered an error due to a problem with job approval.

Another application in Resource Manager Essentials that can run into problems is Access-Control List Manager. The Access-Control List Manager is a Java-based application that loads jar files to the client in order to run. This and other issues with device connectivity can cause problems in ACLM.

Figure 15-45 *The SWIM Log*

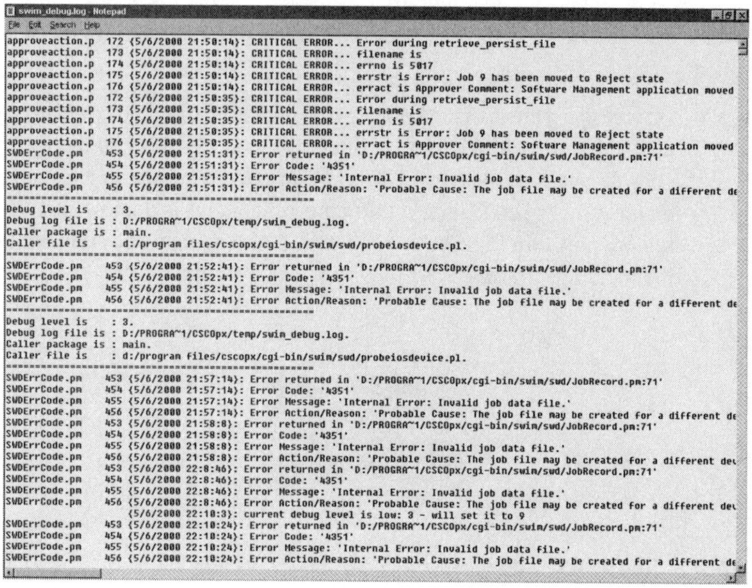

Troubleshooting Access-Control List Manager

The Access-Control List Manager application is an add-on to the Resource Manager environment. Not all versions of ACLM work with all versions of RME.

- Version 1.0 of ACLM is for RME 2.X
- Version 1.1 of ACLM is for RME 3.0
- Version 1.1 of ACLM with a patch from Cisco is for RME 3.1

It is important to keep these requirements in mind when the Resource Manager server is going to be upgraded. ACLM must be installed after RME is installed in order to function.

The ACLM uses Java applets loaded onto a client in order to work. ACLM uses the CAM to install the necessary jar files to the client to improve application performance.

ACLM can create, modify, delete, and download many different types of access lists to devices. This section covers how to troubleshoot the ACLM application process. The first area of concern is launching the application.

Troubleshooting Launching ACLM

The ACLM launches on the client after downloading the necessary files to the end station browser. The following is a list of steps to troubleshoot launching the ACLM client application:

Step 1 If Access-Control List Manager is launched from the server using any alias that refers to the local host address 127.0.0.1, or to the local host address itself, the server will report an error message that it cannot connect to server. This is a known problem and is documented in the release notes. In Figure 15-46, the ACLM Application is not available on the local host name.

Figure 15-46 *Cannot Access ACL Server*

Step 2 If the server is being accessed by the server host name or TCP/IP address and the error cannot connect to server appears, check the aclm.properties file. The aclm.properties file is located in the *%NMSROOT%\objects\ aclm\etc\aclm* directory. In this file verify the ORBagentAddr parameter is set to the server host name. In the AclmName section of the file change AclmName to be "*hostname*-**AclmName**" where the *hostname* is the server host name.

Step 3 If the server host name is correct in the *aclm.properties* file but the server is still unavailable, stop the AclmServer process. The process can be stopped by going into CiscoWorks2000 Server; Administration; Process Management; Stop Process.

Step 4 From a command prompt type **netstat –a –p tcp**. Look to see if port 15349 is listed as a listening port. This is the port ACLM listens on. If it is listed after ACLM is stopped, something else is using the port. To change the port number choose a port number not in use between 1025 and 65536. Change the port number in the aclm.properties file in the ACLMPort section.

Step 5 The process can be started by going into CiscoWorks2000 Server; Administration; Process Management; Start Process. Start the AclmServer process.

Step 6 Verify the client meets the minimum web browser requirements. The application requires the client have Java support.

Troubleshooting Using ACLM

ACLM can encounter problems when the devices in the scenario are modified while the scenario is open, or if more than one user opens a scenario that contains the same devices. Table 15-5 documents how to troubleshoot problems with using ACLM.

Table 15-4   *Troubleshooting ACLM*

Problem	Cause	Solution
Unable to modify templates in template manager.	Access restrictions.	Only administrators can modify templates. Log in with administrator privileges.
Job status shows pre-download failed.	Device went stale during download.	Step 1—Select Device in ACLM. Step 2—Right-click the device and select Refresh Device. Step 3—Download to the device again.
Download Job status: "Download Failed" and "Device Results" reports that Telnet credentials did not match.	Invalid passwords.	Verify Telnet, TACACS, or local login and passwords are correct in the inventory. ACLM uses Telnet to download the ACL.

In addition, if another user is using ACLM and the same devices are in two different scenarios, ACLM will display a small icon in the bottom-right corner. This can help to prevent creating conflicting ACLs in the open scenarios.

Summary

Resource Manager Essentials is a series of interrelated application processes. These processes are dependent on server resources to be able to operate properly. All of the components of Resource Manager make troubleshooting a difficult and sometimes unsuccessful task. Following the steps outlined in this chapter can help to solve most of the day-to-day problems encountered in the Resource Manager Essentials environment.

The chapter details step-by-step directions for troubleshooting the different Resource Manager applications. The most common problems encountered in managed networks are device connectivity and maintaining correct information in the databases. When troubleshooting any network applications some of the basic principles modeled here can be followed. Always start at the physical layer and work up. Never assume anything is done correctly until it is verified. Following these two rules and the steps for troubleshooting applications like inventory management, configuration management, software management, and Syslog management will help to correct most of the problems encountered in the Resource Manager environment.

Symbols

A

B

C

E

J–K

L

M

CCIE Professional Development

Cisco LAN Switching

Kennedy Clark, CCIE; Kevin Hamilton, CCIE

1-57870-094-9 • **AVAILABLE NOW**

This volume provides an in-depth analysis of Cisco LAN switching technologies, architectures, and deployments, including unique coverage of Catalyst network design essentials. Network designs and configuration examples are incorporated throughout to demonstrate the principles and enable easy translation of the material into practice in production networks.

Advanced IP Network Design

Alvaro Retana, CCIE; Don Slice, CCIE; and Russ White, CCIE

1-57870-097-3 • **AVAILABLE NOW**

Network engineers and managers can use these case studies, which highlight various network design goals, to explore issues including protocol choice, network stability, and growth. This book also includes theoretical discussion on advanced design topics.

Large-Scale IP Network Solutions

Khalid Raza, CCIE; and Mark Turner

1-57870-084-1 • **AVAILABLE NOW**

Network engineers can find solutions as their IP networks grow in size and complexity. Examine all the major IP protocols in-depth and learn about scalability, migration planning, network management, and security for large-scale networks.

Routing TCP/IP, Volume I

Jeff Doyle, CCIE

1-57870-041-8 • **AVAILABLE NOW**

This book takes the reader from a basic understanding of routers and routing protocols through a detailed examination of each of the IP interior routing protocols. Learn techniques for designing networks that maximize the efficiency of the protocol being used. Exercises and review questions provide core study for the CCIE Routing and Switching exam.

CISCO SYSTEMS

CISCO PRESS

www.ciscopress.com

Cisco Press Solutions

Enhanced IP Services for Cisco Networks
Donald C. Lee, CCIE

1-57870-106-6 • AVAILABLE NOW

This is a guide to improving your network's capabilities by understanding the new enabling and advanced Cisco IOS services that build more scalable, intelligent, and secure networks. Learn the technical details necessary to deploy Quality of Service, VPN technologies, IPsec, the IOS firewall and IOS Intrusion Detection. These services will allow you to extend the network to new frontiers securely, protect your network from attacks, and increase the sophistication of network services.

Developing IP Multicast Networks, Volume I
Beau Williamson, CCIE

1-57870-077-9 • AVAILABLE NOW

This book provides a solid foundation of IP multicast concepts and explains how to design and deploy the networks that will support appplications such as audio and video conferencing, distance-learning, and data replication. Includes an in-depth discussion of the PIM protocol used in Cisco routers and detailed coverage of the rules that control the creation and maintenance of Cisco mroute state entries.

Designing Network Security
Merike Kaeo

1-57870-043-4 • AVAILABLE NOW

Designing Network Security is a practical guide designed to help you understand the fundamentals of securing your corporate infrastructure. This book takes a comprehensive look at underlying security technologies, the process of creating a security policy, and the practical requirements necessary to implement a corporate security policy.

www.ciscopress.com

Cisco Press Solutions

EIGRP Network Design Solutions

Ivan Pepelnjak, CCIE

1-57870-165-1 • AVAILABLE NOW

EIGRP Network Design Solutions uses case studies and real-world configuration examples to help you gain an in-depth understanding of the issues involved in designing, deploying, and managing EIGRP-based networks. This book details proper designs that can be used to build large and scalable EIGRP-based networks and documents possible ways each EIGRP feature can be used in network design, implmentation, troubleshooting, and monitoring.

Top-Down Network Design

Priscilla Oppenheimer

1-57870-069-8 • AVAILABLE NOW

Building reliable, secure, and manageable networks is every network professional's goal. This practical guide teaches you a systematic method for network design that can be applied to campus LANs, remote-access networks, WAN links, and large-scale internetworks. Learn how to analyze business and technical requirements, examine traffic flow and Quality of Service requirements, and select protocols and technologies based on performance goals.

Cisco IOS Releases: The Complete Reference

Mack M. Coulibaly

1-57870-179-1 • AVAILABLE NOW

Cisco IOS Releases: The Complete Reference is the first comprehensive guide to the more than three dozen types of Cisco IOS releases being used today on enterprise and service provider networks. It details the release process and its numbering and naming conventions, as well as when, where, and how to use the various releases. A complete map of Cisco IOS software releases and their relationships to one another, in addition to insights into decoding information contained within the software, make this book an indispensable resource for any network professional.

www.ciscopress.com

Cisco Press Solutions

Residential Broadband, Second Edition
George Abe

1-57870-177-5 • AVAILABLE NOW

This book will answer basic questions of residential broadband networks such as: Why do we need high speed networks at home? How will high speed residential services be delivered to the home? How do regulatory or commercial factors affect this technology? Explore such networking topics as xDSL, cable, and wireless.

Internetworking Technologies Handbook, Second Edition
Kevin Downes, CCIE, Merilee Ford, H. Kim Lew, Steve Spanier, Tim Stevenson

1-57870-102-3 • AVAILABLE NOW

This comprehensive reference provides a foundation for understanding and implementing contemporary internetworking technologies, providing you with the necessary information needed to make rational networking decisions. Master terms, concepts, technologies, and devices that are used in the internetworking industry today. You also learn how to incorporate networking technologies into a LAN/WAN environment, as well as how to apply the OSI reference model to categorize protocols, technologies, and devices.

OpenCable Architecture
Michael Adams

1-57870-135-X • AVAILABLE NOW

Whether you're a television, data communications, or telecommunications professional, or simply an interested business person, this book will help you understand the technical and business issues surrounding interactive television services. It will also provide you with an inside look at the combined efforts of the cable, data, and consumer electronics industries' efforts to develop those new services.

Performance and Fault Management
Paul Della Maggiora, Christopher Elliott, Robert Pavone, Kent Phelps, James Thompson

1-57870-180-5 • AVAILABLE NOW

This book is a comprehensive guide to designing and implementing effective strategies for monitoring performance levels and correctng problems in Cisco networks. It provides an overview of router and LAN switch operations to help you understand how to manage such devices, as well as guidance on the essential MIBs, traps, syslog messages, and show commands for managing Cisco routers and switches.

CISCO SYSTEMS

CISCO PRESS

www.ciscopress.com

Cisco Press Fundamentals

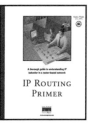

IP Routing Primer

Robert Wright, CCIE

1-57870-108-2 • **AVAILABLE NOW**

Learn how IP routing behaves in a Cisco router environment. In addition to teaching the core fundamentals, this book enhances your ability to troubleshoot IP routing problems yourself, often eliminating the need to call for additional technical support. The information is presented in an approachable, workbook-type format with dozens of detailed illustrations and real-life scenarios integrated throughout.

Cisco Router Configuration

Allan Leinwand, Bruce Pinsky, Mark Culpepper

1-57870-022-1 • **AVAILABLE NOW**

An example-oriented and chronological approach helps you implement and administer your internetworking devices. Starting with the configuration devices "out of the box;" this book moves to configuring Cisco IOS for the three most popular networking protocols today: TCP/IP, AppleTalk, and Novell Interwork Packet Exchange (IPX). You also learn basic administrative and management configuration, including access control with TACACS+ and RADIUS, network management with SNMP, logging of messages, and time control with NTP.

IP Routing Fundamentals

Mark A. Sportack

1-57870-071-x • **AVAILABLE NOW**

This comprehensive guide provides essential background information on routing in IP networks for network professionals who are deploying and maintaining LANs and WANs daily. Explore the mechanics of routers, routing protocols, network interfaces, and operating systems.

Cisco Press Fundamentals

Internet Routing Architectures, Second Edition

Sam Halabi with Danny McPherson

1-57870-233-x • **AVAILABLE NOW**

This book explores the ins and outs of interdomain routing network design with emphasis on BGP-4 (Border Gateway Protocol Version 4)--the de facto interdomain routing protocol. You will have all the information you need to make knowledgeable routing decisions for Internet connectivity in your environment.

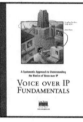

Voice over IP Fundamentals

Jonathan Davidson and James Peters

1-57870-168-6 • **AVAILABLE NOW**

Voice over IP (VoIP), which integrates voice and data transmission, is quickly becoming an important factor in network communications. It promises lower operational costs, greater flexibility, and a variety of enhanced applications. This book provides a thorough introduction to this new technology to help experts in both the data and telephone industries plan for the new networks.

For the latest on Cisco Press resources and Certification and

Training guides, or for information on publishing opportunities, visit

www.ciscopress.com

Cisco Press

c i s c o p r e s s . c o m

Committed to being your long-term resource as you grow as a Cisco Networking professional

CISCO SYSTEMS

CISCO PRESS

Help Cisco Press **stay connected** to the issues and challenges you face on a daily basis by registering your product and filling out our brief survey. Complete and mail this form, or better yet ...

Register online and enter to win a FREE book!

Jump to **www.ciscopress.com/register** and register your product online. Each complete entry will be eligible for our monthly drawing to win a FREE book of the winner's choice from the Cisco Press library.

May we contact you via e-mail with information about **new releases, special promotions** and customer benefits?

❒ Yes ❒ No

E-mail address _____

Name _____

Address _____

City _____ State/Province _____

Country _____ Zip/Post code _____

Where did you buy this product?

❒ Bookstore ❒ Computer store/electronics store
❒ Online retailer ❒ Direct from Cisco Press
❒ Mail order ❒ Class/Seminar
❒ Other_____

When did you buy this product? _____ Month _____ Year

What price did you pay for this product?

❒ Full retail price ❒ Discounted price ❒ Gift

How did you learn about this product?

❒ Friend ❒ Store personnel ❒ In-store ad
❒ Cisco Press Catalog ❒ Postcard in the mail ❒ Saw it on the shelf
❒ Other Catalog ❒ Magazine ad ❒ Article or review
❒ School ❒ Professional Organization ❒ Used other products
❒ Other_____

What will this product be used for?

❒ Business use ❒ School/Education
❒ Other_____

Cisco Press

How many years have you been employed in a computer-related industry?

❏ 2 years or less ❏ 3-5 years ❏ 5+ years

Which best describes your job function?

❏ Corporate Management ❏ Systems Engineering ❏ IS Management
❏ Network Design ❏ Network Support ❏ Webmaster
❏ Marketing/Sales ❏ Consultant ❏ Student
❏ Professor/Teacher ❏ Other _____

What is your formal education background?

❏ High school ❏ Vocational/Technical degree ❏ Some college
❏ College degree ❏ Masters degree ❏ Professional or Doctoral degree

Have you purchased a Cisco Press product before?

❏ Yes ❏ No

On what topics would you like to see more coverage?

_____

_____

Do you have any additional comments or suggestions?

_____

_____

Thank you for completing this survey and registration. Please fold here, seal, and mail to Cisco Press.

Cisco Enterprise Management Solutions, Volume I (1-58705-006-4)

Cisco Press
Customer Registration—CP0500227
P.O. Box #781046
Indianapolis, IN 46278-8046

Cisco Press
201 West 103rd Street
Indianapolis, IN 46290
ciscopress.com

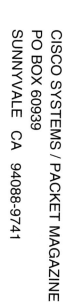

PACKET

Packet magazine serves as the premier publication linking customers to Cisco Systems, Inc. Delivering complete coverage of cutting-edge networking trends and innovations, *Packet* is a magazine for technical, hands-on users. It delivers industry-specific information for enterprise, service provider, and small and midsized business market segments. A toolchest for planners and decision makers, *Packet* contains a vast array of practical information, boasting sample configurations, real-life customer examples, and tips on getting the most from your Cisco Systems' investments. Simply put, *Packet* magazine is straight talk straight from the worldwide leader in networking for the Internet, Cisco Systems, Inc.

We hope you'll take advantage of this useful resource. I look forward to hearing from you!

Jennifer Biondi
Packet Circulation Manager
packet@cisco.com
www.cisco.com/go/packet